UNDERSTANDING RESEARCH

Successfully completing a research project is a major milestone in most university degrees, and the cornerstone of an academic career. This text is an accessible, real-time guide to conducting academic research in international and cross-cultural settings.

It provides advanced undergraduates and graduate students practical and theoretical guidance on how to begin, execute, and then communicate the outcome of research projects undertaken at the intersection of the arts, humanities, and social sciences.

Understanding Research:

- explores the decision-making process at all points of a research project and the implications of these decisions in the longer term;
- outlines the practical and philosophical conundrums around specific techniques for gathering and analysing material;
- examines moments of disconnect, overlap, and potentially mutual benefit for researchers working at different points along the quantitative–qualitative divide that underscores popular and scholarly debates about the relevance of academic research;
- explains how to cope with a divide that is both real and imagined, in all its experiential, institutional, and conceptual variations.

Focused explicitly on the needs and experiences of students and including a wealth of practical tips, this work is an essential resource for all students embarking on a research project.

M. I. Franklin is Reader and Convener of the Global Media and Transnational Communications programme at Goldsmiths (UK). Previous books include *Resounding International Relations: On Music, Culture, and Politics* and *Postcolonial Politics, the Internet, and Everyday Life: Pacific Traversals Online*.

UNDERSTANDING RESEARCH

Coping with the
quantitative–qualitative divide

M. I. Franklin

Routledge
Taylor & Francis Group

LONDON AND NEW YORK

First published 2012
by Routledge
2 Park Square, Milton Park, Abingdon, Oxon, OX14 4RN

Simultaneously published in the USA and Canada
by Routledge
711 Third Avenue, New York, NY 10017

Routledge is an imprint of the Taylor & Francis Group, an informa business

British Library Cataloguing in Publication Data
A catalogue record for this book is available from the British Library

Library of Congress Cataloging in Publication Data
Franklin, Marianne, 1959–
Understanding research : coping with the quantitative – qualitative divide /
M. I. Franklin.
   p. cm.
Includes bibliographical references and index.
1. Political science—Research—Methodology—Textbooks. I. Title.
JA86.F69 2012
001.4–dc23
2011046383

ISBN 13: 978–0–415–49079–5 (hbk)
ISBN 13: 978–0–415–49080–1 (pbk)
ISBN 13: 978–0–203–11886–3 (ebk)

Typeset in Garamond by
Keystroke, Station Road, Codsall, Wolverhampton

CONTENTS

ILLUSTRATIONS

TABLES

FIGURES

▌ BOXES

ACKNOWLEDGEMENTS

Is there really 'no such thing as a stupid question'? Maybe not. However, budding researchers quickly learn to avoid looking 'stupid' at all costs, so leaving many questions about the research process frequently unasked. In this sense, borrowing from that erudite social commentator Woody Allen, this book could well be entitled *Everything You Wanted To Know About Academic Research But Were Afraid To Ask*, or afraid to answer. My first acknowledgement is to other authors in the methods and research skills literature that informs this project: *Respect*.

Closer to home, this book has been the product of a particular sort of collaboration. A number of people have shared with me their own experiences, wisdom, teaching material and, in some cases, let me watch them first-hand conveying some of the insights presented here; thanks to Susan Banducci, Chris Berry, Niko Besnier, Terrell Carver, Tim Crook, Matt Davies, the late Alex Fernandez, Des Freedman, Julian Henriques, Jeannette Hoffman, Jeff Karp, Harry Kunneman, Laurens ten Kate, Meryem Marzouki, Liz Moor, Hans Radder, Philippe Rekacewicz, Anne Sisson-Runyan, Richard Smith, Susan Stocker, Kent Wilkinson, and Sally Wyatt. Thanks to Pasi Väliaho, my 'partner in crime' in developing a department-wide research module at Goldsmiths.

Others took time to read various versions of the manuscript, in whole or in part; offering concrete advice and suggestions from their own point of view, contributing examples and substantive material as well. First and foremost I'd like to thank Susan Banducci for her contribution, not only for the part she played in the genesis and development of the book's rationale but also her input on specific topics: the nuances of quantitative research, supervision, ways of coping, research design, and politics. Her unflinching eye as dispassionate reader of a substantial part of the manuscript early on and her generous sharing of teaching resources and her own research experience have been formative and inspiring. The wit, pragmatism, and perspicacity she has brought to our conversations about these matters over the years are also greatly appreciated. I hope that the book does justice to these ongoing discussions.

My gratitude also to Zeena Feldman, Zab Franklin, Zlatan Krajina, Marieke Riethof, and Yu-Kei Tse for their invaluable reading of the final draft; whose observations, editorial suggestions, and quizzings made a big difference just in time. A number of colleagues along with former and current research students provided an equally important input to the development of my thinking and writing. To James Curran, Nick Couldry, and David Morley my thanks for the institutional-level support for the book's approach and the spirit in which it is written. My thanks to Asad Asaduzzaman, Kath Geraghty, Jowan Mahmod, and Dong-Hyun Song for raising important issues during their Ph.D. research. Thanks as well to Keith Hubbard for all those weird and wonderful web-links, and to Marcia Pacheco and Richard Mulindwa-Kavuma (M.A. cohort 2010) for their pertinent inquiries and encouraging words along the way.

To Pierre Florac, Zab Franklin, Taka Hosoda, Jochen Jacoby, David Reynolds (my 'let's get writing' pal), Pollyanna Stokoe, Belinda Watt, and Claire Young, I am very grateful for all the on-the-hoof input, positive energy, and attention to my well-being. My gratitude to Tadgh O'Sullivan for his intuition and indexing services that went beyond the call of duty. And a very special thanks to all those artists who have generously allowed reproduction of their cartoons and strips for our enjoyment.

Sections in Chapter 3 and Chapter 5 draw on previously published material: Franklin, M. I., 2010, 'Media Research in the 21st Century', in *Journalism: Cutting Edge Commentaries on the Critical Issues Facing Journalism at the Practical, Theoretical and Media Industry Level*, Paul Lashmar (ed.), London: Henry Stewart Talks Ltd, www.hstalks.com/?t=MM107256S-Franklin; Franklin, M. I., 2009, 'Sex, Gender and Cyberspace', in *Gender Matters in Global Politics: A Feminist Introduction to International Relations*, Laura Shepherd (ed.), London and New York: Routledge, 328–49.

Finally, I dedicate this book to all my students – past, present, and future.

Without their questions, crises, disappointments, challenges, relief and satisfaction on completing their various research projects, this book would never have got off the ground let alone written.

Amsterdam
26 August 2011

PERMISSIONS AND ATTRIBUTIONS

Introduction

Topics covered in this chapter:

- Aims and objectives
- Who should read this book
- Using the book in context
- What is *academic* research?
- On divides – real and imagined
- Key concepts and their various uses
- Chapter organization

Successfully completing a research project is a major milestone in a postgraduate, and many an undergraduate university degree. It is also the cornerstone of an academic career. Research in the round is both process and product; it has an important temporal element (starts and finishes), practical limitations (know-how and want-to) and intellectual puzzles (why), which together have cumulative benefits that reach beyond more pressing requirements to get the end-result out the door. In traditional academic terms, the objective is often the successful completion of an academic dissertation. More advanced research projects are disseminated as published and accredited research reports, conference papers, journal articles, books or, increasingly these days, in web-based formats. At various stages progress – and outcomes – also need to be communicated, formally and informally in oral or written form, to various audiences. Designing and then getting through a piece of research seldom proceeds in a tidy straight line upwards. Success is defined as much by our completing the project (at all if not on time) as well as how others rate the outcome of our efforts.

This book treats these at times conflicting demands in four respects. First, it looks at those decisions we all need to make along a certain path that has a point of destination in mind and the implications of these decisions in the longer term where apposite. Second, it unpacks these issues as they emerge at key points in the execution and production of a research project; specific techniques and tools for gathering and then analysing the 'data', broadly defined, and how bringing these two aspects together in some sort of coherent way relate to philosophical and practical issues; the 'theory–method relationship'; intellectual allegiances; and shifts in our own research identities for instance.

Third, the book identifies key moments of disagreement, overlap, and potentially mutual benefit for students working at different vantage-points along the *quantitative–qualitative divide* underscoring popular and scholarly debates about the social relevance of academic research. This dividing line weaves its way through and between departments, disciplines, and institutional geographies in various ways. What counts as 'good' or 'bad' science, the right way of conducting a research project, and the best way to communicate the outcomes frequently pivot on conflicting ideas about the role played by ways of gathering and presenting quantifiable (the 'power of numbers') or qualitative (the 'power of ideas') sorts of knowledge.

These disagreements also pepper methods textbooks, fuel ongoing theoretical debates, inflect employment and funding opportunities, and underscore reiterations of the 'war of the worlds' and related *paradigm shifts* in the history of western science.[1] The corollary division made between qualitative and quantitative modes of research lies at the heart of much confusion and frustration for researchers, experienced and starting-out, during the life-cycle of a research project. Talking about *understanding* research encompasses ways of thinking, general skills, and specialized techniques for gathering and analysing material, the formative role played by worldviews, and academic idioms. It means coming to terms with such divides; in their stricter and more flexible formulations as well as their interdisciplinary and *intra*disciplinary contours.

What all approaches have in common nevertheless is an awareness of the varying pressures of time factors (all those deadlines), practical obligations ('do I *have* to?!'), and intellectual genealogies (whose ideas count, and why) confronting any researcher in any setting. Completing small and larger research projects, as a novice or experienced researcher, seldom proceeds snag-free. Progress is more often measured in fits and starts, clarity of thought and precision of the knowledge produced looking more like a spiral that is, hopefully, not a downward one. Onlookers and new arrivals to academic research often assume that on the other side of this entry-threshold all research unfolds in the same way; once you complete the first project, theory or methods course to good effect, all subsequent ones will fall into place. Working realities soon prove this assumption to be wrong, particularly for those looking to advance up a degree level.

So, in a fourth respect this book is about developing ways of *coping* with a divide that is both real and imagined; its experiential, institutional, and conceptual variations. And, where possible, finding sustainable ways of building bridges along the way by treating research in a holistic and not simply compartmentalized way; understanding the professional and personal dimensions in a wider context whilst working to complete a project in the immediate term in a satisfactory way and with a sense of achievement.

AIMS AND OBJECTIVES

A key premise of this book is that no matter what your educational background, intellectual identity, or hands-on skill-base may be (e.g. in market research), the way this divide works for and against effectively completing an academic piece of independent research is useful to consider from both sides. A second premise is that all research undertakings entail a degree of adaptation, adoption, flexibility, and pragmatism in actual practice. The book has been conceived as a real-time 'rough guide' to academic research. Both theoretically informed and consciously pragmatic, it is a companion volume to the diverse generalist and specialist literature on ways to conduct research in contemporary academic settings. To this end, it provides research students – and their supervisors – both commentary and practical advice on how to deal with seemingly intractable differences about the best way to begin, execute, and communicate the outcome of a research project at the intersection of the arts, humanities, and social sciences; differences that can be passionately defended on a personal and institutional level in everyday research practice.

With *coping* the keyword for these broad aims, the main goal of the book is to enable you to complete a research project in good time and in such a way that you can do so to the best of your abilities and as far as your own personal ambitions allow. This breaks down into the following objectives:

1 Describe, contextualize, and update key distinctions and overlaps between *qualitative* and *quantitative* approaches to academic research in historical context.
2 Unpack and analyse these distinctions, and intersections with respect to the tightrope that spans theoretical debates, everyday research practicalities, and the milestones you need to get through to complete a research project; e.g. choosing a topic, constructing a research question, doing the 'empirical' part, analysing, and presenting the findings.
3 Develop a holistic and pragmatic approach to creative thinking and puzzle-solving when faced with the diversity of methods – ways of gathering and analysing your 'data'; as self-contained or consciously combined methods.
4 Provide explanations of specific research skills (how to) with the analytical tools (understanding why) necessary for scenarios where competing approaches can have consequences for seminar presentations, job placements, research funding, and publication.
5 Outline existing and emerging ethical issues around the research process, formal and unwritten codes of conduct. Understanding methods, along and despite this divide requires a greater awareness of ethical considerations for doing research in increasingly computer-mediated and international – viz. *globalized* – research settings.

A caveat: this book is not setting out to trivialize what are diverging research paths in many other respects or provide a comforting drop-down menu of methods, as if these decisions can be made in a vacuum, de-linked from institutional as well as sociocultural, political or economic considerations. Rigorous scholarship, by any standards, and supermarket-shopping are not one and the same thing. What it does provide is a focused and open-ended approach to understanding research as both process and product.

Even when both feet are firmly in one disciplinary or methodological camp or another, where their respective ways of doing things and value hierarchies set the priorities, this book can help student researchers keep a sense of perspective. It will help you articulate what your research is about in ways that make sense to you and your supervisor or examiners, adhering to mandatory assessment criteria yet resonating with more philosophical conversations accordingly. The point is to provide ways of working through rather than be stumped by entrenched positions on divisions that can and do matter to the successful completion of an original piece of research.

WHO SHOULD READ THIS BOOK

Students undertaking independent research projects as part of a degree programme, from undergraduate through to Ph.D. level, bring to this task previous education and even work experience based on a variety of approaches to gaining knowledge. Some have had technical training or experience in statistical (i.e. purely quantitative) analysis whilst others may come with characteristically qualitative educational backgrounds in literature, the performing arts, and anthropology for instance. Others, particularly from the US, have received exclusively, or a combination of, liberal arts and social science education; others again arrive well versed in western and non-western philosophical thought.

Primarily this book is tailored for any student undertaking an original research project, from final year bachelor, through master-level dissertation students, through to Ph.D. students, with various degrees of previous knowledge, experience, and confidence levels.[2] There is a second readership in mind: research supervisors and tutors, some of whom may also be students completing research for advanced qualifications, or teaching staff striking out in new research directions of their own.

To students: The book speaks to you in two respects, whether or not you classify yourself as an 'absolute beginner', 'dummy', or 'advanced postgraduate'. It provides practical clues for those of you who may be well versed in broader, more abstract philosophical or theoretical frameworks but who are struggling with practical decisions about how to get these off the ground in terms of the 'what' of research let alone *how* to go about it. Second, it is aimed at those of you who, whilst you have a clear object of inquiry, case-study, issue-area and even 'method' of choice, start to come unstuck when you need to communicate, make sense of your choices for others in practical and, by association, conceptual terms.

At the same time I will be alerting you to some of the tough debates residing between the lines, particularly in light of how quickly student researchers identify with one approach, over-hastily putting unfamiliar techniques or ideas into the 'not *my* thing – *your* thing' or 'no-can-do' box; staking claims for 'newness' or transcendental critiques of the 'mainstream' by recourse to *ad hominem* or *strawman* arguments.[3] The book provides a way forward in what is a competitive context for obtaining university degrees in such a way that enhances your ability to remain intellectually curious and not afraid of collaboration; both of these tend to be penalized if they are recognized at all.

To supervisors: The aim here is to provide support, and additional pointers for getting around the daily impasses, misunderstandings, and frustrations that can arise when advising students in mixed departments, those where references to research skills or methods is either a highly contentious issue or a deceptively non-existent one. The book articulates some of the often unspoken conundrums of the supervision process itself and our role as working researchers, supervisors, and teachers looking to enable students to get on with their research, and ways to get on with our own work. It provides a handy reference to familiar key issues, the latest literature, and intellectual support that affirms as well as informs you in your own research or when supervising others.

Based on a 'dialogic' understanding of teaching and learning (see Franklin and Wilkinson 2011), the discussions and puzzles presented here do tend to assume a certain 'ideal type' of research project and model research student. However, it would not be unfair to note that many students completing university-level research projects today simply want to tick the boxes, and get the project over and done with. Likewise that many supervisors want their research students to think for themselves and indeed 'get on with it'. For both readerships, this book provides you with the basis for ticking those boxes and getting on as well as a look into some of the rich debates, challenging ideas and specific challenges that are also an integral part of effective and satisfying academic research work.

USING THIS BOOK IN CONTEXT

This section outlines very briefly the methods/research skills literature at large. It is not a comprehensive survey or the sort of critical discussion that characterizes the *literature review* element of research dissertations (see Chapter 4). These texts have inspired and influenced me during the course of writing and consulting with others on this book so they will be referred to where appropriate along the way.

Marketing mechanisms in the publishing industry and the way publishing catalogues are designed often sees books categorized along disciplinary lines; reproducing the quantitative–qualitative divide in all its various guises accordingly. That said, this is a large and diverse range of titles that is constantly in a state of renewal yet also rooted in oft-cited classics; from those that encapsulate a particular philosophical position or side of an ongoing theoretical debate, or epitomize a particular methodological approach for a disciplinary mainstream, or its critics.

Navigating this complex and wide-ranging literature is often not a job many students see as their first task when setting out on a research project; students who are often introduced to this literature either through prescribed or recommended reading. Which texts are preferred depends on the discipline, the predominant methodological approach (media studies and economics are different enterprises for instance) or the particularities of how methods training vis-à-vis research skills are treated as educational elements in degree programmes. Moreover, as we will be discussing later on in several ways, there is often a gap between our expectations of the sorts of answers any literature can provide to our particular quandaries and how they actually end up making sense for a project (your dissertation, this book) in the long run. Managing this disconnect often means realizing that there will never be an exact fit between what various authors have to say, the examples they draw upon, and what we think – need – to know; 'the catch in all research – making the switch from the literature at hand and our material'.[4]

For these reasons, methods books have a idiosyncratic role in our work. They are often consulted either too early, or too late, assuming they are consulted at all. Moreover, the way they can help us make a distinction between the more general questions we might ask of a particular literature (theoretical or more practical) related to a field of inquiry and the particularities of the *research question* we need to develop to guide the project on hand is too often overlooked.[5] Paradoxically this is often because learning by doing, trial and error, is integral to understanding research. A lot of information this sort of literature can provide at the time we need it most does not really sink in until later for this reason. Nonetheless, being able to get research done effectively also generates its own research needs; we need to learn about the principles, procedures, and wider implications of this process on its own terms.

Which book for what purpose?

The literature can be roughly divided into more or less comprehensive how-to sorts of books that cover various *data-gathering* methods; an important cluster in its own right. A second category focuses on the practicalities of getting through a project, guides on how to write academically, or books focusing on specific skills such as literature reviews.[6] There is a substantial category of books nowadays that look at both aspects; this one included. Underwriting all of these, are those books dealing with more abstract discussions of issues arising from particular tensions within an approach, topics from the philosophy or history of science, and disciplinary interventions looking to challenge methodological orthodoxies or present new visions. These are closely related to philosophical treatments and public debates about the relationship between science, culture, and society.[7] The latter contributions often only start to make sense once you have actually done some sort of research, acquired some hands-on knowledge of certain data-gathering techniques, or come out the other end of your 'theory' or 'findings' chapters.

Along these axes, the literature then diversifies. First, books speaking to or from within discrete disciplines where the methods presented – or critiqued – are grist to debates or divides within said discipline.[8] These titles stressing social and political research contrast with those referring to ethnography, cultural studies, or history[9] on the one hand, and those with terms such as 'interpreting', 're-imagining', or the prefix 'post' on the other.[10] A second diversification is into specific *methods* books with a wider purview. This is the aforementioned corner of the how-to methods market and one that some titles above fit into as well. These titles take a more eclectic approach to methods in order to achieve some level of coverage, applicable for either qualitative or quantitative methods courses.[11] Then there are those texts that are unapologetically either quantitative or qualitative. These sort of books can, by definition, go a lot deeper into the nuances of those methods covered in ways that more general, more synthetic approaches cannot.[12]

Then there are those that can be clustered together as critiques, and radical alternatives. Here I would include those working from critical, feminist and postcolonial standpoints either within or across disciplines.[13] These are books that look to overturn longstanding working assumptions and lacunae in terms of the politics of doing research, and knowledge-production from the geographical 'periphery' of the Global South vis-à-vis the richer regions in the 'centre' of the Global North.[14] This includes alternative frames for undertaking research into non-western societies that engage with many issues broached here drawing on postcolonial and feminist critiques assessing mainstream western academic research from outside, along with corollary inflections from debates within academe by its own internal critics. Such titles are self-contained, working across our concerns here yet influential resources nonetheless. As these are advocatory approaches that aim to improve if not reinvent academic research practice from the ground up, they are mostly more meta-level interventions.

New issues, new approaches

The above literature has been diversifying of late in the wake of previous decades' focus on interdisciplinary methods, literary turns, postcolonial, feminist and post-structuralist critiques in the social sciences, borrowing heavily from the humanities in doing so. Another, more recent impact on methods texts is the impact of 'new technologies' or 'new media'; *information and communication technologies* (ICTs), the internet, the web, and automated data-gathering and analytical tools, and electronic databases. This time-sensitive and growing literature roughly corresponds in terms of the tripartite division outlined so far; how-to books, discipline-based, or more abstract methodological exegeses.

All aim to guide research students through what is an emergent terrain circumscribed by various digital media (the web, 'social media', mobile communications devices, and older computer-mediated communications like email and discussion forums), the impact of ICTs on conventional research practices (automated research tools, web-mapping and data-mining software for searching the web, general-purpose search engines), and even new notions of the research field (virtual or cyberspatial domains), research subjects and topics (avatars to computer games, to simulations), to specific sorts of internet-based research tools and digitalized research techniques. Not only have these developments re-opened older methodological debates, but they have also upped the ante here in terms of the appropriate role, added value, and scientific status of the internet, ICTs, virtuality, and other mediated fieldwork scenarios in academe.[15] Chapter 5 looks at these issues in more detail.

Because the point of the exercise is not to reinvent the wheel, this book traces a path through this rich literature, referring the reader to conceptual and practical insights provided by others where apposite. In that spirit the next sections tackle some key concepts, both practical and more abstract. First we take a look at what is actually meant when we talk about *academic* research. This moves us into a more complex discussion about what is at stake when talking of a quantitative–qualitative divide. From there we can tackle some specific terms of reference that crop up in the preparation and the execution phases of an academic research project.

WHAT IS ACADEMIC RESEARCH?

Set aside for the moment any current notions you have about the social relevance of academic pursuits; old hands are often as cynical as onlookers in this respect – of how research *should* be done or for what purposes. Step 'outside the box' for a moment As others eloquently note, good research is not confined to academe (Creswell 2009, M. Davies 2007, Gray 2009, Morley 2006: 87 *passim*). Research, that is *actively* and methodically finding out about something by consulting various information sources, is something people do everyday. In academe research is of a different order, however. Emphasis is laid on formalized procedures, presentation formats, spoken and written idioms, codes of practice alongside informal conventions around the production and communication of one's knowledge; all of which have to withstand *intense* and *concerted* scrutiny over time.

Academic practitioners aim – indeed they are required – to produce work that engages with that of others and in such a way that allows all aspects to be eventually authenticated, replicated, or developed further. From philosophy through to experimental psychology to astrophysics, our work is constantly held under the magnifying glass. These 'others' can be our direct mentors or colleagues, co-practitioners in a discrete research group, sub-discipline, or part of a broader 'epistemic community' that shares a 'set of normative and principled beliefs' – and disagreements – about the matter at hand (Haas, cited in Cinquegrani 2002: 779).

That is the theory in any case. Criticism is the life-force of all scholarly work. We are bound to disagree: dispute resolution or 100 per cent accuracy, even in the most quantitative or scientifically adamant of corners, is an ideal rather than a given.[16] Yet as students we learn very quickly that affirmation is the Holy Grail; being caught off-side in a methodological or philosophical war of words is a common and discomforting occurrence. How different researchers handle and articulate these margins is where the most potent differences lie.[17] As Niall Ó Dochartaigh points out, in academic settings research

> is not simply about finding the answer to a question. It involves learning about the main issues in a particular area and identifying the central arguments made by those on all sides of the ongoing debates. . . . The research process is not only about generating a piece of work. It is also about becoming an expert [in relative terms] on the sources and on the literature in a specialized area whose boundaries you help to define [even modestly] in the course of your research. This expertise is one of the most valuable outcomes of the research process.
>
> (2009: 1–2)

This is why academic knowledge and thought processes are of a different genre to 'common sense', general knowledge, or even intuition; though a good dose of all three certainly comes in handy in the research lab, the field, and examination. Nor does it communicate outcomes – these are the research results – in the easy-to-read digests of popular science publications, science television documentaries, or investigative journalism. That said, all these genres of knowledge production draw on academic scholarship and vice versa, depending on the setting. So whilst there are many points in common, academic research-work requires paying explicit attention to articulating the *act of thinking* itself, as a specialized practice; the design, format and argumentation are as important as the outcome of your work. This includes making your sources and affiliations transparent, explicating the steps taken in gathering and processing evidence and linking them to an articulated and annotated conceptual rationale, presenting the results and then offering conclusions; all of which then gets wrapped up in a particular format and idiom for a particular audience.

The various 'planning regulations' for completing a research dissertation as part of a university degree, philosophical eddies, data-gathering technicalities, and written presentation formalities have all developed over time in a zigzag fashion; behind the scenes and in the crucible of intense debates amongst not only researchers but also other interested parties. That aside, and contrary to archetypes of how (usually male) genius works, from Galileo to Einstein, or what many students think, academic work is not a hermetic act; it does not take place in either a sociocultural, political, or economic vacuum even when you are locked in your room with the hand-in deadline looming. Inspiration and benefiting from social interaction are virtues in academic research life as well.[18]

That said, self-sufficiency, fastidiousness, and developing an eye for detail are also indispensable; the life-blood of academic research as they manifest themselves across the disciplinary spectrum. The ensuing infinitude of discussions around meaning on the one hand and empirical – evidential – nuances on the other, all 'purely academic' – pedantry in other words – is often a source of exasperation for students starting out. These attributes of contemporary academic practice, 'knowing an awful lot about not much at all' are also the target of radical critiques of its role in ethnocentric, 'western' dogma about what counts as scientific knowledge.

Perhaps this is why academic work and ensuing publications are often perceived as far removed from everyday life, only good for arcane debates within the hallowed halls of the ivory towers of the university (a standard image in film and television costume dramas in the UK, including the *Harry Potter* franchise) or barely read journals. These hallowed halls exist and, to be frank, the latter archetype of academic publishing is true enough even if it were true that subscription numbers were all that counted here!

This other divide, separating 'town' from 'gown' does not mean to say that the downstream effects of academic research, from the natural to the social sciences to the arts, and humanities, are negligible or irrelevant; hair-splitting at the sidelines of major events. Far from it, as successive generations of *critical, postcolonial, feminist*, and other alternatives to research conventions continue to argue.[19] This notion of there being an irrevocable disconnect between academic and 'real life', so to speak, is considerably more permeable in practice. For instance many academic practitioners sit on advisory councils or policy think-tanks. Others have come to academe after careers in the public and private sectors. The point is that public imaginaries and internal debates around the social relevance of academic knowledge wax and wane in any case; as do the socio-economic stakes, cultural ramifications, and geopolitics.

Whatever your misgivings may be of the point of academic ways of working *grosso modo*, the point to note right now is that these practices and ideas did not come ready-made. Even the most widely accepted analytical frameworks within which an object of analysis is studied and understood have changed over time; e.g. planetary movements as codified in Aristotle's cosmology vis-à-vis how they have come to be charted and understood in contemporary astronomy and astrophysics since then. As philosophers of science tell us, advances (and retreats!) in knowledge of the world around us occur less as giant leaps – the cliché known as the 'Eureka!' moment – but rather in more incremental steps. Such *paradigm shifts* in the history of western science take place over time, if not hundreds of years (see Chalmers 2004, Kuhn 1962). The furore over challenges to the widely-held belief in mediaeval western Europe that the sun revolved around the earth is another well-discussed case in point. The current stand-off in some parts of the world between the, once maverick ('heretical') and now orthodox view of the origins of the human species, evolutionary theory ('Darwinism') along with its core concepts ('natural selection') and corollary disciplines (e.g. palaeontology, primatology) and the rise of theories that question its underlying precepts ('Creationism', or 'Intelligent Design') is another example.

More about just how the legacy of these sorts of debates matter for our purposes in the next chapter. First we need to present the ideas and conventions of academic research practice into perspective and in their own right.

Academic research: aims and objectives

Let's take a step back and look at how two broad traditions of quantitative and qualitative research line up if we strip things back to fundamental statements of intent; a discussion of what these terms mean for this book is below. First, consider Table 1.1, which distils a range of characterizations of what various modes of research state as their intention. Reflect for a moment; what do you consider to be the *primary* objective of *academic* or, if you prefer, *scientific* or *scholarly* research?

Your initial answers need not mean you are confined to either side with no way out. Nor does this schematic resolve other thorny issues around the definition and relative importance attached to terms that these two broad bands have in common, or how researchers are engaging in more than one sort of activity, spending time in the other camp at any one time; e.g. a critique may well be in the context of a project aiming to empower a sector of the population, recommendations ensue from making predictions, or generalizations, objects of inquiry may require the application of statistical and linguistic modes of analysis.

What Table 1.1 distils are oft-repeated ways of characterizing the object of the exercise from either side of this working divide. Look more closely though at those terms they have in common. For instance, in practice all researchers are *analysing* or *interpreting* their 'data' or 'findings', making a case based on the 'empirical' evidence

Table 1.1 Academic research objectives

Qualitative researchers	act on the data by	in order to	
analyse/interpret	Deconstructing Generalizing Inferring (Re)assembling	Critique Describe Discover Empower Expand Explain Improve Nuance Recommend Understand	the phenomena the object of analysis policies/law-making social/political debates ideas/debates knowledge groups/communities behaviour/motivations/choices cause and effect truth/s & laws injustice hypotheses
Quantitative researchers	act on the data by	in order to	
analyse/interpret	Deducing Generalizing Inferring Testing hypotheses Validating	Describe Discover Explain Focus Improve Make causal inferences Refine Replace Predict Recommend Understand	

or form of reasoning – argumentation. In this respect analysis and interpretation are primary concerns shared by all researchers in some way or other (Radder 2006, Ulin 1984, van Zoonen 1994). Moreover, *explanation* is a primary motivation and objective in common. For instance, research drawing on German generations of *critical theory* (Burchill et al. 2001) or the Anglo-American pragmatist tradition of empirical research such as *critical realism* (Burnham et al. 2004) are also as preoccupied with explanation – ascertaining cause and effect – as are experimental traditions in cognitive psychology, or their counterparts from Freudian, Jungian, and Lacanian schools of psychoanalysis.

The visual and written means by which an explanation is made, thought processes by which a conclusion is reached, however, is where paths diverge; between and within these broad bands. For example, interpreting – or analysing statistical evidence based on a statistical *reduction analysis* of the data arrayed as numerical values, is quite different from interpreting – or 'reading' the written word or visual images by applying a form of *semiotic* method.

Take a discipline such as history as another example; explaining historical events by consulting people's diaries, private correspondence, government archives, personal memoirs, travelogues, or charting agrarian or industrial output figures over a given period of time all use different sources, requiring different ways to gather and make sense of the empirical material, residing in official archives or community libraries; coming up with competing explanations of the same historical moment as they do so. Philosophers of history duly diverge in their view of 'the' archive as the only reputable source for empirical research, the relationship between *primary* and *secondary* sources, and what counts as a source when it is a recording of someone speaking.

The ante is upped when quantitative data is integral to prediction; stronger still when predictions have implications for macroeconomic policy decisions by governments, corporate R&D, and households. Economics is an example of one discipline, firmly embedded in quantitative methods, recently put on the defensive as it became apparent that obscure statistical 'financial instruments' (e.g. futures) used by stockbrokers and investment banks had no small part to play in the 2008 global financial crisis and its aftermath (see Lanchester 2010).

Apart from these overlaps in how all researchers are engaged in analysis, interpretation, and explanation in varying degrees, quantitative and qualitative modes line up with and against one another in a number of other ways:

1   All would concur that successfully completing any research *project*, large or small, calls upon intertwined skill-sets – analytical, hands-on, and organizational – in upwardly spiralling levels of intricacy and demands on the researcher's patience, time, and material resources.

2   Conducting an 'independent', 'original' piece of research according to certain 'criteria of excellence' and within a certain time frame is a major part of successfully completing a research dissertation across the board. It bears pointing out that in the workplace too, academic-level research is also conducted under strict time-pressures; by journalists, political lobbyists, NGOs, central and local governments, think-tanks, PR and marketing firms, and businesses.

3   That said, what sets the latter sorts of – applied – research apart from academic work, deadlines aside, is a lively but also enervating tension. On the one hand academic qualifications have the satisfactory completion of an independent piece of research as one of the formal requirements for a university degree. They both entail certain expectations about what the key elements (see Box 2.1) are in a research project.

4   On the other hand, where they diverge from other sorts of research is the stress laid on explicating the theory–method interrelationship and in the degree to which they engage with wider debates as noted above. For any research tradition such pressures are as much philosophical inquiries as they are dry technicalities and organizational hassles. This includes conflicting ideas over what counts as acceptable, what not, and then how the respective *savoir-faire* is best passed on to the next generation. Differences about this relationship become pressing for research students, even before they have settled on a topic.

5   Another aspect in common, albeit less readily admitted, are respective ebbs and flows in fundamental thinking about research, as both a practical and reflective pursuit. Sea-changes in research practice and conventions are more incremental; once highly regarded ways of conducting research become superseded, returning again in the wake of disenchantment with the once-new trends that supplanted them.

It would be tempting to characterize all aspects of these debates as a stand-off between the new and the old. Whilst there appears to be a chronological progression in narratives, it is more of a dialectic in that new and old co-mingle; intellectual fashions work in this sense both ways. Much of the time, though, would-be new and so-called old co-habit departments and faculties, sometimes amicably and sometimes less so.

Time now to consider what is at stake when speaking of divides; particularly the one ostensibly marking out quantitative and qualitative research territories for student researchers in the first instance, but also in the theory and practice of everyday research, supervision, and assessment.

ON DIVIDES – REAL AND IMAGINED

Running through these entry-and-exit points is a line that traces divergent positions on the form and substance of *academic* research; a particular way of producing scholarly – *scientific* – knowledge about our natural and social worlds. Research communities – and larger schools of thought – comprising contending worldviews and research practices crystallize around points along this line; in shorthand, the *quantitative–qualitative divide*.

There are as many ways to define and then slice this divide as there are terminologies to describe and contest its influence on research practices. A sense that there is an underlying division between research findings relying on counting and numerical measurement and those that do not prioritize these ways to gain knowledge pervades modern higher education and research institutions nonetheless. It has come to govern how researchers, instructors, and students not only go about doing any particular piece of research but also how they think and talk about their projects, how they present and defend the validity of any knowledge produced. It inflects the conceptual and technical idioms we use when reflecting on the merits of a completed piece of research; its 'impact' or 'contribution to knowledge' for instance.

At times polarized and at other times evident only as a quiet but steady undertow, this dividing line also influences how researchers assess the prospective and ongoing work of others in our varying roles; as teachers, external reviewers, examiners, team-members, and students. We may well be making these assessments in more than one capacity. For instance, dissertation supervisors can also be in the process of submitting proposals to funding bodies themselves or working on their own or within collaborative research projects. Students, even as they embark on their first major piece of academic research, may already have data-gathering and analysis skills and so conceptions of what it takes to do good research – from the workplace, in journalism, PR and marketing, or NGO work for instance.

This fact of academic life, an occupational hazard in many ways, is backed up by a formidable corpus of literature across the disciplines. That said, talk of a divide is not to propose either an absolute or intractable rift. This means being aware of where and how it operates as a hard-and-fast rule, or as an implicit imperative that sees students, supervisors, and colleagues getting irate, talking across one another in a research seminar Q&A. It means being able to tell when these tensions divert us from the task at hand as we grapple with conceptual confusions or practical obstacles during the course of a research project. Expressions of seemingly intractable differences often disguise a number of actual and potential points in common. This requires we develop a sixth sense so we can take note of how differences *within* various approaches can be as intense as those between them.

That said, even carefully talking of a *divide* assumes that everyone agrees on what, and where to draw this particular line. It also assumes there is some sort of consensus about what the terms *quantitative* and *qualitative* mean, along with corollary key concepts. The one thing that is clear is that there is no clear agreement; more on this in due course. Nonetheless, many working researchers – and students – are quick to state which 'camp' they, and others belong to if asked; often before being asked. For those undertaking research in settings where one approach predominates – in a natural science department, within a larger research project, or as a prerequisite for funded research, these meta-level distinctions are often a non-issue.

In other settings – in faculties professing an interdisciplinary approach, those with diverse or international teaching or student bodies, or where sharply diverging research approaches co-habit in the one department – students are expected to proceed as if these distinctions and what to do about them during a research project are self-explanatory.

When embarking on your first or even successive piece of substantial research, in even the most inclusive setting, all topics and methods for getting information ('data-gathering') appear to be equal. The stated objective for you is to design, undertake, and write up an 'original' piece of research under your own steam; as an 'independent' researcher. Quite early on though, even the most inclusive environment can become less accommodating; what you consider to be original, innovative, or a 'hot' topic is met with comments such as 'that's been done to death', disinterest, or disapproval. As different staff members give conflicting advice or no advice at all, the formal requirements for research dissertation work in your institution and informal expectations appear increasingly opaque if not at odds with one another. In the meantime you are struggling to get off the starting block.

These setbacks are commonplace, for students and full-time scholars working within the various disciplines and institutional geographies that now make up the social sciences and humanities. We are all regularly confronted with thorny practical and philosophical issues regarding the nature and purpose of the research we are undertaking. The ante is being constantly upped by calls from society at large, usually voiced by state or private funding bodies for scholars to undertake research that is applicable – *relevant* – to public policy priorities, a greater good, or towards some sort of national or regional competitive edge in research and development.

Where the line gets (re)drawn and its impact on research practice differs from place to place, and over time; here readers can, and will draw on their own experiences. Apart from its role as an organizational device, in this book I use the term less categorically than *heuristically*; as a framing device for unpacking both opposing and intersecting approaches to designing, carrying out, and then communicating the outcome of a research project. Knowing where the pitfalls lie helps anyone starting out to achieve this goal with some modicum of success and sense of a job well done, whatever your level or ambitions.

Let's turn now to some more specific terms and their various usages; these often trip up first-time researchers undertaking projects in consciously or organizationally mixed research contexts, as well as those interacting with others working on similar or overlapping research topics yet doing so from the 'other side'.

KEY CONCEPTS AND THEIR VARIOUS USES

All along the spectrum spanning qualitative from qualitative to quantitative in theory and how these translate into practice, seemingly common terms of reference can belie complex and longstanding debates. These terms create an undertow in that any researcher is both the

> beneficiary and the victim of the linguistic tradition into which he [sic] has been born – the beneficiary inasmuch as language gives access to the accumulated records of other people's experience, the victim in so far as it confirms him in the belief that reduced awareness is the only awareness and as it bedevils his sense of reality, so that he is all too apt to take his concepts for data, his words for actual things.
>
> (Huxley 1954: 23)

The following section looks at several of these terms in so far as their various usages relate to this book's approach to understanding research in interdisciplinary and intercultural settings.

When people refer to *qualitative* or *quantitative* research modes, what sort of distinction is being made here for practical purposes, and what do these signal about deeper philosophical differences? Basically, leaving aside the way polemics can confuse things, the terms designate how proponents understand

1   the role of observation in getting an outcome; and
2   the types of data gathered during the research;
3   differences in what counts as *empirical* evidence; quantitative (numerical) values and measurements, or qualitative ones (field notes, interview transcripts, ideas); how these are processed, analysed, and then presented.

Observation

Whether exploring post-conflict scenarios, how different ethnic groups find expression in, or are excluded from mainstream political processes in liberal democracies, or the relationship between globalization, neoliberalism, and the internet, you may notice that these first conversations revolve around certain assumptions, sometimes explicit sometimes not, about which facts are based on which observations, whether your observations 'fit' your theory, or conversely whether your 'theory' – or hypothesis – has sufficient evidence to back it up. Indeed you may sense that some topics are synonymous with approaches that concentrate on gathering evidence or, conversely, approaches that treat evidence, and the way such evidence is gathered, more as a theoretical endeavour. As Hans Radder notes, that which

> is observable and what it is that we observe at a particular moment depend, among other things, on the available conceptual interpretations. In this sense these

conceptual interpretations can be said to structure the world. . . . [H]owever . . . concepts also abstract from the world . . . In conceiving the world, we aim to go beyond the set of observational processes we happen to have realized thus far.

(Radder 2006: 179)

Not only have these different positions 'been the subject of fierce philosophical debates' (Radder 2006: 1) over the ages, they continue to splice the quantitative–qualitative divide in everyday research settings.

The usual image is that quantitative modes of research support regard observation (getting the 'facts') and conceptual interpretation ('theorizing') as separate issues whilst qualitative researchers regard them as connected; observations make no sense without some conceptual apparatus by which to interpret them. This stereotype is not entirely correct, as we will see in subsequent chapters. That there is a connection between these two activities has been accepted in quantitative domains for quite some time (see Figure 1.1).

The actual dividing line is a practical one; which sorts of questions and the means by which we get there best provide us 'with justified knowledge about an independent world' (Radder 2006: 2; see also Adorno 1976).

For both modes, separately and together, the relationship between, first, observation and then data, however, is not a clear correlation; what you see is not always what you (think you) get; more on these matters in Chapters 1, 3 and 7. Contrary to stereotypes, even *quantitative* modes of social research use relatively blunt instruments for measuring when compared to those employed in the natural or physical sciences; the relationship between the act of observation and the data observed – *facts* gathered – is always moot.

Figure 1.1 How we/cats see the world

Source: Nina Paley: http://www.ninapaley.com

No matter how they regard issues around fact and observation, the role of objectivity vis-à-vis standpoint, researchers across the board are engaged in some sort of observation in varying degrees; asking questions, taking field notes, reading historical documents, setting up experiments, or running focus groups. However, in quantitative work the researcher's concern is to *minimize* two elements: first *errors* in observation and, second, to understand the source of the error – whether it is the result of ill-defined concepts, poor instrumentation, *bias*, or poor preparation on the researcher's part. For qualitative researchers these concerns are considered more a point of departure than a problem to be resolved; in varying degrees that are also informed by underlying *worldviews* and research identities. At the end of the day, most researchers would concede that 'seeing' is not always 'believing'.

Data and evidence

The key point here is that there is no immediate consensus about what is meant by *data*, let alone the adjective *empirical*, in either case, even when there are clear distinctions between how the 'data' are collected, processed, and then used as substantiating 'evidence', or *proof* in some quarters. For practical purposes it is still possible to make two clear distinctions.

First, *quantitative data* refers to the types of information that can be counted or expressed numerically; expressing a certain quantity, amount or range. For example, weight expressed in stones or kilos is being referred to as a quantitative indicator. Usually, there are smaller measurement units associated with the data such as pounds or grams; inches or centimetres with respect to feet and metres as in the case of height or length. Quantitative approaches imply that arithmetic operations will be applied to the *data*. Therefore, simple and more advanced statistics are used as well as presenting the outcomes as values in graphs and tables.

Second, *qualitative data* refers to types of information that are non-countable or not expressed numerically. This information includes elements that are termed 'intangible', or 'immeasurable' because they express qualities, values, states of mind, and ideas; in themselves open to any number of qualifications. To use the same example as above, weight can be expressed in terms like 'heavy' or 'fat', 'chubby' versus 'light', 'thin' or 'skinny'. These terms are qualitative indicators and whilst they correlate in some way to numerical measurements, what these terms mean alone and relative to one another is not simply about their respective numerical value.

Often these differences are understood as objective versus subjective measurements of weight, but I would argue this is too simplistic. As in the case of weight perceptions for those people who are anorexic or bulimic, in light of what friends and family think or recurring public debates about the rights and wrongs of 'size 0' supermodels or concerns about obesity, what someone quantitatively weighs as measured in stones or kilograms, may have little bearing on how they see themselves, or others see them in qualitative terms like 'fat' or 'thin'; 'Rubenesque' or 'Twiggy-like'. When couched in such value-laden terms the numerical values assigned to fatness or thinness then take on a double-life; as literal and figurative notional values.

Within the quantitative tradition, data can also be treated in qualitative ways (see Chapters 1 and 7). In other words, these two notions of data-types are not necessarily mutually exclusive in practice, everyday life or academic. Moreover, the significance attributed to numerical values also differs over time, cultures, and between generations. An *a priori* strict division between quantitative and qualitative data and therefore how to treat them is more polemical than practicable. For instance, the standard numerical indicator of an optimal weight-to-height ratio in western societies, the body mass index (BMI), is as much a qualitative measurement as it is a quantitative indicator, the optimum position to which increasingly over-nourished and under-exercised populations are supposed to aspire.

However, in other parts of the world the converse is the case; a position towards a BMI that indicates too much body 'fat' is indicative of well-being, beauty and relative wealth. The 'measurement units' at stake in this case are numerical yet overlaid with social and cultural judgments. So, here not only are aesthetic, social, and cultural criteria implicit in the terminology used even when statistics may well be employed to underpin these qualitative indicators, but so also are the points on the scale itself. The difference between these numerical and non-numerical indicators of body mass, size, or body-image is a question that incorporates the uses of qualitative and quantitative modes of conducting research about these matters, and the conclusions we draw from them.

How do these distinctions work in practice?

Quantitative researchers may think of data as discrete observations presented by numeric values or points on a graph. For example, when conducting surveys of voters after an election, a researcher would ask them for which party they voted, then record the response they give as a numeric value that is intended to represent a particular party. These bits of information about all respondents in the survey are then recorded and compiled into one file. This is a *data set* – a set of data points or observations (see Figure 1.2). This quantitative treatment of data is based on the root meaning of the word; 'data' comes from the Latin, *dare*, to give, and means 'that which is given'. In the quantitative tradition, data-collection often involves technologies of observation and of record that are themselves anchored in previous, often hard-won results, or data sets.

This interplay between previous knowledge and subsequent accumulation is modelled after research conventions in the physical sciences; for instance where you might envision scientists extracting certain data from observing and recording the results of a (controlled) collision in a particle accelerator, collecting data on ice flows, or on planetary motion with increasingly powerful and refined telescopes.

Qualitative modes tend to eschew using the term. For a variety of reasons to be sure, but the implicit discomfort for approaches that do not work at all with numerical indicators, let alone statistics of any kind, is that 'data' has become identifiable with quantitative – numerical – expressions of scientific knowledge, legitimated by statistical methods of analysis.

"Same graph as last year,
but now I have an additional dot."

Figure 1.2   Post-doc presentation
Source: Vadlo: http://vadlo.com/

**TIP: When starting out, be aware of fundamental differences in perception and conceptualization of research itself; it can be counter-productive to set out on a research project convinced that the one or the other type of data represents the sort of research you are *not* doing. Most research today, those engaged in pure theoretical projects aside for the moment, involves the gathering and analysis of various sorts of empirical evidence, or data.

Empirical versus conceptual ways of knowing?

For the sake of argument, and in order to establish some common moment of departure, there is no real reason why non-numerical sorts of data cannot fall under the rubric of the original Latin, *dare*; philosophical and practical debates about what can, or cannot be taken as 'given' in social relations, communications, or behaviour notwithstanding. That which is 'given' can also be taken to be a non-quantifiable, i.e. non-numerical, entity that need not involve arithmetical calculations: ideas, attitudes, written texts, images, various categories of 'meaning-making'. In addition the conditions in which these 'givens' occur can also be interrogated. Turning the latter into numerical entities or not and their re-presentation is where the quantitative–qualitative divide boils down to graphs versus pages of text in the final product. The upshot is that these idioms become synonymous with oppositional views about the whole enterprise (Figure 1.3). As Creswell and others note, much research lies somewhere between these two extremes; the various elements indicate a tendency, even a preference for nominally qualitative, quantitative, or – a combination of the two – 'mixed methods' (Creswell 2009: 16; see also Berg 2007, M. Davies 2007).

Figure 1.3   Differences between the humanities and social sciences

Source: Jorge Cham: http://www.phdcomics.com

As we see above, different usages for the same terms of reference, or misconceptions of terms specific to a particular way of conducting research, can be off-putting enough, also compounded by the implications continual organizational (re)mergers have for how far different approaches go in order to accommodate each other in the conduct of their research affairs. The virtues of multi/interdisciplinary work are often asserted more often than they are put into practice, a function of interdepartmental reshuffles rather than concerted attempts at methodological synergies or definitional rigour. In addition, *intra*disciplinary differences, whereby the terms of reference sound the same but operate very differently can also be hard to get to grips with in everyday research work. The same word, sometimes a deceptively simple term, can have a meaning and use that is peculiar to a particular method or even sub-discipline. It can also be the bone of contention within a community.

So, where does that leave us in this maze? Can all researchers take the term *empirical* to be an applicable adjective for evidential material as data broadly defined? How direct does any observation have to be before it can be regarded as empirical? Conversely, how much conceptualization is needed in social research scenarios before putting this to 'the test' in some way or another? Rather than attempting to respond to these questions about the production of knowledge and how the latter can be expressed and then valued – a job for philosophers and methodologists – let's consider things more pragmatically. For instance, it might well be that numerical indicators can throw light on a textual analysis or an understanding of how values like weight are what many qualitative researchers, feminists particularly, call 'socially constructed' or 'co-constituted' (see Harding 1998a, 1998b).

> **TIP: Before getting too hot under the collar, and this happens sooner than you might think, it is time well-spent to think about the key terms of reference that inspire you or relate to the topic you want to investigate: (1) Take a blank page/screen and make some initial commitments about what *you* mean before worrying about the 'right' reference or buzzword; (2) then go search the literature; take note how ideas are conveyed as a variety of concepts and arguments (see Chapter 4). Settling on your own point of departure and selectively reading

relevant literature even at this early stage helps you in navigating competing terms of reference in your area of interest.[20]

CHAPTER ORGANIZATION

Whilst these problems and ensuing debates are relatively easy to pinpoint, getting past them in order to make sense of a project is another matter. This book is organized around such bottlenecks, for student and supervisor alike. The topics covered are grounded in practical research realities yet resonant with tough debates that still resonate in academic corridors and seminar rooms, intermingling with the murmurs of debates from seemingly bygone eras.

Whilst the emphasis is on postgraduate dissertation projects (the *master's* degree) this trajectory also applies to undergraduate and Ph.D. research levels. In this way the book distinguishes a research project as two broad phases, shared by all traditions more or less. Part 1 deals with 'Divides and Designs'. Chapters 2 to 4 cover topics such as key terms of reference, research design, research question formulation, the role literature reviews play in all of the above. Part 2, Chapters 6 to 8, is about 'Coping and Communicating'; concentrating on gathering data, analysing the material, writing it up and going public.

Bridging these two parts is Chapter 5 which deals with the skills, practicalities, and methodological innovations in what is a particularly fast-moving domain: internet research skills and emerging sorts of *online research*. As most research these days is conducted using the web, or indeed is conducted entirely or partly online, these practicalities and wider implications for understanding research straddle the preceding and subsequent chapters. Chapter 9 reflects on some underlying themes arising from the previous chapters; signposting an exit for some but also able to work as an entry portal for others.

Successive chapters are organized around two working insights: (1) that each new research project brings with it unforeseen and familiar challenges, for first-timers and more experienced researchers alike; and (2) that all research projects entail a journey of some sort, seldom in a straight, upward line but a journey nonetheless in that any research project has a point of departure and, hopefully, an exit. What happens in between and how a researcher manages, indeed copes, along the way is the heart of the book. For this reason, a distinguishing feature of the book is the way in which themes covered within each chapter are organized along two intertwined strands:

As noted above the discussions, particularly the 'how to' sections, trace research paths well-trodden in terms of a sequence of practical considerations along the course of a standard research project; e.g. coming up with a topic, formulating a research question, working up a work-plan or formal proposal, gathering and analysing data, and then writing it all up.

However, instead of front-loading the earlier phases of the enterprise with every conceivable conceptual consideration that students are usually told are integral to successful research projects before or at the point they need to get started, a number of these discussions have been distributed through the book. For instance, a discussion of questions about the *theory–method relationship* comes early on, whilst a look at how different modes of reasoning impact on analysis is left until Chapter 7. Notes on the supervisory relationship, citation formalities, and research ethics span Parts 1 and 2; returning as the stresses and strains they exert on the research shift along the way.

This approach departs from conventional treatments, which tend to start with theoretical considerations before moving on to practical 'how-to's. This organizational logic is reflected in methods and research skills curricula. In real-life research practice, however, we are often not confronted with some of these more abstract issues until later on.

The advantages of a chapter organization based on a redistribution of the abstract and concrete is twofold: (1) a reader can follow the book from start-to-finish if they choose – the 'road movie' dimension; (2) those looking for guidance on specific topics, practical or more conceptual, can browse the contents as need be – the reference dimension. A disadvantage is that the unbundling of all things conceptual and then treating them throughout the book could disrupt the sense of forward momentum that many researchers, 'newbies' and old hands, often look to maintain. That said, in increasingly web-based research cultures, this organization allows the reader to browse the contents as they might online material; 'power-browsing' and hyperlinking reflect the way successive generations of research students engage with literature and information resources in a digital age.[21]

To supplement the narrative, text boxes permit some focused discussions for further thought. A glossary is included for quick-reference for italicized terminology, and various figures highlight contentious issues or look to capture a terrain in visual terms. Finally, a note on the role played by cartoons and other illustrations: included to leaven the dough, they remind us all to keep our sense of humour in an endeavour that whilst being a serious matter needn't always take itself too seriously all the time. Laughter is a great way to learn too, to cope. These images make me chuckle, and groan, so I hope you the reader will also enjoy the insights, wisdom and irony of these illustrations. My thanks to all the artists who have allowed their work to be reproduced here for our enjoyment.

NOTES

1 For more on this turn of phrase see Carver (2004); see also Bleiker (2009: 7–13). The term *western* here connotes several centuries of cross-fertilization between Anglo-American and western European societies, and their respective histories of science and scholarship. Together they have come to operate, or have been imposed as the 'gold standard' in theory and research.

2 As students, working researchers, and educators we often differentiate between 'real thinkers . . . and the rest . . .'; thanks to Zab Franklin for this observation (personal correspondence, 12 August 2011).

3 The first expression is for arguments that are based on personal attacks (e.g. writing style, religion) rather than a reasoned and fair engagement of the opponent's point of view (what someone is actually saying); as in sport, the aim is to 'play the ball' not the player. According to Aristotle (384–322 BC) in *The Art of Rhetoric*, *ad hominem* arguments, whilst effective for short-term point-scoring, are weak; 'fallacies' based on appeals to the emotions and without supporting evidence. Another fallacious form of argumentation is the 'strawman' one, in which the opposing point of view is presented in its weakest

rendition, if not in as caricature; a fallacy of deception and diversion because it misrepresents your opponent's view in order to make your own look stronger.

4 Zlatan Krajina (personal correspondence, 22 August 2011) based on his own experience when starting out; 'I had to accept that the [methods] lit is only there as raw material which doesn't have the answers I need – I'm looking for those answers, that's my job' (Ibid.).

5 My thanks to Marieke Riethof for this insight. For example, some students only twig right at the end of a project, the writing-up phase, and then ask which methods book they should refer to in order to attach the 'right' etiquette to their method. At other times, recommended methods titles remain unread, or misunderstood in terms of how they inform the larger project; ending up as a disjointed mini-literature review after-the-fact or long treatises on meta-level issues. Neither are really substitutes for a clear outline of the specific ways in which evidence, or data has been gathered, and why.

6 This includes titles such as *Your Research Project: A Step by Step Guide for the First Time Researcher* (Wallman 2000); *Doing a Successful Research Project: Using Qualitative or Quantitative Methods* (M. Davies 2007); *Research Design: Qualitative, Quantitative, and Mixed Method Approaches* (Creswell 2009); *Doing Research in the Real World* (Gray 2009); *How To Research* (Blaxter et al. 2006); *Conducting Literature Reviews: From the Internet to Paper* (Fink 2009).

7 Titles in this category broach topics such as: *Case Studies and Theory Development in the Social Sciences* (George and Bennett 2005); *Logics of Critical Explanation in Social and Political Theory* (Glynos and Howarth 2007); *Interpreting the Political: New Methodologies* (Carver and Hyvarinen 1997); *Methodological Imaginations* (Busfield and Stina Lyon 1996); *Bridges and Boundaries: Historians, Political Scientists, and the Study of International Relations* (Elman and Fendius Elman 2001); or *Ways of Knowing: Competing Methodologies in Social and Political Research* (Moses and Knutsen 2007).

8 Take for example, titles such as *Research Methods in Politics* (Burnham et al. 2004); *Political Research: An Introduction* (Harrison 2001); *Theory and Methods in Political Science* (Marsh and Stoker 2002); *Theory and Methods in Sociology* (Hughes and Sharrock 2007); or *Theories of International Relations* (Burchill et al. 2001).

9 Media and communications methods-based titles tend to straddle this distinction.

10 For example, titles such as: *Inside Culture: Re-imagining the Method of Cultural Studies* (Couldry 2000); *Media Research Methods: Audiences, Institutions, Texts* (Bertrand and Hughes 2004); *Reflexive Ethnography: A Guide to Researching Ourselves and Others* (C. Davies 2007); *Doing and Writing Action Research* (McNiff and Whitehead 2009); Morley (2006).

11 For instance, *Research Methods in the Social Sciences* (Frankfort-Nachmias and Nachmias 1996); *Practical Social Investigation: Qualitative and Quantitative Methods in Social Research* (Pole and Lampard 2001); *The Comparative Method: Moving Beyond Qualitative and Quantitative Strategies* (Ragin 1987); *Social Research Methods: Quantitative and Qualitative Approaches* (Neuman 1997).

12 Take for instance titles such as: *Statistics Explained* (Hinton 2004); *Qualitative Research Practice* (Ritchie and Lewis 2003); *Qualitative Research Methods for the Social Sciences* (Berg 2007); *The Sage Handbook of Qualitative Research* (Denzin and Lincoln 2005); *Working with Qualitative Data* (Gibson and Brown 2009); *Qualitative Research* (Silverman 2011).

13 Useful titles here include ones such as: *Feminist Media Studies* (van Zoonen 1994); *Gender at the Crossroads of Knowledge: Feminist Anthropology in the Postmodern Era* (di Leonardo 1991); *Constructing International Relations: The Next Generation* (Fierke and Jørgensen 2001); *The Politics of Social Science Research* (Ratcliffe 2001); *Decolonising Methodologies: Research and Indigenous Peoples* (Smith 1999); *Creative Social Research* (Giri 2004); *Method in Social Science: A Realist Approach* (Sayer 1999); or *Against Method* (Feyerabend 1978).

14 See Wallerstein (1974).

15 Key titles and more recent ones in this highly volatile area include; *Virtual Ethnography* (Hine 2000); *Qualitative Research and Hypermedia* (Dicks et al. 2005); *Politics on the Internet* (Buckler and Dolowitz 2005); *Internet Research Methods: A Practical Guide for the Social and Behavioural Sciences* (Hewson et al. 2002); *How To Do Your Literature Search and Find Research Information Online* (Ó Dochartaigh 2009); *Conducting Research Literature Reviews: From the Internet to Paper* (Fink 2009); *A Guide to Conducting Online Research* (Gaiser and Schreiner 2009).

16 Thanks to Susan Banducci for this reminder; '[no-one would ever] claim 100% accuracy however hard the science there is always a margin of error also in terms of something as complex as human behaviour, attitudes and opinions the objects [of inquiry] are even more mushy' (private correspondence, October 2010).

17 The distinction and overlap between the terms scholarly and scientific will be broached in the next two chapters. For now, *scholarly* refers to more inclusive understandings of what constitutes *scientific* knowledge in academe.

18 That said, there are qualities to research cultures and careers, along with the waxing and waning of their social status that are particular if not peculiar to these settings. The literature in this respect is massive. For humourous and serious commentaries see for instance, Pierre Bourdieu (1984), C. P. Snow (1993 [1959]), Hannah Arendt (1953), and Malcolm Bradbury (1975).

19 See Smith (1999), Giri (2004), Said (1994), Harding (1987), Ratcliffe (2001).

20 My thanks to Philippe Rekacewicz for inspiring my students – and me – with this tactic for generating ideas; a 'blank piece of paper' approach to refining our own ideas and learning-curve is often more effective than the 'I have to read everything first' one.

21 See UCL (2008), Franklin and Wilkinson (2011), for instance.

PART 1 DIVIDES AND DESIGNS

CHAPTER 2

Putting research into perspective

Topics covered in this chapter:

- Key elements of a research project
- What is a dissertation/thesis?
- What is originality?
- Getting started – deciding a topic
- On theory, method, and methodology

INTRODUCTION

First-timers may well notice early on that *thinking* and *talking* about the nuts and bolts of academic research often diverge from the daily grind of *doing* it. It is cold comfort to hear that this goes with the territory or that like other endeavours in life full understanding comes with hindsight. Nonetheless, a first step in acquiring the skills you need to deal with this disconnect when it creates tensions in your own work is to have a sense of what lies ahead. Rather than taking a leap in the dark with your eyes closed and your fingers crossed, time taken getting a sense of the larger terrain early on is well-spent.

With this aim in mind, this chapter addresses some of the themes and terminology that underwrite initial decisions we take on getting a research project off the ground. This, and the next chapter will not be giving a blow-by-blow account of all the *epistemological* and *ontological* issues – about knowing and existence respectively – at stake in different takes on these matters. Indeed many of these shuttle to-and-fro across the quantitative–qualitative divide if not seek to redefine this very term of reference. Moreover, not all of them are pertinent at the outset.[1]

Whilst the debates discussed here have a timeless quality to them – are endless debates in effect – all projects have an end-point in mind. Here we look at how these issues inflect the everyday practicalities of getting started on a project that will unfold over a given time period; the road ahead in other words, which means certain milestones to pass, whether officially or informally, in order to complete the journey and do so *successfully*, as Martin Davies (2007) notes.

In tandem with Chapter 3, this chapter gets to grips with one of the most difficult aspects of this journey – getting started on the right foot (completion is the next hardest part). This chapter looks at some basic questions, often questions many students hesitate to ask for fear of being seen as a 'dummy'. We then move on to ways of choosing a topic, how to get a better sense of the distinction between the ways the 'theory' and 'method' parts of formal academic projects work together and separately. This puts us in good stead by the next chapter where we tackle formulating a 'doable' *research question*; a moment that confronts all researchers. There are common pitfalls involved in research (question) formulation, planning, and use of various literatures. This is having to tailor our ambitions to available resources, knowledge and skills, as well as the time available.

Because details create pressure points and tunnel vision of their own – e.g. the best size, or randomness of your *sample*, how many (or how few) *focus groups* you need to organize, how many books you should read – the aim here is to provide a wider perspective on how details have abstract, philosophical and practical, puzzle-solving dimensions. Any readers who prefer to grapple with practicalities, get to the how-to before considering more abstract matters, are free to browse. That said, philosophical concerns create their own pressure points in a project as well; so no time like the present.

First though we need to address how these initial practicalities relate to the specific form and substance of academic research projects (see Chapter 1).

KEY ELEMENTS OF A RESEARCH PROJECT

Students often ask themselves, and then their supervisors even several months into the time allotted to complete their research project, 'Where do I begin?' As a student, you may have attended a workshop or module on how to write a dissertation or thesis and the instructor put up a slide with x number (fill in the blank) of steps to the research process. And then looking at this slide it may appear that the research process is simply a matter of ticking the boxes and crossing off tasks on the to-do list: research question – done, lit review – done, data – done; collect your diploma at the exit, and move on. However, you may well find yourself asking the question, 'Where do I begin?' *after* you have already ticked some boxes.[2] This section takes a look at the research process as whole.

Instead of setting out along this path, one way to keep your bearings is to consider a research project in spatial, rather than temporal terms. Box 2.1 provides an overview of the key – compulsory – *elements* that research projects from all approaches have in common. They also are core elements in developing a plan of work, and then presenting this as a research proposal. Take a look and isolate which of these elements are already familiar to you, echoed by those around you? Which are not? Which elements do you currently rate as the most important; the ones you see as your top priority?

BOX 2.1 KEY ELEMENTS OF AN ACADEMIC RESEARCH PROJECT

- The WHAT: (i) general topic-area; (ii) specific object of analysis; (iii) research question/hypothesis.
- The WHY: (i) aims and objectives; (ii) researcher's motivations (personal) or project brief (funded research).
- The HOW: (i) conceptually – theory/key concepts; (ii) practically – method/s; (iii) rationale (methodology).
- The WHERE and WHEN: (i) time and place; (ii) intellectual context – theoretical debates/research literature; (iii) sociocultural, political and economic dimensions.
- The WHO and FOR WHOM: (i) implications; (ii) consequences; (iii) applications.

Working these pieces of the research puzzle into a coherent whole is integral to successful research, in theory and in practice; from choosing a topic, formulating and then refining a research question so that you don't bite off more than you can chew, plotting how to get the information you will need, presenting the project before it's begun in a formal research proposal form, gathering the information (*data* for the sake of argument, see Chapter 1), assembling and then analysing it, right through to writing it all up and presenting your findings in such a way that you can account for, and defend the decisions you made and, thereby, the analysis and conclusions you make from the eventual outcome.

As counter-intuitive as it may seem in competitive and international classrooms, doing research is not the same as competing in sport as such; it is not a speed-race. You are not going for a personal best, world record, or gold medal. Deadlines have their uses nonetheless; they create an end-point for a piece of work and in larger projects this is a comforting thought. You will, indeed you must finish this work at some point; for communal deadlines (dissertation hand-ins for instance) everyone is working against the clock. Nonetheless how the results are assessed does not depend on who was quickest off the mark all those months back, nor who claims to have got their final version printed out first. The tendency for students to judge their progress by how much further along their classmates may be along the way is the source of much anxiety, precipitous decisions, and demoralization.

Whatever your response to where you are 'at' with regard to these elements, it bears repeating that they do not unfold in a neat and tidy sequence. Whilst they all need to be present in some form in the research proposal and adequately covered in the final report/dissertation, they do need to be attended to in some sort of order of appearance; one that consists of overlapping, cyclical chunks of time as well as in the sense of moving forwards. As research projects are completed within certain timeframes, respective delivery dates and *deliverables* within the one project create stress at different points and in different measures. At any one stage, you may need to return to an earlier stage and revise text or remind yourself of the main objectives of the study, reformulate the research question if need be. At other times you, and your brain may need to take a break. Here intellectual effort does bear similarities to sport; the human mind, where 'reason' and thinking resides can improve its fitness levels as well.

All well and good but there are a couple of other, more pressing questions that tend to go begging as supervisors, mentors, and classmates urge us to put our 'best foot forward'.

LOOKING AHEAD: MILESTONES, DESTINATIONS, AND EXPECTATIONS

Many students, even those with research projects (bachelor level or work-related) behind them are reluctant to ask three fundamental questions; often taken as read by supervisors and mentors.

(a) What exactly is expected in producing a *thesis*, or *dissertation*?[3]
(b) If the dissertation is the destination, then what exactly is expected when having to submit a formal *research proposal*, or (often less formal) research *outline*? How are (a) and (b) related (see Chapter 3)?
(c) What is meant by *originality*, or *independent research component*? How does this fit what is expected in mandatory literature reviews (see Chapter 4)?

Let's pin each of these down one by one.

What is a dissertation/thesis?

This document is a formalized presentation of the whole process, as a completed project. As an integral part of degree awards, the particular features of a dissertation and what distinguishes it from other work in a degree programme, such as an exam, presentation, or term-paper, is usually seldom talked about beyond references to university regulations. Even though the actual dissertation may seem far away and its exact contours are still hazy, getting a sense at least of what the end-goal, the deliverable, involves in formal terms can help allay initial anxieties. This section will, at the very least, indicate the destination point, even if the way you will take to get there is still unclear.

The short answer to the question, 'what exactly is a dissertation?', is that a master-level or Ph.D. academic degree, and certain bachelor degrees, require the successful

completion of a substantial piece of written work based on the outcome of a personally designed and carried-out piece of original research. This is what is being
referred to by the terms *dissertation*, or *thesis*. Below is a generic definition:

> A dissertation is a formal written presentation of an original piece of individual
> research undertaken on an approved topic and completed under the supervision
> of a [assigned or approved] supervisor/s; of a [specified] length, according to the
> general and specific criteria of academic excellence of the degree-awarding
> institution/department where stipulated, submitted no later than [specified date]
> according to the [specified or recommended] formats of the respective institution
> or department.

It pays to check out your course handbook, degree regulations, and other official
sources from your institution to be sure what is expected of you for your degree
qualification. That said, these specifications are technical rather than substantive. So,
what do they actually mean in practice?

A dissertation is more complex in substance (content), organizational, and formatting terms than a term-paper or essay. In the UK it is less than a book yet more
than a research proposal, research paper, or research report/work report even though
it shares elements with all of the above. It is a record of the process and outcome of
time spent doing research on a project, which requires you to work independently on
conceptual (theoretical), practical (methodological), and formal (written and analytical) levels. Some of the skills and aptitudes needed you may well already have. Some
will be new to you; e.g. organizing and sustaining the writing of a considerably longer
piece of work for instance; 12,000 words and upwards depending on your location.

The dissertation proper is the end-phase of a research project; a piece of academic
writing in its own right with all the issues of style and presentation and expression
that any specific sort of writing task entails. In this respect, not only planning but
writing, and rewriting this document, in part or as a whole, is integral to the process
of completing the *dissertation* part of the research project as a whole. As process and
product the dissertation is a substantial part of the degree programme; comprised of
mandatory and optional elements.

So a more comprehensive response to this foundational question would take the
following distinctions into account: that between

- a research plan and process; the dissertation as the outcome of both;
- an initial idea, larger debates in the literature underscoring an eventual topic,
  and how all these emerge as a specific research question;
- different sorts of research procedures in their own right, role in schools of thought,
  dissertation formats, and institutional requirements;
- expectations in depth and breadth of knowledge for undergraduate, postgraduate,
  and Ph.D. levels of work; including the total number of chapters, word-lengths,
  chapter titles, section headings, and other formalities;
- argumentation as/in writing vis-à-vis substantiating evidence in the form of
  graphics, images, calculations, and other sorts of non-textual material (e.g. audio,
  multimedia);

- eventual evaluation criteria and marking schemes (e.g. double credits), formatting requirements, depending on department, institution, or geographical area.

That said, there are general elements common to all dissertations whatever the level; bachelor, master, on up to a Ph.D. dissertation. Irrespective of how you characterize the general and specific research path you take, or whether you opt for a 'classic' or alternative dissertation format (Blaxter et al. 2006: 236; M. Davies 2007: 211 *passim*) these are:

- The 'head': a title (and sub-title if desired); a list of contents (that tells the reader something substantive about this dissertation); an abstract (200–300 words); 5–6 keywords (optional and terms that are not in your title).
- The 'middle': the 'chapters' or chapter sections in terms of their function; these *can be given other, more substantive and informative titles*:
    - Introduction: aims and objectives, research question, argument, chapter outline.
    - Review of the background literature/theoretical framework.
    - Overview of the research design: methods used/methodological discussion of these choices.
    - Background (historical) of *case study* where applicable.
    - Presentation of the findings.
    - Analysis of the findings.
    - Comment on findings in light of theory/literature and methodological considerations.
    - Summary and conclusion.
- The 'tail': references (endnotes/footnotes); literature list; appendices and/or glossary (optional).

In sum all the above ideally add up to a dissertation that presents

- a well-formed research question/problem or hypothesis; this is the *heart*;
- evidence of previous knowledge about the field; in the literature review/theoretical framework; this is the *brain*;
- evidence of 'empirical' work that involves a creative application of concepts or analytical tools to make sense of the data gathered, material or ideas being addressed; the *eyes and hands*;
- has an argument, substantiates that argument, and understands opposing views; this is the *backbone*.[4]

What is a research proposal/outline?

A second term of reference is the form, timing, and eventual role played by a formal *research proposal* – or *outline* – in the larger dissertation project. Although self-contained, the latter piece of work does have a bearing on the eventual outcome of your project if not part of a course assessment. For this reason research proposals and outlines need some separate treatment.

Chapter 3 looks more closely at this first milestone in many departments and its role in various sorts of research designs. In light of how both dissertation and research outline go about organizing the main elements of academic research projects (Box 2.1 above) for their respective audiences, the following points will suffice for the time being:

- A research outline is a plan of work for a *proposed* piece of research; a roadmap, or feasibility study. Proposals also include the academic equivalent of a sales pitch.
- Paradoxically given the increasing emphasis laid on research planning and proposal writing in academe, the most coherent articulation of a research project as a proposal and work-plan often crystallizes once the research and analysis has been completed. Our best proposal-writing is in retrospect.
- However, the working reality is otherwise; research projects need to be planned and presented before we know what the outcome is. Students in particular are planning and designing research in unfamiliar terrains, with assessment and awarding of a degree as an arbiter.

What is the difference? Basically, the final product – the dissertation or report in the case of funded work – can and will differ from any outline, or formal proposal. Indeed it can in some cases emerge as quite different in key respects. After all, this document is the outcome of the research once it has been completed and writing up these results, making sense of them conceptually as well is a process in itself. This is why the future-tense use of the proposal form changes, indeed needs to be changed to past tense. It is also why results, analysis, and eventual conclusions may well differ from initial claims presented in earlier outlines.

A third question that students often are afraid to ask is 'what counts as *original*, or *independent* research?'

What is originality?

> Highly original research is very unusual, and you are probably setting your sights far too high if you try aiming for it. The corollary of this is that your research is almost certainly original in some way, always providing, that is, that you are not slavishly copying someone else's earlier research.
>
> (Blaxter et al. 2006: 12)

Reference to dissertations being assessed for evidence of 'original' if not 'independent' work beg the question of what exactly amounts to originality. Is there anything new under the sun, as the saying goes? As the authors cited above point out, coming up with something 100 per cent 'new' is a once-in-a-lifetime event, if that, for anyone. For students starting out, exhortations of originality can create anxiety about the 'worth' of their chosen topic or ability to undertake research under their own steam.

To all intents and purposes, in practice notions of originality (not 'slavishly' replicating others' work) and independent (autonomous) work operate in tandem;[5] discovering or understanding something yourself, on your own terms, in your own time and in your own words is, in itself, something original. By the same token, an academic research project requires you to understand something about what has been done before, if not being done at the moment as you come up with your own ideas; gather your own findings with reference to theory and research literature already 'out there', by whatever means or reasons you have for doing so. The analysis you make and conclusions you draw emerge out of work that, ideally, is something you want to 'own' rather than disown! In terms of those setting out on the quantitative path, originality can be construed as adding some new data, or a new case to an existing body of research on a topic. You may find a way of adding a new variable (see Chapter 3 on research topics) or new concept as part of the hypothesis to be tested; in other words set up a new relationship between concepts from research that treats them in another relationship. References to originality and by association 'contribution to knowledge' are not an issue of quantity alone.

So, originality on both sides of the divide is a relative term as, indeed, is 'newness'; both are claimed more often than they are substantiated. For instance, Blaxter et al. (2006: 13) list fifteen definitions of originality that span from 'setting down new information in writing for the first time' to 'adding to knowledge in a way that hasn't previously been done before', passing by 'using already known material but with a new interpretation' (ibid.).

Perhaps start with what is 'new' to you; rather than the whole of humankind. Striving to do your own thing, being innovative, and ticking the boxes, that is completing the required elements to the best of your ability, and then being satisfied with the final product as a whole is, clearly, a tall task and so more than enough in itself. As Martin Davies notes, the learning curve of the process you are embarking upon straddles the fine line between overly cautious and over-ambitious expectations, learning the tricks of the trade, and settling on 'a question that is realistically answerable and will enable you to make a *modest* contribution to your discipline's knowledge-base' (M. Davies 2007: 18, emphasis added; see also Blaxter et al. 2006: 249).

That said, anyone reading your work or assessing it will more often than not react warmly to something that is innovative, adventurous, and engaged rather than the 'same old song' Baxter et al. 2006: 236); sometimes, like modesty, a little brashness goes a long way. So, for those readers who feel that all these caveats and words of caution are too restrictive or stultifying creativity then go for it. Innovation and originality do emerge by bucking the norm; a calculated risk that once again is not impossible to bring off. By the same token, originality does not always reside in the level of emphasis we might lay on our research project's claims to be doing something unequivocally 'new'. Remember too that different research communities send different, if not mixed messages about the limits of possibility in terms of how far terms like innovativeness, creativity, and risk-taking are encouraged or tolerated. What is 'new' in one department is old hat in another.

> ****TIP:** when beginning a research project or even a conversation with your supervisor or peer-group about a research project, start with an idea of what *you* are interested in doing or, if you are really stumped and open to all possibilities you could also ask your supervisor, or others, what they would consider an interesting topic or line of inquiry.

In some research cultures, students are effectively completing projects as research assistants for work being done by their professors. In other cases, in the US and Canada for example, research proposals are not part of the admission process for the Ph.D. degree. The eventual project and its form (along the lines conveyed above) take shape as the student works in consultation with supervisors, mentors, and seminar groups. Finally, just how individual the idea of originality is depends on these sociocultural inflections of your research community.

The next part of this chapter turns to the task in hand; getting started by coming up with a viable research idea and then turning it into a doable research project. After that it is time to broach an even thornier, albeit no less fascinating distinction that has implications for how an initial idea is fashioned into a research question, or hypothesis: what is meant by references to *theory* and *method*, and by association, *methodology*. These three terms are the sources of confusion and misunderstanding between supervisors and supervisees particularly. But, first let's get the ball rolling.

GETTING STARTED AND DECIDING A TOPIC

The hardest parts in any research project are, as a rule, the starting-out and the completion stages, assuming nothing untoward happens in-between. For now though we shall concentrate on getting started.

Getting off on the right foot

Martin Davies (2007) has a very helpful set of ten tips to help you to the starting blocks in the right frame of mind. Extrapolating with reference to others and my own experience and those of colleagues and mentors, consider the following:

- recognize you need a supervisor; being positive about supervision is beneficial;
- with their permission, make use of your peers, your family, friends, if not other tutors and lecturers;
- embrace brainstorming, avoid the temptation to second-guess;
- accept that criticisms, especially early on, will arise; they help you move on;
- get a sense of available resources, close to home and further away;
- don't get too set on a topic/research question too early or too hastily; keep your options open . . .
- . . . but do decide eventually! This is not your life's work;
- plan what you want to achieve for group or individual supervisory sessions;
- 'RTFM', i.e. become acquainted with mandatory and optional formalities for your institutional setting; ignorance of the 'specs' (e.g. word-limits, formatting) is not an argument;
- keep track of useful and inspirational resources; return to them to touch base;
- assess the time, resources, and current skill-sets you have; particularly if you want to set out in a new direction;
- plan, plan, and plan again; revise and reschedule where necessary. Time flies!

There is nothing like a deadline to get you going. Many students and working researchers, in academe and the workplace, rely upon – indeed thrive on – the impetus an approaching deadline provides. However, for a research project that leads to a dissertation which will be then be graded, how you get ready (get set, and then go) has implications for how to manage moulding your initial ideas or sense of a general topic into a feasible research question; moreover, one that you can live with, let alone one you want to, and can do, over a sustained period of time. So, moving on: What *is* your research actually going to be about; the *topic*?

Coming up with and committing to a topic

Unless stipulated otherwise the topic is up to you; how this emerges as a research question and in a larger context is another matter. This is easier said than done, particularly when you may be overwhelmed with new information, or unable to decide between several ideas.

Here are some tips to help you when deciding on a topic:

- figure out just how much choice you have and how motivated you are;
- start with those topics that interest, inspire, or concern you; thinkers, theoretical streams, ideas, or debates that have caught your attention;
- ascertain which terms, thinkers, debates, and areas of research are developed within your programme, and the department at large;
- look up the staff research interests and personal profiles in your department and programme for cues, inspiration; or for rejection purposes;
- look up previous dissertations; they are available online or in the library;
- in light of the above; consider what kinds of research is being done in institutions nearby, or in collaborative projects within your department;
- think about continuing a previous project (many do). Alternatively, eliminate that from your options (many do again);
- 'start anywhere' (see Blaxter et al. 2006: 32–3); why not?
- put all your favourite ideas in a hat and pick out one. Don't like it? Well that much is clear already;
- brainstorm, alone but even better with others; 'good ideas tend to generate others' (Gray 2009: 47);
- in light of the above, set a time or another sort of limit to the expanding list of ideas to avoid becoming overwhelmed; here deadlines are very useful;
- don't overlook, or underestimate how you may already have a topic in mind based on the reasons for enrolling in this programme, university, or past experience; 'go forward with confidence' in this respect.[6]

Some things to keep in mind about searching for any topic: the subject should be timely in as much that the previous research done on the topic leads to an interesting puzzle for you to investigate. For example, previous research may have left a particular explanation or concept unexplored or there may be research that led to inconsistent results; your research proposes to address these anomalous findings. This is where you can use your research project as an opportunity to be creative – this is a sort of *originality* as well.

> ****TIP:** If the research topic is too speculative or considered too 'left field' in your setting, you may find it difficult to find an appropriate supervisor to support your research.
> - So, along with striving to be creative and independent some compromise may be necessary.
> - Be inclusive but be realistic. You should really enjoy the subject and want to spend a significant portion of your time on it.

At the end of the day, though, you do need to settle on a main theme; what you do decide to do need not take on hugely life-long implications. This need not be your life's work. Agonizing too long over which topic on the basis that this will define you intellectually, confine you in your future options, or must be *directly* applicable to your future career ambitions is often misplaced, particularly at the undergraduate and master level.[7]

For Ph.D.s these questions can take on a larger personal or professional dimension. But even then I would argue that academic careers are not necessarily made or broken on the one research topic, or methodology for that matter. Right now, decisions need to be made. Furthermore, many such concerns get ironed out; even early on in the design stages we need to enrol, enthuse, 'pitch' the idea, get it out of our heads and onto paper where sympathetic and sceptical listener/s, experts and lay audiences can get a handle on it and challenge us to improve.

From the general to the particular

This shift is not a straightforward one; any new research project shuffles between our own 'grand designs', our view of precursors in the research literature as inspirations or competitors, and the need to knock a topic or an idea into the shape of a so-called doable research question. All researchers are looking to find 'the puzzle and gaps' in a particular area.[8] For this reason:

- making notes and committing your earliest ideas in writing is indispensable to moving you along (see Creswell 2009: 78–82); an often overlooked role of research proposal-writing (Chapter 3);
- as is breaking down topics arising from your studies and reading, or dissertation projects from students in previous years.

For example, which of the topics below, all taken from the initial ideas of eventually completed research, are more general? Which are more specific? How could you make some of the broader topics into more focused questions?

- 'body-building'
- 'the anti-sweatshop movement and globalization'

- 'political blogs and democracy'
- 'gender and voting behaviour'
- 'anti-immigration policies in the European Union'
- 'states and markets after the Credit Crisis'
- 'young women and urban violence'
- 'popular culture and world politics'
- 'multilateral institutions and new social movements'
- 'actor-networks and social activism on the web'.

Once you have decided on the subject-area, or areas you are interested in, your research *topic* usually boils down to one sentence or phrase. This can designate both a general rubric, sub-themes and ideally (for supervisory meetings especially) a specific issue. So, if you look at the above examples again, and you can see that they point to any number of more specific questions, you could ask which can be broken down into sub-topics and how you would go about breaking them down (e.g. by geography, periods of time, groups around gender or ethnicity, older or newer media).

> ** TIP: If you want to do something that is counter-intuitive or against the grain in a field, then the 'burden of proof' is greater.

- Note that listeners will voice reservations quite quickly if a research topic is unusual, too narrow, or too broad.
- That said, most research starts out as topics that are too broad. So if you get this comment in the early stages don't take it as a condemnation.

There are two additional points around these initial steps when you go about deciding on a topic and then move on to formulating a research question, or hypothesis if this is the preferred formulation (see Chapter 3):

1 What happens if you are in the luxurious position of not being able to decide between several topics or, conversely, discover that your topic of choice is considered not-doable or inadvisable?[9] The basic answer to this is to acknowledge, preferably in consultation with your supervisor or trusted others, the point at which you will make an executive decision; hovering between options for too long is a form of procrastination.
2 Once you have a Plan A think of a possible back-up, Plan B. Put it this way: in the early phases, don't be afraid of changing your mind or topic. That said, and depending on how your institution sets deadlines in this respect, if changing your mind, do it sooner rather than later and be clear as to why. In a pressure-cooker situation like a one-year dissertation programme, beware of losing too much time changing your mind; this is the converse of putting off making a decision.

Now that you have decided your topic, more or less, the next step will be refining the *research question*; the next step in sequential terms albeit one that can take more then several tries before it sounds, reads, or feels 'right'. Take note that:

- deciding on our topic does not mean we have devised a research question. A research topic is not quite that same thing;
- formulating a question that guides the inquiry entails some sort of larger 'puzzle' that is articulated as 'doable', i.e. in the time allotted and with the requisite resources;
- different sorts and styles of research questions, hypotheses, have respective articulations pointing to different research paths in turn, e.g. literary excursions or large-scale surveys.

Chapter 3 addresses diverging and converging approaches to developing research questions, or hypotheses. These point to respective sorts of research planning and execution. Whilst all approaches would concur that a successful piece of research is in the final analysis 'all about the research question', they part company on the weighting given to whether this aspect needs perfecting early on or whether, at the other end of the spectrum, it is something that necessarily evolves during the research itself.

So, already, we are on shifting sands. The boxes we want to tick start to shimmer and shudder under the weight of our own desire to get on with chosing the best method to pursue the topic, usually resisting admonitions that we take our time, do undertake a selective or comprehensive search of the literature, write these findings up as our 'literature review' (see Chapter 4), or reconsider the topic as we are told to refine or 'develop a research question'. Students literally wriggle in discomfort at this point during supervisory meetings when asked to 'focus' or to 'go away and refine your research question'. They are not the only ones; researchers dealing with negative comments in these sections of a proposal for research funding do so too.

To understand why even this earliest point can create pressure, we need to take a step back from the *perpetuum mobile* of a formal research trajectory in order to move up a level of abstraction.

THEORY AND METHOD – OF CARTS AND HORSES

Here is some more food for thought:

- What is (a) theory?
- Is theory singular or plural?
- Isn't theory the same as methodology?

- What counts as (a) method?
- Is method singular or plural?
- Isn't method the same as methodology?

- Which should come first – the theory or the method?
- What *is* research?

Which of the above terms of reference relate to which aspect of our proposed plan of work? When are they analytically distinct, how do they interact in our larger project, and how do we deal with them organizationally – in the final report?

Easier to ask than they are to answer satisfactorily, these FAQs (frequently asked questions) beg a number of thorny questions beyond their functional role in the jargon of degree-specification or supervisor-speak around the mandatory elements of your eventual dissertation; the 'methodology chapter', the 'theory chapter' as cases in point. Getting to grips with the way in which these distinct yet *interdependent* elements often have the researcher, newbies particularly, going around in ever-decreasing circles are amongst the first, and last hurdles to jump. This is because arguments about their definitions and practical implications are at the heart of debates about the form and substance of credible scholarly knowledge, let alone whether the latter can only be encapsulated as knowledge acquired by application of *scientific method*; detractors and defenders line up along the quantitative–qualitative divide accordingly.

The next chapter explores some aspects of these debates more closely. Suffice to say, they have been raging for centuries, going as far back as ancient Greece. Some great minds and lesser mortals have thought about these issues, and fought long and hard with opponents about them. Indeed, in some cases books have been burned, and high-profile figures ridiculed or even killed for daring to counter accepted wisdoms of the time. Whilst hindsight has vindicated many or condemned others, the jury is still out in other instances. Successive iterations of these debates are the scholarly 'back-story' and cast of characters in the history of modern science; as incarnated in western European and Anglo-American renditions of this particular story, its critics and counter-narratives.

How (i) and how (ii)

At the outset of any research project these terms can be addressed as two roughly equivalent parts of the *how* element of a research project (see Box 2.1). Each will get its equivalent weighting and attention within and across research traditions; for example, in some settings references to 'methodology' are construed as synonymous with 'theory' whilst in others, experimental psychology for instance, a full account of specific methods used to design and carry out the experiment is indispensable, for instance the role of a *control group*, sampling criteria, and what sorts of consent are involved.

1   The first aspect of the *how* is abstract; conceptual frameworks, specific concepts, philosophical considerations; *theory* in so many words.
2   The second *how* is on the more practical side; specific ways of going about getting data, or information – the facts of the matter if you like, of investigating your object of inquiry; commonly referred to as *method*, or methods. Each has their own literature base.
3   Nestled, not always comfortably, between is a third notion, often referred to as *methodology*. This term is often used to underscore how the conceptual (abstract)

and concrete (pragmatic) dimensions (namely theory and method) are insepar-able. How this interconnection is explicitly addressed, or whether the relationship is seen as an integral, or peripheral issue for the research at hand pertain also to various *worldviews* (see Chapter 3).

This push and pull between how we represent the conceptual – abstract, and the concrete – practical dimensions of a research undertaking is where overtly competing approaches collide (see Moses and Knutsen 2007). But this is also why as we look to hurry our research design into getting into what we consider to be the research proper we can 'hit the wall'; if one aspect of the *how* is considerably less thought through it becomes the 'weakest link', as the TV quiz show has it, when it is put under pressure.

So let's try and make some sense of this terrain, by taking each element one at a time – theory, method, methodology – as analytically distinct albeit practicably overlapping one another.

On theory – how (i)

The two excerpts below each put their finger on what is often the sore point within and between research methodologies; the 'T' word – theory; as something pragmatic so 'messy' or, rather, as something quintessentially abstract; elegant and economical with words.

> [R]esearch ... is more than a mere pragmatic activity; behind it lies the foundations of academic theories that have emerged through the process of scientific inquiry and investigations over many decades and centuries.
>
> (Gray 2009: 5)

> A theory is more that a definition; it is a framework that supplies an orderly explanation of observed phenomena. ... It should systematically unify and organize a set of observations, building from basic principles ... Theories have practical consequences, too, guiding us in what we value (or dislike), informing our comprehension, and introducing new generations to our cultural heritage.
>
> (Freeland 2001: i)

At the risk of sounding trite, theories come in all shapes and sizes along these two poles, from grand narratives explaining historical change over time, how the universe began, to highly specialized 'propositions, or hypotheses, that specify the relationship among variables (typically in terms of magnitude or direction)' (Creswell 2009: 51), to more fluid interrogative formulations.

Similarly, different categorizations of theory, or theorizing, also make sense at different levels of disciplinary recognition with respect to their being statements about ambitions to generate truth-statements about the world. These ambitions are evident in micro-level (where details and focus count) through to the macro-level (where generalizations and range matter). More recently, a move to generating 'mid-range' theories looks to accommodate these two poles (see Callon and Latour 1981, Creswell

2009: 52, Foucault 1984, Neuman 1997, Rosenau 1999). In short, the sort of tightrope researchers walk continually (often gesticulating at one another from either side) in this respect spans:

- one end of the spectrum where there are definite ideas about what is meant by theory, taking their cue from the natural sciences;
- to the other end where there are some very definite ideas about what is *not* meant by theory.

The next chapters will discuss these relationships and respective differences in modes of reasoning as they arise. For now, let's take an oft-cited working definition of theory from the social sciences by Kerlinger and Lee. They propose that theory is a 'set of interrelated constructs (concepts), definitions, and propositions that present a systematic view of phenomena by specifying relations among variables, with the purpose of explaining and predicting phenomena' (cited in Creswell 2009: 51, Gray 2009: 5; see Berg 2009: 21–2).

This conceptualization, steeped in how theory and theorizing have been codified and contested in the natural sciences and philosophy of science, has a relatively restricted focus. It also lays the stress on aiming for explanation and prediction. Whilst there are significant differences amongst scientists, and philosophers of science, about the relationship between said 'theory' and the 'facts' to which it is referring, the former effectively boils down to the formulation of an 'appropriate conceptual framework' (Chalmers 2004: 13) for the appropriate data set (facts).

More pragmatically, theorizing is by definition thinking at a certain level of abstraction; to theorize, posit a theory/theory about something, is to do more than describe, annotate, or classify what you see – observe; recall the discussion from Chapter 1). It means to make explicit the underlying assumptions that govern the description, the annotation, or the classification. Stronger still, theoretical physics, mathematical theorems, and the models put forward in the 'high theory' of modernist and postmodernist thinkers in the social sciences and humanities all take leave of absence from the material – empirical – world in order to extrapolate and postulate; leaving the proof of their veracity for later generations (e.g. Einstein's theory of relativity, or the state of sub-atomic theories today). The degree of reference made to alleged facts (historical, contemporary, physical, or symbolic) varies in the social sciences and humanities.

So where do the core differences lie?

Here, keeping one's balance is crucial given the more strident expressions of research variants that emphasize *parsimoniousness* as the deal-breaker for anything claiming the title of 'theory':

- Here, theory is tantamount to hypothesis-formulation and accompanying causal models ('laws'). This is by definition exclusive and narrowly defined and closely allied to work looking to predict, explain, or generalize on the basis of facts gained by observational techniques (see Box 2.1).
- This restricted notion of theory, as hypothesis-testing, will not do for its opponents; if for no other reason than whilst there are observable patterns in the social

world and human behaviour these are neither as predictable as assumed nor as universally applicable as claimed. As the argument goes, the laws of physics do not apply to human subjects, social relations, or cultural practices. People and societies are notoriously fickle, the argument goes on. This distinguishes the social world from the natural world, cultural practices and artefacts from animal drives, instincts, or behaviours.

- Less categorical approaches to these questions from both sides of the polemic, would go along with the Kerlinger and Lee definition as far as this: theory – or theorizing – entails the articulation of a 'set of interrelated constructs (concepts), definitions, and propositions that present a systematic view of phenomena . . .' (see Creswell 2009: 62–4).

As we will see, these positions are taken from within often diametrically opposed working assumptions about whether the natural sciences, e.g. the laws of physics, are best practice for all scholarly research undertakings. The history of scientific discovery, famous debates in the philosophy of science, and their corollaries at the intersection of twentieth-century social sciences and humanities suggest otherwise (see Chalmers 2004, Radder 2006, Schulz 2010).

- Whilst many such approaches – those looking to critique mainstream assumptions – do not shy way from explanatory frameworks, if not cautious sorts of 'predictions' about the future, they use theory more as an orientation device. It is regarded as a more inclusive notion, a heuristic as opposed to an open-and-shut hypothesis that 'specifies the [causal] relationship among variables' (Creswell 2009: 51).
- And then there are many research modes that eschew the term altogether, opting for references to theoretical lenses, perspectives, conceptual frameworks (see Burchill et al. 2001, Peterson and Runyan 1999). The view here is that 'theory', or 'Theory' is too much of a straitjacket for investigations that are less concerned with locating cause and effect ('why?') or prediction.
- The term also appears in some well-known models about how the natural world, the cosmos, or the human psyche works, and why. These are also brand names: Einstein's Theory of Relativity, Darwin's Theory of Evolution, Newtonian Physics, Quantum Mechanics, Freud's Theory of the Unconscious, World Systems Theory, and so on. The same term can be applied to trends if not broad rubrics in the social sciences and humanities for multiple positions and their main representative thinkers: Postcolonial Theory, Postmodern Theory, Literary Theory, and Feminist Theory being cases in point.

So what are our options? Another way to pin down this elusive term, beyond its evocative powers, is to ask where it fits in with the aims and objectives of the project. As noted above, the natural sciences and their quantitative cousins in the social sciences privilege theories that can underwrite models for explaining and/or predicting outcomes. Other approaches look for frameworks that can interpret and critique the same, if not transform or 'deconstruct' underlying assumptions; for example, of hypotheses that investigate how humans may behave in structured ways; patterns that certain sorts of observational research can uncover and so understand.

As such theorizing is treated as a process, not a product, and so an inter-textual endeavour; couched as a sort of open-ended dialogue, an ongoing conversation with others albeit in written form. This is why theory for qualitative work is so closely allied to a discussion of the pertinent literature, accompanied by cross-references and notes. This is in contrast to hypothesis-construction whereby the reference points are to planned observations: an experiment or survey-based exploration designed to 'test' or 'prove' the hypothesis – part of a larger 'theory'. The thing to remember is that theory, however defined, operates as both container term and contested terrain within and between approaches.

**TIP: Whether the world, or particular phenomena being theorized about come first, or are conjured into existence by virtue of these theoretical reflections and hypotheses, has been the subject of much debate over the ages; with little prospect of this abating.[10] In the meantime, taking the working definition above on board for the sake of argument, and as far as you are comfortable in your supervisory and institutional setting, your 'theoretical chapter' needs to aim at articulating a 'set of interrelated constructs (concepts), definitions, and propositions that present a systematic view of phenomena . . .' (Kerlinger and Lee cited in Gray 2009) relevant to your inquiry.

For the moment, no matter what your viewpoint, theory whether it be with a little 't' or a capital 'T' is when you work at a more abstract, more generalized level of thinking, speaking, and writing. To 'theorize' means to abstract, to take a certain distance from the immediate object of analysis by stepping back in order to distinguish the literature's wood from the trees of your inquiry. In some quarters, theory – understood as an organic practice – is not only there to facilitate how to understand, or explain phenomena (namely 'data') but is also open to being challenged by these data (see Adorno 1976). More on these matters in Chapters 2 and 7.

On method – how (ii)

Moving on now to another loaded term for many: method/s. The characterization of method offered by two social epidemiologists below, who also know how to bake, encapsulates this second dimension to the 'how' of research designs for most of us. Namely that methods are

rules and procedures employed by those trying to accomplish a task. Sometimes such rules and procedures are written down. For example cookbooks provide recipes for baking better cookies and cakes. In much the same way research methods are rules and procedures that researchers working within a disciplinary framework employ to improve the validity of their inferences. . . . [R]esearchers who abide by good research methods may more reliably produce valid inferences. . . . *There are always exceptions but the point seems to hold generally.*

(Oakes and Kaufman 2006: 5, emphasis added)

Exactly which unwritten and written 'rules and procedures' are considered to be the tried and true ways to accomplish the task is where paths diverge once again; philosophers speak of 'philosophical research' (Radder 2006), linguists may speak of 'semiotic methods' (see Scolari 2009), political scientists may speak of 'critical realism' (Burnham et al. 2004), feminists of 'gender mainstreaming' (True and Ackerly 2010).

The point of knowing which recipe you are following and to make what sort of dish, to extend this analogy, is a first-base distinction in terms of method/s. A second-base one, to continue the baseball analogy, is that by learning how to do things a certain way we are also learning to know things a certain way. Immediately, this takes us into the terrain of what counts as the best way to *follow* a particular recipe; leaving aside for the moment questions of why this recipe (see section above). For instance, two key criteria for *empirical* researchers, two criteria for assessing the mettle of any research design and the *inferences* its results rest upon, are *replicability* and *transparency*.

1   Whether someone else – another student, colleague, or lay person – could undertake another research project along the same lines, using and being able to access the main sources of information accordingly (written texts, similar sorts of people, raw materials).
2   Could someone else consult your 'data set' or array of evidence, go to where you conducted your fieldwork, locate your source literature, if not to compare their conclusions against your own then to double-check the source on which your findings rest?
3   Unlike investigative journalists, and depending on the ethical terrain at stake in the project, academic researchers do have to reveal their sources.[11]

For less rules-and-procedures bound ways of conducting research, these general criteria hold as well. For most though, to speak of method is about how you went about things; I went here to talk to whomever, I accessed this space with permission from whom, I took part in an internet discussion group with permission or prior knowledge, those ideas from others I cite can be found on such and such a page, this many respondents did my survey. However, the term also entails more complex criteria, and issues about the strengths and weaknesses – and appropriateness – of the chosen method/s given the stated aims and objectives of the project and the research question.

This is why method/s are not innocent in the sense of being neutral. One size does not fit all because all methods (recipes) can be applied and used in various ways. They also arise from various layers of understanding of the processes, and outcomes which they are laying out; e.g. various sampling techniques, questionnaire formats, experimental parameters, dependent versus independent variables, primary versus secondary sources, software analytical tools, on-the-ground participant-observation versus – or alongside – online (web-based) ones.

In addition, certain broad categories of methods are distinctive, 'brand names' in their own right; for example, *regression analysis, semiotics, psychoanalysis*. Their defining role in particular debates, lines of intellectual allegiance and professional qualifications also means that opting to use some particular sorts of methods for the 'data-gathering' pertinent to your project brings certain conceptual vocabularies, authors, and expectations with them. In these cases, your nominal method speaks for itself even though nuances reside within debates generic to these approaches.

BOX 2.2 CLIMATE CHANGE OR GLOBAL WARMING?

In the first decade of this century supporters of this positive correlation between global warming and human activities over the centuries and those with the view that global warming is a gradual, autonomous aspect of climate change over time have been locking horns, in academic conferences, UN meetings, and the media; prominent scientific reports (e.g. the Stern Report in the UK, the ICCC reports and their authors, 'sceptical environmentalists', economists, politicians, governments from the Global South such as India, and representatives of major petrochemical industries all take diametrically opposed positions. Where scientists differ is not only on the underlying criteria by which they analyse the data and on this evidence they then use in making *predictions* about the future of the planet, in order to offer recommendations to governments and industry about ways to minimize the human element as an integral causal factor. They have also been hotly debating the very integrity of the data used; the methods by which it was collected, how it was then conveyed as statistical probabilities.

The key point here is to note how the scientific community is deeply divided about whether global warming and corollary effects is something that 'naturally' occurs or is the outcome of industrialization, large-scale agriculture, deforestation, and other activities over the last few centuries. Whilst there have been exposés of sloppy research methods, the main contentions also pivot on philosophical issues and political stances about the ecosystem and humanity's legacy. Today's debates have their precursors in the 1970s and 1980s when ecological thought first made inroads in the public debate, and ensuing research; William Lovelock's *Gaia* notion, first presented in the 1960s, which posited the earth's various components (from the oceans to the atmosphere) as a large complex ecosystem where all parts worked in delicate balance, has been influential (Lovelock 2000).

This example highlights how the methodological integrity of truth claims and high social status enjoyed by Science (with a big S) straddle public and scholarly debates. When fundamental errors or ambiguous modelling – some call it 'fudging' – come to light in areas as politically and economically sensitive as this one, the debate becomes quickly polarized, pitting not only environmental scientists and environ-mentalists against one another but also different schools of thought within these respective camps. Who is right or wrong about the causes, speed, and responsibility for climate change shows how predictive modelling, where computers generate graphs based on an array of complex data sets, inform governmental budgets, industry research and development, domestic energy bills, and even big power politics at the United Nations (see Maslin 2009: 60 *passim*). It could be that both sides have got it right, as well as wrong (see Schulz 2010).

Nonetheless, this second side to the 'how' question is actually not that mysterious; it involves us taking the time and space to provide simple, though not mundane explanations of what exactly we intend to do (proposals) or what we did do (afterwards); advantages and disadvantages included. What these techniques, tools, or combinations will provide in terms of 'facts', 'data', 'insights', or 'experiences' and what they cannot do are the baselines for any project's claims and achievements.

What has 'methodology' got to do with it?

But what is the distinction between your method/s you are employing, your theory – conceptual framework – and the need then to talk about *methodology*? At times, little point in that the latter is used synonymously with methods; both refer to a 'description of the methods or procedures used in some activity' (Sloman 1977: 387). Then there are those instances where methodology is pronounced as 'merely as a more impressive-sounding synonym for method' (ibid.: 388), its often unintentional use as a synonym for theorizing notwithstanding. But there is more to it than this.

This term also refers to a particular sort of undertaking, an 'investigation of the aims, concepts, and principles of reasoning of some discipline, and the relationships between its sub-disciplines' (ibid.: 388). In this wider sense, methodology can also be an object of study, an academic discipline in itself. There are theorists and philosophers whose specialization is methodology. Moreover, every discipline generates its own set of methodological conundrums, in turn those who specialize in asking each other and working researchers awkward questions about a research practice, particularly those that become standard procedures or ways of talking about the 'right' and 'correct' procedures in any domain as if they were beyond question (see Oakes and Kaufman 2006: 7 *passim*).

Moses and Knutsen distinguish between the two 'm's' in their likening methodology to the toolbox and respective methods to the tools in the box (Moses and Knutsen 2007: 4–7); different tools need different sorts of toolboxes. Creswell opts for the expression 'strategies of inquiry' instead, which may help those who are not into DIY (Creswell 2009: 11), when he distinguishes between methodology as *strategies* and the particular techniques – *methods* – used to conduct the research . . .

How do these nuances actually pan out in general practice? In the day-to-day grind of getting a research project done do we need to be so concerned about such analytical distinctions? Whatever the response, you need to engage at some level of methodological explication, including the pros and cons of this chosen approach; sooner rather than later.

Here are some general things to aim for even before you know exactly how you want to go about your investigation:

- First, take note that a discussion about 'methodology' entails more than a description of particular 'methods or procedures' or literature review-like exegesis of generalities (e.g. 'participant-observation'). The practical specifics need to be there, as well as make sense for your statement of purpose, if not encompass an understanding of your own worldview and why this approach is suitable for this project.

- Then, relax; laying out the specific data-gathering techniques (methods) you plan to use, and then actually do employ is relatively straightforward writing; unless of course you do not have a clear idea about the 'rules and procedures' (Oakes and Kaufman 2006) you are employing or believe, erroneously I would argue, that there are none worth mentioning.
- In formal research proposals, and dissertation formats, you need to deal with these aspects in relatively simple language. A straightforward description of how exactly the data was gathered and under what conditions – method in the strictest sense – is indispensable information; indeed obligatory if others are to be able to assess the findings, duplicate the research, adapting or countermanding it accordingly. As mundane as it is, the method/s section, wherever its place in the proposal or final report, tells a reader a lot about the working premises you are using to investigate or argue your case.[12]
- What lifts the more descriptive aspects of any 'method chapter' or 'methodology' discussion up a level, is how effectively you discuss the implications your chosen approach has for your research question, eventual findings, and conclusions.

How do these rules of thumb play out within, and across the quantitative–qualitative divide, particularly in the early decision-making and planning stages?

For those working in the quantitative tradition, and even those working with qualitative data and relying on an understanding of *scientific reasoning* (see Chapter 3), the above privileging of methodological discussions, with a big M, is less evident in either a research proposal or final report. The following provisos may well apply to your project if not expectations arising from your disciplinary setting:

- When working with an approach where the *empirical data* gathered, or produced are through forms of (in)direct observation (see Chapter ?????? section), the rules and procedures for carrying out these observations constitute method in the stricter sense.
- For more quantitative sorts of projects, in the written research plan or report itself there is seldom reflection on broad, meta-level methodological debates; for example, around the relationship between the observed and the observer.
- Unless these might relate to problems with (mis-)measurement; for example, human error, or the statistical instruments used, or considerations of how a researcher may need to minimize the impact of his or her presence (e.g. in experimental set-ups). Then these would be discussed in the context of how they need to be taken into account; for example, how they may influence the results and then any inferences drawn from them.
- This is different from seeing such discussions as integral to the aims and objectives of the project. In these cases, specific and more general considerations may actually comprise the research question. Methodological questions, as outlined above, can also be research topics. That said, these too need to be rendered as a particular research question; one that is of a different order and register than in quantitative empirical projects.

Bottlenecks: when 1 + 1 + 1 ≠ 3

There are several bottlenecks, however, no matter which way you look at things. To recapitulate, research proposals and the reports that ensue often stand or fall on what peers, supervisors, and examiners, make of the practical side of things; how the data was gathered, and then analysed (see Gray 2009: 57–8). Before considering ways of dealing with a number of recurring bottlenecks, let's look at them more closely:

- Critics of approaches that keep all broader methodological discussions at arm's length see this as 'uncritical'; a convenient way of compartmentalizing intractable issues which, if addressed would indeed raise questions about the very rationale behind any chosen method; for example, why embark on a double-blind experiment, or conduct a large-scale survey when human behaviour is so notoriously unpredictable?
- Reference to the data-gathering or analysis tool, for example, the swathe of statistical and content-analysis software packages currently available, does not constitute an adequate presentation of your methodology in the round.
- Misperceptions and mutual misunderstandings aside, certain qualitative approaches do baulk at having to present method is such matter-of-fact ways.
- Conversely, others have little truck with research reports that do not deem it necessary to provide any indication of the procedures used to get results, or sense of the various sorts of sources upon which the conclusions are being drawn; for example, when a primary source (first-hand, or 'raw data') is usually privileged above a secondary one (second/third-hand); or the significance of choosing to undertake a survey with a highly selective sample when making generalizations.
- Whatever the larger conversations may be, these silences can hold you up in getting to grips with the practicalities that apply to your research project (e.g. your questionnaire questions, the sorts of focus groups you intend to set up, the archival sources you need to consult, or communities you plan to observe). As fascinating as these meta-methodological debates are:
  - At the planning stage not coming to terms with the admittedly mundane ways in which you are going to proceed can lead later to scrambling around in methods texts to identify said method at the last minute, with no time to understand discussion about their respective strengths and weaknesses.
  - Worse still, you may find yourself being lost for words when asked (in a Ph.D. defence for instance) 'So, tell me, what *was* your method?' When there is lack of engagement with 'method' in practical terms to speak of, pages of meta-level methodological discussion make little sense.
- That said, unless you are very clear about your intentions, avoidance here can result in two sorts of bifurcations in the final report:
  - one in which the theoretical and empirical sections diverge completely, seldom referring to each other and related to different sorts of questions;
  - in other cases, the description of the procedures used and then discussion of any findings assumes that issues broached in the preceding theoretical exegesis (often in the form of the 'literature review') are done and dusted; it may well

be that the findings being presented actually support a different set of issues that those presented.

Either way, not having an idea about what position to take and why leaves you open to not only tough but also fundamental criticism about the very point of your work; the relevance of the data-gathering approach you opted for, and by implication the quality of the findings and conclusions made. These need not come from less sympathetic audiences from the 'other side', or hostile external reviewers. They may well be valid points raised from within your own scholarly circle-of-choice or affiliation.

Next: how to deal with these headaches, especially early on when positioned on either side of the divide?

- One rule of thumb, in the *qualitative tradition* at least, is that presenting any chosen method/s requires you to present its corresponding theoretical under-pinnings; what this approach brings to bear on the research question in particular. However, recall that the converse is not always the case; much theoretical work, philosophical explorations for instance, can be achieved without a separate section on 'method'; unless the latter is the object of inquiry.
- Similarly for research requiring quantitative techniques. A researcher is concerned about making an original contribution in a chosen area of study. There are different ways to make clear how that contribution relates to the data-gathering approach you want to take, which requires you to engage with the literature on methods in this field. For example, if your research proposes to make an advance in the study of voting behaviour or media effects, you would be remiss to ignore quantitative studies given that the quantitative approach dominates in these areas. However, this does not mean that innovative studies on citizens and political participation, media effects, or audience response cannot be conducted using qualitative methods (see Franklin 2010, Gunter 2000).

In short, some baseline rules apply to most of us when setting out:

1 do not presuppose that a method explains all, resolves the larger intellectual puzzles for you;
2 nor that a theoretical or methodological exegesis is a substitute for resolving the nitty-gritty details of how you will gather and then make sense of your material for you;
3 nor that multiplying methods will cover all your bases; sometimes less is more in this respect;
4 even if you have just completed some sort of methods instruction, or read a book about methods, avoid nominating your method first; more on this pitfall in due course.

CONCLUDING COMMENTS

So to sum up: *theory*, however defined, speaks to the conceptualization side of things, the philosophical underpinnings of a piece of research. On the one hand these underpinnings are integral to certain *worldviews* (Creswell 2009: 5–11); implicit and articulate beliefs and understandings about what the nature of the world is (*ontology*), the form and substance of appropriate knowledge about the world (*epistemology*). On the other hand, these worldviews inform more formalized procedures; some follow the two sides of the divide explicitly, other *research methodologies* look to straddle if not bridge the quantitative–qualitative divide.

When speaking of *method*, we are addressing particular methods techniques, or tactics within the design of a larger 'research strategy' (Creswell 2009), that allow us to go and collect data; this needs collation, analysis, and then shaping as we come to conclusions about them. Both these dimensions need considering in all research. To what degree is where we see the field diversify into varying levels of abstraction, typologies of theories and/or methods and, by association, topographies of disciplinary research paradigms (ibid.: 5). How codified and rigorously adhered to during the course of project planning, design, execution and eventual outcome, the interrelationship between the theoretical and methodological parts of the work distinguish quantitative modes of research design from qualitative ones; mixed methods or anti-method approaches claiming to fill the would-be void that separates them.

From the view of where to put each of these elements in a research proposal and then later into your final report, John Creswell notes that the 'theory section' is worth separate treatment (2009: 57) for the sake of coherence and clarity, particularly in undergraduate and postgraduate research projects. By the same token, and this is a particular occupational hazard for empirical research drawing on qualitative research's diverse theoretical literature, this does not mean to say that the object here is for you to construct a 'theory section' that has to be watertight; a straitjacket, or container into which any findings are poured (Lather in Creswell 2009: 65). The converse holds for how you present, and place your eventual 'method section' and/or 'methodological discussion' as well.

This all sounds easier said than done given that often our best methodological discussion is the one we (re)write after the research in question has been completed, results written up and presented. That said, and even at these early exploratory and designing stages, it is not advisable to settle your method first, before you've formulated a research question or even come up with a topic (this happens more often than it should). Why not?

1 Whilst you may naturally start here based on past successes, preconceived ideas about your own ability, or as part of your own research identity politics (see Chapters 3, 4 and 7), it is better to move from topic to research question by considering both theoretical and methodological options.
2 This may mean doing a preliminary review of the literature in this topic area before settling on what would work, or

3   deciding, whether or not theory is an explicit feature of your project, 'how the theory will be used in the study, . . . an up-front explanation, as an end-point, or as [some sort of] lens' (Creswell 2009: 64).

4   It helps to think about where in the larger proposal, or report, the theory works beyond its formal role as 'my theory chapter'.

5   The converse holds for where discussion of particular methods, along with methodological considerations, end up; alongside the theory, as a separate chapter, in an appendix where your interview questions are there for easy reference, or as a passing reference in those projects based on purely theoretical – philosophical – explorations.

Indeed you may well need to rethink several elements again (see Box 2.1 above) once you know more about the topic. A method is not in itself a research question. Nor is it a theory as such.

Whilst these two dimensions are both vital to getting research done, letting a particular method take the lead in your initial thinking and planning is equivalent to having the 'tail wag the dog'. So, like David Gray, I too would strongly advise you to remember that when 'planning a research project, *never* begin by deciding on what data-gathering tool or approach to use. Begin [instead] by identifying what it is you are actually trying to research' (2009: 34, original emphasis).

All in all, talk of theory, method and/or methodology is an area in which there is a lot of unconscious if not deliberate fudging of terms. This discussion has taken each term in turn and highlighted the analytical and philosophical distinctions they bring to bear on our work. Fudging aside, for this reason from this point on the term *methodology* is taken as a synecdoche for the larger enterprise of research as an undertaking that entails another lively but enervating tension: that between our theory and our method.

NOTES

1   There are a number of excellent texts dealing with these matters across the spectrum as well as those taking more in-depth explorations within respective streams; some of which are touched on here and in elsewhere in this book. It may be more useful to get into this literature in greater depth at a later stage in your project.

2   This problem also occurs on having to complete an ethics form which may raise issues for the committee assessing whether you can carry out the data-gathering.

3   The terminology differs from place to place, institution to institution. I will opt for the term 'dissertation' as a generic one.

4   Thanks to Pasi Väliaho for this metaphor.

5   We will be looking at what constitutes *plagiarism* in due course.

6   Thanks to Zlatan Krajina for this tip; and to Julian Henriques (conveyed to me second-hand) for the empowering exhortation.

7   Many students, often those returning from the workplace and looking to upgrade or make a career switch, get very preoccupied with making their project relevant: how it will get their foot in the door, and so on. Others, particularly when looking at topics that are politically or socially sensitive back home, get concerned about their future careers, and at times safety (this happens). Both these sorts of premeditation are understandable. However, too much time on these issues before you have explored the possibilities is

putting the cart before the horse. First, many skills and items of knowledge gained in pursuing any inquiry are transferable in their own right. Second, human research subjects are not there entirely to serve your ends, surely! Third, there are ways to protect yourself from political ramifications, some of which are dealt with in codes of ethics. If a topic is too loaded, then you need to leave it alone. Finally, the aim is to undertake a topic that interests you enough to pursue it for a length of time.

8 Thanks to Marieke Riethof for this phrase.

9 See Gray (2009: 45–9) on the sorts of 'topics to avoid'; Creswell (2009: 18–20) uses the term 'research problem' instead of topic or research question.

10 For a classic in this area of debate, and one in which the terms 'theory', 'empirical', 'critical' and 'positivism' have a prominent role, see Adorno (1976). See also Petrocik and Steeper (2010) for one example of a critique within political science of how too much attention to theorizing creates blind-spots for researchers observing data sets of voting behaviour; thanks to Susan Banducci for this example.

11 See Chapters 3 and 5 on research ethics.

12 As a dyad, method–methodology is more commonplace where empirical research takes place. In the more philosophically inclined corridors of academe, these practicalities amount to reading and knowing the literature, thinking about things, and constructing an argument in written form; here writing and thinking are effectively theory and method; literary studies, social/cultural theory, cultural studies, and postcolonial studies (partially), fall into this category. Here too however, there are projects whereby the topic, and thereby the underlying approach, is about the 'principles of reasoning of [the] discipline, and the relationships between its sub-disciplines. . . . [including] attempts to analyse and criticise its aims, its main concepts . . ., the methods used to achieve these aims, . . . and so on' (Sloman in Bullock and Stallybrass 1977: 388).

CHAPTER 3

Research in practice

Designing a research project

Topics covered in this chapter:

- Main stages in a research project
- Why plan? Presenting a plan of work
- Formulating research questions and hypotheses
- On science and worldviews
- Research ethics
- Supervisors and supervisees
- Methodological survival guide

INTRODUCTION

The last chapter looked at ways of getting prepared, in the right frame of mind for embarking upon an extended research undertaking. It looked at initial decision making alongside some of the thornier conceptual and operational issues that emerge even in these early stages. We now turn to research design – project planning in so many words. These are the ways in which we show that we are clear about how we can put our intellectual investigation into action, and achieve our objectives in the time allotted. Here variations, large and small, between and within disciplines will come to the surface according to which elements are prioritized. The same applies for which form and stylistic conventions are favoured when submitting a written work-plan, our first feedback – formal and informal assessment – often for the *research proposal*, or as is the case for dissertation projects, *research outline*.[1]

In both instances these plans need to arrange those key elements (see Box 2.1) in some sort of *temporal* sequence and developmental logic (Box 3.1 below). The more attention you pay to these elements as aspects that all require some forward planning, the better; for example, which books or articles to study first, to selecting or formulating key concepts, to outlining how you will tackle a key thinker's work, get access to an online community, or find suitable experimental 'guinea-pigs' or interview subjects. As you field questions, criticisms, and alternative suggestions from supervisors, classmates, and others, you will also become aware of inherent weaknesses in the idea, the planning, any underlying assumptions that may cloud your thinking, as well as deficiencies in your knowledge of research literature pertinent to your inquiry (see Chapter 4). Ironing out these glitches in these first phases could well prevent you from major (as opposed to the usual) setbacks and disappointments later on; unforeseen events notwithstanding.

For these reasons alone the challenges of developing an explicit, coherent but also flexible action-plan by which you will carry out and complete the research are shared by all approaches. They also share the working knowledge that getting to the requisite level of coherence – feasibility and persuasiveness in other words – entails a certain degree of initial research, knowledge that may not explicitly find its way into your final report. In some cases you may need to complete some *pilot research* if not a *pilot project*.

Keeping with this book's approach to deal with more complex issues as they arise during the research process, this chapter unpacks the 'mysteries' of research design, in four ways:

1   The *main stages of a research project* and the vexed question, 'Why plan?' These include issues to consider when drafting and then presenting a work-plan. Supervisors expecting evidence of progress and students who underestimate the need to put some elbow grease into the practical planning of any research undertaking (from experiments to philosophical investigations) often come unstuck on this point.

2   Zooming in closer, we look at ways of turning a research topic (see Chapter 2) into a *research question*, or *hypothesis*. Whilst they have much in common in this respect, quantitative and qualitative research modes do have different takes on this matter, employ different vocabularies, and demand different loadings in terms of how the question, or hypothesis are expressed, the degree of step-by-step planning required to convince others that you know what you are doing.

3   Then we take a step back from the nitty-gritty to look at how they speak to some underlying differences in working assumptions about the form, content, and objectives of *scientific reasoning*; the status of Science, with a big S, in society raises a set of issues that overlap those already raised in the theory–method discussion from the last chapter. As research designs are often the first public outing for some

projects, how their viability, relevance, and acceptability are judged by those in a position to veto – or fund – them is where implicit differences in worldview can crystallize as prescription; norms, rules, and values around notions of academic best practice.

4   This section takes an initial look at two aspects to managing our project, and ourselves along the way: (i) research ethics and how codes of practice have implications for your research design and execution; (ii) the supervisory relationship, a primary mentoring or collaborative relationship that can affect how research students – and supervisors – see themselves and their own research in both an institutional and societal context. We revisit both aspects in later chapters as their implications change for a project.

These aspects are brought together in the last section in the form of a methodological survival guide; an orientation device for the more focused discussions in Chapters 5 to 7. Whilst many effective and successful research projects develop in a more organic way, in literary studies or more philosophical approaches, the goal of this chapter is to show that planning ahead can be useful across the board, even when formal research proposals are not mandatory requirements. Being confronted with fundamental methodological deficiencies or ethical oversights is not a pleasant experience in the final lead-up to the deadline or in an oral exam.

MAIN STAGES IN A RESEARCH PROJECT

In light of Box 2.1, Box 3.1 below unpacks these required elements as distinct, albeit overlapping *stages*. Different institutions, departments, and modes of research will expect each stage to be completed differently. This schematic is a general guide, not a one-size-fits-all.

If research can be considered as an uphill journey, one that includes learning particular customs, norms and values, and vocabularies along with a swathe of formal – written – regulations and informal – unwritten – ones, then this journey can be uncomfortably steep. For everyone, research brings with it personal and professional challenges. Like all journeys though, there will be times when it is wise to stop, take stock and, perhaps, even retrace your steps. Like others I too would stress that this process is not a linear one per se; it is more likely to be a spiral motion than a straight line onwards and upwards (see Berg 2009, M. Davies 2007, Blaxter et al. 2006). Besides, with any steep incline, ascending in a spiral is often the more efficient way of getting to the top. If that is the case, let's break down this large chunk of work down into its composite two stages:

Stage 1: Once you have a topic or if you already have an idea for a research topic you need to start refining the topic-area as you develop a research question. Chapter 2 outlined this decision-making process in detail. To recall, these early stages are when you take time to become familiar with research in your chosen area. This process is a line of continuity throughout but particularly as the research plan takes shape, along with your grasp of the literature – the 'field' or fields in which you are working. As

BOX 3.1 THE MAIN STAGES IN A RESEARCH PROJECT

Enter: first decisions and commitments

Stage 1
- Selecting a topic (*What*)
- Formulating a research question (RQ)/hypothesis (H)
- Aims and objectives; motivations (*Why*)
- Designing and refining the approach (*How*)
- Conduct review of available literature
- Articulating a conceptual framework – 'theory'
- Selecting the appropriate method/s to gather data – 'method'
- Presenting a work-plan (*Research outline/proposal*)
- Plan to carry out research within time, resource, and knowledge constraints
- Outlines how to gather data and relates it to conceptual framework and RQ/hypothesis
- Consider and deal with ethical and/or practical limitation to data-gathering.

Stage 2
- Gather the data
- Design, organize, carry-out original/empirical research component
- Literature review: synthesize, refine, and write-up
- Analyse the data
- Present findings and writing up results
- Conclusions (*research paper/dissertation/thesis*; seminars, conferences).

Exit: draw things to a close and disseminate

you make use of such tips, and even after you have narrowed down your options, you can also make a point of:

**TIPS: Browse through journals for new work; keep up to date by reading the latest published articles that are relevant to your research. Attend research seminars on related topics and engage in the discussions where you can. And if not, take note of classes in courses you are still attending that are particularly relevant for you by reading the literature provided and seminar discussions. As you do the above, ask yourself questions such as:
- From where does the author draw their ideas?
- What are their main research questions?
- How do these relate to my research topic?
- What would be some ideas for my own research?
- How, and where would I like to build upon current knowledge?

Stage 2 is where a different sort of work gets going: the data-gathering, analysing, and presenting/dissemination; topics for the second part of this book. For now though, the key to not becoming bogged down in abstract details, or going around in ever-decreasing circles of indecisiveness in these earlier moments, is twofold:

1 Treat work-plans seriously yet as open-ended documents. This means accepting that you will need to plan, plan, and plan again. It also means having to draft, get feedback and then redraft successive versions of your research outline. Write things down, or draw mind-maps; whatever works as a record of your thinking.
2 Be prepared to change plans if necessary – redesign if, after some initial research into the existing literature or try-out ('pilot') data-gathering of your own, you discover certain things don't work, are beyond your means, or access is denied.

Let's now turn to the role that work-planning and formal research proposal and outline writing play in research projects. Chapter 4 will then look at what is meant by the 'literature review' and its role in helping you firm up your plans, and move them into action.

Why plan?

Work-plans can be informal documents or an element in preliminary evaluations or supervisory sessions. Getting your first formal research plan together, particularly when submitted as a formal *research proposal*, creates its own output-related pressure. Despite this sort of document being a stage in the larger project, it often becomes an end-goal in itself; indeed, funding applications and sometimes mid-way grades are given for this piece of work.

Apart from this sort of performance-based output, research plans are tough for other reasons; below are some common conundrums and ways of coping with them.

First, because the level of difficulty is raised when you have to turn an idea into a clear research question that is anchored then in a doable plan of work. It is often at this moment that your initial grasp of the terrain starts to become unsteady, not only as you read more and discover more about what others may have to say about the matter, but also as you start working out the practicalities, realize what is possible, or what is not given the time, resources, or skills you have at your disposal. Not only do new ideas and challenges arise, but so does the often discomforting awareness of how much you still need to learn about your topic before proceeding.

Coping: The sooner you get started, the better. How you decide to go about doing it, from the earliest stages of designing and writing the research in a *proposal* form, has implications for not only the end-product but also for how it is perceived and assessed by others along the way. Realizing this will enhance your chances of being at home with your own decisions, give you some space to 'own' what you are doing, recognize and set your own limits and then be able to manage your level of satisfaction or dissatisfaction afterwards.[2] Whilst researchers, starting out or longer in the tooth, are often impatient to get going, time spent planning in the beginning is saved later on.

Second, for newbies however, these initial steps and decisions they entail do create anxiety. The time-pressures of completing a higher research degree these days sees many students underestimating the value of planning, as they rush headlong into their data-gathering phase or try to write up their work before they have a clear idea of what it is they are doing.

> Coping: Rather than seeing the design phases, and this includes the preparation of a research outline – proposal – as something to be got over as quickly as possible in order to get on with the 'real thing', it is more productive to consider the planning phases as integral to the larger process and eventual product.[3] Those great ideas you discard, various methods and techniques you hope to employ that may have to be left out for the sake of time, lack of institutional, or supervisory resources, will stand you in good stead another day. This is because deciding, eliminating, setting limits and continually refining terms and techniques *is* doing research. You have started already!

Third, forward-planning also needs to allow for contingencies. Becoming so wedded to an initial idea, work-plan, theory of choice, or particular method/s can also lead to rigidity. You need to be open to making changes, adjusting core ideas or approaches. And, if need be, set up a pilot project, or be ready with a Plan B. Sometimes even the best-laid plans do not get off the starting blocks or have to be abandoned later on.

> Coping: There is no reason for anyone to be confined to, or defined by the one research topic, theoretical inspiration, or method/s until the end of time. It is often only afterwards that some things will become clear. Rest assured, mistakes and missteps, underestimations of time needed and overestimations of our wherewithal to achieve initial ambitions do happen. The decisions you make and course you plot, or diverge from, will evolve during the course of the project. Your intellectual acumen, ability to absorb new ideas and analyse complex data, and practical skill-sets for accessing knowledge and resources (e.g. how to use electronic databases, conduct interviews, make statistical inferences) will also ripen.

There are also specific ways of working productively in the planning phases for quantitative and qualitative approaches respectively:

For *quantitative research*: after defining your research topic and as you work on developing a research question, your review of the existing research in the area will most likely guide you towards a particular data-gathering approach. This too contributes to your understanding of the field in terms of the literature (see Chapter 4), pre-existing research findings, and research designs.

- On the one hand, you may want to follow on some exciting strand of research by adding a new quantitative indicator that you think is important to explaining a particular phenomenon; this means adopting and perhaps extending those rules and procedures (e.g. survey tools – see Chapter 6).

- Or you may want to approach a phenomenon from a particular angle because you argue that it will reveal some new and interesting insights.
- Regardless of how you might arrive at any particular data-gathering approach once you do, your research plan should include certain elements common to all research designs:
  - First, it is absolutely necessary that the research plan clearly stipulates a research question, whether or not it is in the form of a hypothesis.
  - Furthermore you need to identify the concepts that are of interest to you as the researcher, not simply list all those available to you in the literature.
  - As with other modes of research the research question, or set of research questions, animates and motivates the research project.

For qualitative research: The above rules of thumb hold true here as well. That said, because many qualitatively inspired projects take research to be a cumulative and open-ended process in the round, you may find that there is less concern with strict protocols.

- Certain philosophical, ethnographic, and textually based research traditions take it as read that because their objects of analysis are neither static nor predictable, the research question animating the project will be plastic as well.
- For disciplines like anthropology or projects working with *action research* approaches where a researcher designs the project together with those they are researching, planning and execution are intertwined, organic and socially embedded processes (see Chapter 6).

Time now to move into the exigencies of work-planning and its role within the larger research design.

WORK-PLANS AND PROPOSALS

Getting through a research project in good shape often hinges on how much thought you put in ahead of time about how to investigate your ideas in practical terms. This is where the formulation of a self-contained research proposal – or outline – comes into its own. Whilst it may be difficult to think how the research will be carried out before actually starting on gathering any data, doing any extensive reading, or deciding how you intend to go about either of these undertakings, a successful research project (defined here as meeting research objectives within a certain timeframe with given resources) requires a thought-out research plan. As there is limited time and resources to complete the research, plans may need to change, so having a plan also allows room for revising initial ideas. Indeed, you should take the need to do this as part of the process; one that involves various levels and degrees of supervisory and peer-to-peer feedback (see Chapter 8).

The proposal in formal terms (for funding and applications), or outline in informal terms, aims to present the above key elements of the research project before substantial data-gathering or analysis has taken place. Sometimes previous research or *pilot research* informs a new project proposal. The point here is to anchor the research in some structured work-plan and rationale. The writing sees the use of the future tense: 'This research project will investigate . . .'. Whilst initial research may well have been undertaken, indeed this often strengthens the research design, a formal proposal, or outline is composed, and assessed as a project-under-construction.

Even though a research plan is the outcome of several stages in itself, a finishing line in its own way, at some point we all need to 'let it go'[4] in order to be able to set out into the terrain of the research-proper. Depending on your institutional and/or supervisory connections, in addition to the sections outlined below, even the earliest research plan can be asked to provide an initial chapter outline in substantive terms (not simply functional), timeline, and ethical approval. This checklist is flexible and adaptable; see Box 3.2 below.

BOX 3.2 ELEMENTS IN A RESEARCH OUTLINE

- Introduction with electing a topic (*What*)
- Research question (RQ)/hypothesis (H)
- Aims and objectives; motivations (*Why*)
- Description of main theories and literature that will be used
- Data-gathering plan
- Describe how data will be analysed
- Ethical and/or practical limitation to data-gathering
- Chapter outline
- Timeline for completing stages of research process.

Note how the above schematic resembles the elements of a research project as shown in Box 2.1. The difference is that a proposal, or outline, arranges these key elements into a narrative; hopefully one that is persuasive and feasible. Departments, research schools, and institutions vary amongst themselves as to the form and tone this narrative takes; from the lyrical, through to the declamatory, through to the executive summary. In all cases, proposals are concise; strict word-lengths force the writer to be brief, clear and inclusive.

Why this particular stage can take on a life of its own is because proposals are also used to gauge output and quality in postgraduate and advanced research; as research skills or methods, course examined papers, but most particularly as part of applications to research places or funding. At a simple level committing your ideas to paper (or screen) in the form of a proposal/plan is a powerful way to move you forward, put some foundations in place and confront you with any gaps in your thinking. This is the moment and the means by which you convince not only others, but also yourself that the project is 'doable'.

Proposal writing is in itself a certain genre of academic writing; in the USA in particular, grant-writing is a career path itself and an invaluable service for non-profits, politicians, and academics who can afford the services of a professional proposal writer. Initially, notions of style and persuasion are less crucial than getting all the above elements together in a coherent yet concise whole; most outline or proposal formats have strict word-limits (1,000–2,000 words maximum). The aim here is to convince and engage supervisors and others (your peer group) that this project has a point, a plan, and a rationale behind it. Sounds simple? In theory it is; practice makes perfect, however. Once again different disciplines weight this stage, and its elements, differently; students discover these differentials quite quickly.

How these sections are organized differs. For instance, research outlines in some parts of qualitative research tend to front-load the more abstract elements: theory/theories as they pertain to thinkers/literature, or fields. The specifics about method often come right at the end and when broached are often in broad methodological terms. Conversely, research based on large-scale surveys or experimental work, front-load the data-gathering method in terms of the layout of a questionnaire, design of the experiment, and statistical foundations.

Even though a research question is integral to all approaches, in qualitative research a cursory look over many students' first research outlines can give the impression that 'theory' is in the driving seat; method is understood primarily as methodology in its more abstract terms (see Chapter 2 on theory and method). The risk here is that there may be a coyness about laying out how exactly the 'data' (texts, images, interview responses) is going to be gathered, under what conditions, and to what ends.

On the other hand, those outlines that indicate that a large amount of time and effort has gone into showing precisely how quantitative empirical data are going to be collected, as is the case in surveys or questionnaires, can give the impression that there is less interest in articulating a theoretical – conceptual – framework, less concern for underlying methodological debates. Like it or not, sooner or later any research design, and its presentation as a formal research proposal or mid-project research report, needs to take into account all the key elements in terms of how they relate to *your* research; it is now time to tailor-make these general rules for your enterprise. This much both sides of the quantitative–qualitative divide have in common.

As noted earlier, this is one reason why the completion of a research proposal, even a first draft of an outline, is often a project in itself, its own end-result. The key thing to note here is that getting over this hurdle is an important milestone; getting past this point can help move (even push) your project into the next phase. It also requires you to move on from that point. For however well presented it may or may not be, neither research proposal nor outline will be the same as the final report, or dissertation.

Within these broad parameters, different traditions go about formulating a research question, an aspect that is distinct from a research topic, in various ways as well. Included here are those sorts of research questions often common to quantitative approaches but not exclusively: hypothesis formulation.

FROM RESEARCH TOPIC TO RESEARCH QUESTION OR HYPOTHESIS

Let's retrace our steps in order to move those first decisions about a possible topic up a level; formulating your *research question*, or *hypothesis*. These in turn designate for many fundamental differences between not only sorts of questions, and how they are asked, but also how they will be investigated. For the sake of argument let's see the term 'research question' as a general term with 'hypothesis' a more specialized one.

1   Quantitative traditions tend towards a research question formulated as a *hypothesis* (Creswell 2009: 132 *passim*; Gray 2009: 57). Getting to this stage constitutes a large part of the preparatory work, as the data-gathering methods employed and integrity of the findings pivot on the viability of the hypothesis.
2   Other sensibilities stress more open-ended formulations where the research question could be couched around a 'how' as much as a 'why' or 'who' sort of interrogation. For these traditions, the eventual outcome as a written piece of work all hinges on research questions that not only generate but also evolve during the course of the investigation.

Let's look more closely at the implications of these differing expectations:

First, the terms *research topic* and *research question* can be used interchangeably in everyday discussions, and sometimes departmental guidelines. To complicate matters, references to a third term, the *research problematic* (or *problématique*) blur this distinction further. Without agonizing too long over these nuances there are distinctions at work, which point to some entrenched debates about the ends, and means of academic research.

What are the differences in practical terms?

*   Recall, that the research topic is the general area of research irrespective of whether you end up engaging in strictly qualitative or quantitative work.
*   In most cases, research questions ask how two or more ideas or concepts might be related.
*   For quantitative research designs, however, a hypothesis asks whether and how two phenomena or concepts might be related by presenting these two phenomena or concepts as two *variables*; in the order of appearance of the directional relationship you expect to them to occur and which you will therefore proceed to *test*. In this respect these hypotheses have to be *testable*.
*   Other approaches may talk about a hypothesis in other ways; as statements or premises of an argument that do not presuppose the above protocol and accompanying expectations.
*   In other words, using the term 'hypothesis' does not automatically lend your research question legitimacy in quantitative, hypothesis-testing modes of work.

How then do these distinctions unfold when designing a project respectively?

Formulating a research question

Chapter 2 covered ways to come up with a research topic; noting that a research topic is not the same as a research question. As Gray points out; 'topics are broad but research questions [are] definitive and narrow' (Gray 2009: 55).5 The challenge is how to move from the broad brush-stroke – the general – to a finer one – the specific. Unless either or both come ready-made, as a specifically funded research topic/question or as a sub-set of a larger project, or senior researcher's research speciality (prevalent in parts of Europe like Germany), the sky is the limit for even undergraduate research dissertations.

Whilst conveying the topic you're interested in is, for all but the most undecided, not too difficult, constructing a research question that encapsulates why you are researching this topic, on what terms and in what ways, is less cut-and-dried. Here are some ways to proceed with the topic/s you have at hand:

1   One way to approach it is to consider your *research question* as consisting of a main question, which can be unpacked into two to three sub-questions.
2   In contrast to the declamatory form of a research topic ('my research is about . . .'), a research question needs to strike a balance between the abstract and the concrete. How far you come down on either side depends on how deeply rooted you are in those research traditions that privilege *inductive* modes of reasoning (see Chapter 7) and so are not so strict about how 'concise and unambiguous' (Gray 2009: 55–7) your formulation is.
3   It may well be that ambiguity is integral to the question itself, the object of analysis. There are those who argue that the research as a whole and the research question are both parts of a larger puzzle, not reducible to sound-bites (see Creswell 2009: 64).
4   However, this need not mean that you are not required to articulate a coherent question, one that encapsulates the intellectual puzzle you are engaging in, if not express a sense of purpose.

So even for projects nominally called qualitative, conciseness and non-ambiguity are not a bad thing. In this respect the research question and 'purpose statement'[6] are both characterized by the use of open-ended rather than closed (yes or no) questions, action words that stress discovery and process, question forms that prefer the 'how' and 'what' over the 'why' and other sorts of open-ended, or 'nondirectional language' (Creswell 2009: 125).

Let's turn now to research question formulation in those traditions where hypotheses are specific sorts of research questions. In light of the above distinction the difference pans out as follows:

- For instance, a research question about immigration policy might be, 'How has the immigration policy of western European countries influenced the diversity of the population?'
- A hypothesis, on the other hand, does something else. It is a statement asserting that a specific variation in one concept results in specific variation in another concept.

- Usually a hypothesis is derived from the research literature currently available in a particular area, which implies that it may also be derived from qualitative work as well; sometimes referred to as 'soaking and poking'.[7]
- The working premise that hypotheses can be empirically verified; a premise that is itself a topic of key debates amongst philosophers and historians of science, as we will see below.

When hypotheses are used it is typical to speak of *variables* as well.

- Variables are qualities or characteristics that take on different values; thus they vary. Age is a variable – though some people may share a birthday within the population, age varies from one person to the next.
- A hypothesis will state a relationship between an *independent variable* and a *dependent variable*.
  - The value of quantity of the dependent variable will depend on the value of the independent variable. So, for example, the temperature outside is a dependent variable because it depends on how much the sun has been shining (independent variable).
  - We can speak of these as X (independent variable) and Y (dependent variable).[8]

Using the earlier example, we could phrase as a hypothesis as something like, 'In countries with stricter immigration policy, diversity will be lower.' That said, there are several different types of hypotheses:

1 Hypotheses might state a causal relationship or simply a correlation between two variables. If the relationship hypothesized is *correlational* then we may drop the terms independent and dependent variable and only use the term variable.
2 The hypothesis might state a conditional relationship where the existence of a relationship between two variables depends on the presence of a third variable.
3 In addition, in research based on statistical analysis we may speak of a null hypothesis; where there is no relationship between the two variables.
4 The direction of the relationship can be negative or positive – a negative relationship is when an increase in one variable is related to a decrease in the value of the other variable/s.

All in all, a hypothesis needs to provide a clear idea about the *unit of analysis* and the *theoretical population*. The unit of analysis is the types or levels of actor, institution or group to which the hypothesis is thought to apply. This might be individual citizens or interest groups, sub-groups that are drawn from larger, theoretical populations to which the hypothesis can be applied or generalized; survey work for instance (see Chapter 6).

In terms of formulating a useful hypothesis certain characteristics need to be evident.

1 It should be stated affirmatively, not in the form of a question; that is a research question as noted above.

2 In order to be verified (or falsified) it must be *testable* with empirically *quantifiable* evidence (see Chapter 1).
3 A hypothesis needs to state how concepts (variables) are related in such a way that the direction of their relationship is clear; e.g. as the independent variable increases in value, does the dependent variable decrease (a negative relationship) or increase (a positive relationship)?

The next two principles are also common to various shades of qualitative research question formulation:

4 As with any research question, the hypothesis should make sense in terms of how it relates to the relevant existing body of knowledge; the theoretical and research literature in so many words.
5 Though it may seem this goes without saying, a hypothesis should be plausible and make sense to others, and yourself at a later date.

BOX 3.3 EXAMPLES OF HYPOTHESES

'The greater the inequality in land-ownership in countries, the greater the civil strife.'

'Local television news stories are more likely to be about crime than network news stories.'

'The proportion of the vote a party receives determines the proportion of seats it receives in the legislature.'

'The greater the number of highway patrol officers per capita in a state, the fewer the number of highway fatalities.'

'Interest groups that spend the most on professional lobbyists receive the greatest financial rewards from government programmes.'

To illustrate, and in order to keep these functional distinctions between hypotheses and research questions, we can turn to a well-known example in American social science literature:

As researchers started to note a decline in *social capital* they also asked what was 'causing' social capital to decline? One theory, advanced by Robert Putnam (2000) in *Bowling Alone*, is that the decline in the status of the family contributes to the decline in social capital. In this case what are the independent and dependent variables? Social capital is dependent on the status of the family in society, according to one explanation of Putnam. Therefore, social capital is the dependent variable and the status of the family is the independent variable; as the family declines social capital declines – a positive relationship (think about why this is understood as a positive and not a negative relationship in normative terms).

Stuck in a rut?

Whatever side of the divide you are currently standing, moving from research topic to research question is often where many students, and professional researchers, get stuck. Assuming that this moment is not symptomatic of a lack of reading, thinking, or consultation, a sure sign of being stuck here is when you, or others, are heard editorializing when asked about your research question, for example: 'Well, I'm not sure yet, 'coz I'm still working on it, and my supervisor and I are meeting this week to discuss it but it sort of, at the moment, about . . .' So what to do if you are not able to articulate your research *question* 'concisely and unambiguously'?

> **TIP: Instead of waiting for inspiration to come – fall from the tree above you as it were, treat your current formulation as work-in-progress.**
> - As you gain more knowledge and insights (usually by reading rather than agonizing) your question will also ripen, your ability to formulate it also.
> - In the meantime note down new ways of phrasing it, particularly after reading more literature, doing some of the data-gathering, or (as is often the case) just before going to sleep, in the shower, or on the way to work – the 'put it on the back-boiler' approach based on psychological theories about how our memories often work subconsciously.

The main thing here, whether or not you are working up a hypothesis or articulating a more open-ended sort of research question, is that the distinction between general topic and specific research question and how the latter breaks down into sub-questions needs to make sense to you and others – supervisor, classmates, engaged lay persons.

Still stuck? Then try the following:

- Having several versions of the topic and research question helps you towards finding a formulation that you, the researcher, can pin down; make it your own as your research plans take shape.
- Sometimes it is more a matter of syntax; phrasing rather than a substantive issue. The lack of a clearly identifiable research question is a common criticism by even the most sympathetic of readers. Try inverting those long statements, lists of propositions or possibilities into question-forms if not declarations.
- Another way is to try rephrasing your initial idea in the conditional form: 'what if', 'if', 'supposing that . . . then what would . . .'. This results in a research question, if not hypothesis, that is recognizable for various audiences.

Rephrasing, or changing the word order is often linked to how the core question develops as you gain more knowledge of the terrain, through a better grasp of the literature/s pertinent to your inquiry but also as your own research progresses, in both theoretical (ideas, concepts, analytical frameworks) and in empirical terms (what you find out).

That said, at some point all projects need to be able to articulate their core question, or set of questions motivating it. Not being able say what sort of inquiry is 'driving' or underlying the project in so many words does not augur well when you are faced with the next set of decisions: gathering and analysing your material (see Part 2). For those stuck on the horns of this particular dilemma, one way out of this cul-de-sac for qualitative research sensibilities is to try stating your research question in its most boldest, and baldest formulation; as a yes/no or a declamatory, straight-forward statement or in hypothesis form. Conversely, you could look at reformulating your provisional hypothesis – to be testable in the strictest quantifiable sense – as a more open-ended inquiry.

The idea behind this sort of role-reversal is that when stuck, taking a counter-intuitive approach to the presiding research culture within which you are working can create openings; lateral thinking is not the preserve of self-help books. As you get on with things, take heart; formulating your research question in the case of qualitative projects, or a hypothesis in the case of quantitative work, is a work-in-progress itself.

Rationale: the 'why bother'? question

> Every research has to start somewhere; typically, the starting point is an idea. The big question, however, is how to go about finding an idea that will serve as a good launching point to a research project.
>
> (Berg 2009: 23)

So what about your reasons, the rationale – aims and objectives – of the project? Sometimes here the research question may well be lurking. Stipulating your personal reasons, as well as your more ambitious aims for doing a project, particularly when trying to decide between more than one idea, gives direction to the project. That direction can, and often does change; aims and objectives get refined, or overturned along the way. When faced with the question 'Why are you doing this research?' or even the more hostile one, 'Why are you bothering?', be straight-up: why do you think this inquiry is worth pursuing?

ON SCIENCE, WORLDVIEWS, AND OTHER BRAINTEASERS

> One's analysis of theories tends to influence strongly the position one takes on issues such as observation, confirmation and testing.
>
> (Suppe in Craig 2005: 1016)

Sometimes the reasons for doing research in certain ways and not in others are obscure, boiling down to sociocultural conventions or unwritten codes of behaviour and allegiance, as much as they are grist to the mill of larger epistemological and ontological debates between philosophers and social theorists.

The first step in project design is where students, and researchers embarking on new projects, find that they too realize that there are many things they don't understand. Recalling the overview of the theory–method relationship from Chapter 2, how we collect evidence and then analyse this material does not happen in either a social or intellectual vacuum; all researchers start from implicit and explicit assumptions about what they (are going to) observe, how they observe it, and how they expect to come to understand it.

Recalling the discussion about observation in Chapter 1, conceptualizing, researching, and underlying worldviews are intertwined. It is often only at moments of tension (when confronted with a counter-intuitive finding) or direct challenge from others that these underlying assumptions make their presence felt; if not in how we respond to any criticism, then how we attempt to articulate these assumptions in order to pre-empt such foundational challenges. A basic truism is at the heart of these discussions: not everybody sees the same thing, or thinks differently about what they think they see (Figure 3.1).

To recap: in terms of how you work out the theory–method relationship pertinent to your inquiry, consider the following elements as decisions about

- Theoretical frameworks – or *substantive theories* – and how these speak to their respective disciplinary precursors.
- How a *worldview* is in play; implicit positions about how the world works, and our place in it, and how these correlate with as well as diverge from quantitative and qualitative demarcations.

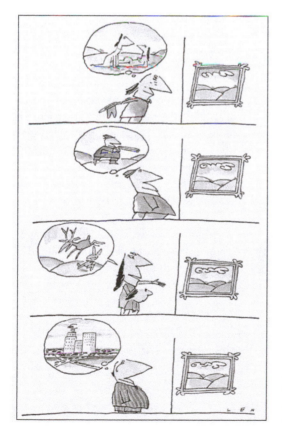

Figure 3.1 Ways of seeing

Source: Len Munnik:
http://www.lenmunnik.nl

- Recall too that no data-gathering (Chapter 6) or mode of analysis (Chapter 7) can be de-linked from any number of 'theoretical orientations' (Berg 2009: 4).
- One way to encapsulate the push and pull between these various elements is to talk of how they all contribute to our design as 'methodological strategies' (Berg 2009: 4) or 'research strategies' (Creswell 2009).

'This thing called science' and you

The notion of science and *scientific method* has become synonymous with the physical sciences, which in turn are positioned as diametrically opposed to the arts. The transposition of these ideas about the correct, right way of doing research has been grist to major rows and partial reconciliations across the modern academe and over many centuries.

One conflict between the lines of the discussions so far, often evoked if not explicitly reiterated, is one that arguably has become more pronounced as disciplinary borders correlate more and more closely with career paths, funding, and 'ideal types' in terms of best practice criteria for research success. This is the notion that the arts and the (natural) sciences do not, and cannot get along (see Snow 1993). Historically this dichotomy can be challenged; there are many examples of individuals being both accomplished scientists, philosophers, and artists. These historical accounts are beyond the bounds of this book. Suffice it to say that its entrenchment and emergence as a truism for academics and the general public alike remains a source of friction even today. Many have lamented it and many still work to surmount what is both stereotype and fact of working life in research institutions the world over. So what exactly is at stake?

Alan Chalmers puts it in a nutshell in his exploration of 'modern views about the nature of science' (Chalmers 2004: xi) when he notes how science is 'highly esteemed. Apparently it is a widely held belief that there is something special about science and its methods' (Chalmers 2004: ix). He goes onto to suggest that this received wisdom begs the question of 'what, if anything, is so special about science? What is this "scientific method" that allegedly leads to especially meritorious or reliable results?' (ibid.). And, as philosophers are wont to do, he then proceeds to state that

> questions concerning the distinctiveness of scientific knowledge, as opposed to other kinds of knowledge, and the exact identification of the scientific method are seen as fundamentally important and consequential. As we shall see, however, answering these questions is by no means straightforward.
>
> (Chalmers 2004: xx)

Take a moment to ask yourself what your standpoint is on the following propositions in Box 3.4: in themselves integral to substantive theories as well as worldviews.

BOX 3.4 WHAT IS SCIENCE?

1   Science is distinguishable by its generating knowledge that is 'derived from the facts of experience [that] can only be sanctioned in a carefully and qualified form, if it is to be sanctioned [as science] at all' (Chalmers 2004: xxi).

On the other hand, there are grounds to argue – as many have and still do – that

2   'scientific knowledge can neither be conclusively proved nor conclusively disproved by reference to the facts, even if the availability of those facts is assumed' (Chalmers 2004: xxi).

Stronger still, if indeed scientific theories, and the knowledge they claim to generate about how the world works, 'cannot be conclusively proved or disproved and that reconstructions [of preceding moments of scientific discovery or philosophical arguments bear] little resemblance to what actually goes on in science' (ibid.), then

3   'science has no special features that render it intrinsically superior to other kinds of knowledge such as ancient myths and voodoo' (Chalmers 2004: xxi–xxii, citing Feyerabend 1978).

Delving into the various ways philosophers address these propositions, with reference to or despite what practitioners claim (see Callon and Latour 1981, Feyerabend 1978, Kuhn 1962) is beyond the scope of this book. Nonetheless, the social and economic status granted to modern science – see proposition 1 in Box 3.4 above – as a set of principles (theory) and practices (scientific method) for objective, truthful and reliable knowledge about not only the physical but also the social and cultural worlds we live in, in recent times is hard to ignore.

The point Chalmers is making, a sub-text of all methods texts and headlines for many critical interventions, is that warranting the claim 'scientific', narrowly or broadly defined, in modern times, is the idea that 'what is so special about science is that it is derived from the facts, rather than being based on personal opinion' (Chalmers 2004: xx). What constitutes a *fact* vis-à-vis an *opinion*, who decides and how any position is supported by the 'evidence' is, again, related to views on the relationship between observation, experience, and scientific, or non-scientific knowledge about how the world works. Referring to different worldviews is a way of encapsulating these deep-seated standpoints.

Worldviews

Various commitments, individual and institutional, to certain views about how the world works can be mapped onto the demarcation lines that often get drawn, rightly or wrongly, between quantitative and qualitative research and their derivative schools of thought. Like others, I would distinguish between the myriad roughly hewn and nuanced positions making up three *very broad* worldviews. The groupings below are diverse and dynamic; the terms of reference used are also in themselves contestable. For your research needs you will need to go a lot deeper than these approximations of often inchoate, and conflicting positions, to make sense of them for your question and design.

The first worldview is one I shall call *empirical-positivist*; often seen as the 'default' position because it is identified as the 'mainstream' position in academe and society at large. This take on things is based on the premise that what we know is down to what we observe, phenomena that are 'given' as empirical data. Any scientific truth based on that data has to be created by objective forms of knowledge creation. From this flow other premises in varying degrees:

- the physical world exists *a priori* to ideas
- humans are rational actors
- human behaviour is observable, and predictable generally speaking
- facts are derived from observation
- knowledge is objective when based on *deductive reasoning*
- scientific research generates general laws.

In practical terms, this view holds that the observation point and the observer exist separately from the object observed; therefore error and bias have to be minimized as much as possible for findings to be valid, results considered legitimate.

One way to illustrate this worldview is in Figure 3.2, a photo taken from the Greenwich Observatory in southeast London. This point marks the Greenwich 'Prime Meridian', the point from which Greenwich Mean Time (GMT) was set in the mid-nineteenth century, and by extrapolation modern international time-zones are measured. The contemporary cartographic and temporal status of this point belies, however, the fact that there have been, and still are numerous 'prime meridians'; in Madrid, Mecca, Alexandria, and Kyoto to name but a few. The point here is that GMT is both an objective point of reference, and an international agreement to synchronize baseline time-measurement (along with datelines). It has, however, only become such over the course of time and for particular geopolitical and historical reasons.

This tension between notions of objectivity, the passing of time, and social convention brings us to this worldview's opposite number; one I shall call the *interpretive-constructivist* worldview (further discussion is in Chapter 7). This is based on the working premise that what we observe is not *a priori* to ideas about it or the position from which the observation takes place. This links then to the following rules of thumb in research practice:

- the social world, and sometimes the physical world, and related systems of meaning (how they are talked about) are inseparable from one another
- social practices, institutions, and phenomena are *co-constituted*
- human behaviour and motivations are not in a one-to-one relationship

- knowledge is partial; science/scholarship also needs *inductive* reasoning
- facts and values are inseparable even though they are not synonymous
- complex sorts of theorizing are integral to, not outside of, the object of analysis.

This worldview sees an intricate interaction between the point of observation, the observer, and the observed. This take on things goes a bit further, though, than purely a question of perspective. Where you stand actually co-defines what you see; how you proceed affects what you see. Hence there are not only multiple ways of seeing but also, ipso facto, multiple things that are observed (Figure 3.3).

The third worldview comprises various positions along the above spectrum in that it is interwoven with strands of both of the above views. This I shall tentatively call the *critical-pragmatist* worldview. Its neither synchronic nor harmonious working premises have their feet in both clusters above. These include views that research is about

- exploring cultural practices, experiences, and artefacts on their own terms
- examining the ways language and practices create societies and cultures
- uncovering and critiquing injustices as well as misperceptions
- looking at how power is exercised; from 'top-down' and 'bottom-up'
- exposing relations of domination, discrimination, mystification
- locating alternatives rather then reproducing that which is 'given' to us
- research is normative by definition; if not then it can be normative in intention.

Figure 3.2   View from Greenwich, UK

Source: M. I. Franklin

In other words, whilst the world as we see it – facts – may exist and there are ways of knowing that are scientific as well as 'non-scientific', what is observed may require our intervention. A number of longstanding alternative or dissenting modes of research, from feminist, to postcolonial, to forms of 'action research' and including those that are 'against method' (Feyerabend 1978) fall under this rubric. As Figure 3.4 below conveys, the social world under investigation may be an objective reality but this does not mean it is a pre-given. It can, indeed must, be acted upon.

What do this rough topology mean to anyone trying to get started on a research project? On the face of it, these complex, often arcane discussions do tend to unfold over the top of the heads of most fledgling researchers, those engaging directly with these debates as part of their research aside. However, at some point or other these issues do raise their heads. How so?

1   In standoffs between advocates of any position within or between the above clustered worldviews, experienced by most students in their 'Classics', 'Key thinkers' or 'Theories of . . .' classes, often regarded as far removed from real-life research (see Creswell 2009: 6).
2   When competing for funding, places in programmes, or approval by senior members of staff, these issues also emerge in the form of intense debates about which, if any, methods best pertain to local (departmental, faculty, or even national) understandings of research 'excellence'.
3   As noted in Chapter 1 it is often when embarking on a major piece of individual research for the first time that students encounter an idea of a particular worldview (your own, or one seen as the opposition) as synonymous with a particular method or cluster of methods.

How to cope, then, when these divisions appear under our feet?

1   For practical purposes, getting too bogged down in these issues, no matter how fascinating, or when they constitute the content of many erudite books on the matter, is not particularly helpful when setting out on a project (see Gray 2009: 34).
2   That said – and this is the balancing act – any one, or combination of approaches you then adopt, or nominate for the time being, as the way in which you intend to gather and analyse your material ('facts', 'empirical data', 'the literature') are not neutral either; their operating principles are also loaded with their respective historical and intellectual loads about what the world is (*ontology*) and how we come to know it (*epistemology*).

Figure 3.3 (above) View of lighthouse, Castlepoint, New Zealand

Source: M. I. Franklin

Figure 3.4 (right) Urban renewal (Prenzlauer Berg, Berlin)

Source: M. I. Franklin

OTHER PRACTICAL MATTERS

Recognizing and setting your limits

An important question to ask yourself when writing your research plan and developing your research project is to ask yourself; is this doable? Consideration of time, resource and even intellectual limitations is an important part of the planning phase. If you pay enough attention to constructing a research project, and thereby a question that is answerable, or hypotheses that can be tested with data collected within the time frame of the project or assignment, then you are further along the path of achieving your goal than you may think.

This is when you become aware of time-limits, what resources you really do have at your disposal in terms of costs and other logistics, and whether you have underestimated either the time or resources available. One way to have some back-up is to keep a record of your 'reject' ideas in case you need to draw up a contingency plan. Setting up a time-schedule thereby has its uses in the research proposal stage, for understanding time limitations is an important reason to make sure the timeline in the research proposal is reasonable, too generous or not generous enough. Be willing to ask yourself as well whether the research you are designing is suitable for the degree being awarded.

Figure 3.5   Valid and invalid claims schedule
Source: Fran Orford: http://www.francartoons.com

There are two other key areas where we may well find ourselves having our limits set for us: codes of research practice and related ethics on the one hand; and on the other, the way a supervisory relationship evolves during the course of a project.

Research ethics and codes of practice: more than ticking boxes

For the most part, this book is addressing academic projects in which a researcher carries out their research in the 'real world'. For that reason alone it is a misconception to proceed as if academic research is immune from social, cultural, and legal concerns, as if a researcher can go anywhere, do anything in the name of scientific (read: 'objective') knowledge. History, past and quite recent, shows how such an approach, especially when backed by a particular worldview, military might, or the 'rights' of imperial conquest, has left its own legacy.[9]

Over the last fifty years or so this assumption has been significantly revised; under the aegis of international human rights, intellectual property rights covenants, and also notions of *corporate social responsibility*, codes of ethics are now integral to doing research in private and public sectors. The statement below encapsulates the underlying principle as one of *socially responsible research*, one that is echoed in institutional and professional codes and guidelines around the world:

Social researchers must strive to be aware of the intrusive potential of their work. They have no special entitlement to study all phenomena. The advancement of knowledge and the pursuit of information are not themselves sufficient justifications for overriding social and other cultural values.

(Social Research Association 2003: 25–6)

How this principle is developed and enforced as mandatory and recommended codes of research conduct is a large area of philosophical debate in itself. It takes many forms, from lecture modules to simple or complex ethics forms that researchers are expected to complete and submit for approval at a certain stage in their project. It also underscores increasing levels of documentation researchers now need to complete when applying for research funding or gaining permission to access funding from their institutions. The oversight resides in guidelines as well as committees, who take a hands-off or hands-on approach accordingly.

Two points bear noting straightaway:

1   In practical terms ethical issues arising either when designing or carrying out research, legal as well as more sociocultural sensitive issues (copyright permissions and access permission respectively) are largely delegated to individual institutions, if not devolved entirely to the individual researcher, in consultation with supervisors, at the end of the day.

2   Things are changing as things move onto the web; as human subjects take the form of avatars, simulations, or game-based creations, we see these issues further complicated for online research scenarios. Chapter 5 takes these initial points further, given the way that changes brought about by the internet in particular in terms of where and how researchers now carry out observations, interviews, or even experiments now include cyberspace ('virtual') domains and computer-created subjects (e.g. avatars, game characters).

This overview looks at the role played by ethical considerations in general and ethics forms in particular at the moments they exert pressure on your research plans and ambitions. All the points raised below are open to further debate within departments; indeed they are often the source of some friction in working research communities given the power some committees can wield. In theoretical terms they are also covered extensively in philosophical critiques as well as professional guidelines and discussion papers.

For the sake of argument and simplicity, I have framed the discussion as if it were a Q&A session between a (frazzled or resistant) research student and their supervisor or tutor.

Researching human subjects

So what is the point here? For the most part codes of ethics have been formulated on behalf of research subjects (people) and their production (texts, words, images). But these codes also bear the weight of varying degrees of institutional liability as well as seeking to look out for the well-being of their students and research staff. There are regional, national, and disciplinary differences in terms of just how far limits are imposed on any individual researcher or team; in theory (in the design and consultation phase) and in practice (during the research and its eventual dissemination). There are also ongoing debates in certain quarters about the longer-term implications the formalities can have on independent thinking, or innovative research project plans anyway. What are complex cultural and moral questions that differ from project to project, place to place, and periods of time, can become inflexible rules and procedures wielded by powerful committees, as is the case in the US in particular.

Who calls the shots? Nonetheless, recent years have seen universities, international academic organizations, and national research bodies developing and refining their respective 'codes of research ethics' to comply with legal obligations but also to keep up to pace with changes in the context and challenges of research today. Anthropology, sociology, and psychology are particularly active in this area, as are medical researchers and those fields where experimental work is carried out. Apart from moral and philosophical inquiries into the origins of ethics, there is a more practical point. As the Social Research Association puts it,

> Poor design or trivial and foolish studies can waste people's time and can contaminate the field for future research. Thus research design itself raises many ethical considerations.
>
> (Social Research Association 2003: 25)

When considering doing research with human subjects, and their avatars (see Chapter 5), all researchers, students included, need to consider whether their inquiry will have an impact, namely a detrimental one, on their interlocutors. The converse is also the case, ensuring that a research project has taken account of any physical or emotional risks; when researching criminal organizations or in post-conflict zones, a research project should not put a researcher in any unreasonable or excessive danger. There is also the whole legal matter of litigation, liability, and responsibility by which institutions, hospitals and research centres look to cover their backs at worst, and ensure their staff and students conduct themselves appropriately at best.

The assumption underwriting unwritten and formalized codes of research practice is that researchers are social actors working with other people directly or in situations where others may be, or see themselves affected by what researchers are doing. Theoretical pursuits such as astrophysics, mathematics, and philosophy do not fall under this rubric on the whole. In addition, as a scholarly and legal pursuit on its own terms, ethics is an area of specialist knowledge. And with the influence and penetration of the internet into everyday research and methodological innovations emerging from there, codes of ethics are being overhauled accordingly; in other words, 'new methods pose new ethical problems' (Social Reasearch Association 2003: 5); more on these matters in Chapter 5.

When should I start being concerned with ethical issues? The main thing to bear in mind is that ethical practicalities, and dilemmas, can arise at three moments: when designing, when carrying out, and when writing up or going public with the results of the project. The good thing about the increasing clarity and referenced guidelines readily available these days, including mandatory forms and permissions for advanced research projects (postgraduate and onwards though not excluding any bachelor level), is that they provide a wealth of information and resources. The downside is that these details can threaten to overwhelm those starting out or confront those who have left these things until the very last minute with some frightening limits to what they can say and eventually claim.

What sorts of projects in particular see researchers having to devote time and consideration to these issues? Basically, any research involving interviews, focus groups, or participation-observation requires 'informed consent', implying some sort of access permission from a gatekeeper, if not a whole community, or a tacit recognition that the observation is happening in a public place. Here too the definition of public-ness is not clear-cut. For conducting interviews and/or focus groups, you need to use, or compose your own informed consent form. These vary from basic to more developed depending on the sort of interviews you envisage doing (see Chapter 6). Do consult with your supervisor about the wording and the eventual use of interview material; these matters will become clearer at a later point and are touched on in Chapters 6–8.

For official definitions and extensions pertaining to your disciplinary home-base or data-gathering approach, I advise you to consult your institutional or respective inter/national association's documentation; most of which are now available on the web. For the time being, the key principles to bear in mind are first those applying to the design and execution phases, and second those related to how we treat the material we've gathered afterwards in terms of its use in the project and storage:

- informed consent
- access rights and obligations
- anonymity and data-use
- data-retention
- transparency and accountability.

Informed consent

This principle is the cornerstone of research ethics today in that how a researcher goes about contacting and interacting with research subjects in an ethical way sets the tone for aspects below. What we mean by the notion of 'informed consent' is that any individual, group, or community who you envisage as your 'research subjects' (and that means they effectively become the object of inquiry) – those you plan to survey, interview, or observe – knows who you are and what you are doing. They then grant consent, in written form usually and where necessary orally. It is up to the researcher in the latter case to show how consent was gained; Appendix 1 provides a template for this sort of request.

> Gaining informed consent is a procedure for ensuring that research subjects understand what is being done to them, the limits to their participation and an awareness of any potential risks they incur. . . . The amount of information needed to ensure a subject is adequately informed about the purpose and nature of an inquiry is bound to vary from study to study.
>
> (Social Reasearch Association 2003: 28)

The basic point here is that active deception or coercion for most social research scenarios, and journalistic codes of ethics moreover, is not acceptable on the whole. There are exceptions whereby covert research is possible; experimental research and in the case of police work and investigative journalism undercover work. The latter are also governed by professional and legal codes and so lie beyond the scope of this discussion. On a more informal level, whilst there are some ongoing debates about whether it is justified to tell a 'white lie' to gain access where normally access (e.g. to sacred or gender-based restricted areas such as married women only) would be denied, it is advisable to err on the side of caution.

If consent is not granted, or is controversial for legal or cultural reasons, then you may need to rethink the object of analysis; some research topics are not feasible for student projects whilst others accepted in one discipline may well be considered inappropriate in another. For academic research the bottom line is that we are not undercover police officers or journalists (see Chapter 1, 'What is *academic* research?') so gaining consent or access by deception is a breach of ethics.

Access

Here the distinction between what is a public place and what is a private one is particularly difficult sometimes for research situations. It is a truism to note that there are cultural, and commercial if not civic variations on what is meant by a 'public' or a 'private' space. Online, in social networking sites for instance a lot of 'private' level interactions are taking place in ostensibly 'public' spaces which some researchers see as not requiring informed consent or access. Carrying out observations in public areas such as railway stations or shopping centres unobtrusively, or conducting surveys with passers-by, may all require you as a researcher to obtain if not access from the 'owner' (e.g. shopping centres are private spaces) then from those you may want to approach.

The way that research on the web makes this shifting line even fuzzier notwithstanding, in most sorts of fieldwork scenarios researchers rely on gatekeepers (e.g. village elders or discussion group moderators, website owners) to grant them initial access (see Chapter 6). However, gaining access is just a start and it is conditional; access can be withdrawn or made difficult. Online, where visibility is less obvious, 'lurking', whereby researchers observe and follow discussions without indicating their presence to other participants, the initial access granted by moderators or website owners often needs to be supported by the larger community.

On the other hand, if a gatekeeper refuses or later blocks access then it is sometimes unsustainable to continue (Social Research Association 2003: 29); not only because gatekeepers hold the keys to a group or community but also because if researchers were to circumvent these people they could create other sorts of disturbance within the community at the cost of the integrity of the eventual findings. Most codes and guidelines will note here the need to account for these eventualities in your methodological rationale; ways to gain access and consent as well as a clear reason as to why you may wish to observe 'covertly'. Bottom line is that an appeal to the need to maintain scientific objectivity, or that the findings will be compromised, is not considered an argument in itself.

Transparency – anonymity

On the one hand academic research is about leaving a clear trail (citations, methodology, data-gathering tracks). On the other hand, most social research with human subjects is based on privacy whereby informants' identities and their pronouncements (written or spoken) are treated anonymously unless they provide consent to be named.

In interviews or situations where your project has you recording or videoing your subjects you also need to gain (usually written) consent to record these conversations, for not everyone wants to be recorded or videoed.[10] In most cases, though, anonymity is the rule rather than the exception; in larger surveys anonymity is a given, and for probability sampling a rule. But when citing interviews or online discussions, and when anonymizing these texts, the ability for others to follow up on these words may be impaired; so here the trade-off between protecting informants' anonymity, ensuring transparency and accountability to keep the integrity of the data clear (i.e. not making things up), and conducting research in an ethical way have to be balanced out.

Using and retaining data

How we use any interview data when conducting qualitative interviews or conversations had in the field (see Chapter 6) is also an ethical matter. As anonymity is the standard rule this makes it easier to be consistent when citing. That also means, though, that the onus is on the researcher to treat others' words in context, to cite accurately, and with respect. When researching other cultures or marginalized groups where controversial topics are at stake, these issues can create their own stress points when analysing and then writing up the results (see Chapters 7 and 8).

For large-scale surveys, quasi-experimental projects and questionnaire-based interviews there are usually nationally set rules for where and how researchers should retain the data they've collected, particularly those data that can identify anonymized informants. In the UK and the European Union this period is between 5 and 7 years. Your job is to know what the regulations are and whether they will affect your project. Keeping identity-based information on a password-protected part of your computer, with disks or tapes locked up is a simple way. Most regulations insist that researchers destroy this material after a certain time period; the UK in particular is very strict in theory on these matters. As we are conducting research and hopefully will be using the material more than once, or want to refer to it at a later date, these regulations do not mean students need destroy their raw material the day after handing in the project. The main principle is to treat it with care.

Accountability: authorship – ownership and control

I mentioned above how research subjects, particularly those with strong gatekeeping power, can exert their own pressure on researchers to grant them full authorship rights, or full access to any transcripts. In some settings where the topic may be politically or culturally charged, government representatives may also demand exclusive rights over your work.

This is a delicate area where ethics and accountability are double-edged. Consult any guidelines, or ethics committee members as well as your supervisor if you find yourself in this position. Remember that the eventual dissertation is an original piece of work of which you are the author (unless this research has been carried out in a partnership with those you are researching, as is the case with *participatory action research*). Research into NGOs, for instance, can lead to demands for co-authorship or full rights over any material a researcher gathers as these organizations wish to maintain control over the eventual results or access to the data.

Starting out – practical survival tips

For beginners, absolute or otherwise, here are some practical tips to consider as your research design starts to take shape. In fact it would be a good idea to incorporate these inquires into your initial reading and research:

- If your department does not have documented ethical guidelines, there should be information available at the faculty or institutional level. These guidelines and handbooks are often written in quite dry, legalistic language as they are often construed in the interests of protecting the institution from prosecution. Nonetheless, it is worthwhile taking a look at these governing codes, particularly in cases where a researcher may be liable or required to gain official permission; researching legal minors (children under 16 in the UK) being a case point, participant-observation of groups engaged in semi-legal or illegal activities another.
- If there is an approval or consultative procedure in place, if not for bachelor/ master level then usually for Ph.D. and most certainly these days for faculty-level research, you need to locate the forms and integrate the time needed to get a response into your planning.[11]
- On that note: ethics form-filling usually takes place in the earlier stages of a longer research project, though usually once you are clear about the question and elected data-gathering mode. In some departments, anthropology in particular, fieldwork cannot proceed until approval has been gained. For fieldwork in some parts of the world researchers also need to undergo a governmental-level approval of access process; postcolonial societies are particularly sensitive to these protocols, given the chequered history of research encounters in the colonial period and since.
- Whatever level you are at, try and integrate this aspect into the research design phase; do a first draft of any ethics forms you may need to submit; in Appendix 3 is one example. Use this as reference point when discussing your options with your supervisor/s or mentors, who may well have quite opposing opinions on the exercise or how you approach it.
- Be prepared to have to perhaps revise your plans if serious objections are raised.
- All these concerns are becoming not only more acute but under more scrutiny in computer-mediated or web-based research. Online research ethics are being written and existing ones adjusted with the rise of virtual ethnographic research, research into virtual worlds and gaming, web-mapping tools, and the boom in user-generated texts (e.g. reader comments on news media websites) where traditional editorial gatekeeping has been arguably superseded if not transformed; more on these matters in Chapter 5.

Figure 3.6 Human–machine ethics

Source: Nina Paley: http://www.ninapaley.com

In short, if you treat the ethics practicalities as more than just ticking boxes, as more than a subsidiary to the project, you stand a good chance of not only getting approval (if required), some productive feedback or suggestions about what to look out for (if this is part of an educative process), but also a more rounded project design.

During the research – taking responsibility

The rules of thumb below are based on what *not* to avoid when considering ethical implications for your project. This is because ethics cut both ways; as negative and positive limitations to what researchers do. Remember that in some parts of the world, fields or settings research is a contentious undertaking.

1 Excesses on the institutional side or cavalier attitudes on the researcher's side (history and scholarly critiques are full of these examples) notwithstanding, ethics are as much a philosophical issue as they are a minefield of cultural and social sensitivities.
2 Belief systems and worldviews play a prominent role here in terms of how ethics are practised in the field, institutionalized in academic departments, or even ignored by some researchers claiming immunity from the above considerations.

You can tick boxes or you can take the ethics protocols on board in such a way as to strengthen the project and ultimately your methodological rationale. Here are those things that are best *not* to avoid:

• Don't avoid looking into whether there are general ethical considerations or specific implications for your project. Thinking through foreseen, and then unforeseen issues actually strengthens your work in the long run.
• For the above reason, don't avoid taking action – adjust, rethink, or desist as need be – further on if an ethical issue emerges or you discover late in the day an aspect overlooked, for example, not having gained informed consent or access permission, or citing words by online interlocutors without their knowledge. A Ph.D. defence is not the place to be confronted with this news.

- For online scenarios in 'open cyberspace', don't avoid checking whether there are ethical issues around observation, access, and informed consent in those forums you are investigating. This is even more pressing if you are working in a password-protected space on the web; even if a member already, this does not mean it is alright to lurk. Many researchers have found out, particularly when in spaces from other cultures or particular interest groups or subcultures, that other participants may not take too kindly to being research objects.

- Don't avoid gaining consent, at the outset and during the research either. If objections arise during the course of your stay, or dynamics change, these need to be accounted for and it is in your interest, in fact, to note how these shifts in access and acceptance affect the observation, and participation.

- Don't avoid dealing with these obligations by stating that (a) a project rests on your doing covert research, or (b) has to be 'objective'. Whilst there may well be interesting theoretical debates on these matters to attend to, at the practical level you will see that all codes of ethics, and forms you may need to fill in, have clear guidelines here.

- Finally, a word on attitude: it is a good idea to avoid cynicism or sarcasm where possible, even if the ethics form is a formality for your work. Ethics cut both ways and also have multiple applications. Even textual analysis (e.g. online texts and images) now fall under overlapping terms of use and reproduction; for instance Facebook and Flickr images reside with these service providers yet ethically permission to use, or cite is also a matter for she or he who posted them, assuming of course that these images are theirs!

Whether or not they are mandatory, ethics forms and, when they arise, dilemmas need not stop you in your tracks. Nor should they prevent you from undertaking a creative, innovative piece of research. Rather, see them as part of the territory; their many facets and non-resolvable nature as integral to the theory–method relationship pertinent to your inquiry.[12]

Further reading – ethical codes and practice

If your department or institution is not forthcoming (though it would be surprising these days if there was no information at all on ethical matters), see the useful checklist provided by the UK-based Social Research Association (2003: 53–56). A comprehensive discussion is the *European Code of Conduct for Research Integrity* by the European Science Foundation (www.esf.org/activities/mo-fora/research-integrity.html). Other associations with well-developed codes and supplementary guidelines online are

> The American Anthropological Association
> The Economic and Social Research Council (UK)
> The Association of Internet Researchers Ethics Guide
> The Arts and Humanities Research Council (UK)
> The British Sociological Association's *Statement of Ethical Practice*.

General discussions and applied topics are also available in Berg (2007), Berry (2000), Denzin and Lincoln (2005), Gray (2009), Ratcliffe (2001), Silverman (2011), and Smith (1999). As for specific ethical issues, practical and more conceptual, pertaining to either an issue-area or within a particular discipline, consult the relevant journals and book catalogues for research-based examples.

The supervisory relationship

A valuable resource is your supervisor. This relationship is one that develops as your project does so all the more reason for you to take a proactive approach to supervision in its formal and informal dimensions. Coping with tensions in the research process brings us to how the supervisor has an important role to play in helping students to overcome these tensions. Having an audience that is both critical (their role is to challenge you) and supportive (they want you to succeed) is something that needs nurturing at the same time, as it is perhaps the first professional working relationship students develop in their research lifetime, in the shorter or longer term.

Oftentimes the supervisory relationship is taken as read; moreover, it can well be a source of anxiety if not tension for some. This introductory section discusses not only the formal role of a research supervisor but also how students can 'manage' their supervisors, along with their own expectations of the supervisory process. Whilst there are many cultural and disciplinary variations to this relationship, one principle holds for all interactions: at the very least, aim to arrive at supervisory appointments prepared and hope to leave them feeling they have been worth the effort even if they have not always been comfortable, or comforting.

First, let's look at it from one side of this relationship; we will deal with the other side in Chapter 8. The role of the supervisor is, foremost, to provide advice on the research topic, provide assistance on sources of material and give feedback on written work. The supervisor is expected to give feedback on interpretation, writing skills, written work, and to provide guidance on academic conventions, and the planning and completion of the thesis. On the other hand, students are responsible for undertaking the research needed to complete the thesis, for formulating the principal ideas contained within it, and for writing up the results according to the formats expected (see Chapter 8); earlier points on how formalities and originality interrelate are a case in point.

However it is gone about, early on the main objective is to get agreement between supervisor and student on key deadlines, meeting times, and mutual expectations. This can only be achieved through regular contact and open channels of communication.

But these exhortations, and many more, beg the question of why a supervisor is necessary for student researchers. In other words, what special skills do supervisors bring to the supervisor–supervisee relationship?

1   First, your supervisor will have successfully completed a research project at least one level higher than the one being undertaken by the supervisee. Or, they have specific skills or knowledge of an area.

2   In the first instance they understand the institutional rules that are in place regarding completion deadlines and they keep an eye on these, nudging you along when it seems time is passing without much progress. They can also offer guidance about reading as well as alert you to substantive issues in your research.

3   Finally, supervisors will also have an idea when your research is complete and ready for submission, or to be defended. For new researchers this is sometimes the most difficult aspect of the research process – knowing when it is finished and what it takes to get there.

One reason why supervisors and supervisees can find themselves at loggerheads is this undertow of mutual expectation; we all harbour ideal-types. So, ask yourself the questions in Table 3.1, depending on your role in the above process.

Table 3.1 Supervisors and supervisees

What sort of supervisee are you?	I want to be told what to do.
	I want to be left to do my own thing.
	I don't like criticism (not really).
	I love criticism (I think I do).
What sort of supervisor are you?	I want students to do as I say.
	I want students to listen to what I say.
	I want students to be independent, not needy.
	I want students to do work that interests me.

Until we return to this relationship and other points about feedback towards the end of a project's lifecycle, the following pointers are for you to consider as you get your project off the ground and get to know your supervisor.

- A good working relationship between supervisor and supervisee requires communication. It is actually up to supervisees to work on keeping the supervisor informed of any major issues, in the research or personal, that may affect the timely completion of the research.

- This means that student-researchers need to more proactive in contacting and scheduling meetings with their supervisors than many think is necessary. This is in order to avoid some common pitfalls such as inadequate planning, misunderstandings, failure to stick to deadlines and the mutual distrust or resentment that can ensue.

- Good communication and being adequately prepared for meetings help anyway. But they are also crucial for pinpointing specific needs; any research training needs can be planned and undertaken, and alternative plans can be developed in the event the initial research plan turns out not to be feasible.

- Even though the dissertation or thesis is an individual research project, working too much in isolation can be detrimental to the research process. Keeping in touch with a supervisor, and others, can ease the isolation.

- However, at some point you will need to do the work, not just talk about all the problems you are having doing it; supervisors and classmates are neither our parents, nor our therapists.

- Serious issues that are affecting your ability to work are best dealt with by a trained professional. If it is all getting too much (and this happens) or if you are dealing with personal distress, let your supervisor know so they can refer you to the appropriate support services. All universities have counselling and health professionals in place for these contingencies.

Time-pressures and a tendency to see what is often referred to as the 'deliverable' as an end in itself and our supervisors as merely instrumental to this end is, paradoxically given the competitiveness of most research cultures, not where the real value of the supervisory relationship and research process as a whole really lie.

Before getting too far ahead of ourselves, this chapter draws to a close by considering the points raised so sfar from a bird's-eye view; the road that lies ahead and its various highways and cul-de-sacs is as much a rule-bound as it is an uncharted territory.

METHODOLOGICAL COPING STRATEGIES – PLOTTING A COURSE

Remembering that our topic, research questions, and rationale are that the dog should be wagging the method/s' tail, one way to plot a course through these philosophical and methodological undercurrents in a way that makes sense for your project is to leave aside this particular distinction. Make a mental note as you must; acknowledge the predominant research culture you are working within as required. In the meantime work on considering whether the course of inquiry you are working on calls for you to make a start gathering your data and from there applying any particular analytical framework to make sense of your findings.

The five areas below describe core methodological approaches in operation today. They are presented here as a sort of survival guide to help you plot a course in practical terms in light of the various theoretical and practical debates that affect our choice of topic and eventual research question. This overview concentrates on these distinctions as practicalities: (1) ways of gathering data; (2) ways of analysing the material. Note too that these are not mutually exclusive terrains by definition, nor are they synonymous with particular disciplines or schools of thought per se. However, each one also has come to be associated with particular disciplinary 'homes'; e.g. surveys in election or public opinion research, focus groups for media and communications studies, participation-observation for anthropological fieldwork on the ground or in online settings such as computer games.

Given that there are various worldviews and positions on the 'What is science?' question underpinning these clusters at any point where they diverge and intersect, how their respective 'rules and procedures' for gathering and analysing the material work is the task of Chapters 6 and 7. At present we are getting a sense of the lay of the land as we firm up the research question, make our first plans, and get acquainted with the literature. The highways and byways of this larger terrain include ways of working that can be characterized as *ethnographic*, *surveying* and *interviewing*, *archival* and *textual* approaches to documents, *experimental* and *alternative* pathways:

Ethnographic

In the field where full immersion (part-time, periodic, or longer intervals) by the researcher engaging in participation-observation research provides close-up, intimate knowledge of the field and its inhabitants, data is gathered in real-time, using field notes, interviews, photographs or diagrams of the terrain, and personal accounts of changing relationships between research subjects as well as between them and the researcher. Involvement in the lives of others, development of closer working relationships, friendships, and trust between researcher and researched are integral. Entries and exits need to be negotiated. The governing style and rationale is 'rich description'. Distinctions need to be made between

- doing an ethnography and designing ethnographic projects;
- how much observation vis-à-vis how much participation;
- degrees of ethical considerations and long-term effects of the researcher's presence in a community or field more complex;
- work traditionally undertaken in cultures/settings foreign to those of the researcher, nowadays also carried out for varying degrees of virtual (simulated/computer game) fields.

Surveying and interviews

Where larger, or smaller selections of human subjects are given a set of questions, designed to elicit responses that test a hypothesis, or provide more complex information about a given topic. Results are collated and analysed by statistical means but not exclusively; e.g. some surveys ask open-ended questions or require respondents to provide their own views. These findings need to be analysed qualitatively as they cannot be easily quantified. Distinctions need to be made between

- Formats for interviews: one-to-one based on semi-structured or unstructured forms of question and response between researcher and respondent provide more personalized information; these can follow on from larger-scale surveys or questionnaires.
- Focus groups: small group sessions where particular tasks or questions are put to the group; the researcher is facilitator rather than participant. The aim is to ascertain how different people respond to the same material, for example, an image, TV programme, film. Focus groups can comprise like-minded or diverse groups. Data is recorded and transcribed for analysis at a later date by the researcher.
- Sorts of question-design along with format and style of the interview/focus-group exchange, recording, and analysis of the responses as both statistical and textual data.
- Whether selection of respondents can be carried out randomly (larger samples) or in concentric circles of nearest neighbour (snowballing) or based on the researcher's immediate networks of friends.

• Generalizations based on whether the findings are in direct proportion to the size and randomness of the sample.

Archival-textual

Where access to original documents, their analysis or 'textual analysis' of images as well as written text are paramount. Within this area a number of specific methods have become codified, all of which concentrate on unravelling how meaning is made through language, or visual images; e.g. semiotics, discourse analysis, framing analysis. These include:

• Textual analysis is a term that can be literally applied to the analysis of policy documents as well as a particular approach to meaning-making (written and visual) in terms of 'social text'. Here various sorts of interpretive techniques and linguistic methods are applied to the material.
• Archival work for historical purposes based on available material and piecing together conclusions based on that. Archives can be hard copy or digital.
• Policy analysis can entail the retrieval, reconstruction of policy output; it can also entail the tracing of policy-making processes (such as drafts, bills, Green/White Papers) as they emerge; the written texts, and those writing the texts can be treated as distinct or linked objects of inquiry.

Experimental

Where testing or observing behaviours of individuals or groups is carried out in a controlled, or semi-controlled setting (laboratory, public place). The design of the experiment; its physical and psychological parameters, ethical issues around the implications for human, or animal subjects, and elimination of bias are controlled in varying degrees.

• This sort of work aims to test a hypothesis in terms of dependent versus independent variables.
• Findings can be analysed statistically but not exclusively in that the researcher's point of observation is integral to the aims and objectives of the experiment.
• Used in audience effects research in media and communication studies, sociological work on social or cultural attitudes such as prejudice or sex–gender stereotypes.
• Based on theories of human behaviour and motivation which come under scrutiny in studies of cause and effect; for example, the Blue Eyes/Brown Eyes race-experiment; reproductions of versions of the 'Prisoner's Dilemma' (most recently depicted in the film *Die Welle*).

Alternatives

Hybrids of the above on-the-ground, virtual (web-based), or semi-virtual (online/offline) settings whereby the data gathered, observation–observer relationship, or analytical techniques diverge from the above in form and substance (e.g. action research, virtual ethnography, simulations, 'virtual methods'). Designs based in 'mixed methods' can fall under this category, along with radical departures based on other cultural models of knowledge production (e.g. Carver and Hyvarinen 1997, Couldry 2000, Giri 2004, Smith 1999).

These broad categories for data-gathering can accommodate both qualitative (non-quantifiable) and quantitative (statistical/quantifiable) findings. They also lead onwards to more detailed, and more nuanced methodological discussions, debates, and alternatives in their own terms. The point here is that as your research project develops, particularly as your research question and knowledge of the field in terms of theoretical and empirical literature already available sharpen, these rubrics can open up avenues that lend themselves to your inquiry.

CONCLUDING COMMENTS

The above coping strategies will start to make more sense as you proceed further into gathering and analysing your material. Let's review these initial stages before moving deeper into the research terrain.

1   There are general and particular rules of thumb for embarking upon what are commonly characterized as qualitative- or quantitative-style research when not a mixture of the two. It is the execution, respective weighting, and presentation of these elements that are informed by deeper, underlying tensions between underlying worldviews and the way any approach develops and gets institutionalized, or not, over time.

2   As we approach the last two chapters of Part 1 where research designs and research divides appear to walk hand-in-hand, I would stress that in order for a project to get out of the starting blocks, we need to make an analytical and pragmatic distinction between how worldviews, research question formulations, and other planning matters impinge on the inquiry and then set our priorities for the time being without undue worry about how the project 'looks'.

3   To extrapolate: rather than pretending that there are methods and accompanying theoretical frameworks that either transcend or can resolve this particular dialectic, or trivializing what are very real power hierarchies at work in terms of which research gets the thumbs up – good grades, public recognition, research funding – or leads to future employment, the best way to cope when these distinctions start to impact on your work is (try) not to panic. Put them off until a later day, take in the lay of the land first or step up to the plate and engage in the big debates, ask these difficult questions of yourself, your peers and your

supervisors. But at the same time make some initial decisions, strike out on a path. You can review, retrace your steps every so often along the way.

Reflect on these matters for sure but do try and keep moving. Ironically, your eventual topic is not *a priori* confined to one sort of method, theory, or broader school of thought. Unless you are doing a research project that focuses on these meta-level or philosophical questions per se (and even then you still need to focus and give shape to them) keep the distinction between these abstract questions and their practical dimensions in mind. This way you can avoid getting too bogged down in a meta-methodological morass.

NOTES

1 To recall, the first is mandatory for research-funding bids or applications to Ph.D. programmes. The second encompasses anything from templates to help students along in their planning, a guide for preparing for supervision meetings, to a written document submitted as a piece of work for research skills/methods courses. Some supervisors may expect you to submit a research plan to them in any case.
2 See the relevant sections in Blaxter et al. (2006), M. Davies (2007), and Gray (2009).
3 See Gray (2009) and Creswell (2009) for some good discussions on using writing as a way of thinking.
4 Wise words from my own research office support staff member on submitting a funding bid.
5 See Berg (2009), Blaxter et al. (2006), Creswell (2009: 129 *passim*, ch. 7), M. Davies (2007), Gray (2009).
6 Creswell devotes a whole chapter to the Purpose Statement (2009: 111–26).
7 Thanks to Susan Banducci for this reference (personal information).
8 These terms might be familiar to some of you from studying maths in school, where you learned the formula for a line ($Y = mX + b$).
9 This topic fills volumes. For references that have certainly helped me along the way in terms of the way they speak directly to, and from hands-on experiences, see, Fabian (1983), Marcus (1995) and Smith (1999).
10 As a research subject in a research project where videos played a key role yet not all interviewees wanted to be identified, the researcher filmed only our hands. I have also done work with people who prefer not to be recorded. Others have been happy to be videoed, recorded and named in any citations yet also wish to vet the sections that appear in the final report.
11 Any funded research these days comes attached with the caveat that an ethics form and committee-based procedure is a co-requisite if not prerequisite for funding.
12 Material for this and other ethics-related sections are based on my role as vice-chair of my department ethics committee and membership of the university ethics sub-committee at time of publication. My thanks to past and current research students for their permission to be able to draw on their dilemmas and material in these discussions (see also Chapter 5). Thanks go out as well to my ethics committee colleague Tim Crook at Goldsmiths, whose legal knowledge and intrepid eye for the practical nuance and limits have taught me much. My own hands-on learning of these matters has also been informed by Helen Lee, Johannes Fabian, and Niko Besnier in particular.

CHAPTER 4

The politics of research

Living with and defending our choices

Topics covered in this chapter:

- Institutional and geographical research settings
- Literature searches and the 'literature review'
- Historical and philosophical context
- Purpose and categories of literature reviews
- Practicalities – pitfalls, rules of thumb, where to go
- Acknowledging sources – what is *plagiarism?*
- (Inter)disciplinary identities

INTRODUCTION

Living with and defending your choices during the lifetime of a research project has not only formal but also social and personal dimensions to it; implicit and explicit levels of accountability which underpin how we are thinking and going about the research. Researchers express these expectations in a number of ways: categorically (for example, basing a decision on the 'facts and figures'), *normatively* (for example, noting something missing in current knowledge that should be covered, arguing how the research serves notions of social justness), or as strategically placed references to publicly available literature (for example, individual publications, statistical databases, White Papers, news reports, or *blogs*) in the narrative.

In all of the above researchers will also quote others directly, *verbatim* or by alluding to publications. These are the most prevalent ways of anchoring our work in what others have done, or are currently doing in our topic-area; the formalities and etiquette of academic citation. Direct quotes, allusions, and paraphrasing are where scholarly hierarchies and peer networks are made visible in academic production; recognized or resisted in various measures in any written report of a research project. This is the power exerted on our work by the so-called *canon* of any given field of endeavour as well as the diffuse pressure of everyday sensibilities about whose work we think is relevant for our project. Dealing with who others think are more relevant is part of the politics of research.

The larger process entailed here, however, is one through which researchers gain familiarity and then come to terms with what others have to say, or not, on their topic and its wider context. This is what your supervisor and teachers are talking about when they refer to the 'literature'. It is also why many supervisory sessions are punctuated by names, references to debates, and references to specific publications.

These expectations – and obligations – often only crystallize at those moments when we have to present work to others or find ourselves having to defend a decision made and its, perhaps unforeseen, consequences for our findings. Learning how these technicalities work within respective methodological, institutional and geographical settings is also what makes academic research so exacting; tedious at times and at worst an exercise in name-dropping or intellectual versions of 'keeping up with the Joneses'.[1] Such moments occur almost from day one; explaining changes in our research plan or inability to tighten up the research question to our supervisor, elucidating aspects of a Ph.D. dissertation queried by the examiners, in the Q&A after a presentation to our peer group. For first-timers, dealing with direct challenges to key decisions made early on can be a disconcerting process, particularly if you cannot come up with any let alone a satisfactory response; either through nerves or, worse still, because of ignorance.

The point here is that whether still in the planning stages or when completed and bound, ready to be disseminated to a wider audience, how we see our project in terms of work done or being done by others is pivotal, requiring different levels of commitment, selectivity, and written expression. It also involves some deft manoeuvring through the material for projects that draw on more than one disciplinary literature (for example, ethnography and literary analysis, politics and media studies) or where supervision is also shared between approaches.

For example, if your project is in psychology broadly speaking, there is a distinction between finding out and then discussing how your research question relates to research done by others on a similar issue-area or even the same topic; within or across the various approaches now making up the larger 'field' of psychology and its sub-fields, for example, behaviouralism (see Chapter 7) or psychoanalysis. How these overlapping domains – those closest to your inquiry in particular – relate to comparable work done by sociologists or anthropologists is another. Which insights from other domains are pertinent, as well as which are not, may well be something you need to explain and defend in itself, particularly if your topic and approach counters the mainstream line of thought in your setting.

Below I will touch on some of the issues around the way inherently multi/interdisciplinary projects, and so literature bases, create both openings and risks. Suffice it to say that in these cases the ideal of work that draws on and addresses multiple readerships involves a trade-off between depth and breadth of coverage, independence and allegiance. Many postgraduate, and not a few undergraduate dissertation students working in mixed or recently merged departments, become acutely aware of these undercurrents, often feeling duty-bound to 'pin themselves down to one discipline for career purposes' at a very early stage.[2]

Chapter aims and organization

To set the scene, the first section looks at how location plays a part in the sorts of research undertaken today in an ostensibly globalized context; international master programmes, interdisciplinary and cross-border collaborative research projects, or research seminars create exciting sorts of synergies and also heighten differences in approach and sensibility. The next section takes a brief look at the philosophical and historical dimensions to these geographies, intrinsically Anglo-Euro-American academe. The core of this chapter unpacks what is meant by literature searches (a process) and the *literature review* (the product); both terms denote a certain sort of research activity – how we relate our work to one or more literatures.

In formal terms, for dissertation work at any degree level, these levels of expected and acquired knowledge converge at two moments in the research process: the preparatory reading – and writing – you do early on in a project, and writing it up in the final report (see Boxes 2.1 and 3.1). In everyday conversations, between supervisors and dissertation students especially, these two phases tend to become synonymous; referred to as the *literature review*.[3] Given its strategic role in research design (see Chapter 3), the writing up of the research (see Chapter 8), and that way you as well as others identify with your project, this chapter aims to help you understand how this element works in academic research in three interconnected ways.

1 As part of familiarizing yourself with the form and substance of the discipline, or disciplines, in which you find yourself or choose to work; location – orientation – matters. As researchers we develop a sense of where our work is located; cognitively, institutionally, and geographically; how disciplinary borders influence the research process, where they matter and where they can be bridged.

2 As part of the mandatory requirements for successfully presenting a completed piece of research for degree programmes, which is quite specific; a chapter or section in the final report. This requirement arguably puts the *literature review* at the epicentre of the research project. Whether you undertake a systematic or a more selective sort of 'lit review' the point here is that you can show you have got to grips with the main debates (and key thinkers) in your area. In that sense

as part of the research process, reviewing the literature is important for helping you formulate a research question and furthering your work-plan.

3   Distinct from doing a literature search, the term 'lit review' and its intertwined relationship with the theoretical component of a project is also a piece of written work in its own right; a mandatory element in many UK dissertations for instance.

Undertaking and then presenting literature reviews is an important resource for learning to live with, and reasonably defend our choices. It also implies that the researcher, absolute beginner or old-timer, can appropriately acknowledge sources (in formal citation formats, through allusions to, and engagements with themes or thinkers). That we know the difference between our own ideas and those of others, and can engage with those others in a reasonable way is where we test our mettle (see Chapter 8).

This brings with it protocols, so before returning to how research communities also create and carry certain identities, we look at more formal skills, technical matters related to how we need to treat the work of others. Whilst being original (see Chapter 2) is the aim, as researchers look to generate new knowledge, both unfold in the context of knowledge and foresight of others. There are rules and regulations about how researchers acknowledge and cite the literature. The chapter goes on to consider:

4   The basic principles of academic citation and referencing; more details to follow in Chapter 8.
5   The question of *plagiarism*: why presenting other people's words, or research results as if they were our own is not acceptable. This term encompasses a range of transgressions, some more clearly defined than others; for example, from claiming a concept is all your own when it may already be in circulation, to 'tweaking' a text to avoid using quote marks (once again), to 'lifting' chunks of text *verbatim* from other sources without full acknowledgement of the source, inclusion of quotation marks, or too much use of quotes instead of your own words.

As with previous chapters, which aspect of the discussions below need attention first as you work to put *your* research into context, and figure out why, is up to you in the final analysis.

DOING RESEARCH TODAY: 'LOCATION, LOCATION, LOCATION'

As a student working toward a particular degree, you may proceed with assignments, essays, and even the final research project without stopping to think more deeply about the nature of the discipline you are studying in: for example, what is the key object of study in politics, media studies, or sociology? What drives these fields; what types of questions are important for researchers? To a large extent we as students and researchers just get on with it. However, these types of questions ask us to think about the discipline we are working within, or against (as the case may be). They also affect the sorts of research we embark upon, certainly in terms of our first major pieces of independent work.

The research process is intimately connected to these discussions about the discipline; therefore, what is new about doing research now is also a story about the development of the discipline that can go way back. Let's take two examples, politics and history. Commentators date these disciplines in many different ways, some as far back as the writings of the ancient Greek philosophers, Plato and Aristotle, Thucydides, and Herodotus. In the first instance, Plato is accredited with being the first political theorist and Aristotle the first political scientist; Thucydides the first international relations scholar, and Herodotus the founder of historical method. Plato, in *The Republic*, was concerned about formulating a model for a utopian society, which would take into account many of the problems endemic to living in society. Aristotle, on the other hand was interested in the design of political institutions based on observations of how a society operates. It has become commonplace to see Plato and Aristotle as representatives of two divergent ways of drawing conclusions from the (observed) evidence; the implications of these two paths for how analysing our findings will be explored in Chapter 7.

The point of this detour into how the ancients have come to occupy foundational positions in institutional differences in undertaking research and then presenting the results is to highlight the undertow of millennia of reiterated assumptions about the correct *savoir faire* in which all researchers find themselves as they embark on a new research topic (see Chapter 2). All disciplines, and constituent methodologies make allusions to these founding fathers [sic] accordingly.

Another way to get a sense of the development of a discipline is to look at the professional associations that have emerged. Not only the historical conditions, but also the geographical and cultural parameters of the first associations can tell us something about both their 'genetic code' and the way they develop as part of any disciplinary 'genealogy' (see Foucault 1973). For instance, political science is considered as an American enterprise. One of the first professional organizations was the American Political Science Association (APSA) founded in 1903. Despite the name it has an international reach with members from over seventy other countries. International relations by all accounts is considered as a British discipline, its origins dated from the first chair in international relations in 1918, named, incidentally, the 'Woodrow Wilson Chair', after the 28th American president, in Aberystwyth, Wales. That said, the International Studies Association (ISA), based at the University of Arizona (USA) was founded in 1959 to promote research and education in international affairs. It currently has over 4,000 members in North America and around the world. A comparable set of overlapping associations, with or without the appropriate use of the term 'international' for US-housed associations, is in media and communications; the International Communications Association (ICA) is based in the USA with spin-off associations such as the International Association of Media and Communications Research, Association of Internet Researchers, and nationally-based or regionally-organized academic associations presenting various methodological predilections and preoccupations likewise.

Both quantitative modes of empirical research and the predominance of *formal theory* have come to be strongly associated with American political science, communication studies, a large part of sociology, and their professional associations (the APSA, ICA, and ISA respectively). Continental Europe and the UK, with their own distinct blends of approaches, represent different academic cultures. Here we see that some of the above 'American' approaches have been adopted whilst in other cases associations identify strongly with Anglo-European traditions; the British International Studies Association (BISA) for instance is where an 'English school' of international studies is strongly represented. In addition, British universities appear uneasy with the American adoption of the term 'political science'.[4] Despite the different names – political science compared to international studies – in attending the annual conference of either of these large professional organizations there is a great deal of overlap in the range of topics and methods used; the quantitative–qualitative divide developing all sorts of cross-cutting inflections accordingly.

As students and professional researchers take part in these associations and related events, we all learn how location in the figurative and literal sense encompasses disciplinary, national, and financial parameters which enable and encroach on our research paths in varying degrees: intellectual and emotional allegiances, professional networks, and job opportunities follow, more or less. As noted above, the two largest international professional associations related to politics and international relations do not necessarily exclude topics or methods from outside their respective 'mainstreams', referred to as *malestreams* by feminist critics (see Carver 2004, Shepherd 2009, True 2001). Even though the term political science is not used in the UK in the same way or same extent as in Europe and the United States, the divide does not always correlate to the Atlantic Ocean, or the Channel for that matter. There is considerable mixing and overlap, so it is too simplistic to suggest here a one-to-one match between the US and quantitative forms of empirical research methodologies, with the rest of the world bringing up the rear so to speak. Within geographical and methodological locations there are shifting mainstreams and their detractors.

This brief excursion into academic institutions and geographies is simply to alert the reader to how these larger histories, ones that predate your project or your entry into academe, form the literature. Given that the objective of this book is to equip readers with the skills to navigate these different approaches at their points of contact and friction, then the point here is to suggest a way to read other writers as researchers undertaking the same task as yourselves; making their point and claims to a particular audience, if not against one. If the aim is to employ techniques that work for the research question at hand then this awareness can assist you in persevering when the going gets tough, when underlying fissures that mark any disciplinary and professional tradition may open up under your feet.

Time now to get down to the practicalities of getting to know which literature, amongst all that is potentially available for any project, is pertinent to your inquiries; which you need to account for as part of the aforementioned kinship structures, and which are specific and indispensable to your project. And to know why.

LITERATURE SEARCHES AND THE LITERATURE REVIEW

The first thing to note is that the very term, *literature review*, is culturally specific; most commonly used in the UK but also in other Anglo-American settings (for example, New Zealand, Australia, Canada). The second point is that the term is shorthand for both a process by which you conduct a 'review of the literature' – let's call it an *overview*, and a product. This particular phrase of the research process does tend to stress the product side of the equation – the presentation of this search as a 'focused argument or set of concerns' (Gray 2009: 122). The various ways a literature review is actually used and where it ends up in the final report is also conditional on whether a project is affiliated to *qualitative*, *quantitative*, or *mixed-method* approaches in general and the local customs of a department in particular (see Creswell 2009: 26–9, M. Davies 2007: 38, Gray 2009: 122–24).

There are comparable distinctions between relative depth and breadth as well, ranging from reviews that are comprehensive, highly selective, or quite cursory; dissertation, journal articles, and books require different weightings in this respect. However, for dissertation work on the whole there are three things to note:

- Depending on where you are carrying out the research and at what level, the scale and scope of this element needs to be tailored to the degree for which you are studying as well as the stage you are at in the dissertation project.
- The review of the literature presented in an initial outline, or formal research proposal, is necessarily more of an overview; distilled and so quite short (sometimes there are word restrictions).
- The one you shape and write up for the final dissertation will need to go into more depth, cover more terrain, or do a bit of both. By this point your discussion will be considerably more refined in itself and be closely related, if not integral to your theoretical framework.

So, straightaway it should be clear that whilst there is no hard and fast rule, there are some general rules of thumb, more on these below, as well as some well-entrenched conventions or unwritten rules that are dependent on time and place. As (part of) the end-product, the eventual placement of your literature review is partly the outcome of how these factors interact with the effectiveness of your search and selection of the literature itself, your own thinking and writing, organizational decisions in the chapter or section outline and, most importantly, consultations with your supervisor/s. They will, if nothing else, indicate what is expected of you in terms of the 'local customs', to use an anthropological turn of phrase, of your department or larger institution.

Either way, approval and criticism of the study often begin and end with opinions on the merits or deficiencies of this aspect; in its own right – who, or what is in, who or what is left out. But more importantly it is about how well it frames the study with respect to what is often called 'the field'; broad debates, intellectual precursors, recent research, a particular (sub-)discipline. In contrast to the *original research component* – the part that you do yourself and by which you develop hands-on knowledge that you can call your own and by which you make your case – this element is largely where you present a *synthesis of others' work*. Either as a self-contained part or recurring element (more on this in Chapter 4) the 'lit review' sends signals about where you are situating the study, in specific and more general terms.

Establishing this point of departure along with your intellectual preferences, or those of others that you've taken on board, means that you are addressing an audience. As I noted above, the more interdisciplinary the study is, the more bases to cover, the more potential audiences there are that have a stake in the outcome. Here, when the overview is comprised of more than one, if not several literatures, the bar is raised even higher.

Lest this deter anyone who is embarking on a research project that straddles more than one specific discipline, learning to be both inclusive (at first) and then selective (sooner or later) is key to surviving and learning from this process. Knowing when to stop, and then being able to live with, if not defend your choices at the end of the day is part of it. This is true for undergraduate work through to advanced research. Whilst searching for, reviewing and then presenting relevant literature is distinct from the research method/s or theories we are engaging with, it also informs and influences them by requiring us to make distinctions and informed choices. In most academic cultures students are expected to go out and find – at least some of – the literature themselves. Expecting otherwise incurs the common complaint about younger generations wanting to be 'spoon-fed'.

Doing well in this part is related to assessment criteria that look for evidence of 'original thinking', 'critical thought' and 'independent research skills'. Literature review is also part of the research process as a whole; neither just a warm-up to the real thing, nor an end in itself if it is to make sense as part of a larger project. In particular, the line between a separate 'literature review' and 'theory chapter' is one that needs negotiating according to local conventions; the latter implies the former. By the same token, your theoretical framework is distinct from how you position your project vis-à-vis the literature.

What do you think a literature review is in practice?

Before we go any deeper into this terrain, try the mini self-assessment below (Box 4.1). Don't think too long about your response to the propositions below. Your initial reaction is the one that counts; besides you need not tell anyone.

BOX 4.1 SELF-ASSESSMENT – WHAT IS A LITERATURE REVIEW REALLY?

- A set of mini-*book* reviews?
- A shopping-basket of Big Books, Big Names, Big Ideas?
- A list of books my supervisor told (or should tell) me to read?
- A list that makes my supervisor happy?

Continued

- Proof that I've read the right *amount* – a lot – of books?
- A close reading of one thinker?
- A survey of several, or more thinkers?
- Everything written on my topic?
- A review of everything I read in my studies?
- All of the above?

HISTORICAL AND PHILOSOPHICAL NOTE

> One of the features of any project is that it should enable you to demonstrate a critical awareness of the relevant knowledge in a field. A comprehensive review of the literature is essential . . .
>
> (Gray 2009: 99)

In western cultures, knowledge – scientific and common sense forms – is largely contained in written texts; a long-term historical development that is regarded as one of the hallmarks of *modernity*, of which higher learning institutions, literacy, and the archive are cornerstones (see Anderson 1991, Foucault 1972, 1995). Since then a plethora of *postmodern*, *feminist*, and *postcolonial* critiques have targeted the value-hierarchy that privileges the written word and its western European/Anglo-American seat of governance as the preferred vehicle for producing and disseminating knowledge (Fierke and Jørgensen 2001, Giri 2004, Ratcliffe 2001, Said 1994, Smith 1999).

Whatever your disciplinary home, the written word is paramount. It is through *the literature* (classical, topical, archival, popular, scholarly) that researchers get a sense of what came before, what is going on now and, most importantly for those looking to break new ground, what has been left unsaid, unstudied or overlooked. As modern academe's credentials are founded on publications, again academic books and journals are the fountainhead of what counts as the 'literature'. More recently online texts, for example, blogs, media portals, web-portals from international organizations (for example, the UN, WTO), NGOs, think tanks and funding organizations (for example, Greenpeace, Economic Social Forum, the Social Science Research Council) jostle for position on the top-ten hits of web-searches; as do individuals' (independent and salaried researchers) web-pages where they post their own work. All these have been pushing the envelope of what may or may not be included in either respective literary canons or literature reviews. At the very least these newer forms and locales are contesting the norm.

In research cultures prone to using this term, the literature review is a milestone in the earlier phases of a research dissertation, often in the first year of the longer process of Ph.D. work. For bachelor- and master-level research projects, this is the case too albeit in different measures. Remembering that some disciplines tend to define the data/research field as literature (philosophy, literary studies, history, cultural studies) as opposed to those that gather other sorts of data, or see data in non-literature forms (sociology, anthropology, political science, media studies, science and technology studies), the tendency to reify this element goes hand-in-hand with a large amount of anxiety and mixed messages.

In the North American scenarios (USA and Canada), the literature review at a Ph.D. level dominates the first year or two years of the research trajectory, encapsulated by courses with terms like 'foundations' and 'classics' in their titles, completed before a full research proposal is developed. Exams are held that assess students' knowledge of a set of literature that is canonical to the field or discipline in which they are enrolled; for example, international relations/politics, sociology, anthropology, media and communications, women's studies and so on.

In other research cultures and parts of the western world, however, these terms are used a lot less. The form they take in the research proposal, and then the final project, is less prominent, more integrated into what is often referred to as the 'theory chapter' or 'theoretical/conceptual framework'.[5] For instance, in parts of continental Europe, the emphasis is on a more selective approach: depth as opposed to breadth. Nonetheless, a grasp of broader debates, fields of literature and the ability to synthesize these in terms of how they serve, underpin, and challenge your project, is still regarded as an early phase, an early section/chapter in the final product. But even in these arguably narrower notions of the literature review and how it is often synonymous with the term 'theory' or 'theoretical framework' there is a fine line between being too selective and not selective enough.

PURPOSE AND CATEGORIES OF LITERATURE REVIEWS

> [A] literature review helps to determine whether the topic is worth studying, and it provides an insight into ways in which the researcher can limit the scope to a needed area of inquiry.
>
> (Creswell 2009: 23)

There are various ways to categorize literature reviews, some of which trace the quantitative–qualitative divide as well as straddle it (Burnham et al. 2004, Creswell 2009: 25, Gray 2009: 123). Broadly speaking we can speak of comprehensive – systematic – literature reviews and more selective – integrated – ones.

For most student research dissertations, the literature review element is selective; you are not expected to literally review everything. Those settings that favour *integrative* and *theoretical* sorts of reviews (Cooper, cited in Creswell 2009: 28) mean both

- summaries of broad themes emerging from the literature; and
- a more focused appraisal of a particular theory, theorist, or theoretical stream.

In practice these two categories overlap, the balance between them depending on the focus, angle, and topic that is being researched.

A third sort of literature review is more difficult, indeed more contested given the way in which 'method' can be either eschewed in some quarters or this term used synonymously with references to *methodology* (see Burnham et al. 2004, Moses and Knutsen 2007: 3–5). The *methodological* literature review is important for studies that engage a particular data-gathering method, or which look to critique or adapt existing ones. Whilst quantitative research projects give more attention to this side of the literature (see also Chapter 1, 'Using this book in context') this dimension to your literature is also important to methodological rationales across the spectrum.

Some delineations do apply to literature reviews for hypothesis-driven research projects, which take a particular format.

- More than describing everything that has gone before, it provides a focused theoretical context and justification for the hypotheses under investigation in the remainder of the paper – or larger report.
- From the objectives listed above, along with justifying the need for this research through reference to the theoretical literature, it also points out exactly how past research has either presented anomalous findings or that there is a gap in the existing research.

In the example below, we see how this mini-lit review sets up the justification for the research, points out existing problems with the past research and sets out hypotheses based on bringing in a different set of literature.

BOX 4.2 LITERATURE REVIEWS IN ACTION – A WORKING EXAMPLE

In a 2008 article published in the *American Political Science Review*, 'Oil, Islam and Women', Michael Ross challenges the long-held belief within gender politics research that women in Islamic countries have been held back in terms of labour force and political participation by cultural values associated with Islam (Ross 2008). In the literature review of the published article, Ross critically assesses some of the major research suggesting that the lack of women's progress in some countries is due to Islam (for example, Norris and Inglehart 2003, 2006). He then moves on to review the economic and political research on women's labour force participation, from which he develops a hypothesis that single resource economies (i.e. those based on oil) have a lower level of women's participation in the labour force due to higher job segregation. This is, he argues, actually the major factor in the lack of women's progress: 'oil, not Islam is at fault' (Ross 2008: 107). The supposed causal link between Islam and traditional gender roles that other literature posits is spurious; based on a assumption that because most countries where oil is the single export tend to be Islamic, the causes for there being fewer women in the workforce are down to religion. Ross argues that the causes are material resources and the structure of the labour market; a quite different premise, set of observations (labour market data) and conclusions drawn to those of others working from different premises about sex-gender roles, religion, and the workforce.

Before tackling the practicalities let's take a look at the first category of literature review, suitable for some projects and fields but not all. Realizing the difference between a comprehensive and a selective sort of approach will help you navigate these ever-increasing and shifting fields.

Undertaking a 'systematic literature review'

Before unpacking the practicalities that all literature searches, and eventual lit reviews share, let's look at the most comprehensive understanding of this element: undertaking a systematic, *meta-level* review of existing studies. This entails regarding each piece of existing research on a given topic as a piece of data, or self-contained information that warrants analysis in its own right (see Fink 2009). In other words, the review treats the literature as individual items of published studies rather than the output of individual authors; all units count. This sort of approach can only be rightly considered as a meta-analysis if it attempts to review all studies in order to review and compare the effects across a body of literature, for example, medical studies of breast-feeding versus bottle-feeding. These sorts of meta-analyses characterize literature reviews in medical studies and the health sciences because they are aiming to assess the overall impact of a treatment as it is demonstrated in the existing research literature.

This approach has some important advantages over more author-centred or concentrically organized forms of searching and engaging with the literature; the 'field' in other words.

- You are not required to second-guess – pick and choose amongst what is often a wide and conflicting range of viewpoints in any one area, running the risk of overlooking a key piece of work.
- Your eventual summary and evaluation of this field is thereby based on content (rather than status). This, according to advocates of this approach, is a method that provides a 'more complete, more explicit, more quantitative, more powerful . . . and, for all these reasons, helpful to the process of [knowledge] accumulation' (Rosenthal 1991: 378).
- Given the danger of over-citations of an ever-decreasing circle of a select group of authors – 'key thinkers' – in any given conventions of the 'canon', the results from a meta-analysis can reveal how research findings, and ideas that appear central in one context may emerge as outliers in the context of a larger data set (the wider literature here). Advocates argue that this inherent preference, bias in other words, has us all focusing on those studies which have large effects (large citations, or reiterated ones). This can lead researchers to overestimate the effects of some literature at the expense of other less-known exponents.
- As this sort of review is essentially a quantitative exercise, making use of software tools (see Fink 2009), it can also show how normally sizable clusters of publications, ones that can fall just short of *statistical significance*, may actually be more important to your field that you think.

So, when is this sort of approach appropriate?

- This approach can help you get a sense of what is really out there as opposed to what you think there is without forcing you to commit before you are ready.
- The more specialized your topic or key concepts are, the more likely it is that you will be able to capture all existing literature in this manner.
- So, even when this approach is not suitable for projects in large fields where literatures overlap, there are advantages to considering a systematic approach when considering your choice of topic, or formulating the research question.
- However, the more interdisciplinary the topic the wider the net you have to cast, so a dedicated software-enabled search tool may be necessary (see Gaiser and Schreiner 2009, Ó Dochartaigh 2009). This then requires a certain investment of time and energy that may be superfluous to the requirements of your degree level.

**TIP: Whether you embark on a selective or a thorough, meta-analytical review of the literature, you do need to set up a database, or keep a simple record (file or notebook) of any studies you find that relate directly to your topic, research question, main hypotheses, terms of reference, and findings.[6]

Bottom line: you need to confer with your supervisor about exactly the pros and cons of this sort of full-coverage approach if you are not sure about its feasibility in the long term. That said, why not start out by making a systematic review of all the published literature in the main area you consider relevant to your inquiry as a preparatory step.

Summing up: across all categories of review, the main aim is to critically *synthesize* the literature in the ways listed below; it should be clear that the review

- justifies the need for this research;
- supports your case for the significance of the research; for example, provides the basis for your conceptual framework, key concepts, or supports your case for how the study addresses gaps in the literature;
- acknowledges and indicates your awareness of precursor and contemporaneous research in your area; which is significant and which is corollary;
- shows that you have grasped not only the specifics but also the broader contours of debates in the field/s you are working with; their implications for this topic and your research plan;
- situates your project in relation to those closer to home (supervisor/s, department, faculty, national research culture) and all those big names, big ideas, and big books from further away;
- shows that that you have read, engaged with, and can distil the main points of a range of texts for yourself but, even more importantly for others;
- demonstrates that you can achieve a balance between breadth – knowledge of the range of debates or key texts on a topic, or intersection of topics, and depth – awareness of nuances, specifics, a selection (several if not only one) of thinkers or ideas.

For summaries of what others consider the key elements in a literature review, see Creswell (2009: 25) and Gray (2009: 116–25).

PRACTICALITIES

Taking all the above on board at once can be more than a little bit daunting. And it may come as little surprise for some to hear that very often undergraduate/postgraduate research dissertations are, in effect, largely literature reviews! Nonetheless, even for a more philosophically inclined project (where the data to be gathered and analyzed is literature – written texts), this is not to say that a research project is reducible to 'the *literature*' in the final analysis; it is necessary but not sufficient on its own.

Still, the 'literature *review*' is something that is much easier said than done; there are various degrees of confusion, for students at all stages, about how much is expected of them from their supervisors and/or institutions, and how much space this element should take in the final report, indeed where it fits in the larger narrative. Moreover, where to start searching for literature is increasingly bewildering in these ICT-embedded, web-dependent, and inter-textual, hyperlinked days.

So what are the main pitfalls? When does a literature search morph into our literature review and what weight does it have in our final report?

Pitfalls

The mini self-evaluation exercise intimates what the pitfalls are when first confronting this particular element. Even if everyday use of the term or its prevalence as a self-contained homonymous chapter in dissertations appears to be nine-tenths of the law, it would be safe to say that there are certain things that readers, and examiners, are not looking for. In other words a literature review is

- not a set of book reviews where each author or book is handled in turn, treated equally and without reflection on where their work fits or does not fit your project, or vice versa; your ideas, central claims, vocabulary, and citations, following the order of author accordingly;
- not an overly reverential presentation of ideas, thinkers, or debates to the detriment of the other side of the story;
- not an over-dependence on one or several texts, certain sorts of philosophical exegeses excepted;
- not an unbalanced critique based on a *strawman argument* that misrepresents complex ideas for self-serving reasons;
- not an array of books or articles randomly picked without due consideration;
- not a list of publications dotted through the main text, as an after-thought, an exercise in name-dropping, or in lieu of argument. This tendency is often signalled by repeatedly bracketed big names/big ideas as opposed to a concerted engagement with them in substantive or thematic ways;

- not an over-reliance on large quotes or secondary sources – particularly common with the Big Names whose work has produced a substantial secondary literature in its own right; for example, Bourdieu, Foucault, Arendt, Machiavelli, Spivak, Popper, Kuhn, Adorno, de Beauvoir, Butler, inter alia;
- not a free-floating chapter or section that bears little relation to your stated aims and objectives, research question, theoretical framework, or methodology.

Where the theoretical and methodological literature intersect, and where they need to be treated separately, is often a major headache during the writing-up phase, particularly when word-restrictions are an issue or when the theory and the method sections start to go in different directions; not uncommon along the spectrum of absolute beginners to experienced researchers!

> **TIP: All the more reason to realize that right from the get-go, there is one cardinal rule of thumb. As John Creswell puts it: a 'first step in any project is to spend considerable time in the library examining the research on a topic. . . . *This point cannot be overemphasised*' (Creswell 2009: 23, 25, emphasis added). In other words, there is a certain amount of legwork that needs doing even if, nowadays, a library is not longer just a physical building but also a virtual, and multiple one now that the internet has become embedded in contemporary teaching, learning, and research practices.

For this reason we need to bear in mind that references to your literature review encompass a process (searching and getting control of literatures) as well as a product (writing this up in a coherent way). Below are some practical rules of thumb.

With some sense of what literature reviews are not (supposed to end up as), let's take a closer look at what we should strive for when searching the literature and writing literature reviews; as process and product.

Rules of thumb

First, some general rules of thumb for getting on with things:

1   No matter where you're setting out on your research in geographical or disciplinary terms, one of your very first tasks is to access, and then get a grasp of the literature/s. Locate and collate, read and digest, then synthesize and critique it (in positive and negative terms) from the point of view of your topic, your research question. This is a two-way street as the more you read, the more focused and well-defined your research question will become (see Chapter 3).

2   Remembering that in terms of writing up or presenting the mass of books and articles you've read, the UK system puts more emphasis on having this part done and dusted quite early on. In continental Europe this is also the case as a rule. However, it is also expected to be significantly reworked later on.

3   Sometimes this means it emerges in another form: interwoven into chapters or sections dealing with historical background, case-study description, the theory/ theoretical framework, and as noticed previously, in the presentation of your

method. Whichever form and location the review takes in the final analysis, it is not advisable to introduce new ideas, thinkers, or themes towards the end of the project.

4 If you treat getting this overview of the literature/s as an integral part of your research as a verb (doing) and a noun (naming) you will be less inclined to see it as such a bugbear. At the end of the day you are expected to show the inter-connection between your own thinking and research in a dialogue with extant research. In short, your study is not happening in a vacuum.

5 By the same token, neither is it entirely derivative. The trick is finding the balance between (wild) claims at originality and (overly) anxious attempts to be onside with everything you have read or been told to read. Hopefully the outcome will be that reading inspires you, rather than sends you into a slough of despondency (see M. Davies 2007: Introduction).

6 A crucial aspect of designing a research project entails getting a sense of what is out there, what has been done, and whether your idea and proposed method/s to get data, however defined, is viable. The literature search side helps you check that you're not setting out to reinvent the wheel, gives you a sense of the lie of the land; sometimes referred to as knowing the 'field' or 'fields'.

7 The point here is for you to broaden your horizons, have your assumptions challenged, allow you to put some of your more ambitious plans (or not so grandiose ones) better into perspective. The data-gathering that follows will be the better for this broader knowledge. In this respect we all stand on the shoulders of giants.7

8 At the very least you indicate that you've read and understood the main texts from the relevant classes you have taken (this is why courses have literature lists; they're there to pave the way). This is why a strong emphasis is put on getting this part done early on, in both senses of the term: searching, gathering a pool of literature and then committing yourself in written form. The view here is that without this aspect well under your belt your research project will come unstuck, make no sense to others, and you could end up revealing your ignorance, not getting finished on time, or submitting a piece of work you are not happy with at all.

9 Even if you are a late-starter with this aspect of the project, or find that later on in the research you discover a key item – book, article, blog/s, online archive – that causes you to reconsider some of your basic ideas or working assumptions, this need not mean you have to throw the baby out with the bathwater. A revision of the initial literature review and editing will allow for these later discoveries to be integrated into earlier reading.

10 When writing up the final report, particularly when putting your research in these larger literature-based contexts, try to avoid over-citation to other people's work. It is your voice and input that counts by this point in that readers are not there to read paragraph after paragraph, page after page of potted summaries of other literature. The 'lit review' section needs to be in proportion to your own work and words. This is why it is useful to consider the final presentation of this part of your research as the moment you put your project in a larger context, not just in terms of those whose work you choose to use, or need to acknowledge, but also those approaches you do not engage with, in full or in part. Examiners in Ph.D.

defences may well ask you to explain why you do not engage with such and such school of thought, or thinker.

These rules of thumb need some breaking-down; first in terms of the process and second with respect to the product side of the coin.

Process and product

For literature searches, and their emergence as your literature review, that are not based on the systematic approach covered above, we need to break things down to the process and the production side of things.

Process-searching the literature

First up: the process, which is the locating, filtering and selecting, and then getting a grip on the relevant literature. Assuming that you have decided upon your topic, and have some sense of your main and subsidiary research questions, this element works along three axes: (1) broad and specific themes, for example *Globalization, Global Warming, New Media, Gender and Voting Patterns*; (2) key authors along with their critics and followers; and (3) how both these dimensions play out in a disciplinary sense: for example, how Pierre Bourdieu's work is relevant for sociologists on the one hand, or is applied in international relations or media and communications on the other; how philosophers of science like Thomas Kuhn and Karl Popper are understood in science and technology studies which is distinct from how philosophers debate their work; how terms like 'evidence', 'proof' or 'interpretation' are treated, and debated by political scientists, literary theorists, physicists, or legal scholars. For undergraduate and master-level dissertations, managing the first two is already a considerable task. For Ph.D. work and onwards, the third element emerges in implicit and explicit ways dependent on how strong processes of socialization – disciplining power – of respective departments and faculties work themselves out along the way.[8]

When starting out on a literature review in the sense of it being a search, you can cast your net wide (drift-netting) or you can start close to home, with a specific topic or thinker or idea in mind (line and hook).

To continue the fishing metaphor – there are many metaphors available (see Gray 2009: 101) – somewhere in between lies surf-casting; standing at the water's edge and casting out a long line and bait into the breaking surf, a slightly larger area. Starting out wide means that you need to narrow the search at some point, sort out what you net. Likewise when starting out closer to home, you need to cast your hook, or net, a bit farther out at some point in order to maintain perspective. For example: consider three places you can go; starting out close to shore and then moving into deeper waters so to speak:

1 Course outlines and their reading lists, including those already completed; an often overlooked ready-made resource.

2   The reference lists in books, and articles pertinent to your project or which you find interesting; again, this is a resource full of possible leads to other work.

3   Keyword searches in specific, academic but not exclusively, databases; for more on this use of the web see Chapter 5.

The paradox to this initial casting about is that often the 'right' literature does not emerge, or you don't see it until your own research question and central proposition have been more refined. Once you have acquired some sense of where the horizon lies, with the help of course literature outlines, supervisors' recommendations and your own searching-surfing around databases, use of search engines to navigate the web, and other sources, the next challenge is filtering and evaluating this swathe of material. This middle phase precedes and accompanies the writing up of all this knowledge into some sort of coherent, synthetic account for another audience, not that audience of one that is you, yourself. Whilst a large part of your search and selection need to be done before the writing up, it should be clear by now that these three phases are closely related; both in turn are then influenced by your eventual findings and how you went about them.

Product – writing a literature review

What does writing up mean? A literature review is not a book review in the conventional sense of the term; presenting a synopsis and then giving it a thumbs-up or thumbs-down. Rather it is a *refinement* of this initial read; something that all methods textbooks and guides stress on one way or another. It's about you showing how you link any author or cluster of authors, idea or big theory, theme, or debate/s to your research topic, your method, and your theoretical framework.

The space between finding and reading book/s and other material and then being able to present that knowledge in its own right, and with respect to your topic entails another stage of work, another level of abstraction than those first notes, first impressions. This is where all the thinking-work happens: before the data-gathering is completed but often afterwards in the editing and reworking phase. This is the difference between taking notes or copying out direct quotes from a text for your own reference and paraphrasing the main ideas as part of a virtual conversation you have been having with others, for other readers.[9]

Alongside variations in how the 'lit review' works with a project's presentation of its particular theory, or conceptual framework (see Chapter 2), there are different levels of expectation for bachelor-, master-, and then Ph.D.-level literature reviews; in terms of the depth and breadth of the literature students need to read and how they present this knowledge in their final piece of work.

By Ph.D. level the student should be able to demonstrate a comprehensive knowledge, and ability to synthesize and apply selected literature, whereas a master-level discussion shows a relatively well-rounded knowledge of the main lines of these debates and key literature. A bachelor-level dissertation (research paper) is one in which the range of literature consulted is narrower. Nonetheless, in both cases for ambitious students, there is not necessarily an upper limit. That said, at some point you will have to stop, choose, and then present what you've read for another audience.

Sometimes fascinating books, articles, or thinkers have to be left out. You can always return to them another day.

To recapitulate, the term *review* is both a noun and a verb; a naming word and a doing word. It is this dual aspect to this part of your work that needs to be borne in mind. Once the search and selection has taken place, and you have the requisite overview of the field/s, comprised of recurring debates, canonical figures, or key concepts, you present this knowledge in a distilled form in such a way that it accompanies and underpins your project.

Finding the literature: the web or in the library?

The web itself (viz. the internet) is in many ways one big library, globally linked clusters of electronic databases connected by what is known as *browser* software; more recently in the form of the ubiquitous *search engine*. This sort of online resource is currently dominated by the registered trademark Google and its derivates like Google Scholar amidst an array of others designed for different needs and with different implications for the search results.

To complicate matters, all of these newer digital and ICT-embedded resources are changing all the time, as are their trade names and compatibility with older machines, university and public libraries' ability to keep up with the play, and more informal conventions of passing on knowledge of key literature. In the latter sense, its well worth the effort of following up on any recommendation, from anyone. You never know what gems you may find that you could have missed whilst trying to find the needle in the virtual haystack that is the web of today. Chapter 5 looks in more detail at how to use the web as a resource and tool for undertaking a literature search. This section deals with the underlying principles.

BOX 4.3 WIKIPEDIA – A NECESSARY EVIL?

The number of literature sources available is exponentially increasing. Traditional libraries and their many electronic databases are now supplemented by innumerable clusters of online bibliographies of major theorists (for example, Foucault, Freud, Hawking) or major ideas (globalization, climate change); every university offers students access to one or more commercial computerized – bibliographic – databases (for example, Web of Knowledge, ProQuest, LexisNexus); there are many other sorts of free-access databases (for example, ERIC, Google Scholar); and traditional encyclopaedias are going digital (for example, Encyclopaedia Britannica) as fast as they are able in order to compete with the latest innovation in web-based encyclopaedic production, Wikipedia.

Opinions about whether this radical shift to peer-to-peer practices of generating and editing knowledge through ICTs and for use on the web is better or not than traditional editorial boards are still divided (O'Neill 2009, see Brabazon 2007) but the general consensus is that the internet, and resources like Wikipedia are increasingly the first stop for research students on their literature quest (see Creswell 2009: 30–33, Gray 2009: 104–13), as it is for many experienced researchers and teaching faculty.

I take the view that Wikipedia is a treasure-trove (see Chapter 5) but like any general reference resource, it needs to be consulted in conjunction with other sources: the principle of *triangulation*.

These days many students starting out on a research project assume that the web and other sorts of electronic databases or digital books and articles are the first port of call. Increasingly the journey (see Gray 2009: 100–1) that is entailed in conducting a review of the literature before you start writing it up is taking place in front of a computer screen. It's the fingers that are doing the walking rather than the researcher's legs and eyes scanning a bookshelf. As more libraries have their stock out back than on the shelves, more and more news is produced for web-accessed reading and downloading, and policy documents and other sort of primary sources are available online, the very locale and nature of the search process is changing.

But the ease and facility of digital forms and search tools brings with it an increase in possibility. It is not uncommon to hear students complaining that they are suffering from a over-abundance of literature sources rather than a dearth. How to cope in this huge domain?

- One tip is to make a point of learning how search engines work – Google Scholar in particular, as its automated filters do a large amount of selection and filtering for you; there is an up and a down side to this sort of user-friendliness in web-saturated research cultures; see Chapter 5.
- Another tip here is to go back to basics, of a sort, and start with the required readings, bibliographies that you have accumulated during your course of study. You can use the reference sections from these works as texts for further research using the references in the original text to guide your search. This is another sort of 'systematic literature review'.
- Third, when overwhelmed, try consulting the literature cited in books and articles that you consider central to your topic, your interest, or the approach you want to take or critique, whatever the case may be. This is the snowball principle of gathering literature and keeping your bearings; starting at the centre and moving outwards. There are other ways to conduct a literature review, however, a 'systematic literature review' can be an effective way to grasp a specific field of work that is relatively self-contained.

In the worst-case scenario this part of the work is a box that has to be ticked, often seen as a necessary albeit tiresome first base, one to move on from as quickly as possible. Moreover, a common problem in those settings where the literature review is part of an early assessment stage, is that once done in that first year, first few months, it is treated as a hermetically sealed product.

> **TIP: Returning to your earlier versions, refining and revising them accordingly later on the project, is creating a virtuous circle, not a rerun. Without this, all too often these sections in a dissertation read as dated (quite literally) and disconnected from the original research sections and analyses because they have not been touched since first written. However distinct this element may be regarded as, or held up as a self-contained item, it needs to be part of the larger conversation that is your project.

In the best-case scenario, the process is an indispensable generator of knowledge and insight, one that hopefully emerges as a well-rehearsed synthesis of core texts, key debates, and larger 'fields'. A knowledge and awareness of why certain texts or fields do *not* belong to your project is also part of this knowledge; what to leave out is just as crucial as fields continue to increase in scope and depth. What you are doing here is getting to know and then being able to show how you know your way around the literature.

- This first part of the process also socializes and situates the researcher in a community, whether this be of choice or circumstance.
- The second part, as part of the written, completed project, a review of the literature, puts the project in perspective by conveying both the broad, and the more specific fields in which the research took place, to which it speaks, and the direction it wants to take.

Presenting, and referring to the literature – the 'field' – confidently is also performed in non-written contexts: in research seminars, Ph.D. defences (the viva voce), conference panels, research funding interviews, and so on.[10]

Remember, that as with the study itself this part of it remains work-in-progress. Instead of second-guessing about what you think is expected of you, becoming bogged down in all sorts of 'musts' and 'shoulds' (see Creswell 2009: 24–5), or trying to cover all the literature bases and related fields at once, see this element as an integral part of your planning process, part of the research itself (see M. Davies 2007: 12–15), your learning and knowledge-acquisition that accompanies your own research-part, and then as a formative part of the writing process you engage after you've gathered, collated, and analysed both the literature, your 'data', and your findings.

Getting started and completing the literature review is a snapshot of what it means to learn to be selective and part of a larger set of conversations; something that is one of the hardest things to do when faced with a sea of possibility.

SOURCES AND RESOURCES THAT MATTER

Acknowledging sources

Citing others is the principle way academic writers locate themselves vis-à-vis their immediate, or larger *epistemic community*. Many first-timers in fact consider copious quoting the essence of being 'scholarly'; academic writing must include lots and lots of quotes, or references to Big Thinkers (whether or not they are pertinent to the project). The why's and wherefores of these attitudes aside, when citing directly, i.e. using the words written or spoken by others and indicating this with 'quotation marks' or as an indented passage on the written page, the writer is assuming responsibility for (1) citing *accurately* and as much in context as possible, and (2) for indicating *exactly where* the quote comes from. Chapter 8 takes a closer look at how these basic principles work out in terms of citation formalities; an integral feature of academic style that can vary across geographical and disciplinary boundaries. For example, different conventions for citing authors, using what format and where these references are placed, exist between the social sciences and humanities, between the US and the UK.

This next section looks at a particular occupational hazard of research undertakings today; this is a tension between aspiring to produce an original piece of work (see Chapter 2) and obligations to 'situate' your project within a particular 'field' by way of the literature (see Chapter 4) and then produce a piece of formal writing (see Chapter 8). Or to put it another way, how much of your own words, your own ideas

"You should spend the next week typing down names of all co-authors on your paper."

Figure 4.1 All the authors?!
Source: http://Vadlo.com

are acceptable in academic work? Many students, depending on where they were educated, embarking on a major piece of independent research think that the bulk of their writing has to come from other sources; that their own ideas and insights are less important. The emphasis placed on acquiring, and showing knowledge of the field, including various bodies of literature, pulls them in one direction and exhortations to be original in the other.

Before addressing the way these confusions, and the performance stress of completing much academic output today, relate to issues of plagiarism as a rising or steady problem in intellectual labour in a digital age, one tip is worth bearing in mind. As you draft and rewrite the more theoretical parts of your work, notice how much of the page is your own words, including acknowledgement of sources and inspirations as appropriate, and how much consists of allusions or direct quotes. Are there more than two paragraphs, or even more than two pages in which your own 'voice' is not clear? If readers get no sense of what you, the author and researcher, have to say bar what you tell us about others, why continue reading?[11]

We now need to turn our attention to the issue of plagiarism.

What is plagiarism?

Plagiarism is the term used for cases when an author uses another person's work as if it were their own; evidenced by passages of the work being copied ('lifted', 'cut-and-pasted') word for word, or all but directly from another source. Indiana University puts it succinctly: 'Plagiarism is using others' ideas and words without clearly acknowledging the source of that information'.[12] Clear acknowledgement entails certain sorts of signals in the text: quotation marks, indented extracts, which are all accompanied by references to the source, or allusions in notes if the source is not a published one. More on this in Chapter 8.

However, plagiarism not only occurs through technical oversights or inexperience with formal citation systems; when engaged on a systematic if not conscious level, this practice is considered a legal and ethical transgression in academic research, published (and so falling under intellectual property jurisprudence) and unpublished.[13] This is why, in academe unlike music-making or peer-to-peer communities, 'file-sharing' or 'sampling' without clear acknowledgement of your sources is not a sign of respect.[14] The double-edged nature of plagiarism in a context in which original ideas are currency within wider traditions of ideas, is encapsulated in a position statement from Duke University's online guidelines. I cite at length:

> Rarely, if ever, do we develop ideas in our individual minds, free of the effects and influences of others' previous findings, claims, and analyses. This is not to suggest that writers never forge new ideas; rather, the majority of one's thoughts – and certainly the intellectual thinking that we do in university settings – is prompted, shaped, and changed in response to and in light of what has already been stated by others. Our ideas emerge in response to reading others' texts, in sites of conversation and verbal exchange, with and against the grain of the words and formulations of others. . . . the university. . . . requires that its members formally

recognize who has made which sorts of statements in what settings. Scrupulously citing the origin of quotations, summaries, and other borrowed material included in your paper enables the social value of respect to exist within intellectual circles of research and scholarship around the globe. *Not to formally recognize the work and influences of others in your writing is to plagiarize, violating an ethic of mutual regard.*[15]

As the web becomes the main source of information and research resource for successive generations of students, and working researchers, the ease with which anyone can access, download, or cut-and-paste from digital documents does not mean that this sort of citing lies outside academic citation conventions. Citing online sources is no longer a guessing game as publishers and high-profile universities codify these practices. And as a response many institutions sign up to digital, web-based software programs that than monitor students' work before and as they 'turn it in'.

A popular platform is Turnitin, a tool based on quantitative indicators, that 'compares students' work to a range of other electronic sources (including other students' work) and highlights potential matches between texts'.[16] Whilst there are limits to what the results of a Turnitin search can tell about forms of plagiarism that are not discernable by quantity alone is an area of debate in itself.

The point here, particularly for those who are unused to the way academic citation codes and etiquette work in terms of written output, is to remember some underlying principles. These are covered briefly below as skills you need to have and attitudes you need to nurture.

Skills you need to have

- Always, and I reiterate, *always* provide clear proof that a section is being quoted verbatim. Err on the side of caution here.
- Do not make a habit of 'tweaking' a passage by changing one or two words and then assuming that this is no longer a citation; this is still plagiarism. Experienced readers and software can still figure this out. Moreover, if found out this practice implies a certain level of premeditation; your defence of 'accidental plagiarism' no longer holds water.
- However counter-intuitive this sounds in an age marked by the ease provided by digital forms of reproduction (the 'cut-and-paste' functions of word-processing software), make a point of copy-typing out the passage. You may be surprised that you are actually reading it (as opposed to pasting it in).
- In all cases indicate the source directly afterwards and depending on the citation convention you are using.

Attitudes that you need to nurture

- When rereading and editing your work, ask yourself (particularly when word-length is an issue) which quotes really must stay, and which can go. Most of the time we need a lot fewer direct quotes than we think. Keep returning to your text and whittling down the quotes when doing final edits.

- Read the quotes you wish to keep at various points in the writing; do they serve your argument or are you a 'slave' to what others have said?
- When reading your narrative in line with your direct quotes, ask yourself if they make sense together; what are the links to and from the quote in question? Are you engaging with the text you are citing?
- If a quote looks like it has been 'parachuted in' as a substitute for your argument or your own words, think about why this quote is in this place. Could you state the point in your own words and simply allude to the source?
- Have you really understood what the author is on about in longer passages; have you understood the quote in its own context? Are you citing this passage in such a way that fairly represents another's argument – particularly when setting out to critique them?
- When balancing your own voice against all those authoritative ones in the literature, note that most readers prefer to see more of your voice.
- Ask yourself, when you become aware of overburdening your text with direct quotes (unless this is a deliberate device, but this is another matter), whether your reliance on direct quotes really does reveal your knowledge of the canon. Or is it actually an indication you are still grappling with these ideas? Can you paraphrase them? If not, then perhaps you should reconsider!
- For those writing in a foreign language or having difficulty with academic writing (see Chapter 8), note that direct citations do not do the work for us.

Once you have these working principles clear, learning how to apply various citation formats in your work will make more sense, whether or not you have a choice or are required to follow one particular format. Chapter 8 looks at these technicalities in more detail.

RESEARCH COMMUNITIES AND (MULTIPLE) DISCIPLINARY IDENTITIES

In light of the above practicalities and their underlying cultural and institutional dimensions, before moving on, a further word on research identity politics in and beyond the printed word.

Whilst researchers move between specific research methods and broader disciplines, others do specialize. The level of disinterest or ferocity with which researchers, individually and as communities, critique other practices or defend their own are socioculturally encoded. Sometimes these codes are evident as behavioural traits (for example, the cut and thrust of a research seminar Q&A), writing tone (qualified to matter-of-fact to polemical), or as the statement of intent (for example, for projects looking to do a 'critical analysis'). Sometimes these codes surface when certain sorts of research go public – in scholarly or lay circles – as underlying assumptions or misapplications become subject to scrutiny by its critics (see Eberstadt 1995). Current debates around global warming and climate change (see Box 2.2) are a case in point. The role played by researchers ranking physical morphologies and attributes along racialized lines during the colonial era is another example (see Canales 2009, Chowdhry and Nair 2002, Smith 1999). Newspaper rubrics on what counts as 'bad science' is another popular rendition, if not exposé, of these codes.

Whilst most research in social science and humanities faculties is undertaken and assessed on an individual basis, the research process is not hermetically sealed from these sorts of identity politics. Recall, no researcher is an island; research is an activity that is inherently an 'intersubjective' endeavour, embedded in social relationships and institutions and their respective systems of recognition and reward. None of these stand still over time either. One of the areas where a lot of double-speak and contradictory messages occur is about the pros and cons of research that is strictly disciplinary, interdisciplinary, or multidisciplinary. The gap between theory in terms of rhetoric and everyday practicalities of research contexts in this respect can be pronounced. It inflects the literature review element in particular ways as well.

Let me illustrate this point by way of some common miscommunications that can occur between supervisors and research students along these lines. Some of these stem from differences in training based on research traditions, countries, or even departments. Others are based on varying receptions of numerous and contradictory cues from more diffuse sources: our classmates (where 'gossip, rumours, and fact' intermingle), departmental seminars, out to funding agencies and educational watchdogs. These days, researchers are often negotiating varying ideas about how interdisciplinary research deserves special recognition and the assumption that a research question approached from multiple disciplinary approaches must, by sheer numbers, be better than a single disciplinary approach. The converse is also a pressure in those settings where one disciplinary way holds sway.

Wilson has referred to interdisciplinary work as *consilience*-the 'jumping together of knowledge' across disciplines 'to create a common groundwork of explanation' (Wilson 1998: 8). Wilson proposes that a merging of the natural sciences and the social sciences could equip future humankind with the analytical and predictive capacity to identify inherent principles underlying the entire human endeavour, and suggests that interdisciplinarity is the most promising path to scientific advancement and intellectual awareness. C. P. Snow, in his turn, pleads for a cessation of hostilities between the arts and sciences for comparable reasons (Snow 1993 [1959]). From another vantage point, Donna Haraway (1990), Sandra Harding (1998b), Linda Tuhiwai Smith (1999), and others, have looked to refine an empirical mode of research between different sorts of approaches to the gathering and analysis of research material – data in its generic understanding.

Most of those looking to investigate their object of inquiry in inter- or multidisciplinary ways, however, have a slightly less bold objective than the formulations of a unifying theory of human behaviour or society; or hybrid methodology for that matter. Both terms imply fields of study that cross, link up, or combine traditional boundaries between academic disciplines or schools of thought; based on shifting priorities, emerging professions, or disciplinary/institutional realignments that merge disciplines once housed in separate departments. Notably the terms have earned much wider usage, such as when applied to new professions (for example, sociobiology, science and technology studies, internet studies) and to older fields such as psychiatry where the professional must have advanced credentials in several fields of study – a medical degree to start with. Attempts to consciously forge interdisciplinary, multidisciplinary, or even 'transdisciplinary' research across existing disciplines by applying a battery of mixed methods approaches, come and go out of favour.

Because target audiences and literature bases are often the sub-text to why such attempts often come adrift, the 'lively but enervating' tension' referred to on page 12 of Chapter 1 also resides in the trade-off that has to be made between the exclusiveness of disciplinarian urges (less is more) and the inclusive ideals of inter/multidisciplinary work (complexity is everything). The need to hone the focus of a research question notwithstanding, moving beyond strictly set disciplinary boundaries brings interesting and encouraging results despite protestations to the contrary. Indeed, many areas of research – communication and media studies, women's studies, and even area studies – are interdisciplinary by nature in that they combine substantive – theoretical and practical – methodological knowledge and research practices from various disciplines.

Other models of interdisciplinarity include research undertaken by teams of researchers drawn from different disciplines or by one researcher working beyond his or her discipline in order to engage intellectually with another discipline. Within these models, there is a continuum that ranges from a confrontation or dialogue between two or more disciplines to address a particular issue, or to a full integration of theories, concepts and methods across a wide range of approaches.

Some suggest that the natural complexity of questions asked in the social sciences and humanities, means that research, in the past and today, is increasingly multiplex in nature and thereby requires a multi-pronged approach. One discipline alone is not capable of tackling themes or issues that involve a diverse set of actors, institutions and social, cultural, biological, technological and political relationships; recent debates around the form and substance of climate change being a case in point.

> **TIP: Instead of feeling you must cover all the bases, or hang onto one angle anxiously for fear of losing ground or not getting a good grade, it is more prudent to start with the current topic, and initial formulations of the research question you are considering, then move outwards to how these are usually associated with particular ideas or data-gathering techniques. Starting close to home-base, then moving outwards, *snowballing*, may lead you into some degree of interdisciplinarity or even, if need be, greater disciplinarity. Indeed, either may happen without a conscious effort or need to belabour these terms of reference in your initial stab at outlining your research project as a whole and then planning just how you intend to find out what you want to know.

As I noted earlier in this chapter, the point of researching the literature as you consider the approach you eventually adopt, where you want to call 'home' in (inter)-disciplinary terms, the literature-base for the inquiry, is to inform and so guide you in the formulation and execution of the research question.

CONCLUDING COMMENTS: LIVING WITH YOUR CHOICES

To bring this chapter to a close, the recapitulation of key points to bear in mind covers more than one research location, intradisciplinary forms of deference, and accepted wisdoms about which works (and authors) do or do not warrant inclusion in any academic literary canon. Successfully undertaking a literature search and then writing up a suitable literature review entails:

1 Understanding that selecting and then presenting what 'everyone else' has to say about our topic, let alone the implications larger debates have for our own project, is one thing. Considering how, and where to put our project into a specific context or vis-à-vis a major figure in the area we are working in is another. Deciding what, or who to leave out of our discussion is another. This 'sifting and tagging' process is what researchers are doing when they locate their research with reference to 'the literature' or a 'field'; if not fields, selected thinkers, debates, or schools of thought.

2 As one of the first things on a research project's to-do list, this task is in essence the first piece of original, i.e. independent research we will probably undertake. It has us consciously (re)reading books and articles written by others, targeting literature lists for titles, browsing through library catalogues (less often), or relying on search engines to beach-comb the web for us (see Chapter 5). This is before we have possibly finalized the other research elements, and it continues into the writing-up phase. Sometimes these decisions, and oversights, can haunt us long after submitting the final piece of work; something we have to learn to live with, if unable to defend our decisions adequately.

3 This task, 'situating' or positioning your project in context, is the moment when many students notice that they are undergoing a particular process of socialization around expectations of knowledge and awareness. By *socialization* I am referring to the conglomeration of specific skill-sets (referencing), customary behaviours (when to reference), linguistic conventions (how to make the reference), intellectual attitudes (critique and counter-critique), and norms and expectations (who (not) to reference) that come to characterize local research communities, signal more trenchant inter/intradisciplinary identities, and define institutional access and ongoing affiliations.[17]

4 Something to note though not to get too bogged down about: Peer recognition, social status, and rewards that follow from the above are anchored in such *kinship patterns* – networks of respect, intellectual 'food chains', citation and even funding flows are embedded in the literature. These are the poles around – and against – which researchers understand their work not only in terms of hierarchical and peer-to-peer relationships but also in line with academic conventions. The cues we get and give as we locate our work (and sometimes ourselves) negatively or positively vis-à-vis others are to a larger extent rendered in written form: our review of the literature and accompanying literature list.[18]

5 The larger navigating process of establishing your literature, reviewing and presenting it as part of your conceptual framework, also entails a specific skill-set: learning about the different conventions for citing and referencing literature

and then making them as much 'second nature' as possible. Dry as dust as these techniques may be, and as far removed as they appear to be from more scintillating theoretical debates, they are indispensable nonetheless. Even with software-aided ways to reference the literature, learning these ropes serves you in good stead.

6   Learning how to read, and digest a literature list – drawing inferences and making judgments about the piece of work you have read or are about to read – is a powerful way to understand how a particular piece of work interacts with those around it. At the writing stage, software tools aside, as most researchers do not have recourse to professional copy-editors to correct their bibliographical referencing for consistency and accuracy, for those readers who are keen to do well in their examination, sloppy referencing is not an option (see Chapter 8).

7   On the psycho-emotional level, research students often experience the 'literature review' requirement as a necessary evil. When not experienced as a form of oppression from those with the authority to judge our work before it has matured, recommendations to read such-and-such article or book can appear condescending. Others take this on enthusiastically, referring to as many books, and as many of the 'top ten thinkers' as they can.

8   This leads me to one important paradox in terms of everyday practicalities about the role of this element, often overlooked. Many students, as well as relatively experienced researchers, regard literature reviews as somehow disconnected from the research proper; something to get over and done with; hopefully our supervisors will give us the right cues about which literature. In any case, when not being put off – and this happens – many try to get this aspect out of the way or as cursorily as possible in order to get on with the 'real' research. On the other hand, and this is quite legitimate for projects based on *philosophical research*, the literature review can be regarded as the research proper. If so, then the depth of knowledge and ability to create a coherent narrative and argument raises the bar even higher.

In short, literature reviews, broadly and narrowly defined or executed, are not only a core research skill, sensibility, and form of writing; they are also research. All proposals, plans, and written-up results improve as our knowledge of the literature deepens.

These literatures now come to us in printed – hard copy – form and increasingly in digital, web-embedded ways. The implications of the internet as a resource, a research tool, and a new methodological domain in its own right, is the subject of the next chapter.

NOTES

1   I have had research students with a background in journalism noting this shift in attention to sources, and the citation trail entailed, as something that marks academic from journalistic forms of investigation. The former draws out the acquiring of new knowledge and insights well past the enjoyment, or use-by date.

2   Marieke Riethof, email correspondence (18 August 2011).

3 Thanks to Susan Banducci for her input into this chapter; her expertise on systematic literature reviews and institutional histories in particular.

4 With the exception of the London School of Economics and Political Science, departments related to the discipline of politics do not have 'political science' in their title. Thanks to Susan Banducci for her input into this discussion.

5 In continental Europe, master and Ph.D. level dissertations (theses) are seen as books, many being published in book form at the time of the public defence; this is not the case in the UK and Commonwealth countries.

6 A detailed account of how to conduct a meta-analysis can be found in Lipsey and Wilson (1996). There are also several digitized and web-based tools freely available for creating a literature database as you search. These then form the basis of an eventual literature list (see Chapter 8 for more on citation conventions). The most popular at time of writing are Bookmark, and Zotero; InVivo is also a tool that can be put to good use in this respect (see Chapter 5). Their creation of hyperlinked references that take you from your document to the web is indispensable for many. For others, like me, using 'old school' manual methods, this functionality is useful in moderation. Either way they do not in themselves create deeper knowledge of what these references actually have to say; they flag rather than reveal substantive content.

7 Here are some best practices, not exhaustive by far: Jürgen Habermas' collection of essays, *The Postnational Constellation* (1998); Foucault's major works (as they are based on a particular notion of reviewing literature), *The Order of Things* (1973 [1966]) in particular. Another, earlier exemplary one is in the first chapters of Simone de Beauvoir's *The Second Sex* (1949).

8 See *Discipline and Punish* by Michel Foucault (1995 [1975]).

9 Overheard in an academic conference, an off-the-cuff remark from a guest speaker (who shall remain anonymous): 'Personally I don't like literature reviews; they are seldom done very well!' Many would agree.

10 There is a wonderful scene in Gus van Sant's 1997 film, *Good Will Hunting* (where the hero, returning student/college janitor and unknown mathematical whiz-kid – Matt Damon) is confronted in a bar by a leading member of the student elite claiming superiority based on citing the right literature. What happens next is an astute commentary on how quantity is not always quality, as well as how citation is not in itself an indicator of understanding. Umberto Eco's book, *The Name of the Rose*, presents a more historical take on the subtle interplay between knowledge, early modern Europe, and the book as a cultural, and subversive artefact. Contrast this to other forms of learning and knowledge acquisition based on oral rather than written transmission, community-based rather than authorial notions of accumulated knowledge (Smith 1999, Giri 2004; see also Foucault 1984 [1977]).

11 There are some readers who refuse to read further if more than two pages of text are devoid of the writer's input. Thanks to Susan Banducci for relaying this golden tip.

12 Indiana University (2004); www.indiana.edu/~wts/pamphlets/plagiarism.shtml (21 July 2011).

13 Not only are there cultural differentiations at stake here but also disciplinary issues. The arts and humanities, and social sciences are by and large 'intertextual' communities where mutual forms of cited recognition are part of the kinship structures, underscoring epistemic community-formation, pedigree, and success. However, there are areas of academe that see students completing research projects and submitting dissertations without any training on how to cite, whether to cite, and who to cite. In some cases I have seen, and heard of students assuming that they have to use others' words because these are the experts. These scenarios reveal a gap in the teaching curriculum, I would argue. As such they are very different from recent high-profile controversies (in the UK, the Netherlands and in Germany) where public figures have been accused – and found culpable – of plagiarism or employing a ghost-writer. The latter is the same thing in academic terms because of the requirement that all research work is submitted as an 'original' piece of work, i.e. written by the named author.

14 Even in 'online tribes' (see O'Neill 2009) where software platforms are developed, or open web accessed sites like Wikipedia, other forms of 'crowd sourcing' or explicit forms of anonymous activities (e.g. Wikileaks, and the 2011 debates around other activist/ whistle-blowing actors on the web like 'Anonymous') there are codes of behaviour and 'good practice' within communities where sharing is the modus operandi. These codes and how they pan out in everyday practice are constantly evolving; under scrutiny even given that the creative industries, publishing, arts and entertainment fall under intellectual property rights legislation at the national and global level

15 Duke University (2009): http://library.duke.edu/research/citing/plagiarism.html (21 July 2011, emphasis added).

16 Goldsmiths (2011): www.gold.ac.uk/gleu/resources/plagiarism/ (21 July 2011).

17 See Bourdieu (1977, 1984) and Foucault (1973 [1966], 1995 [1975]) for detailed studies of the intersection of socialization processes and social institutions, e.g. schools and universities. David Lodge's novels take a satirical angle on these matters (1993).

18 Thanks to Margaret Tibbles, university librarian *extraordinaire*, for reminding me of how often people conflate these terms.

CHAPTER 5

Online research and web-resourcing skills

Topics covered in this chapter:

- Terms of reference
- Internet (literature) resources
- Digital data-gathering and analysis tools
- Online research: fields, relationships, ethics
- Web-analysis: sites, maps, links, communities

INTRODUCTION

> As computer protocols enable individuals to interact in new ways, they open new spaces and forms of interactions that warrant research. Likewise they make it possible to conduct research in new ways.
>
> (Gaiser and Schreiner 2009: 5)

The quote above captures how the internet, however conceived and experienced these days, plays multiple roles in a researcher's life, and the life-cycle of a research project. As intimated in the last chapter, it is a powerful resource for locating empirical material, general information, and specialized literature. It is also a domain – a research field – and access point for more and more projects across the disciplines. Moreover, there is a plethora of tools – products and services, and functionalities that are peculiar to the internet that signal new methodologies if not fundamental reconsiderations of existing ones.

Getting a research project underway and successfully completed has become increasingly dependent on computers, computer-mediated communications, and software packages; a fact of life encapsulated by how the internet has become par for the course in higher education and research cultures around the world. There are two broad avenues to explore in this respect: first, the practical skills, formal and informal know-how, for making good use of the internet for academic research purposes. Second, issues that arise when designing and carrying out any level of *online research*; for example, from participant-observation when researching internet communities, to studying blogs, conducting a textual analysis of web-content, carrying out internet-based surveys – large or small, mapping web-based networks, to studying the private lives of *avatars* or computer-mediated intimacies between humans.

Because these two paths cross one another at regular intervals, making an effort to think about the role *information and communication technologies* (ICTs), the web especially, play in your own research is time well-spent. Frequently asked questions from research students include ones such as:

- How do I go about finding literature and other resources on the web?
- What is the best way to process and archive web-based data?
- What counts as data, access, and transparency in online settings?
- What is the relationship between observer and observed online?
- What are the limits to researching the web? *Are* there any limits?
- Are online resources, for example, Wikipedia, legitimate academic sources?

Some of these point to particular skills needed for doing effective internet-based research; technical practicalities about finding and using internet resources. Others overlap with topics covered in previous and subsequent chapters, fuelling debates about the legitimacy if not the practicability of not only online research but also web-based literature and information. They cut across all modes of research in terms of the challenges and opportunities presented by the internet as a research tool and the web as a research terrain.

The main distinction for research that occurs at any point between each end of the qualitative and quantitative spectrum is the degree to which the automated and computational powers of content-analysis software, web-based survey tools, and statistical programs are put to use. This chapter concentrates on the following aspects to conducting online research, and related internet research skills:

- finding academic resources on the web;
- best practices when re/searching the web;
- using software packages and web-based research tools;
- referencing, archiving, and presenting web-based findings;
- ethical and legal issues;
- emerging web-based, web-driven methods and topics.

For some skills, such as locating and organizing literature and other sources of information, and methods like surveys or interviews, best practices for conducting these effectively in 'real life' – offline – also apply online. But they also bring with them particular pitfalls for web-based situations.

In the second instance, designing an online research project confronts researchers sooner or later with a number of practical and ethical decisions; for example, the rights and obligations for anyone wanting to research password-protected groups on the web, if not observe interactions taking place in open-access spaces. Research into computer games or computer simulations also brings with it issues specific to the way data, and research subjects, have acquired digital form and corollary computer-coded legal identities in recent years: the IP address of your computer, or the repertoire of login names and passwords that many of us need for everyday and scholarly internet access are cases in point.

These considerations have implications not only for research design conventions in social research generally, but more importantly for how respective codes of research ethics are dealing with these concerns across academic disciplines, administrations, and funding bodies.

This is a fast-changing area where terminologies are quickly out of date, indeed 'date' the author even more quickly. As this book goes to press, and I update yet again the technical details and terms of reference for this particular chapter, the way the internet is a moving target in all its multifaceted applications for research, as well as for everyday life, underscores the inbuilt 'sell-by date' of pretty much 99 per cent of any specific brand names, goods and services mentioned from here on in.[1]

However, with an eye on developing an understanding of basic principles, and given that many critical functionalities of the web remain constant since its early years (back in the 1980s if not before), the following objectives will hopefully bear the test of time, namely that even if you are not undertaking some sort of 'online research', by the end of this chapter you will have

1 familiarized yourself, updated, or deepened knowledge about the internet as a resource, research domain, and object of research;
2 a sharper sense of the practicalities and pitfalls of online fieldwork;
3 extended and refined current internet skills for *research* purposes;
4 a greater awareness of ethical issues and accountability for conducting online research;
5 a clearer idea of the emerging areas of web-analysis and their implications for how you go about designing an inquiry located online, in part or in whole.

The chapter covers a range of topics in a question and answer format; this is an ongoing conversation and evolving set of values and principles for not only research practice but also everyday life. My thanks to past and present students for their contribution to these conversations and the way they keep me on my toes.

SETTING THE RECORD STRAIGHT

Whether or not the internet figures strongly for your research project, it has acquired a ubiquity in research communities the world over. The hardware and software of the *information and communication technologies* (ICT) that make the internet at once a highly personalized resource and the quintessential local–global universal connector are now indispensable to how we think, communicate and undertake research. From philosophers at one end of the humanities spectrum through to social scientists, through to microbiologists at the natural sciences end, computers – as individual machines and as the interconnected networks of the internet today – perform vital research-related functions.

Modern-day computing has also contributed to an increase in the *quantity* of empirical data available, the numerous forms in which evidence is produced, analysed, and presented; all of which have created distinctive *sorts* of knowledge, research fields, and controversies as research communities actively (or reluctantly) develop approaches for dealing with computer-mediated research.

Working researchers and their students tend to fall into two broad camps, depending on geographic location, the level of internet infrastructure, and research culture:

1 For many educator-researchers, and certainly for upcoming generations of undergraduates, the internet – the web – is the first stop, if not the only stop for accessing literature, getting facts, or exchanging ideas and plans with our peers and assessors. This is its strength, but it is also its weakness as the web is huge, the information available there expanding, and the rules governing access and

Figure 5.1 Information superhighway
Source: Chappatte: http://www.globecartoon.com

comportment under scrutiny. At the same time vast amounts of information, still viable resources, and online communities are disappearing from view as they go offline, are archived, or deleted from the visible web made accessible to us by search engines.

2   For others, the web is their research domain – field, sub-topic, or community – of choice; to locate particular sorts of online communities, enter various virtual worlds, or investigate textual/visual content. Some may conduct research that is entirely immersed in online domains, using methods developed by and for these computer-mediated undertakings. In this respect the term *online research* refers to the gamut of digital content, computer-mediated communities, relationships, and networks.

Whilst in computer-mediated scenarios many of the decisions governing respective disciplinary conventions of what constitutes viable research come under existing methodological rubrics, others see research students sometimes stranded in what is relatively uncharted territory. Here traditional boundaries and methodological working practices have less traction or are being transformed; whether anthropologists doing various sorts of 'virtual ethnography' are really doing fieldwork, how they get close to their 'local inhabitants', is one example.

For this reason online research is exciting and challenging for researchers – students and supervisors. There are new notions of 'mixed-method' or 'multi-sited' research design along with emerging disciplines based on the internet and/or the web as an object of theory and research in their own right.

Taking stock

The ways we use the internet in our everyday lives and workplace add up to a set of internet competencies: forms of 'computer literacy'. This hands-on knowledge develops in generic and individual ways, for instance how we go about searching the web, manage incoming and outgoing emails, identify ourselves when registering for online services or interacting with others online in open or restricted-access web-spaces, locate reliable sources of news and information, or find out what's on this weekend.

Many of us already have some idea about how to access, format, and handle *digital* data – as textual, multimedia, or visual content – when we file our email messages, comb an online catalogue for the latest literature such as journal article abstracts, register on *listservs* and *research hubs* in order to keep abreast of developments in our field of interest, or when we want to track down an item (person, gig, news, music, book) by any combination of the above. Indeed, many readers may already be quite well-advanced in designing and maintaining websites, computer-aided graphic design, using spreadsheet programs (for example, MS Access, or MS Excel), in manipulating images, or in layout design for desktop publishing. Some of you may already write your own software programs, run an internet service provider or related service, or are proficient in accessing or adapting pre-existing software; or be members of *hacker* communities and proud of it.

Figure this: can you imagine designing, carrying out and then writing up your research project without access to a computer, the web, or email?

Computer-skills are cumulative, ones we learn-by-doing over time; once we have got over that first entry-threshold, that is. Whilst there are indeed varying access thresholds and respective 'levels of difficulty', including an unwritten hierarchy of expertise and jargon amongst high-level user-groups, genders, generations, and parts of the world, many of us also regularly engage in low-level computer programming without realizing it. For instance: when we edit our profile on social networking platforms, download software in order to bypass more expensive products and services, when we set up our new laptops, or mobile phones, when we set up new programs or edit our images, or when we find ourselves having to re-install faulty, virus-infected, or malicious (*malware*) programs.

Don't I need to be an advanced computer user to conduct an online research project; beyond accessing the web for ideas, background information, or free literature, that is?

- No you don't. However, if you are uncertain do a self-evaluation of your skills, financial resources, internet access, software and hardware set-up first.

Do I have to use the internet, or use an online research method in my research project?

- No you don't. But if you do, then remember that any internet-based method/s you may be looking at need to make sense for your research question.

All this know-how, and accompanying assumptions about what should work best, is evident as we set about using the internet for general research purposes or set about a piece of *online research*.

The web-based fields, internet resources, or software tools we encounter as researchers have a different dimension to those we use everyday or professionally: for example, the effective use of various techniques for carrying out a keyword search with any *search engine* (i.e. searching, or 'browsing' the web by typing in keywords, scanning a document by using an integrated 'find' tool), keeping track when navigating the *open web* (see Ó Dochartaigh 2009: 59 *passim*) as we move backwards, forwards, or sideways between *hyperlinks*, organizing and then archiving, *bookmarking* websites for later reference, learning how to create or use *web-caches* to *code* a document. In sum, education, funding flows, and academic research have all become inseparable from three generic sorts of computer-mediated practice: word-processing, electronic correspondence, and web-based search engines (see Brabazon 2007, Latour 2007, Lazuly 2003).

Do you think the way you search the web, use your word-processing package, or set up your computer is the only, if not the best way?
- Not necessarily. There are many ways to perform these functions, some already written into the program, as *defaults*. Others evolve through use or when someone shows us another way.

- There are few *wrong* ways of accessing or navigating your way around cyber-space as there are many ways to get around the web or use a computer; i.e. if it works, it can't be wrong!
- However there are many other, sometimes more effective, more satisfying ways of doing so, particularly for research purposes.

When these habitual actions become integral to achieving a satisfactory outcome in research terms, they can appear to be less well-honed, less self-explanatory.

BOX 5.1 FREQUENTLY 'UNASKED QUESTIONS' ABOUT ONLINE RESEARCH

These are a number of assumptions that remain moot in classroom, or supervisory sessions.[2] After all, these technologies are those of today's generation of students and as such there is a certain level of assumed knowledge.

- I don't need to learn anything about research and the internet; I use the web everyday/am a website designer/hacker/media practitioner.
- Observing an online community/social network/listserv is OK if it is open-access, i.e. not password-protected.
- Accessing a closed (password-protected) community only requires the administrator's approval.
- If I disclose my researcher status to an online community it will bias my findings so it is preferable to stay hidden ('lurk').
- I can back-up all my research data/findings in a 'cloud' archiving service.
- Using a software data-analysis tool cuts down on the work, does it all for me
- Citing an internet source is easy: just cut-and-paste the URL (internet address).
- Email-based interviews are not as good as face-to-face ones.
- Email-based or other software-based surveys are easier and save time.
- Google is the only search engine worth using because its results are the best.

Surfing the web is not the same as (re)searching the web

What works for us at home when we are web-searching or interacting with others online can be put to good use in our research project, and so it should. However, some readers may think that this is all they need to know; no need to be given instructions on how to use the internet as a research resource, learn about or upgrade our internet (research) skills, and little need to bother with ethical issues because the internet is, by definition, the research tool and resource for the 'today generation'. For instance: any reference to services or programs from further back than last year is prehistoric; the web is a public space so 'all bets are off': researchers can roam freely and observe with impunity; information online is free – for the most part if you know where to go; findings can be easily stored on a portable device or, even better, backed up by depositing it in an archiving service based on *cloud computing*. Just as our photos and contact details, and those of all our friends are backed up for us by our social networking site or email service provider, low-cost or free data-archive services are now available to archive our research findings too.

I am already an advanced user/IT professional so there isn't much more to know.
- Great; that knowledge will stand you in good stead. However, conducting online research is another level of difficulty.

These services, and our accumulated know-how, need to be put into perspective when engaging with them as researchers. Broader sociocultural, political, and economic contexts have always informed research practices, and changes in research ethics; ICTs and the internet raise the ante in this respect in overt, and not so obvious ways. For instance many of the free products and services we take for granted in our everyday, professional, and research online lives are provided by corporations; where we go online, how we get there, and who owns, controls, or monitors these activities is an area in which corporations and governments alike have a keen interest. They are the object of huge R&D investments, hi-tech security measures, and marketing techniques, or where covert agencies use software applications that track internet traffic for financial gain.[3]

These trends have been a target for social mobilization as people become concerned about electronic privacy, data protection, internet censorship, and surveillance techniques. These issues are also objects of research and scholarly debate. In contrast to the internet of the previous decades, critical researchers have shown that web-based information and access to key services are becoming more complex by the minute in terms of ownership, control, and legal accountability. The point here is that whilst these services are intended to be user-friendly, their effective use for concerted research purposes is not self-explanatory.

Whatever your personal view of these matters, as researchers we need to bear them in mind. When designing an online research project in whole or in part, accessing an online community, conducting online surveys or email-based interviews, considerations about the practicalities and legalities of digital data-collection and data-storage are interconnected.

Terms of reference

Suggesting that research can be carried out these days without using the web, that automated, computer-aided research existed before the arrival of the internet, or that document analysis and scholarly writing did, and still occurs without computer-mediation arguably separates the 'Google generation' from the 'silver surfers' (see UCL 2008). Nonetheless, like any significant technology in terms of its impact on society, politics, and culture (think of electricity, the telephone, printing, or photography), the internet too has a history. It too has changed over time and will do so again, sooner rather than later in this case because what is striking about the internet technologies is that this history is relatively brief; not even that of a human lifetime.

Moreover, many aspects of this 'short history' remain disputed; the ownership, control, and future design of the internet are currently in flux, making it a fast-moving area for internet scholars, students, and researchers.

BACK TO THE FUTURE: A QUICK PREQUEL

> The internet is not an organized system. No-one is in charge [yet]. It is not primarily a network or even a network of networks. Above all it's a simple fact – the fact that millions of computers across the world can communicate with each other.
> (Ó Dochartaigh 2009: 3; see Gaiser and Schreiner 2009: 7–9)

The internet, as a particular combination of ICTs that permitted computers to communicate and computer-users to navigate these interconnections in a 'user-friendly' manner, the world-wide web and its family of internet protocols, was developed in the late 1980s.[4] It took off in the 1990s with what is now called the 'dotcom boom', a bubble which collapsed around 2001. Up to then it was the preserve of computer geeks, government military establishments, and software designers working in IT corporation and government R&D departments.

Perhaps you may even think it irrelevant to consider that it was not so long ago that teaching, assessment, and supervision took place face-to-face, by phone, or in written form; virtual learning environments or digital uploading of essays were a thing of the future. This is the first distinction you need to make; the difference between the internet's core functions and its underlying architecture on the one hand and, on the other, the plethora of products, services, and gadgets that flood the market. Only hindsight can tell which of these were fads and which were there to stay.

Technical aptitude or familiarity with website design, a particular computer code for software development, does not automatically add up to proficiency in internet/online research. Expertise in one area may well be equalled by relative ignorance in another. Why?

- First, because computer programs are like languages – closed code systems, so fluency in one is not necessarily fluency in another.
- Second, the web is vast; the amount of data available there, everyday traffic, and cumulative know-how is as well. So know-how and want-to is not only relative but also time-sensitive.
- But it is also easily shared, iterative and so cumulative.

So which web – internet – is at stake here? There are at least three generations of the internet, i.e. computers communicating with each other as we know it. Some would argue, going back to the 1960s, that this is also not strictly correct. For the sake of argument we stipulate here that what is generally understood as the internet proper refers to three overlapping periods:

- 1980s, when academic and early internet communities were developing ways for computers, and then people via computers, to communicate; for example,

ARPANET (USA), Minitel (France), word-processing software, and the personal computer.

- 1990s, when hypertext transfer protocol, and hypertext markup language and accompanying web-browsers emerged as the world-wide web. This is the age of giants like IBM, Microsoft and Intel, inter alia; also the years in which mobile telephony, and slowly mobile internetting, take hold.

- Since the early twenty-first century, when Web 2.0 (i.e. social networking) applications, *smart phones*, and other devices began to merge email, image, and sound into one integrated multimedia and interactive platform. This is the era of 'social media', internet giants like Google, Yahoo!, YouTube, and the global success of social networking sites such as Facebook.

Conceptual issues worth thinking about

There are some terms we need to keep distinct even as they tend to be used both interchangeably and as disciplinary markers; the predominance of one or other of these terms indicates differences in philosophical, empirical, and even political disposition towards the role of the internet in society, as a research field, resource, or source of disquiet.

Cybernetics: This term was coined in the 1940s for theory and research into human–machine interactions based on how 'feedback loops' function in social and automated contexts. A discipline, if not a general paradigm, emerged around the Macy Conferences for Cybernetics (1943–54), which brought key figures from computer science, biology, mathematics, and anthropology together. This line of thinking is integral to the computational logic at the heart of information technology. Hayles (1999: 8) notes, as do many others, the term's etymological origin in the Greek for 'steersman'; now extended to R&D into ways of furthering 'the synthesis between the organic and the mechanical' (ibid.). Three principles are at the heart of the cybernetic paradigm: information, control, and communication (Haraway 1990, Ramage 2009, Spiller 2002).

The next two terms tend to be used synonymously in everyday language. However, they are not synonyms; the internet is the overarching architecture within which the world-wide web (or web for short) functions. Because the latter is the part most people, researchers and students in particular, use and access on a regular basis it is easy to forget that this is a particular system of internet servers based on hyperlinking software; web browsers, search engines, graphics, audio and video singly or together have developed in the wake of the web's *hyperlinking* facilities.

The internet: Because the internet is the largest network of connected computers across the globe, it has become a generic term for the means and medium for all manner of computer-mediated communications; email to computer-dating to gaming; electronic commerce to e-government to political fund-raising. These various functions based in the PC, laptop and increasingly the mobile phone, connect through servers around the world and are enabled by layers of computer codes and the 'user-friendly' icons on our screens. In simple terms the term denotes 'a network of networks'. The way the internet works is by a particular software constellation based on two protocols, TCP and IP (Transmission Control Protocol/Internet Protocol). These effectively connect a host (for example, your PC or mobile phone) with server/s. It is the backbone of computer-mediated communications as we understand them today.

The world-wide web dates from the 1990s and was key to the internet's rapid and popular uptake and the corollary 'dotcom' boom, which lasted until the new millennium. Its hyperlinking software protocols characterize today's internet; these are what allow us to jump from one website or document to another: *hyperlink*. In distinction to how the internet's origins are rooted in the US military establishment, the web was developed in Switzerland by a British–European consortium led by Tim Berners-Lee in the late 1980s. Not all servers that make up the internet are part of the web.

Web 2.0/social media: To all intents and purposes commercial social networking sites (for example, Facebook, MySpace, YouTube) that bundle text, images, and moving images into a single, individually based 'social network' have become synonymous with the web. On going to press, the global brand-leader, Facebook, had reached the 500 million mark, the number of registered users outstripping the population of many countries. Email and static websites linked by browser software (for example, Explorer, Firefox), the bread-and-butter of internet communications, may be on their way out. Time will tell.

Cyberspace: A term with many inflections and a rich literary genealogy in science fiction. For our purposes here the term encompasses the experiential, phenomenological dimensions to how the web functions in technical terms or how the internet's architecture is configured. Tim Jordan's definition should suffice for now: 'Cyberspace can be called the virtual lands, with virtual lives and virtual societies . . . [that] . . . do not exist with the same physical reality that "real" societies do . . . The physical exists in cyberspace but it is reinvented' (Jordan 1999: 1).

Virtuality is also an elastic term that looks to capture the way ICTs have become embedded in ways of thinking about and living with/in our organic bodies. The 'strategic definition' put forward by Katherine Hayles pinpoints this tension and everyday fact of life: 'Virtuality is the cultural perception that material objects are interpenetrated by information patterns. . . . [This] definition plays off the duality at the heart of the condition of virtuality – materiality on the one hand, information on the other' (Hayles 1999: 12, 13–14).

Technical terms worth knowing about

Websites, web portals, web-pages

A *website* is a formal presence on the web. For that you need a web address, which in turn is comprised of several elements; see pp. 134–6 below. How a website is set up and designed differs from individual, to organization, corporation, and governmental body. But all have a home page; the first thing that opens when you enter the site. Sometimes this home page comes after or doubles up as a web portal. As the name suggests, a *web portal* is a gateway website; it leads you further into a range of options for a website. Larger organizations use portals but not exclusively; the United Nations at http://www.un.org/is a classic case; a web portal is comparable to a front door, 'shop window', or 'welcome' sign.

Websites are comprised of *web-pages*, variously made up of text, images, sound, and video material. The website's organizational hierarchy, multimedia applications, and layout are down to graphic design decisions, expertise, access to a range of software applications, computing power, and bandwidth capacity. As the web becomes increasingly made up of sound, still images and video, websites are less text-heavy yet require more transmission capacity (*bandwidth*). That said, (hyper)text still underpins web-content. Older websites or those without access to enough bandwidth (including electricity), the latest plug-ins or web design know-how are immediately apparent for their larger amount of static, textual content. Questions of looks, taste, and cultural distinctions also count in twenty-first century cyberspace.

Websites, and their composite web-pages, are linked together, and then in turn linked onwards to the web by a computer protocol called HTTP – *hypertext transfer protocol*. The way that they can be located is, as in 'real life', by having an address; one that is recognizable and consistently locatable. In web-speak this is the URL, the *universal resource locator*. The address given for a website's home page provides you with the URL in its simplest form.

Understanding web addresses

When someone refers to the *URL* (Universal Resource Locater) or *web address* they are talking about that line of words, numbers and slashes that appear in the strip at the top of the screen when you use a web-browser; for example, Firefox, Explorer, or Safari. How this address contracts, expands, and operates as you move to and from it is where researching the internet, rather than surfing it in varying degrees of interest or absent-mindedness, really begins in earnest. For instance, http://www.un.org/ is the URL for the United Nations on the world-wide web. This address brings you to the UN's website by way of this web-portal/home page. Once you've opted for your language option, from there you enter a matrix of interconnected web-pages.

Let's take a closer look by taking this screenshot (Figure 5.2) from Goldsmiths' website (2010) as an example. As you go deeper into any given website (see the screenshot) this address (URL) gets longer, depending on how its composite pages and links have been organized, and coded accordingly. Learning how to interpret this first strip of information as you are browsing (this is a way of moving through the web in a less structured, more open-ended way) is one thing. Ascertaining its usefulness when searching (using a search engine or tool in a focused search) in a glance can save you time.

At this point many of you may well be aware that searching the web in our research tends to follow web-surfing practice; namely the use of the 'back' button/arrow icon on the top left-hand side of our browser as we 'browse' the web. This forward and backwards movement gets most of us where we want to go; at times though it has us lose our place because not every part of the web address is linked in the same way. So, habits and the ease with which most of us search/browse in this way aside, there are ways to be more focused in this respect, especially as we face search results as a list of top-ten hits. Let's look again at the web address shown in the screenshot close up (Figure 5.3).

All web addresses have three main elements:

(a) The *protocol*. The most common one is *Hypertext Transfer Protocol* (http:// or https://). Another common one for those familiar with news-feeds is rss://. Anything before the :// designates the protocol. These days most web-browsers (for example, Explorer, or Firefox) automatically include this first part whether or not you type it in.

(b) The *domain name*. This is the core element because it tells you the key information. It has three parts in turn:

(i) the name of the server – or host (usually www);

Figure 5.2 Screenshot (i)

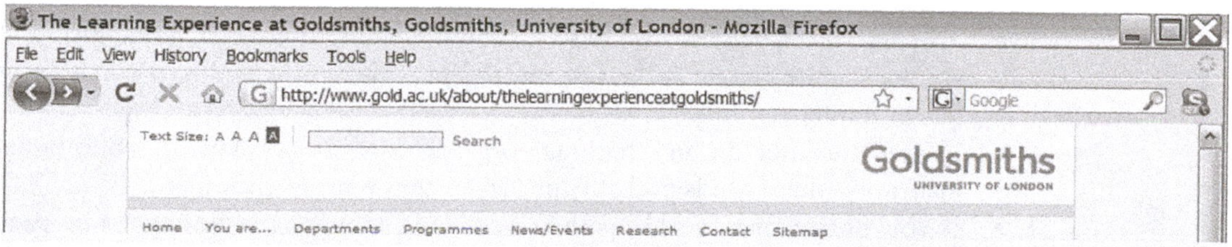

Figure 5.3 Screenshot (ii)

(ii) the name of the page, i.e. the service, you have accessed, such as the name of the institution or organization; 'gold' in this case stands for Goldsmiths;

(iii) the top-level domain. This can be a generic one, which indicates whether it is an educational (.edu or .ac), governmental (.gov), an (international) organization (.org), or commercial service (.com). This domain is also denoted by *country codes*; for example, web addresses based in the United Kingdom end with .uk; those in New Zealand end with .nz, those in India with .in and so on; 'gold.ac.uk' in this case indicates that Goldsmiths (gold) is an educational institution in the UK. US educational institutions often simply end with .edu; for example, http://www.mit.edu/, which is the Massachusetts Institute of Technology's web address.[5] Country codes are usually key indicators for content, national, and legal affiliation of a product or service, though not necessarily the actual whereabouts of the website owners.

(c) The *file path*. This last part comes after the first forward slash (/), including other forward slashes. This is the part of the web address that can give you vital clues about how the website is organized and where certain segments of information are housed: the first, *about*, and the second, *thelearningexperienceatgoldsmiths*, respectively.

When *citing web addresses* certain rules now apply; the whole URL is required along with the date you last accessed the site as a rule (though some citation style guides differ on this point).

Along with these two criteria, an author-name, and document title are also mandatory; if the author is an organization then that will suffice. If the only document title you have is the one designating the web-page, then that will suffice. Whether you incorporate web resources into your literature list or as a separate list depends on your institutional setting as well as whichever style or citation guide you are using. In any case, simply listing URLs in your literature list is not adequate.

Every website owner or administrator has to register their web address; whether they opt for a generic top-level domain name or a country-code depends on availability, commercial, cultural, and political considerations; a whole story and area for advocacy and research in itself.[6] The governing body for this process at the global level is ICANN (the Internet Corporation for Assigned Names and Numbers), a corporate entity based in California, USA.[7]

I don't usually pay much attention to the web address because I can usually see straightaway if the web-page/website is relevant.

- True. However, you can also tell a lot about whether it is worth going further if you look more closely at the web address provided at the end of the first set of search results – or hits.
- If you are after an international organization rather than an educational institution then .edu is probably not where you want to click first.
- If you notice that the file path is very long then this indicates a web-page embedded in a website. A closer look can tell you whether it is a lead worth following.

- If you find a worthwhile website whilst linking from another one, make a note of the source URL. Hyperlinks between websites are not always two-way streets and have limited shelf-lives.
- These architectural features, and their accessibility/aesthetic functions may be an aspect of specific sorts of website analysis, or mapping (see below).

THE WEB AS RESOURCE

Increased reliance on the big search engines provides a large part of the explanation for a rapid rise in student use of poor quality and unreliable sources in recent years.

(Ó Dochartaigh 2009: 1; see UCL 2008)

Do you agree with the statement above? If so, why? If not, why not? Internet research skills and online research more generally entail more than 'Googling' it, cutting and pasting text from Wikipedia, 'lurking' about on listservs, online communities and social networks as an invisible observer, or visiting virtual worlds by proxy (through an avatar).

Academic sources online: specialized databases/search engines

Setting out to search the *whole* web is like trying to find a needle in a haystack. It also assumes that all references are of equal weight, value, quality, and relevance to your needs. As this is academic work you're engaged in, starting with traditional 'print' publications, as they are available online, in part or as e-publications, is as good a start as anywhere. You can branch out later.

How do you keep your head above water when starting out doing a literature search on the web? There is so much information out there! Which databases, which journals, and which categories matter?

- Whilst the border between the humanities and social sciences, let alone the points at which they intersect, differ from place to place, isolate now the broad domain in which your topic or interests currently reside.
- Then proceed with a more focused rather than a generalized search through these standard disciplinary fences to locate the pertinent databases; for example, humanities for visual cultures, or social sciences for political science topics. Start there with a keyword search relevant to your current topic.
  (a) No luck? Now consider either narrowing your search terms further or widening them.
  (b) No luck? Now consider visiting other disciplinary databases: for example, internet-related researchers in both the humanities and social sciences cover topics so look in both zones.
  (c) No luck? Take another look at your keywords; whilst they may be your key concepts and make sense to your topic, perhaps you need to look at possible synonyms, or close relatives; for example, sustainability may emerge by looking at 'climate change' or 'carbon emissions' or 'global warming'.

Books and journals

Despite ongoing predictions to the contrary and advent of hand-held digital devices such as the Kindle reader, books and other printed matter are still the core business of academic publishers, who are also branching out into various forms of e-publishing. Here, the reference to *print publications* refers to those publications (printed or electronic) that have gone through the academic review and editing process.

These publications – books, journals, and encyclopaedias – are all readily available on the web in publishing house catalogues, and university and online databases. Again, use a snowball technique and dedicated database rather than head straight to general reference web-sources.

- Why not start with the university's e-resources – databases by which the university has access to journals and book abstracts, and thereby you too? There is more than enough information there to get you going before diving into the depths of the open web.
- If using the open web, apart from the various offshoots of Google Scholar (for example, http://scholar.google.co.uk/) there are other academic databases worth checking out. For instance:
  - www.britannica.com/; Harvard University, or Stanford and other reference services from major academic institutions;
  - various publishers' online catalogues – a very valuable resource for the latest publications;
  - other library catalogues e.g. www.worldcat.org/.

It is not uncommon for research students to overlook the knock-on benefits of assigned texts, or one important to you, and its references. From these sources you can then head out into the open web. With one foot firmly on the terra firma of print publications, finding parts of or whole books online, and for free, often follows more quickly than an aimless keyword search in a generic search engine.

- Do not underestimate the goldmine of information, already cross-referenced and sometimes even annotated by your lecturers, that is your course reading-lists; those you already have access to as well as from online syllabi from other universities, or departments that work in the areas of interest to you.
- An often overlooked and under-rated source of help is your department or faculty specialist librarian: highly educated and trained staff whose knowledge of databases, and desire to impart that knowledge, is hard to match.
- And then there are the references listed at the end of most entries in Wikipedia, a runaway success in online encyclopaedia projects at www.wikipedia.org/. As with all encyclopaedias, the best way to approach this resource, and eventually cite from it (under advisement and with care) Wikipedia entries work best as an initial source; the more developed pages provide extensive literature lists which stand on their own merit. Many academics look askance at Wikipedia, not just because, rightly or wrongly, they have doubts about the do-it-yourself aspects of its peer-to-peer working-model, but because of the uncritical way many students use this

resource. An increasing over-reliance on citations from general reference material, i.e. dictionaries or encyclopaedias, along with the indiscriminate use of the 'cut-and-paste' function in student essays, compound the problem.

For journals, the terrain is even more convoluted as there are many, many journals available. The quantity, quality, and scholarly standing of online peer-reviewed academic journals have all been on the up in recent years; *First Monday* which specializes in social sciences approaches to the internet (http://firstmonday.org/) is a pioneering example. For cultural studies and related fields, *Transformations* is another one (www.transformationsjournal.org/journal/index.shtml).

Journals reside in databases; bibliographical reference/abstracts only or full-text ones. More and more these are becoming linked as libraries and commercial search engines both collaborate as well as try and stake out their respective claims to be gatekeepers of an ever-expanding cyberspace for scholarly and related resources and sources.[8]

- To get off on the right foot, ask your supervisor, tutors, lecturers, and subject librarians for their ideas on where to locate online access to books and journals in your topic area.
- If the web is your preferred ecosystem, then you will find quite quickly various sorts of university library-based e-resource portals. These have gradations of open-web or enrolled student ID access, so trial and error will establish these limits for anyone accessing from outside the respective infrastructures.
- There are several useful online access points for academic books and journals that link up national and disciplinary geographies developed by library services.
- JSTOR (Journal Storage) at www.jstor.org/, is another useful, US-based not-for-profit resource for scholarly research where you can go for back issues (more than three years old) of many journals; it is linked to many university library e-resources, some of which can be accessed from outside the university system and depending on which journal subscriptions your library has.
- INTUTE, at www.intute.ac.uk/, a free online database made available through library e-resources, has been an important way for universities with lower budgets to provide online literature for their students. Mid-2011 this valuable resource lost its funding; however, it has been archived, i.e. it is still available but will no longer be updated.
- However, in its place two other online, academic-based resources on the web are available as supporting organizations which embrace the open-access principle of many web-based activities; first is the Directory of Open-Access Journals at www.doaj.org/; second is the Open Access Publishing in European Networks (OAPEN), an online library and publication platform at www.oapen.org/home.
- To get further look for the OpenURL links – for example, SFX or MetaLib – within the database entry you are on (for example, the Goldsmiths online library catalogue). These will take you to online copies if your institution has it. If not, then where else can you go? This is where Google Scholar or Windows' latest vehicle, Bing, may come in handy; but now you know what exactly you're looking for!

- Are you looking for the full article or trying to get a sense of what is out there? If the latter, where abstracts of articles are also provided, then if you know which journal, head to its website, where abstracts and sometimes full articles are available. If looking for articles generally, then try *indexing* databases, for example, library catalogues, or citation indexes like
  - ISI Web of Science: Social Sciences Citation Index and the Arts and Humanities Index.
  - The Virtual Library at www.vlib.org/.
  - BUBL Information Service at www.bubl.ac.uk/.

Other tips

Try searching for oft-cited authors' home pages or Wikipedia entries, as the better ones have fully annotated and usually updated linked-in bibliographies. Many classic texts and key thinkers' works can be located this way.

1   When your library does not have an electronic version of a book (e-book) or you cannot find a 'freebie' there is also Google Books. Whilst currently in dispute (and for some, disrepute), these partial scans of many academic publications will give you enough inside views. These are not full texts and they are awkward to read onscreen.
2   Commercial outlets, for example, Amazon at www.amazon.com, and publishers are providing increasing access past the cover-shot; 'inside this book' and sample chapters can help you decide whether a title is worth pursuing.
3   Publishers, and book vendor web portals like Amazon employ a range of digital marketing techniques based on users' searches; recommended titles can provide useful leads.

Online versus traditional academic resources

The arrival of web-publishing, do-it-yourself knowledge-exchange and the way in which computer-mediated communications have created opportunities for creative artists, authors, and scholars to cut out the middle person (record companies, publishers, and editorial boards respectively) means that there is an enormous amount of good, well-researched material available in purely online, or non-traditionally academic nodes online. This is where personal home pages, blogs, webzines, and a plethora of research hubs run by NGOs, international organizations and funding organizations come into their own. A lot of earlier drafts, older editions of classic articles, and conference papers where you can find out about the latest research have now been uploaded to various websites, personal, professional, and institutional. Some find their way into the top ten if not the top twenty hits of a general keyword search. Some you may come across through links provided by friends and colleagues, or newspaper articles, specialist online publications in a given areas, or in blogs.

There is no reason for these to be dismissed outright because they have not passed the 'acid test' of external review processes or academic publishing. Nonetheless, like the printed book, there is as much good material as there is sub-standard material. Double-check and cross-check, as in cyberspace the foundational hyperlink can also facilitate iterations of spelling errors, misrepresentations, and lots of baloney masquerading as 'true facts'; the power of dominant search engines to define the terrain has no small role to play in this respect.

General search engines

A keyword search for terms at the start of a research project with these services will always throw out something for you to follow. At present Google dominates this part of the internet. However, the diversity, quality, and depth of your search results will be variable; a search engine is not infallible. For academic research and particularly when your research question and literature review need to be refined, commercial internet search engines, along with *meta-search engines*, open-web databases, and general subject guides are rather blunt instruments (see Ó Dochartaigh 2009). At worst they are time-wasters and divert you from really getting to grips with what is out there in scholarly terms, online and in print.

This is not to condemn browsing per se, or to imply that any material you come across by chance, or via another unrelated browsing-session is suspect. More to the point, consider making a *distinction between everyday browsing/surfing of the web and conscious researching*. The former can support the latter but it is neither a substitute for doing the legwork, figuratively speaking, nor is it a shortcut to instant research findings; online literature searches are time-consuming and, as many students discover, demand patience.

BOX 5.2 TRY OUT – ANOTHER SEARCH ENGINE?

TRY OUT – type in your current research interest into a variety of search engines:

- Bing at www.bing.com/
- Google Scholar at www.scholar.google.com/
- Open Directory at www.dmoz.org/
- A meta-search engine, which amalgamates results from multiple search engines, such as www.dogpile.com/
- A few academic (university and commercial) publishers: Oxford University Press or MIT; Routledge, Blackwell, Sage, or Palgrave Macmillan.

What do you notice?

Now refine your search using 'advanced search'. What do you notice?

Increasing your web-searching success rate

'Sorry! File not found – 404 error'.
'404 not found – wait, yes it is'.[9]

There are ways of browsing the web and ways of searching it in a more focused way. In both instances we make use of two closely connected sorts of software applications designed for the internet: *internet browsers* and their variously integrated *search engines*; for example, Microsoft Internet Explorer and its Bing search engine; the partnership between Mozilla Firefox and Google (by far the most popular), the various browser and search services provided by Yahoo!, Safari, and others.

Based on the principle that these services are 'free' albeit tied to their service provider in various ways, both these applications are needed to navigate the web. The key difference between them is that a browser locates and displays web-pages. Search engines on the other hand, particularly those developed for the internet as a whole, are programs that automatically search the web or a specific document for a combination of terms and phrases as specified by the re/searcher. The 'top ten' search hits list is where most everyday users, and researchers for that matter, begin and end their search. As search engines, and their browser-based goods and services, increase in sophistication and marketing savvy, the effectiveness of this initial search has been also increasing. To date, Google leads this hit parade.

If searching the web is more than simply browsing, or surfing it, and assuming that there is more to be gained than relying on a Google search for a particular core concept, big name, or issue area central to your research project, then what else do we need to bear in mind? The pointers below pertain to how the aforementioned computer literacy and everyday know-how that budding or experienced researchers bring to their work when setting out to research in web-based settings, can be both a hindrance and a blessing.

1   In response to many a student's frustration at not being able to find anything useful when first conducting a literature search on the web, the basic rule of thumb when starting out is to try and develop focus earlier rather than later; start with a narrower set of criteria for your initial search. You can branch out as you go. Ironically it is only after achieving greater focus that our success rate when searching improves; as your research question, aims and objectives become more refined so do your searches.

2   In response to the truism that states 'if it isn't on Google it doesn't exist', in other words that no other search engine is worth bothering with, I would like to suggest that this is not necessarily so. There are generalized search engines and respective searches, and there are more specialized ones; Google Scholar is, again, a specific service designed for academics as is its would-be nemesis, Microsoft's Bing, launched in 2009. Whilst the former is to date the most powerful and most successful program around for providing an instant overview of which websites, documents, or other sorts of web-content are most prominent based on a (still top-secret) calculation of how your terms crop up in any web-page along with how

frequently it has been visited by others, it is not a 'true' representation of what is out there on the web.

3   No search engine is fully 'live'; all are selective and the web they search is cached (a just-in-time archive stored in huge server-bays); if for no other reason than the web itself changes continually as do the algorithms governing how the software works. For example, the frequency your words/phrases appear against how often that website is accessed against how much some website owners pay for 'preferred placement', versus how ad-tracking intermediaries facilitate the above as they piggy-back on millions of searches a second.

4   When starting out on a web-search, particularly if you are looking for easy-access literature (where you don't need to leave home, use the library, or pay) about your research topic, there are several things to bear in mind:

(a) A *simple search* will provide you with a swathe of information; more than you can deal with. Alternatively it can result in a list of commercial products and services rather than substantive information or sources. For academic sources, use academic tools.

(b) So, here, why not start with those websites that you already know are useful: your library online catalogue, publishers or online book vendors, the ubiquitous Wikipedia, or international organizations. Why start with the open web when you know already that your topic is about one of the United Nations organizations, an NGO, or corporation? Start there and move outwards.

(c) If an initial search is disappointing, try other terms. Even if they are not the exact terms you want to use, crucial links and information may well be contained under other ones; for example, 'climate change', 'global warming', 'greenhouse effect', 'carbon credits' are overlapping phrases. Stubbornly persisting with the same phrase or combination of terms despite disappointing results (no hits at worst) is not recommended. That said, sometimes the same search on another day throws up different results.

(d) This is when an 'advanced search' comes in handy. Look for this option at the top of the web address window in your search engine/browser window. Here you will have a set of options for refining your search. Like fishing, it sometimes helps to bait the hook in certain ways to attract the fish you want; for example, restrict or open up the dates between which you want to look, include or exclude certain items that get in the way of creating diversity in a simple search. Here big names or global brands can be excluded if they are not what you're looking for.

(e) As search engine designers look to make searching easier and easier, if not predict where we want to go by providing us with previous search terms as a matter of course, finding the right phrases to ensure the best results for your purposes is an art as well as a science. As you become more familiar with your field, your topic and how certain terms and phrases characterize your literature base, your ability to search (when you need to) will improve.

(f) So the golden rule is not to get too reliant on one search engine, one web-service provider when researching. Given the commercial stakes alone, it never hurts to see what you can find using two or three search engines; if nothing else you will get a sense of which websites, personalities, and articles feature prominently.

(g) There is a time-honoured set of search principles when combining search terms: *Boolean search terms*. See Box 5.3 below for more information. Sometimes it works better to eliminate terms from our search parameters rather than attempt to add to them. The line between too broad and too narrow is a fine one. All the more reason to try different ways before giving up and going to the pub!

BOX 5.3 BOOLEAN SEARCH TERMS

A *Boolean search* is named after the mathematician and philosopher George Boole (1815–64) who invented the algebra that came to govern electronic databases. *Boolean logic* is a way of refining a search by narrowing, or broadening your terms; the four key operating terms are AND, NOT, OR, and NEAR. Either you write this in full or you can use symbols as listed below:

And   can be shortened to '**+**'.

Not   can be shortened to '**-**'.

Or   This is the default setting, i.e. unless you indicate otherwise a search engine will conduct an either/or search for all terms provided.

Near is designated by putting quote marks around your key phrase: '. . .'. This tells the software to search for appearances of those words in that order, or as close as possible to them; useful when looking for an article, document, or website you've lost track of as well as for keeping your search focused.

These principles are inbuilt features of search-engine design; the advanced search option in your search engine uses them too and most of us figure this out by trial and error, or by the example of others. However, search engines differ in degree and effectiveness in how they have incorporated these principles in their design; for example, the NEAR option can result in hits where proximity is within ten to twenty-five words between search engines, rather than strictly together; when using the full words, certain search engines require their capitalization.

(h) Finally, *nothing* works? You keep getting a '404 not found' message when searching for your research topic? No-one out there in cyberspace is interested in what you are? Your key terms don't exist in a Google context? First, check your spelling! Second, try another day, try another combination of search terms, try another tool, ask someone for advice.

(i) Or, overwhelmed with too much information? Or, on looking closer you realize that this over-abundance of information is actually the same website, product, or article reiterated in the top ten/top twenty hits? At the end of the day, dedicated databases and their search engines such as library catalogues, mature research hubs, and many inter-governmental organizations' websites will provide you with more than enough without having to venture into the open web or use generic search engines. Literature lists, print and digital, are a mine of information.

Getting past Google and why bother

What do you think might be the problem with relying entirely on search engines on the open web, Google in particular? What is good about them?

'To google or not to google, that is the question'; In a very short time, Google has established itself as the predominant ('free') search engine on the world-wide web, superseding predecessors like Gopher, File Transfer Protocol (FTP), Usenet, and contemporaneous search engines like Alta Vista and Yahoo!, inter alia. However, Google's 'spider web', algorithmic search functionality with its hierarchy of top 'hits', is based on the ordering of citation frequencies rather than the random filtering of keyword frequencies. Incredibly efficient, this principle means that keyword-placement and citation by other websites has become increasingly strategic, for website designers/owners and advertisers alike (parties pay for a position in the top ten hits) as they situate their websites' content accordingly. Web surfing and information access is now inseparable from 'product placement'. The upshot for researchers particularly is that relying entirely on Google leads you, more often than not, to a selected few websites or highly cited online sources, and often the same ones in different guises, rather than a selection of various websites or online sources that also relate to your keyword selections. There is a host of sound, high-quality material that doesn't always get to the top of the Google hit parade.

DIGITAL TOOLS FOR ONLINE DATA-GATHERING AND ANALYSIS

Online researching has opened new environments to researchers that move beyond traditional research and challenge some of our notions of what it means to research, how people engage online, and so forth. . . . These new environments not only offer new ways for learning, but also new ways in which to conduct research, creating simulations and testing conclusions.

(Gaiser and Schreiner 2009: 5)

More and more research students are engaging in doing research into, or gathering information from, domains that are entirely, or largely web-based (see Gaiser and Schreiner 2009: 83–9, 90–2, Ó Dochartaigh 2009: 98 *passim*). This emerging field has two dimensions: specific sorts of digital tools used to mine, map, or collate 'raw' data directly from the web; web-based domains, groups, and activities that are the object of research and/or designated field in which a researcher carries out their data-gathering by various methods (for example, observation, interviewing). These emerging research environments include:

- Social networking sites: Facebook, YouTube, MySpace, and other sorts of social media-based portals, and their constituent groups.
- Internet communities: These predate and co-exist alongside the above. Often using a mixture of 'old-school' bulletin board services (BBS), Newsgroups, and listserv set-ups, they are core constituents of many grassroots activist groups, NGOs, and special interest communities. Moderators and passwords keep track of 'who's who' in varying ways.
- News and entertainment portals.
- Blogs: the many individual blogs, professional and amateur, that make up the 'blogosphere'.
- Web portals and websites of intergovernmental organizations (the UN, WTO, or World Bank for instance) and those of NGOs, large and small.
- Political party websites along with politician's blogs or home pages.
- Computer games and virtual worlds; for example, Second Life, computer gaming communities, games like World of Warcraft, The Sims, and such like.

Entering to access, observe and/or participate in the various sorts of communities, readerships, or documentary resources made available in these domains brings with it a host of familiar and new practical and ethical challenges for the researcher. But before taking a closer look at these issues, we need to consider how web-based data can be collected and then analysed; by what means (digital – automated, or manually), and to what ends.

Making sense of the data: web-based and software tools

This section looks forward to a more in-depth discussion in Chapters 6 and 7 in light of the growing market in software designed to aid and speed up qualitative data-analysis; particularly when large amounts of (digitized or web-embedded) material is under investigation.

Quantitative analysis tools such as SPSS have been a staple of quantitative modes of research for some time, as statistical analysis is integral to modern computing. Home office products all include spreadsheet and database programs for collating and crunching figures; basic statistical functions can be used without using more extensive software. Qualitative sorts of content analysis can be done manually, indeed quite reasonably for smaller to medium-sized fields or data such as interview transcripts, smaller-scale focus group work, or a well-defined set of policy documents.[10]

For long-standing email/listserv text, internet communities, or intersecting ones on a larger portal, the quantity of text can be too large to handle by manual means only. Here, new qualitative digital tools are being launched and refined all the time. That said, any software program will have a certain degree of 'default' built-in, which will have an impact on your eventual findings. If you don't know what you want to do with the material and to what ends, you will be putting the cart before the horse and more than likely spending a lot of time for little added benefit. So, first do a self-evaluation; ask yourself the following questions:

1   What is my realistic level of computer-use, skills, and equipment?
2   What length of time will I spend doing this research? Answers will differ according to whether this is an undergraduate or postgraduate, (post)doctoral project.
3   Where will I be storing the raw data, and in what format? As software formats are often exclusive, not always compatible for other formats, the best advice its to keep your data in a relatively or widely available format (e.g. text-only, or RTF formats), rather than locked into a high-end or proprietary format (e.g. Photoshop). You need to think about being able to access this data after you have updated your operating system, laptop, or mobile device.

Software analysis tools

Making use of software programs is a digitized way of collating, organizing, and then analysing textual, and visual content; bringing order to an array of material gathered during the research in order for some sorts of conclusions to be made, an argument substantiated. These products have been gaining momentum in academic research as the quality and flexibility of programs improve. One thing to remember, however, is that automated searches and then coding of any content are *not in themselves a method*. They may do a lot of work for us, such as sorting out terms according to criteria such as the 'nearest neighbour' or particular word combinations – collocations. But they need to be in service of our analytical framework. Coming up with findings based on word frequencies, syntax, or patterns of placement in a document is the outcome of criteria that are built into the program and then put into action by the researcher according to her/his priorities and respective analytical method.

Qualitative software tools are designed for 'any kind of research that produces findings not arrived at by statistical procedures or other means of quantification' (Strauss and Corbin 1990: 17, cited in Gaiser and Schreiner 2009: 114). Quantitative tools can accompany this sort of research in that counting keywords, tagging, or figuring out significance entails a level of quantification. However, in methodological terms, the key distinction remains for quantitative content analysis tools: these are 'by definition about numbers' and analyses by using statistical techniques (Gaiser and Schreiner 2009: 121). So, once again, which is best for your project relates to your research question, research design, and rationale.

Qualitative content analysis

So, what kind of *qualitative software* that can facilitate in collating and then analysing large amounts of text is currently available? Remember, try out these various offers *before* committing time and resources to them if they are not made available to you by your institution. If so, check how long your access rights last.

- Nvivo: www.qsrinternational.com/; www.softwaresales.bham.ac.uk/az/nvivo.shtml
- Hyperresearch: www.researchware.com/
- Atlas/ti: www.atlasti.com/

- Ethnograph:www.qualisresearch.com/
- MAXQDA: www.maxqda.com/

The above are currently available and in use. Content analysis software is improving steadily. And with that the complexity of the programs is also increasing. Licensing costs, for students as for full-time researchers, depend on institutional and commercial factors.

Looking ahead to Chapter 7 for a moment, note that these programs are automated albeit sophisticated versions of what many people do when reading a book or article; using post-its, or colour highlighters to mark significant passages for later reference. When we want to analyse texts, and images, using any particular *coding scheme* or analytical approach, these programs can be put to good use.

- That said, setting them up in order to have them work for us, in the way that we want them to and to serve the purposes of our analytical method, is more time-consuming than many would believe.
- The promise of automation and digital formatting belies this preparatory and decision-making phase particularly for qualitative content analysis programs, where manual forms of interpretation are still more than a match.
- For statistical analysis, software tools have a longer pedigree, general and more specialized. Their effective application requires preliminary knowledge and understanding of the principles of statistical work as well.

When considering whether or not these software packages are feasible, indeed even appropriate for the sort of research you are doing, it bears reiterating that it is highly recommended you take the time to try them out; here trial offers offer a first taste, many universities offer free tutorials, and the user manuals are an invaluable way to test your willingness to persevere as well as provide insight to how user-friendly the program really is. Sometimes trying out various software packages can help in moving you forward in designing your analytical framework, even if you end up not using a package extensively.

Still convinced that these will solve your data-gathering and analysis puzzle? Perhaps, but first note:

- It bears reiterating; these tools are not in themselves a method. Their use is not a methodological shortcut, or explanation per se.
- Find out how others have found any of these packages; only once you have taken a look yourself, though, as then you will not be wasting other people's time with base-one queries. Here user-group listservs and websites are invaluable sources of information.
- If you are someone who checks out the reviews and comments for new consumer products and services online, then why not do the same with something as important as a piece of research software?
- Make sure you confer with your supervisor about this option, in principle and practically. If they do not show much enthusiasm, and there could be many reasons for this, try and have a better response to the question 'Why use this tool

instead of doing the analysis manually?' than 'It is free' or 'Because it can do the work for me'. It can only do the work for you up to a point. Then you still have to make sense of the findings, and justify them on your own.

It is better not to be too hasty about adopting the latest software tool (at time of writing Nvivo was top of that hit parade) without being sure about what its role, and the disadvantages thereof, is in your project. Committing yourself, and your raw data, to a software package without your supervisor knowing, without due consideration of the methodological pros and cons, or without preliminary practice (better still, a practical workshop if offered by your graduate school or support services), is more often than not a recipe for disaster.

Quantitative analytical tools

In this area quantitative data-processing tools have been around a long time, before the web in fact. However, their availability and existence online have also developed with the web. Again, these are tools not a methodology and as always you need to learn how to use them, know why you want to use them for your inquiry, and then apply their functionalities in analysing your material and drawing eventual conclusions. The main ones used are:

- SPSS, a program developed by the IBM corporation, is a mainstay in many social science departments. Apart from the company website, consult university resources such as www.ats.ucla.edu/stat/spss/. The point here is that using powerful tools such as these requires an understanding of basic statistical analysis to make proper use of them. For anyone conducting smaller-scale surveys that generate quantitative results, you could rely on the functionalities provided by either you own spreadsheet program or online survey tools.
- Stata (standing for statistics/data) is the trade name for a popular package. See www.ats.ucla.edu/stat/stata/ for a useful online resource that includes tutorials and specific sorts of actions. If you are still not sure, or even if you are absolutely sure that statistical analysis is what your inquiry requires, then consult the useful link on this page entitled 'What statistical analysis should I use?' at www.ats.ucla. edu/stat/stata/whatstat/default.htm. The table provided there provides a comprehensive overview of terms and parameters with links to the relevant tool.
- SAS (Statistical Analysis System) is another statistical computing package with specific functions. See www.ats.ucla.edu/stat/sas/default.htm for an online primer and links.

In sum, all these packages are computing tools that consist of 'powerful data management tools, a wide variety of statistical analysis and graphical procedures'.[11]

Again, before committing, if you have not been introduced to these tools as part of a methods training course, then you need to trial them, or take a course beforehand. Here some products offer online training, or university computing departments make their learning resources available in the open web, as is the case with UCLA above.

A final point: make sure that there will be terms under which student access and use of these tools, namely via their institution, may have a shelf-life; think about how and where you intend to store your data (for example, survey results) and the way these tools process them, for later reference.

Crossover tools

There are a number of software tools that are useful for more than one sort of research methodology: online and partially free survey tools and low-cost tools developed by academic researchers.

- Surveys: for smaller (up to ten questions) and more complex surveys, Survey Monkey, www.surveymonkey.com/, is an attractive and easy to use tool. For those on a limited budget and doing a BA or MA level project, it is a good exercise to restrict yourself to ten questions. Before sending out the survey to your target group (something that needs preparation), try out the survey yourself, and with a pilot group. Only then will you see whether your questions are well-formulated or in line with your aims.
- Web-mapping. For those looking for connections, linkages, and undertaking any kind of network analysis, one readily available and low-cost tool is Issue Crawler, at www.govcom.org/. The online tutorials and research results are both useful ways to consider whether this approach to researching the internet might offer you an avenue for your topic. That said, the maps that get produced with this tool are not in themselves self-explanatory. They often raise as many questions as they answer. This particular product is one of several sorts of web-mapping tools available.

The web as archive/archiving digital content

There are some practicalities to bear in mind as we gather and depend upon the web to also store our notes, writing, interview material or other forms of 'raw data' and access it to find literature, do fieldwork, or contact interviewees by email.

Whether you opt to archive your work on your own hard drive, in a portable storage device, or by using a cloud computing archiving service, the rule of thumb is threefold: back-up, back-up, and back-up. Two different back-ups should suffice. If you want to include hard copy as well as digital formats of your work then this brings it to three. University and/or workplace servers, and commercial cloud computing archiving services are great when you are on the move or using different hardware access points for your work. However, if the server crashes or goes offline you are in a fix; particularly stressful as deadlines near. Sustainability over a longer period of time is another key consideration. Remember internet products and services are a particularly volatile domain; what is available today may not be next year, or even tomorrow.

ONLINE RESEARCH: FIELDS, RELATIONSHIPS, ETHICS

> [T]he online environment represents new ethical challenges for researchers that require thinking outside of the boundaries of traditional research. Informed consent, confidentiality, anonymity, privacy, the nature of what constitutes private and public spaces, virtual personae, copyright, and more, take on new meanings and require fresh insights when you are conducting research in the online environment.
>
> (Gaiser and Schreiner 2009: 27)

The web as a self-contained research field, as distinct from the research tool or medium for interpersonal and professional communication and collaboration, has been causing methodological stress for some time. Its legitimacy is at the heart of some heated debates within and between scholarly communities in the social sciences as well as the humanities about what these developments mean for existing research practices and future ones. Key issues in this area pivot around four axes:

1 New, and longstanding questions and codes of ethics for conducting research on human subjects or animals as they are transposed into online fieldwork settings.
2 Burgeoning legal rights and obligations for researcher and research subjects alike when interacting in contexts subject to various sort of 'digital rights management' rules and regulations: for example, in the case of how the entertainment and media industries watch over downloading – P2P sharing – of music, film, and computer games.
3 What counts as real-life research as online domains, experiences, and relationships that only make sense in cyberspatial terms stake a claim on what counts as a social fact, a physical fact; empirical data in short as traditionally understood and argued about for some time already has been undergoing a sea-change (see Chapters 2–3, 6–7). Digital data, digital persons, and virtual worlds have an impact on how these philosophical questions are debated today and their methodological effects on research practices in the short and longer term.
4 Reconsiderations of what counts as scientific knowledge, participation and/or observation, authenticity, transparency, and replicability when research is conducted with or in computer-mediated settings with research subjects (for example, avatars as interviewees in a virtual world like Second Life, or The Sims). As above, these concerns underscore longstanding ontological and epistemological debates about what knowledge counts.

In all cases, the jury is still out; local, national, and even international trends and power hierarchies debate about what is credited, accredited, and duly legitimated as bone fide knowledge in computer-mediated or web-based research cases is still underway. Research students are often caught in the crossfire. Those who persist and develop innovative approaches to these questions, particularly by undertaking research in these newer domains, are instrumental in moving the debate along.

Figure 5.4 Spam

Source: Chappatte: http://www.globecartoon.com

Research ethics

To recall (see Chapter 3), it is nowadays mandatory for academic researchers – staff and doctoral students, with master and bachelor-level research students increasingly included – to go through a formal ethics approval procedure. Par for the course in the medical and natural sciences where research (experimental or trials) is carried out on human beings or animals, these considerations also apply to any research in which human subjects – and their avatars – are the focus or means for gathering data. Each institution has an overarching code of practice to this effect; and within them each department has its respective procedures and forms to fill in on this count. Ethical considerations cover research that entails gathering material through interviews, focus groups, written texts by 'living subjects' for example, diaries, personal correspondence and such like. The formalization of research ethics considerations is also inseparable from any work involving varying degrees of participant-observation, any sort of experimental work, and intentions to carry out covert forms of observation; permissions criteria for the latter are particularly stringent.

To recap, the core principles of all codes of research ethics, whatever variations there may be in national or institutional renditions of basic human rights legislation to protect personal privacy, data, freedom of information, press freedom, and freedom of speech, are:

1 informed consent: permission is granted to access, observe and/or participate, and then use material in the research findings;
2 protection of subjects' identity and right to privacy by insuring anonymity;
3 proper and respectful use of any data gathered under conditions of informed consent that is then used only for the purposes of the immediate project;
4 obligation on the part of the researcher to ensure transparency and accountability with respect to the research subjects – their words, deeds, and way of life; during and after the research process.

Nowadays these criteria encompass research on communities, individuals – as physical and digital entities – avatars, virtual worlds, access to and citation of various sorts of web-content; written and visual texts produced by living research subjects in online settings.[12] The fact that visibility is of a different order in web-based research domains, or that there are increasing amounts of research still to be done on what is going on, as well as being produced in open-access parts of the web (for example, readers' comments pages in online news media, chat-rooms that are not password-protected), does not constitute a *passe-partout* for any online research. Far from it; there are several aspects that need to be considered right from the outset:

Lurking – undercover observation or gatecrashing?

Bearing in mind from Chapter 3 the principles underwriting professional and academic codes of ethics for conducting research with human, and also animal research subjects, we now turn to how these work out in online research settings.

Online research ethics is an area still under construction; sometimes existing codes of ethics have been revised or extended with respect to interviews, surveys, or participant-observation in computer-mediated fields. Sometimes specific codes of ethics have been developed: those developed by the Association of Internet Researchers (AoIR) for instance (see Chapter 3). As is the case with standard research ethics considerations, from formulating a written consent form for your interviewees or simply checking with them if you can use their real names or 'tags', for online research this aspect is an integral part of your research design. It too is more than ticking boxes; the decisions you make or avenues you cannot pursue because of ethical considerations all help you in the long run to refine the question and the theoretical assumptions you bring to the original research component.

Just as in 'real life', research involving interviews (by email), surveys (for example, using Survey Monkey or other facilities), and particularly participation-observation (for example, of a Facebook group or internet community) requires you to obtain access permission at least once, and under review, and deal with informed consent and anonymity when online. As participants or as researchers, the ethical dimensions to online forms of participation-observation, partial or full immersion, have theoretical, empirical, and epistemological implications.

So what are the main distinctions between these standard considerations and how they pan out on the web or when conducted in computer-mediated ways?

1 For *participation-observation* research in many online scenarios the researcher is either wholly or partially invisible to the research subjects. Covert observation, referred to as 'lurking' when the observer has not announced their presence formally, is much easier to do. For some students this is inviting as they can conduct observation without 'biasing' their findings, or so they think. However, as anthropology, feminist, postcolonial, and action research scholars have pointed out for some time now (long before the internet), all observation is a form of participation, (quasi-)experimental work notwithstanding, but that is another matter.

As avatars, thumbnail identifiers and (decreasingly) signatures can cover for our on-the-ground identifiers this does not mean that web-based identifiers (nicknames, avatars singularly or in combination) have no meaning for people. Online anonymity is a relative thing; one's nickname is also cherished as a 'real name'. In this respect, the conditions by which your access and presence on an online community is accepted by your interlocutors – research subjects or perhaps even collaborators – can also be dependent on your taking care to anonymize these quasi-anonymous 'handles'.[13]

2   *Conducting online surveys, email-based interviews, or analysing web-content* produced by a community of users, readerships, or members of the public is also easier in one key respect: much of the text is there already. We only need to cut-and-paste; no more transcribing. No more note-taking. This is true in many respects.

However, many a researcher has discovered, sometimes too late, that setting up an email-based survey or online questionnaire does not necessarily lead to an increase in participation. The success rate for email-based questionnaires is quite poor. Moreover, in cases where anonymity is not an integral part of the questionnaire design, permission to name or cite is not a given either. Finally, the sheer volume of text produced by online communities or groups is in itself reason to consider what limits and selection criteria need to apply for you to achieve viable results, or conclusions, in the time you have.

3   *Access* permission for any community online is comparable to access permission to any community on the ground. Because access can be granted technically before it is granted officially, for closed communities entry access is not necessarily a long-term prospect for research purposes. Some students, whether or not they are already active members of a community, such as a (P2P) file-sharing site, have found themselves the subject of 'flaming' or overt criticism when their status changes from co-participant to researcher. The longer you wait before announcing your presence as a researcher the more chance there is of this sort of negative reaction. When communities are already engaging in semi-legal or socially marginalized interactions (for example, pro-anorexic sites, political organizations, sexual minorities), the need for researchers to obtain permission is also to protect themselves as well as their informants.

Philosophical disputes about the epistemological legitimacy of 'cyberspatial practices' and those digitally constituted 'beings' that produce these practices aside, online research has been raising the ethical and the methodological stakes across the board. This can be daunting for research students. By the same token it is thanks to cutting-edge projects and the trials and errors of fledgling internet researchers that fascinating topics and more rounded codes of ethics are emerging. Two cases drawn from the work of several researchers (students and others) illustrate the above distinctions.

Dilemmas – two cases

The following scenarios (several projects have been condensed here into two cases) really happened; the researchers involved found themselves obliged to make significant changes in their research projects as a result. Their respective ethics committees, supervisors, and colleagues all had different takes on the matter.

In the following situations, what would you do?

1 *Overt vs. covert observation*: Is it acceptable for a researcher to observe a password-protected online community without revealing their identity or purpose?
   - What if the researcher has gained temporary access already and wants to continue?
   - What if the researcher realizes they need official permission well into the research; permission from the administrators let alone from community members is still pending?
   - Is the moderator's approval enough or should all members be asked?
   - How often should this access permission, once granted, be renewed?
   - Is there a case where *covert* research, even in online settings, or particularly for online settings where the research is investigating issues around self-disclosure or illegal practices, is acceptable?

2 *Researching peer-to-peer practices*: Should the researcher, having access permission and having provided full disclosure of their role as a researcher with others in a peer-to-peer file-sharing community they have been a member of for some time also engage in downloading content that is protected by intellectual property rights law?
   - Or should they change their research aims and objectives given the *potential* danger of becoming liable for prosecution by eventual copyright-holders?
   - Are they answerable to the community, their research institution, or the integrity of their original research plan, now compromised by these considerations?
   - Is the moderator's approval enough or should all members be asked? How often should this request for access permission, once granted, be repeated?

One thing all these research projects had in common was a shared anxiety by the research student that revealing their role as a researcher (before or even after the fact) would compromise their findings. Put it this way; on-the-ground participation-observation in particular communities also requires permission, reveals us as researchers. There is a distinction between close-up observation within a community and observations made in public spaces such as railways stations and squares. In the latter cases as well, care is needed when approaching individuals to ask them questions. Not everyone appreciates learning that they have been the subjects of systematic observation; would you be in all circumstances?

WEB-ANALYSIS: SITES, MAPS, AND HYPERTEXTS

To recapitulate, with the web comes an array of new places to go, relationships to follow, and sorts of digital (computer-mediated) data to collect; from user-log statistics, to hyperlink hubs, to web maps based on density, distribution, or traffic flows between websites. Some of these data are provided by freely available, commercial search engines and service providers or as part of a website's display. This information is a first stop for basic information; for example, how old a website is and how often updated, how many registered users it has, and how many there are at any one time.

Digitally constructed, web-dependent domains have also created a burgeoning literature on 'digital methods', or 'virtual ethnography' or 'hypermedia research' where their newness predominates and innovative approaches to gathering and analysing the interactions and subjects populating cyberspace, new topics and recharged older debates (for example, about privacy and surveillance in social networking sites, editorial control in user-based domains, peer-to-peer practices) are proliferating. Wikipedia, Second Life, Facebook, and Twitter, are at the time of writing the research domains, and topics of choice, in their own right or their role in major events of the day, for many research students.

Whilst online and computer-mediated, and thereby trans-border and covering ever-expanding research terrains are characterized by the exponential increase in terms of quantity, time (compressed synchronous but also asynchronous) and intensity of volume (increasing all the time) online research also engages tried and trued data-gathering methods. Interviews online are conducted more or less following long-standing principles, as is focus-group work whatever form the participants take (see Chapter 6). Surveys are also increasingly carried out online, if not within communities or user-groups then by using survey tools (as outlined above). Various sorts of 'content analysis' in quantitative terms, visual and 'textual' analysis from interpretative traditions are also perfectly viable for approaching website content and design, as a whole or in part; for example, changes in layout and editing for web-formats, or themes and debates in discussion forums or user-groups. Chapters 6 and 7 will cover these points for online settings where relevant.

In that respect, a lot of research carried out entirely or partially by means of the internet overlaps established research traditions. However, apart from the distinct features that web-based practices and production bring with them which impact on research methodologies in turn, there are differences.

1 First, in terms of how text online, as written, audio, and visual material is constantly in motion; website content is constantly updated, archives are not always accessible or kept up to date, participants come and go or adopt various personae for their online identities, access and interaction occur at various levels of mediation.

2 There are differences in the relationship between researchers and research objects/subjects based on non-proximate and non-visible, textual exchanges where computers mediate and frame the encounter. These dynamics affect the ethical rights and obligations for both researcher and subject (see Chapter 3).

3 There are practicalities peculiar to studying a website or cluster of websites, or web portal as the primary object or research, for these are multimedia and multilevel sorts of domains: visuals, layers, functionalities, populations, and content. This is also the case when an inquiry wants to map or trace particular sorts of hyperlinked relationships (between participants, or websites), or focus on images and digital texts from web-sources in their own right as cultural or aesthetic artifacts. Or when an online community (however defined) of gamers, or an ethnic minority, or a larger newsgroup (e.g. Facebook group) is the main focus.

All in all, web-spaces are multi-user, multimedia, and multilevel domains for researchers. They offer expansive and overlapping sorts of data to collect, create new ways to navigate, sort and then assess the material, and a seemingly accessible range of potential interviewees to access in ways that are as exciting as they are difficult to contain. For the time being, and making sure to consult more detailed and focused explorations in the literature, note the following analytical distinctions:

- Those between the sorts of research you may be doing, where on the web you intend carrying out the work, and how these relate to, indeed may well be, the main object of inquiry.
- Depending on the question and objectives, the internet may be more than a cornucopia of free or accessible information and academic resources. It may well be a key factor in the phenomenon you are studying if not the research field itself.
- In addition, and this truism bears noting; the internet and the web are not only huge but also moving targets. Any research project in this domain needs to be specific about which part is the main focus; for example, a particular micro-blogging service, or social networking site for a particular setting (Chinese ones are different from American or European ones).

Web-mapping

This is a developing area where software tools are coming into their own, designed for consumers (Google maps and spin-offs, GIS devices) and researchers (specific tools with licensing arrangements). Like all sorts of mapping, this sort of research as data-gathering and analysis has its own methodological weighting; implying a geographical, topological approach whereby an area, spatial relationship, and other sorts of distribution are primary. Some researchers have achieved interesting results by manual means; for example, following leads and hyperlinks and creating a repre-sentation of these pathways from a clear starting point (for example, home portal and back). Others are more interested in investigating a particular, or comprehensive area based on traffic flows, concentrations, or access points.

The point here is that this research makes use of our 'digital traces' (see Holmes 2007, Latour 2007) as well as creating online traces of its own (see Rogers 2000); the digital footprint is both means and object of the research. In this sense the *hyperlink* (how texts are linked from one to another) is a key unit of analysis, the way the researcher gets around in digital terms, and an indicator of certain hierarchies (for example, where one website is a central hub, i.e. linked to and from many others).

Hence, like all cartographic instruments, exploratory projects and their underlying operating principles, digital hyperlinking or web-mapping research tools and their programmed rules and procedures are not neutral mining or representational devices. Their conception and deployment are related to an objective notion of what is being looked for.

That said, they are generating new ways of looking at cyberspace and understanding how the internet and web function behind the user interface and content production that preoccupies a large part of online research projects to date. But they are also playing a role in its future architecture. Nonetheless, hyperlinking and web-mapping can be put to use for inquiries where web-embedded relationships or flows rather than traditional content production or producer identities are the main focus.

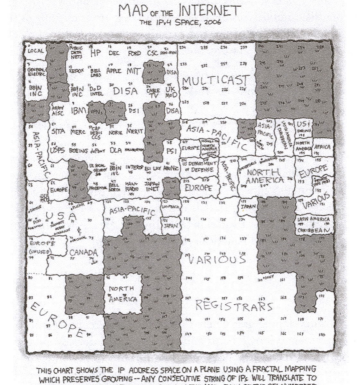

Figure 5.5 Map of the internet

Source: xkcd: http://xkcd.com/

Hypertexts – hyperlink research

The links themselves can also be an object of research. So here the practical issue is how best to isolate and then connect up these relationships which only make sense as digital relationships and in computer-mediated formats; their dynamism and ability to define online power hierarchies are lost in translation onto the written page.

Most researchers rely more than they realize on commercial search engines to do the linking, present the results, and then archive them. As Google dominates at present for navigating the open web, it is difficult for most student researchers to even envisage using another way to get around the web; moreover, specialized ones cost money. Here too, as above, note that no search engine, no matter how effective, is neutral either. They do not work by random selection but are designed according to hierarchies of citation and generate income by embedded forms of ad-tracking.

If your web-based project is relying on a freely available search engine then bear this in mind in terms of the claims you make, where you store the raw data, and your eventual findings as well (see Lazuly 2003, O'Neill 2009, Rogers 2000). As 'Twitter feeds', i.e. the sorts of traffic and content generated by micro-blogging practices and their web-access points, become a common feature, methods to track, collect and then analyze them are also being developed, some based on quantitative indicators and others based on signs, symbols, and relationships.

Website analysis

This is more than simply creating a screenshot and making some general comments. If websites and wider portals are the central focus then you will need to consider how exactly you will set up criteria to study them, why, and to what ends in terms of your research question: Do you need to study:

- How a website is designed; layout, colour, images, multimedia operations?
- How this website is part of a larger conglomeration, may or may not be a 'hub' or more peripheral? Here web-mapping tools may help.
- What people ('users') are doing when visiting this site? Can you gain enough information from user statistics provided or do you need to talk to the moderators? If they are willing can you access the log-files (data of traffic and 'hits'); if you do access these how will you use and then present the information?
- The frequency of visits in general ('hits') or who is visiting and why? Can you do this from the website itself, from your access point? Or do you need to contact these visitors?
- The content itself, either as keyword frequencies or positions using content-analysis coding and interpretation (quantitative and/or qualitative) or in terms of meaning-making?
- What people are saying thematically, as an online space for deliberation or debate or in comparison to offline relationships?
- The more technical features? For example the layers of software design governing functionality or how users can freely contribute.
- The role a website or portal plays in a larger setting? For example, for an international or local NGO? As a fund-raising platform or social mobilization tool?

In other words, web-analysis (a very general term) or website analysis requires a methodical approach that can focus on the interface (what we see onscreen), the traffic coming and going, the stuff that gets produced (uploaded and accessed) on its own terms, the community using and running the site, or behind-the-screen functions. You could combine any of the above but as always it depends on the question. You could also simply treat a website as you would newspaper or television content, to access and code accordingly. That said, websites are always in flux, archives not always consistent or accessible, and user statistics an amalgam of hits, individuals, and double-ups.

Online communities

This is where anthropologists and those using ethnographic approaches have been active from the early days of the web. It is also where traditional ethnographic issues and newer, more digitally inflected issues intersect (see Chapter 6). If your work is based on observation – and so participation by virtue of being online – of a community, a group, or a discussion forum (often part of a larger community) then your project has particular ethical considerations that are longstanding and also embedded in the 'multi-sited' nature of cyberspatial fieldwork: see Chapter 3 and specialized discussions to help you in the initial planning. As you are observing-participating in any online group, or larger community by logging in, accessing or browsing around the site, you too are leaving digital footprints. These in turn can become a 'partial object' in some other research project.

An important corollary to communities online are computer games and virtual worlds, which have existed as long as the internet itself. These comprise all the above features in terms of where to go, how to navigate, and then how to present the material in a traditional dissertation. Not only is there a rich research literature focusing on gaming and virtual worlds in their own right using emerging and longstanding methodologies, but there is also a fast-growing area in IT law and policy analysis that looks at governance mechanisms such as the *terms of use* and the *end user license agreement*. These can be researched in their own right as well as how they are being rewritten and contested within user-groups and gaming communities (see e.g. Gaiser and Schreiner 2009, O'Neill 2009).

As these are new areas, student research is often where some of the most exciting and innovative methodological advances and conceptual debates are emerging right now. These technologies and their everyday, political, and economic impact are those of today's 'Google generation' (see Franklin and Wilkinson 2011, UCL 2008) and this generation is now the upcoming generation of researchers.

SUMMING UP

To some, the online environment as a shifting research environment may feel daunting. We believe, though, that it offers an exciting shift in the possibilities for research and provides a wealth of opportunity.

(Gaiser and Schreiner 2009: 159)

Whilst its basic functions – email, web-browsing or searching, online databases or web portals – remain relatively constant, the internet that concerns researchers these days has quickly become characterized by the multimedia and interactive software platforms that in the first decade of the twenty-first century transformed the largely text-based world-wide web of the 1990s into multimedia, integrated platforms known as 'social networking sites' or 'social media'.

To date (circa 2012) the internet is dominated by a handful of corporate internet service providers and activities; web-search engines (Google), social networking (Facebook), encyclopaedic information (Wikipedia), visual media (YouTube), voice-over-internet-protocol (Skype), email, news and entertainment. Here social networking sites, blogs, increasingly powerful search engines, portals, or instant messaging/ chat/micro-blogging tools like Twitter, and any number of news and entertainment platforms bring with them new opportunities, new topics, and new challenges for researchers (as well as marketers!).

All of the above have only taken root in the last five to six years; relatively recently by even the internet's brief lifespan. How people use standard applications such as email, word-processing packages or search engines, differs widely. There is a tendency for quick judgment about what counts as 'skill' or 'knowledge' with respect to the use and application of the internet and related software or web-based tools for academic research; fashion and trends also contribute to the way successive generations of internet users and developers regard one another, and have variable shelf-lives. What was cutting-edge last week can be yesterday's news by the end of the year.

For this reason alone, it is worth reiterating that familiarity with the latest service or brand is not tantamount to honing sustainable and adaptable internet research skills or developing a feasible online research project. The key objective is to develop internet research skills and online research methodologies that are sustainable and sound, able to deal with change and continuity in this domain.

A word to the wise

At this point, and in view of the way online research methods, ethics, and theoretical frameworks are all very much under construction as today's Web 2.0 makes way for whatever is around the corner, I'd like to close this discussion of internet research skills and emerging online research methodologies, circa 2012, with some general comments about the broader context in which research is being conducted today.

Ownership and control

Ownership and control of the internet, the web, and rights to all that travels through and within these computer-mediated communications are currently in flux, fiercely contested at the highest international level, and increasingly dominated by

Figure 5.6
Cyberpolice!

Source: Chappatte: http://www.globe cartoon.com

commercial interests. In short, and the concerted actions of open-source software activists and advocacy organizations, and *creative commons* countermoves to proprietary property rights law notwithstanding, less and less online is actually free. The price ordinary users and researchers pay for so-called free access, goods and services, is an increasingly sophisticated level of tagging and tracking – surveillance – by corporate and government entities. Whilst such concerns are not new (digital databases and CCTV cameras predate the internet), transparency has a price-tag that is not yet clear.

Electronic privacy and transparency

As an everyday user and researcher, protect your privacy and access to personal information online in ways that make sense to you on the ground. As a socially responsible researcher, laid out in all codes of ethics, you are also obliged to protect the rights and privacy of your research subjects. Lurking online is covert observation; a form of research that is considered unethical, key exceptions notwithstanding. That is for your ethics committee to decide.

Archiving and retrieving digital or web-based data

As noted above, when backing up your work, remember that the internet is a volatile domain; formats change, programs become obsolete, freebies disappear or, worse still, start charging. Keep strategic material close to home and in more than one format as well if you opt to use a server-based archiving service.

Figure 5.7 Welcome to the medium of the future

Source: Nina Paley: http://www.ninapaley.com

Screen-lives

Finally, remember that in cyberspace and computing generally, an everyday version of *Moore's Law* applies.[14] Namely, as readers will note in the cartoon above, in cyberspace the speed in which *things change, links come and go*, is considerably faster than on the ground, as a rule. Successive generations of 'digital natives' assume, like their predecessors, that their user-based knowledge and idiomatic terms are here to say. Not the case; what is new today on the web will be yesterday's news before you know it, perhaps even before a project has been completed.

Further reading

This is an area where the date of publication can be quickly superseded by the latest developments. Nonetheless, as the web did not start in the last five years with the arrival of 'Web 2.0' and its 'social media' there are many insights and principles available that even go back to the 'old days' of the internet, the 1990s.

For discussions based on ethnographic-based or 'digital methods' research, see Franklin (2004), Hine (2000), Latour (2007), Miller and Slater (2000), Rogers (2000).

For more methodological discussions see Dicks et al. (2005), Fink (2009), Gaiser and Schreiner (2009), Hewson et al. (2002), James and Busher (2009), Ó Dochartaigh (2009), and relevant chapters in Silverman (2011).

For recent research-based insights see journals that focus on ICTs and related media such as *Information, Communication, and Society*; *New Media and Society*; *Journal of Information Technology and Politics*; *The Information Society*; *Communication, Culture and Critique*.

NOTES

1 For the record, the bulk of my own research has been in this area. This does not mean to suggest, however, that I have IT training, am a hacker, or a blogger. An engineering degree or software design skills are not prerequisites to conducting online research, or web-constituted topics. What it does mean though is that my own research experience and working knowledge predates those products and services currently falling under the 'Web 2.0' rubric; perhaps that makes me a 'silver surfer' in computer years (see UCL 2008).

2 These have been collected, offered, and overheard from students and colleagues over the years.

3 For instance, a report by Symantec, the anti-virus software developer, in April of 2010, noted that every second 100 attempts are made by hackers, of varying levels of expertise, to break into people's personal data such as online banking codes; with an attempt being successful every 4.5 seconds according to Symantec's calculations. Computer infections with bugs and viruses grew by 71 per cent in 2009; reportedly enabled by programs now being designed to facilitate these sorts of activities. See www.symantec.com/business/ theme.jsp?themeid=threatreport (last accessed 21 April 2010).

4 Here we are picking up the story of Tim Berners-Lee and his colleagues' work at CERN in Switzerland because the internet that concerns us here, and most research students, is

the popularized form of computer-mediated communication known as the world-wide web. This means we are not looking at the preceding, and overlapping roles played by the US military establishment, former vice-president Al Gore's role in promoting a US version of the internet's 'global internet infrastructure', hacker communities and software developers in the USA from the 1970s, and preceding decades when cybernetics ideas and R&D criss-crossed pioneering internet communities and advocates such as the WELL and the Electronic Frontier Foundation on the west coast of the US. Neither are we looking at the role played, and claimed by French IT developers in the 1980s and 1990s who developed an internet prototype, the minitel.

5 That US-based web addresses are generic to the internet and so dispense with the country code relates to the economic and technical dominance of US (state) actors and agencies in its short history; a contentious and cantankerous topic in itself.

6 For example, the.xxx domain name furore (a top-level domain name for adult content), or the consequences for IP addresses as top-level domain names such as .com reach saturation.

7 For more information on web addresses, protocols, and the increasingly important IP (internet protocol) address that is unique to every computer, see Ó Dochartaigh (2009: 69–75). For a good glossary of abbreviations and jargon related to the internet, see Gaiser and Schreiner (2009: 160–4).

8 See Ó Dochartaigh (2009: 28–9).

9 This message can mean several things: a spelling mistake or language-based confusion about spelling, the deletion of the website from the internet, that the URL address has been changed or is no longer in use, or that certain authorities have blocked (censored, or filtered) access to that content. 404 error messages are becoming antiques also, but where they do pop up they are not then end of the story either; sometimes they are temporary glitches, so try again. These two phrases come from two spoofs on this once frequent occurrence; see http://bcn.boulder.co.us/~neal/humor/marvin-the-server-404.html; www.sendcoffee.com/minorsage/404error.html (26 August 2011).

10 For a useful synopsis see Gaiser and Schreiner (2009: 113–14).

11 UCLA: www.ats.ucla.edu/stat/sas/modules/intsas.htm

12 See Chapter 3 for an overview. See also the UK Economic and Social Research Council's 'Research Ethics Framework' at www.esrc.ac.uk/ESRCInfoCentre/Images/ESRC_Re_Ethics_Frame_tcm6–11291.pdf; the UK Social Research Association's 'Ethical Guidelines' at www.the-sra.org.uk/ethical.htm; the UK Government Social Research Unit guidelines at http://www.gsr.gov.uk/downloads/professional_guidance/ethical_assurance/ethics_guidance.pdf

13 Thanks to Marieke Riethof and Jowan Mahmod for noting this double-edged side to anonymity when citing participants by their online handles. Sometimes 'silencing marginalized voices is also a political/ethical choice' when undertaking ethnographic work with marginal online communities (M. Riethof, private email 18 August 2011). Other times, to claim that a nickname is not a real name and so taking the additional step is not necessary in the final report cuts no ice within the community, as 'everyone knows who everyone is already'. Sometimes academic conventions put too much stress on 'transparency' based on civic notions of identity; our 'official' names and 'real name' email addresses (see Franklin 2004, Jones 1999). And sometimes, online visibility is only the tip of the iceberg (see Franklin 2007, O'Neill 2009).

14 *Moore's Law* refers to the – now folkloric – accuracy of the predictive model developed in 1965 by Gordon Moore, co-founder of Intel, the global brand leader in microprocessor manufacturing, that computing power will increase exponentially; doubling every 18 months to 2 years.

PART 2 COPING AND COMMUNICATING

CHAPTER 6

Doing research – gathering data

Topics covered in this chapter:

- Data-gathering techniques review
- Surveys and questionnaires
- Interviews and focus groups
- Ethnographic fieldwork and participant-observation

PREAMBLE: INTRODUCTION TO PART 2

It is a good feeling to get a research inquiry off the drawing board and into motion. As I noted in Chapter 2, being on the road in a research project generates its own pay-off. There is a certain sense of satisfaction to being finally underway in itself, but also because once underway an inquiry starts to generate its own 'critical mass' as we learn more and become more confident about the direction we are taking.

The second part of this book (Chapters 6 to 8) focus on the nitty-gritty of *doing* research; some of which we need to address when planning and designing, and some of which present their own conundrums and decisions to make as we are in the middle of things. In that respect, with the overview of both the main elements and the main stages of a project (Chapter 2) and the survival guide from Chapter 3 in mind, these two chapters walk through selected ways by which researchers generate, gather, and analyse their raw data, or empirical material. These specific techniques along with various intradisciplinary and cross-cutting schools of thought about their respective 'rights' and 'wrongs' are foundational for much research undertaken by student, and faculty-level researchers in the humanities and social sciences.

For the sake of argument the act of gathering and that of analysing our core material have been split. First, this chapter takes a look at established 'rules and procedures' (viz. *methods*) for generating and gathering material directly from social actors; in quantifiable or qualitative form, as existing empirical material (for example, public databases) or data generated by the researcher themselves. Chapter 7 looks at approaches that put the stress on ways to develop and then apply analytical procedures on the activities and outcomes of social interaction. Here the larger object and specific units of analysis are observed – and conceived – as 'content', 'text', or 'discourse'.

In this respect these two chapters work in tandem. Given the range – from highly specialized to more generic methods – available today for achieving all levels of research projects, three distinctions govern the way the material is covered in these chapters:

1   The distinction between ways of generating and gathering data on the one hand and, on the other, analysing this material work in tandem in that the researcher generates and communicates the findings, inferences drawn, and arguments made as knowledge.
2   For methodologies that place analysis centre-stage, the material under investigation could be generated and gathered by the researcher. It can also be pre-existing, pre-sorted publicly available material; for example, a historical archive, set of policy documents, television programme or series.
3   In both cases we see that approaches to certain ways of conducting analysis and how the data is gathered are both interconnected and distinct; for example, notes or transcripts of interviews we conduct can be analysed in several ways. Conversely different sorts of specialized techniques of *visual analysis* apply variously to respective media – still photographs, audio-visual material, film (digital and acetate).

In light of our ongoing goal to understand research as a pragmatic and intellectual endeavour, the areas covered from here on in are selective discussions of principles and techniques that need adjusting and reappraisal perhaps according to their role in your inquiry, the wider context in which you are carrying this out, and the various rights and obligations that these all bring with them.

CHAPTER AIMS AND ORGANIZATION

The aim of this first chapter of Part 2 is to engage with a cluster of techniques that focus on researching human subjects and ways of generating and gathering data particular to but also shared by quantitative and qualitative research sensibilities.

These are (1) surveys and questionnaires; (2) interviews; (3) focus groups; and (4) participant-observation and ethnographic fieldwork. This latter category encompasses the first three as well as denotes a locale for conducting the work by way of varying degrees and levels of (partially or fully immersed) *participant-observation*.

In this chapter and the next, the discussion is along three axes: general principles, practicalities (how-to), and wider methodological considerations. Any 'rules and procedures' presented here are not intended as one-size-fits-all models. Moreover, they are not always compatible in that they encompass both overlapping and divergent ways of assembling evidence; textual or numerical, experiential or performed, spontaneous or produced.

> ****TIP:** As each aspect touches on vibrant literatures and ongoing debates that pertain to both general and highly specialized points of agreement and contradiction within and across even sub-disciplines, you need to become more conversant with these details before committing.

- Some further reading is provided at the end of each section.
- Touch base with mentors and supervisors as need be.
- At some point though, you need to get on with the thing; deal with the outcomes as part of your findings, discussion or argument.
- Trying out some of these techniques as part of a pilot (try-out) can be productive and instructive.

As a bridge, and in light of the last two chapters, the following section reviews key distinctions between data-gathering and analysis as commonly understand by quantitative or qualitative research traditions.

DATA-GATHERING TECHNIQUES – REVIEW

First, *qualitative* data-gathering and analysis entails material that cannot be, or need not be counted:

- Using non-statistical means of collating, analysing the material, and then drawing conclusions.
- This material encompasses 'meanings, concepts, definitions, characteristics, metaphors, symbols, [experiences] and descriptions of things . . . [that] cannot be meaningfully expressed by numbers' (Berg 2009: 3; see also Creswell 2009: 173–6, Gray 2009: 493 *passim*).

Three broad sorts of data-gathering and analysis techniques flow from here:

A *Researching human subjects*: face-to-face and/or computer-mediated contexts; interviews, surveys (small-scale), focus groups, auto-generation of contemporary archives (diaries, narrative work) in settings where the researcher encounters selected individuals or groups at set times and places.

B   *Research in a field, with/within communities or groups* – human and/or virtual; fieldwork carried out by participant and/or observation (partial or full immersion, short-term or long-term) and accompanying records of observations, events, and interactions; the researcher may set up interviews, focus groups and other sorts of spontaneous or premeditated interactions with research subjects close-up and 'in situ'.

C   *Researching documents and other 'social texts'* – hardcopy and/or digital; where the research accesses historical archives, policy documents, visual depositories, online production to conduct forms of content/textual analysis; these texts are treated as self-contained and/or interactively generated written, visual, or multimedia items.

These preferred approaches need not rule out the incorporation of quantitative data-gathering or analysis techniques.

Quantitative data-gathering concentrates on collecting material that is countable or measurable:

- The form the data takes is numerical and is made sense of primarily by the use of techniques of statistical analysis i.e. making *inferences* on the basis of statistical probability.
- Research designs in these cases are largely set up to test *hypotheses* to make informed generalizations about past behaviours, or generate predictive models (see Berg 2009: 342).
- Data is collected under controlled conditions in standardized and replicable ways; in both a large scale and smaller scale
- Automated analytical tools and the requisite skills required to use them go hand-in-hand.
- Many quantitative projects make use of publicly available data sets; for example, national census results, government statistics.

These sorts of techniques and their accompanying conditions need not exclude qualitative sorts of data or their application in mixed-method projects.

A   *Survey-based research on human subjects*: large-scale questionnaires and/or standardized interviews comprise this work; media effects, audience research, and media uses (for example, ratings, website clicks) make use of these techniques; combination and comparisons of existing data sets, for example elections, census results, land and survey data, apply statistical and modelling techniques as well.

B   *Content analysis*: the counting, codifying, and collating of quantifiable manifest content of written text; for example, keywords, 'nearest neighbour' analysis (e.g. relationship between negative terminology and terms such as 'teenage boys' or 'homeless people'. For web-based texts, this also entails the counting and coding of hyperlinks and online 'hubs' as visualizations of quantifiable web-uses (search engine results, tweets, web-link 'hubs').

C   *(Quasi-) experimental*: to test behaviour under entirely controlled – laboratory – conditions (experimental); social scientists also set up semi-controlled (quasi-) experiments, for example, on the effect of violent images on subjects' neurological or physiological readings.[1]

As noted above, these are not necessarily mutually exclusive approaches. For instance:

- some initial survey work can isolate potential interviewees for more in-depth interviews, prepare the ground for focus-group work;
- a discourse analysis of the sub-text of a particular sub-set or genus of government policy-making could be accompanied by a comprehensive content-analysis of recurring or significant keywords or phrases;
- policy-makers could be interviewed to provide the 'back-story' of the drafting process.

This is not to suggest that all combinations are equally feasible, all data-gathering techniques viable for all research questions in an unproblematic way. It is up to you to consider the implications of each approach for *your* inquiry; some data and the ways to collect them suit certain research questions better than others, others are more adaptable, others require more set-up time whilst others may be easier to carry out but produce copious amounts of data to process and analyse. It should be apparent by now just how mobile and intransigent some of these distinctions can be within and across academic disciplines and geographies.

Let's start with a mainstay of much social research and, arguably an approach that exemplifies the quantitative modes of gathering and analysing large amounts of data: conducting surveys based on standardized questionnaires.

SURVEYS AND QUESTIONNAIRES[2]

Surveys are suitable when a researcher is looking to capture attitudes, opinions, or gain insight into how people behave (based on what people tell you). When the aim is to gather this information from a large group of people, survey instruments – based on questionnaires and the statistical collation of the findings – are a well-established practice.

Second, surveys are used to garner detailed information in order to describe a particular population; national census surveys are one example. Survey work presumes that the population it looks to study is accessible and available for surveying; for example, by phone, on foot (door-to-door polling for instance), or online via the web or emails.

General principles

The optimal survey instrument you use or adapt for your inquiry is one that can generate as accurate a representation of the people's opinions, preferences, or behaviours as possible. The information yielded comes in three broad categories:

1 Reports of fact: self-disclosure of basic information (demographic for instance) such as age, gender, education level, income, behaviour (for example, which candidate voted for).

2   Ratings of people's opinions or preferences: responses gathered here are evaluative in response to a statement; for example, levels of satisfaction, agreement, dislikes (e.g of television programmes, or university course evaluations).

3   Reports of intended behaviour: here the questions would be asked in such a way as to get people to disclose their motivations, or intentions about some action (for example, likeliness or willingness to buy or use a product if it were offered in a certain way).

Most of us have probably been asked to participate in a survey at some point in our lives; agreeing or refusing as well. So, recall how you yourself may have chosen to respond, or not respond to any of the above sorts of surveys by lecturers, marketers, or pollsters, and remember when compiling your own survey questions or approaching others! In everyday life, journalism, marketing, and political surveys such as public opinion polls generate important data sets for use in the social sciences. Large or small, the promises held out by survey work come with a number of trade-offs.

First the up-side. Survey work can be:

1   An effective way to represent opinions across a population/s as well as representing information about individuals and groups of people. They provide the means by which researchers can describe populations they cannot, or need not directly observe or personally interact with.

2   This approach comes with a large literature that debates and lays out the generic and disciplinary-specific rules and procedures for effective data-gathering and their quantitative analysis. The aim is that the results can be replicated by others; rerun and reanalysed as need be.

3   A productive way to ascertain baseline information about a group for more in-depth interviewing, or focus group work. In other words, survey work is not necessarily the antithesis of qualitative modes of analysis.

The downside of survey work is that

1   Drawing *causal inferences* from limited survey-based observations is difficult. On a larger scale, the premise that probability sampling best proves or predicts human behaviour is an ongoing debate (see Ginsberg 1986, Lewis 2001, Lippmann 1998).

2   A survey stands and falls, whether it is large or small-scale, on the strength of its questions; weakly formulated or inappropriate questions create unsatisfactory results and response-rates.

3   People can misreport; deliberately or through carelessness, lack of attention; in long surveys especially.

4   Moreover, many people do not want to do surveys. In short, getting an adequate response rate for the population you want to survey is not a pre-given, it takes work.

5   People can react differently to the same question; culturally ambiguous or controversial questions can generate strong emotions (see also the discussion of interviews below).

On deciding whether or not to embark upon a survey, large or small, note that for inquiries looking to find out what people think or experience, or those based on how people behave or interact in groups, whether this is in a simulated or naturalistic setting or over time, survey instruments will not produce the sort of data you are looking for; participant-observation, focus group work, or perhaps an experiment may well be better suited.

Practicalities

Key practicalities entail being clear about the difference between (1) the *population* for the survey and the *sampling* of that population (not all surveys study all things equally); (2) different ways of administering a survey; (3) sorts of questions and question design; and (4) the need for pre-testing before carrying out the survey proper.

Sampling

This refers to the selection made once the researcher has established the *population* from whom they will contact a group of respondents; the size and composition of the sample relates to the aims and objectives of the inquiry. Basically, you need to ascertain the characteristics of the target population, and how many from that population you need/want to survey.

- This implies that the sample should be *representative*, i.e. that all possible permutations of the population are accounted for within the sample. *Representative samples* generally permit stronger generalizations in the final analysis; one reason why *random sampling* is indispensable for larger survey instruments.
- Once you have drawn up a comprehensive list of identifiers for this population you can then sample; for example, one population could be international students; comprised of students from respective countries, doing different sorts of study, speaking different languages or coming from one area/language group. You may need to include the age-range, academic background, gender, and income-support relevant to this larger population, and so on.

In short, populations need to be clarified in terms of the research question. Moreover, the criteria by which you designate your sample are not always self-explanatory.

- You need to define your population clearly before setting out; then consider how to sample, by random or other means.
- A sample here can be arrived at from a population systematically as well as randomly. For example, by putting all the names of all international students enrolled in your programme in a hat and picking out the first ten, or more.

This brings us to the various *types of samples*. There are several sorts of samples along the spectrum, from fully random to highly selective.

- Samples based on *statistical probability*, based on the assumption that every element or unit in the population has some likelihood – a *non-zero probability* – of being in the sample.
- The thing to note here is that *only samples based on probability can be analysed according to theories of probability, including statistical estimations of margins of error.* In short, if your sample is not based on probability/forms of random selection, then applying an advanced level of statistical analysis on your findings is inappropriate.
- This does not mean to say that other samples are not possible, particularly for smaller projects. Samples based on *non-probability* include:
  - Starting with your own friends and then their friends in what is called the *snowballing* technique is a popular and useful one.
  - Or using your classmates in what is a *sample-of-convenience* can also generate some interesting results.
  - As can more targeted forms like *quota sampling*; for example, asking students from one part of the world within a certain age group to respond up to a certain total, or
  - What some call *accidental sampling* (for example, on-the-street surveys that stop passers-by or whoever is sitting near you in the canteen).
  - Another sort of sample is to consciously select key actors; those figures who are important to an event or decision-making process; for example, registered participants in an international summit; cabinet members or civil servants.
- Often used alongside other, qualitative forms of data-gathering and analysis, non-probability samples can provide useful insights. Any conclusions drawn are done so on the basis that these are not random samples and so basing these claims on this level of representativeness is conditional.

This brings us to the next major decision (best taken before setting out, by the way).

How big should a sample be?

The first response to this question for individual researchers is that the size of your sample depends on time and cost restraints as well as the nature of your research question and role any survey is to play in the larger inquiry.

Size also relates to how much precision is required. For instance, larger samples selected on the basis of probability, or high-response rates from a surveyed population (for example, a class of students evaluating a course) provide more bases for generalizations; the larger the sample the closer it correlates with the population. This is why more heterogeneous populations (for example, national citizenries) require larger sample sizes to make sense.[3] Sometimes the answer to how large your survey needs to be can be ascertained by doing a pilot survey and considering the viability of not only any results but the response rate.

Figure 6.1 Surveys – a waste of time

Source: Fran Orford: http://www.francartoons.com

Methodological considerations

How you administer any survey, large or small, based on probability or not, requires some forethought and experimentation. Likewise for designing the questions and which questions to ask; readily available survey tools and services on the web do not get you around this part of the work; a survey tool is not in itself a method. The main pros and cons of survey work were discussed above.

Two other points relate to broader methodological considerations when doing survey work as well as ascertaining whether this approach is best-suited to your inquiry.

Modes of administration

A survey can be administered by getting people to do it themselves or by asking them the questions directly. Although the former is more convenient, and greatly enhanced by web-based or email access to potentially ever-expanding populations out there in global cyberspace, it is worth considering the trade-offs for each approach.

1   *Self-administered* surveys see subjects responding to ready-made questionnaires, digital being the most efficacious at the data-gathering point. Here respondents can be asked longer, more complex, or even visually-based questions they can answer at their leisure and without influence from others around them (not the case in classroom evaluation surveys!).

But this is the downside: little direct control over the administration, the need for questions to be well-designed, all contingencies covered, and with respondents who will understand the questions asked. No point carrying out a text-based survey with people who cannot read or write at the requisite level (very young children, non-literate people). For projects looking to ask open-ended questions which generate complex and diverse responses, then reconsider, or consider how you will process this information in the eventual analysis and presentation.

Figure 6.2 Don't have a category for that

Source: Joseph Farris:
http://www.josephfarris.com

"Sorry, but we don't have a category for that."

2   *Directly administered* – on-the-spot or phone interviews – are ways of carrying out a survey when you approach respondents personally. The advantage here is that there is a greater chance of getting full cooperation in completing the survey. You can also be sure that all questions are answered, answered adequately or after due thought.

The downside is that this approach is time-consuming and expensive; why marketing and polling research projects using phone-based surveys have huge teams and big budgets. You also need to have the skills to deal with cold calling and negative responses from the public when approached for face-to-face surveys; not everyone appreciates being approached in this way.

3   *Online/digital surveys and questionnaires*: It may seem self-explanatory, especially for cash-strapped students, that these days email, instant messaging, or texting are the best way to access people; email lists, address-books, or your own Facebook group providing a ready-made sample for you to use.

However, issues about sampling aside (see above) many a researcher has discovered that email-based and even more user-friendly web-based survey tools do not always provide satisfactory results.

•   Email surveys: The upside is that they can be sent directly to a respondent, with an automated receipt-acknowledgement message built in. They are low-cost, easy to design (cut-and-paste the questions into the message or attach a file); easy to return as well, a click of the reply button only, and require little technical skill to administer on that level. However, there are several catches:

- Because of the do-it-yourself and text-based formats of emails and pasted-in questions the design can be simplistic and unattractive to people, many of whom have over-charged inboxes already. Email surveys need to be short, very short, to get any response rate.
- Once received, the researcher then has to copy the results into some sort of spreadsheet, create a database in order to analyse, and then present the findings in graphic form. Straightaway the chances of data-entry error and escalating time taken to do this work presents a major impediment to effective execution.
- Before administering, all email addresses need to be valid, requiring preparation time. Moreover, if the results are supposed to be anonymous – a basic premise of most survey work – emails immediately undermine this principle. Some respondents may trust the researcher to treat their responses in confidence, but in many cases people respond differently to anonymous and non-anonymous surveys.

4 *Web-based survey instruments*: These products and services (see Chapter 5) deal with many of the above problems in email surveys; layout options allow for higher production values and attractiveness for easy use. They collect, collate, and statistically analyse the data for you. Their question templates are very helpful in framing questions and ordering them in the best way for your purposes; try-outs and revisions are possible before launching the survey itself. Anonymity can be integrated into the responses, and research populations are accessible by virtue of being on the web (assuming the survey is placed in the right spot to reach them).

However, note that whilst they are very cost-effective for surveys of ten questions or less, samples of 100 respondents or less (as is the case with Survey Monkey), graphics and extended analyses require annual subscriptions and these can be costly.

- If you rely on these tools to do the 'dirty work' for you then these additional costs may be a disadvantage. You still need to do the legwork to ensure you get enough responses to warrant this outlay.
- As web-surveys become more common, sent to respondents via email, you may well find yourself with similarly low responses. Moreover, a web-survey product does not do the question formulation for you. Nor does it resolve any major deficiencies with your initial sample or unsuitable questions.
- Finally, these tools are not failsafe; technical problems can arise and render them non-functioning, links inactive.

These drawbacks notwithstanding, web-based survey tools are handy research aids; a good way of teaching yourself the basics of survey design and actually quite fun to set up and carry out. Fancy formatting aside, how useful the findings are for your project in the final analysis is up to you to ascertain.

BOX 6.1 CURRENT WEB-BASED SURVEY TOOLS AND RESOURCES

Where these options come into play are covered in Chapter 5. For easy reference though, consider these useful services:

www.zipsurvey.com
www.surveymonkey.com
www.questionpro.com/web-based-survey-software.html
www.createsurvey.com/demo.htm
http://lap.umd.edu/survey_design/questionnaires.html

On doing so, be sure to check the terms and conditions of use, access, and storage; including registration fees and licensing.

Questionnaire design

The results you get depend too on the types of questions and response formats you opt for. Here there are two basic categories: open-ended and closed-ended questions. Each has their uses and disadvantages.

- *Closed-ended questions*: These are recognizable as a list of predetermined, acceptable responses for respondents to select from. These create more reliable answers for quantifying purposes. For these reasons they lend themselves to relatively straightforward analysis. However, it could be that a respondent's choice is not among listed alternatives, which defeats the purpose. They also generate the sorts of responses that are meaningful to the researcher and question. However, because these questions tend to be most closely allied to the researcher's intentions, closed-ended questions may be simply generating self-fulfilling findings, the kind of response wanted.
- *Open-ended questions*: These are formulated so as to permit respondents freedom to answer a question in their own words (without pre-specified alternatives). These allow for unanticipated rather than predictable answers. They may also reflect respondents' thoughts and worldviews better and so provide incentive to complete the survey. They also help when you find yourself composing a closed-ended question that has an excessively long list of possible answers. For *action research* project designs, these sorts of question can also move the project forward in ways that make sense to those who will be involved in the outcome; for example, company department, hospital ward, community group.[4]

Administering surveys

The above section on question design can be summarized as rules of thumb for doing survey work; also relevant to more standardized formats for interviewing and focus-group work, which are discussed below. Whilst off-the-shelf and web-based survey tools go a long way in coaching survey makers in this regard, you will save time and headaches by ensuring that that when setting up (semi-) standardized *questionnaires* you aim to

- ask clear, easy to understand questions; how you word the questions will provide incentive or discourage responses; for example, avoid double negatives or long preambles;
- provide a clear estimate of time needed to complete the survey (less rather than more is an incentive);
- provide an orderly organization of the questionnaire, i.e. what logic are you following, are your questions consistent? Differences in responses are supposed to relate to differences amongst respondents, not inconsistencies, ill-defined terminology, objectionable or irrelevant questions;
- begin with easier, information-based questions; move from the general to the more specific;
- formulate questions that make sense to the population and respondents, i.e. know your population; consider the context and attitudes in which your questions may be taken;
- keep the list short, if you can; do you really need more than ten questions? Do you really need so many sub-questions?
- allow for expressions of variability, and include the 'don't know', or 'neutral' response in multi-choice questions;
- try mixing up the sorts of questions between single answer to multiple answers to avoid *response bias*. Minimize questions that generate judgmental responses (unless this is the aim, in which case a survey may not be the best approach).

BOX 6.2 OVERVIEW – MODES OF SURVEY ADMINISTRATION

- questionnaires: standardized/non-standardized or semi-structured
- face-to-face interviews
- face-to-face administering of questionnaires
- telephone interviews
- (snail)mailing/manual distribution of printed questionnaire
- emailing/web-based questionnaire.

When designing a questionnaire, or indeed setting up interviews and focus groups (see the section on interviews) always do a try-out, on yourself and some others, before launching the survey; at the very least have your supervisor take a look. Take a second look yourself, for the first version is seldom the final one. This includes always checking the spelling, grammar, and other factors (for example, culturally insensitive formulations). Get some feedback on the questions before going public. Your survey will be better for it.

Be prepared for a disappointing response, or no response. If responses are not what you expected consider whether this is down to the questions or, in fact, whether these findings are results. If your project depends on survey results then ensuring an effective dissemination and working on getting responses requires time and energy. Even for limited surveys, set-up and administration time can often be in reverse proportion to the final outcome and role in the dissertation.

On that note, while surveys can be both challenging, stimulating and fun to compile and carry out, you may need to ask yourself whether you need to generate these data yourself. Have you considered using or searching for existing survey data? There are several reasons for this, including:

1   The quality of the data is more likely to be higher in that these surveys have been carried out by established agencies or research teams, questions tested and samples larger.
2   Why reinvent the wheel when you can use, adapt, or be inspired by these surveys? That said, the results usually require a level of skill in reading complex data-analysis packages, and being able to assess the findings and discussions of published work on these surveys. Nonetheless, public-access databases are out there, more on more coming online all the time.[5]

BOX 6.3 CHECKLIST BEFORE TAKING OFF

- Does survey-data already exist? Can it give you ideas for questions?
- Know your population, understand your sample.
- Ask good and appropriate questions.
- Be aware of alternative formulations of your questions and related responses.
- Choose an appropriate mode of administering the survey.
- Analyse the findings, don't just reiterate the tables and figures.

Analysing responses

More on these points in the next chapter. Suffice it to say that the basic steps for analysing the responses and then working with results of larger surveys where statistical analysis and random selection govern the design proceeed as follows:

- Collate results by producing tables/graphs.
- Make sense (and double-check) the numbers.
- Write up the analysis – at least one or two paragraphs per table.
- This is also when you need to pay attention to writing up exactly how you went about the survey, and why; the methodological/data-gathering methods section.

Survey work across the divide

Formalized ways of gathering personal data from human subjects also provide invaluable information for qualitatively inflected research inquiries. The basic rules and procedures follow those outlined above. Incorporating surveys can be suitable for:

- Research projects that need to generate baseline knowledge, as a preparatory phase in setting up focus groups, or (self-)selected interview candidates; an initial survey can cover a lot of ground.
- As pilot research; to clarify whether the object of research, and related research question are feasible, i.e. doable in the time and with the resources available. The difference lies, however, in the relative weight given to the statistical analysis of the survey results, questionnaire design, relative size of the sample and sampling technique used.

In light of the downside of survey work covered above, take note that

- For research projects that produce or focus on textual material, for example, responses provided to open-ended questions, the time needed to carry out a survey and eventual results may need to take the back seat in the final analysis.
- If survey results are a lead-in to in-depth interviews and/or focus-group work then the collating of these transcripts and how their analysis is woven into the presentation of your findings and analysis are more important than a lengthy account of the survey itself; the usual requirements of your methodological explication notwithstanding.
- Even when web-based survey tools and services do the work for you here (as noted above), a common misjudgment is to still lean on these outcomes too heavily on what may well be relatively modest findings. The end result can be that the more substantive, and for these projects more interesting material (for example, transcripts of people talking about complex personal issues) is left under-analysed, less well-presented.

"I can prove it or disprove it! What do you want me to do?"

Figure 6.3 I can prove or disprove it. . .

Source: http://Vadlo.com

- Statistical analysis is more than the final percentages spat out by the program you may be using here; the numbers are not in themselves a conclusion and percentages are just that, percentages (see Berg 2009: 181, Eberstadt 1995).

If a survey is in fact the bulk of the research then the sampling technique, questionnaire design, size of the sample, and eventual findings and analysis thereof move you into more specialized, statistically-based forms of research. This then requires you to be well enough versed in the finer points of survey design and execution to make the point relative to your research question, aims and objectives.

Summing up

You can still carry out survey-based research, if not make use of survey work available in the public domain, if you keep in mind the following ground rules for achieving and evaluating good quality quantitative analysis:

1 The first step is to keep a record and then clearly report the process by which the data are generated. In this respect, you need to be sure that you understand the procedures required to get this information; for example, constructing a standardized questionnaire or basic knowledge of sampling and statistical analysis (even if the actual number-crunching is done for you by automated tools such as Survey Monkey).

2 Aim to collect data on as many observable implications as possible within the timeframe and scope of the investigation; extrapolating from one, or limited observations unawares could undermine the strength of your eventual conclusions if not taken into account in the set-up and execution; for example, omitting to consider age, occupation, or gender in the survey yet drawing conclusions which assume, or could be influenced by these indicators.

3 This means that you need to aim at maximizing the *validity* of the measures by assuring that you have 'good indicators'; meaning indicators that actually measure what you intend to measure with respect to your inquiry, and governing hypothesis.

4 Maximize the *reliability* of the measures; for instance make sure that all measures are consistent in themselves (e.g. measures of frequency are different from total measures), and *consistently* applied. This means to say that applying the same procedure in the same way should always produce the same measure; double-check or retrace your steps before drawing conclusions.

5 Make sure that all data produced is *replicable*; others may wish, or need to follow the procedures used to arrive at the same data and thereby engage with, or reconsider your findings.

6 For smaller samples (for example, a limited survey), beware of over-using percentages in order to suggest a larger sample and more significance than may be the case. In short, a percentage value is not necessarily more legitimate than a more qualitative assessment when the group interviewed or surveyed is a small one; if you have responses from only ten people for instance, it makes more sense to talk about 'one out of ten surveyed responded to the negative' rather than '10 per cent . . .'. Percentages need only be cited up to the first decimal point for medium-

sized samples, and rounded up for smaller. Basically, a percentage does not tell the story; statistical values provided to the 'nth' decimal point are not an indicator of accuracy or efficacy in itself.

Finally, as is the case across the board, trial and error, 'pilot research' in other words, before embarking on the formal data-collection phase is indispensable; standardized questionnaires need trying out, interview questions revised and tried out on willing guinea-pigs, software programs practised and applied in try-out examples.

Further reading

Useful overviews are in Fowler (2002), Harkness et al. (2003). A review of web-based surveys is in Couper (2000); principles for asking sensitive questions are covered by Tourangeau and Smith (1996); Baehr (1980) is an example of surveys using in-depth interviewing; Lewis (2001) is a look at mass surveys and their role in public opinion research from the 'other side'; for a cultural studies perspective see Deacon (2008); Deacon et al. (2007) address surveys for communications research.

INTERVIEWS

Whilst some surveys are based on interviews, this section looks at interviews as a generic form of data-gathering in their own right.

Interviews conducted without depending on a standardized questionnaire are a well-known and productive way to gain insights from people, those in the know, ordinary people, or particular groups. A derivative of interviews – *focus groups* – is particularly popular in media and communications, business studies, and marketing. Some of the same rules of thumb laid out in the previous section apply to setting up and designing interviews and interview questions.

Interview and focus-group research generates large amounts of textual, including visual and audio material, the content of which requires time and attention to sorting and analysing the data, either in quantifiable form (word/phrase frequencies or volume) or by other, interpretative means; see Chapter 7. A combination of analytical interventions is possible, interpreting and then making use of interview material in strictly qualitative inquiries is heavy on text, citations as well as the commentary on them. In both cases, transcripts of interviews are your raw data.

General principles

As Berg puts it, interviewing is 'simply conversation with a purpose' (2009: 101). As such they are a core ingredient of much social research, the bread and butter of news and entertainment journalism, and used in various forms extensively in market research.

In distinction to large-scale and medium-sized surveys based on anonymous questionnaires or polling, a research interview is generally held between two persons.

It can be highly structured, using standardized questionnaires, relatively formal along a set of prepared questions, or very informal where interviewer and interviewee engage in an undirected conversation. The form an interview takes, its role in the data-gathering phase, and thereby decisions about how many interviews are sufficient for any project, depend once again on the aims and objectives of the inquiry; what sort of research question is at stake and what sort of information is being sought?

There are various ways of demarcating various sorts of interviews along with related techniques and reasons for undertaking each approach (see Berg 2009: 105, Gray 2009: 371). This discussion clusters them into three broad approaches, all of which are open to adaptation and the unexpected in real-life research scenarios. Three concerns are shared by all sorts of interview formats and their methodological implications:

1 Research interviews take many forms and can be carried out in various ways (for example, face-to-face, by phone, or using VOIP services). They will produce middling to large amounts of text (the transcripts or notes), all of which may not be pertinent to the inquiry, or able to be analysed as/in the findings. Individual differences in insight, experience, and knowledge amongst interview subjects provide concurring and conflicting ideas and perceptions of the topic on hand. This diversity is what non-standardized interviews are made of; in contrast to standardized formats conducted as part of larger-scale surveys which are, by definition, designed to elicit consistent sets of answers available for statistical analysis.

2 What is the 'right' number of interviews to carry out is a question of degree level as well as research design; some projects conduct one to several interviews to add 'flavour' or nuance to other findings whilst others (particularly at Ph.D. level) rest on more substantial numbers of interviews, or more in-depth explorations requiring varying amounts of time to complete the interview and corresponding amounts of text produced per session. This material – the interview data – then needs sorting, coding, and eventual analysis of these findings.

3 Interviews, whilst popular and convenient, are not mandatory for every qualitative research project looking to engage with people yet not undertake surveys. Moreover, having contacts or knowing people in the organization or activity you want to study does not presuppose that they will make suitable interviewees for the project in themselves. Interviewees do not provide ready-made conclusions; far from it. An individual's view is partial by definition, although some individuals may have more overview than others. Nominating interviews as a primary source of data may not be sufficient as an articulation of your methodology in itself, unless they form the core research component. Even then they need explication in design terms.

As is the case with survey design, interview questions require time and thought, and try-outs should be done before the research proper can begin. This is important because the working assumption in these sorts of interviews is that what respondents say they do is in fact what they do, or what they feel, so questions need to elicit an appropriate response (see Berg 2009: 105). Below is an overview of the different forms interviews can take, with accompanying pros and cons.

Standardized formal interviews

The working assumption here is that all respondents need to understand and respond to questions in a similar enough way so that responses can be collated in quantifiable terms, and then statistically analysed; the inferences drawn will then depend on the size and composition of the sample. When the researcher is looking for clear answers from, usually but not exclusively, a relatively large group of respondents – for example, news and entertainment preferences, shopping habits, voting behaviour, public opinion polling – 'how often', 'when', and 'what' sorts of questions, singular or multi-choice, characterize this category. Standardized interviews are particularly suitable for research questions interested in gaining information, or in ascertaining the views, attitudes, or behaviour of respondents in a controlled manner; hence their use in survey work such as polling and market research; telephone-based research uses standardized questionnaires for one-to-one interviews that are randomly selected.

This format is not suitable for interviews premised on the interviewer playing a substantial role in the conversation and in that respect jointly generating the 'raw' material to be analysed. Open-ended, narrative-based or autobiographical sorts of inquiry do not lend themselves to standardized interview formats. This because the aim with this degree of formality in the interview is to obtain a standardized response, cover a particular territory, or ascertain a trend or set of behaviours across the sample; political pollsters use this format to good effect. Here the findings, and quality of the analysis, stand or fall on correctly formulated questions. You cannot collate or compare results across (groups of) respondents if the questions are too 'fuzzy', open to many sorts of answers, involve question and answer forms such as the interviewer asking 'why?', or ' tell me more about that', or if a crucial question has been omitted.

Semi-standardized formal interviews

Most interviews are formalized, somewhat artificial interactions in that the researcher has approached their interlocutor with a clear aim in mind, then assumed the lead by steering the conversation. However, working with human subjects brings with it always a degree of the unexpected; this too is accounted for in standardized formats through the 'don't know', or 'neutral' response category. In practice, most interview situations are a subtle interplay between interviewer and interviewee; both an explicit agreement between the two parties, based on *informed consent*, about the reason for undertaking the interview, and an implicit sort of 'meaning-making occasion' for both (see Chapters 3 and 5; Berg 2009: 104). This is why interviewees are known to go on record, or comment afterwards about how the interview generated new ideas, insights or even memories for them as well.

The most popular sort of interview is the semi-standardized, or semi-structured one to which the researcher-interviewer brings a set of predetermined questions, or a line of questioning to the meeting. Sometimes the interviewee requests, or can be sent these questions in advance. In any event the interviewer comes prepared for the respondent to digress, or for the direction of the interview to change along the way. How far the interviewer allows the interview to develop in various directions, or judges when it is time to return to the main theme, or lets the interviewee take control of the conversation (this can be consciously or unconsciously) depends not only on the sort of information the researcher wants to elicit but also the underlying rationale of the project.

In less structured settings, interviewers also need to contend with those moments when a line of questioning becomes too sensitive, a question misunderstood or tensions develop between the interviewer and interviewee; some questions may be out of bounds for official reasons (as with government officials), emotional or cultural ones (traumatic memories or inappropriate references by the interviewer). Sometimes the conversation generates less 'significant' material; but how insignificant may well require closer analysis at a later date.

Non-standardized, informal interviews

At the other end of the spectrum from the standardized interview/questionnaire format, and moving away from the more directive even if more open-ended approach of the semi-structured interview, are scenarios that consciously forego a preconceived set of questions, or expectations about the response.

- *Narrative research* is one approach where the flow and content of the interviewee's contribution is left to them, their words not directed or interrupted (more or less) by the interviewer.
- Another example is during fieldwork in which participant-observation is a key element in the data-gathering (see below). Here researchers often find themselves undertaking informal interviews when they ask people questions 'on the fly'; this approach (when handled ethically) allows for people to talk about what interests them in a less stilted way than a more formal interview moment; these are research interactions that can provide interesting insights, add nuance to a proceeding, or provide another standpoint into the research topic.

Sometimes, however, informal interviews do not start out as such; semi-formal interviews can often morph into one-on-one conversations. Whether this is desirable or not is a moot point and many first-timer research interviews can end up like this. Either way the net result is that the more informal the interview, the greater the input the researcher will have into the material generated. This affects how the same researcher handles the eventual material in the analysis phase. Indeed, it often takes a supervisor or examiner to notice that these sorts of interview transcripts often provide important insight into the researcher's underlying motivations of the research, their assumptions and goals predicating the interviewee's input.

When applied consciously, the unstructured approach is also suitable for certain sorts of settings: with people who may not feel comfortable or respond well to a more formal interview format, for example, those in unfamiliar cultural contexts, or disadvantaged groups. That said, the principles of informed consent and anonymity for these sorts of interactions still need to make sense within the working principles of research codes of ethics (see Chapter 3, sixth section).

Cutting across these generic types is another designation: in-depth interviews. By definition these involve interviews with fewer people, over a longer period of time albeit not necessarily, or spread out over several meetings rather than one single comprehensive interview (see Berg 2009: 119–21). In normal parlance, when a research project undertakes 'in-depth' interviews the researcher/s is working at the semi-unstructured part of the spectrum.

Administration

A number of the practical considerations when preparing and carrying out interviews, whatever the eventual format you opt for, overlap those for surveys and questionnaire design. Others are specific to the more open-ended structure and expectations of the sort of material interviews will generate.

(a) Preparation matters: Preparing a set of questions, including the key topics you want to discuss as well as basic information about your interviewees, is highly advisable for all but the most open-ended sorts of research interview. Even the latter requires preparation; more on this below.

That said, note that for most interviews, even the most well crafted questions can and will provide all sorts of responses; from different people and sometimes from the same person as they contradict or correct themselves during or after the interview.

The output of the interview – recordings and/or notes – can also vary; some highly relevant for the research question, some digressing, and some challenging as interviewees take the researcher and the topic on. Sometimes they render little material because they digress, or because interviewees – as humans are wont to do – find ways of avoiding the topic.

At the outset of an interview the interviewer needs to establish rapport. This can be small talk or by way of preliminary information-eliciting questions (see Berg 2009: 112–17) before the more substantial questioning begins. Later, as you analyse the outcome, note how silence or diversions in the conversation can also speak volumes; comparable to a statistically significant result in standardized questionnaires in the 'not applicable', 'no opinion', 'neutral', or 'don't know' category.

(b) Sorts of questions: Again, these practicalities overlap those for questionnaire design. For interviews based on qualitative sorts of questioning (i.e. open-ended rather than closed-ended questions and fewer of them), working on how to formulate as well as order the questions you want to ask helps you focus and refine your core questions; gets you to consider closely why exactly it is you are engaging this sort of interaction. Bearing in mind general pointers about question formulation, pitfalls to avoid when conducting interviews across a range of formats and context include:

- Asking double-barrelled, or overly complex questions.
- Over-lengthy preambles when in fact you are looking for a specific response to a specific question.

- Culturally inappropriate or 'red flag' questions or formulations; for example, some settings require preambles to questions (i.e. the reverse of the above). In others being too abrupt can create barriers. In others certain sorts of questions can be red flags; for example, Berg talks about how Americans can respond negatively to the question 'Why?' (see Berg 2009: 118).
- Lack of facility with group-lingo or jargon which means you miss cues, sub-texts, non-verbally conveyed information, or misinterpret these later on.
- Not being up to speed with key issues of concern for your respondents – revealing your ignorance of the terrain does not enamour you to busy respondents.
- Losing your orientation when interviewing experienced people (for example, politicians, corporate executives, media professionals) who can obstruct the flow, take over the interview (by asking you questions instead), or use the range of human ways to avoid answering the question, (un)consciously (see Goffman, in Berg 2009: 128).
- Sometimes persistence is not a good thing. Showing respect for a person's non-response may be wiser. You can try again later by gently probing but don't insist.
- Taking everything that is said as the primary message when in fact this could be simply what is for the record; note any differences between on-the-record and off-the-record comments when talking to officials (government or corporate representatives).

(c) Sorts of settings – which is best? I often get asked by student researchers setting out to conduct interviews about the right, correct setting for an interview. As research becomes increasingly predicated on information and communication technologies, web-based media, products and services, the convenience of VOIP services (Skype being by far the most popular at time of writing) for interview purposes appear a given, yet create uncertainty about their validity.

(i) Interviews conducted over the phone, Skype included, are perfectly legitimate particularly if time and resources are limited for a face-to-face appointment. If the interview is to be recorded, then this practicality needs to be prepared for in advance. Otherwise it is down to the researcher to take notes as they ask and listen. Phone interviews are also acceptable; sometimes people respond better in mediated rather than face-to-face settings.

(ii) Emails have become a cost-effective and shortcut way of generating interview material. Strictly speaking this is not an interview. However, a Q&A session conducted by email for those willing or preferring this form of interaction can be productive too. Note here though that the material produced is already written (versus spoken) text. Some email interactions see the respondents spending a lot of time writing and editing their responses. This is a gift for the researcher who 'only' needs to read and analyse, code and interpret.

(iii) Written responses to written interview questions do require a different level of engagement with the text, though, than with the transcript or interview notes of a spoken session where memory of the voice, setting and other factors can add nuance (and this is why taking side-notes is useful). Not worse necessarily, just different. That said, the point of an interview for many is the spoken word, spontaneity and human interactive aspect.

But rather than set up premature hierarchies of value, the setting and manner for conducting the interviews, or mixture thereof, bears noting and considering in the set-up phase and eventual analysis and methodological explication. In this respect the variety of computer-mediated and technological mediations for facilitating interviews (including here video-conferencing or web-conferencing) are there to use. There is also research that has research interviews and focus groups (see the section on focus groups) conducted in purely online settings: virtual worlds (for example, Second Life) and between avatars. Again, this depends on the inquiry.

Wherever the interview takes place, these architectural aspects do play a part in the flow, pacing, and outcome of the interview; the significance of which is up to the researcher to consider.

(d) Dealing with tensions and disappointments: A brief word on tensions and disappointments, some of which have been mentioned already in passing, and some of these can be avoided, even for the novice research interviewer, by preparing the ground beforehand as well as expecting interviews to differ. Preparation, though, is your best means to avoiding major disappointments in projects with short time-spans.

Issues can arise beforehand, during, and afterwards.

Beforehand

Getting people to agree to be interviewed, if not in person then to respond to an email question list, can be harder than you think; people in businesses, NGOs and governments, and media professionals are often very busy. A refusal can be outright (here, 'no' usually means 'no') or conveyed by silence. If the latter, there is no reason not to try one more, if not two more times. An initial silence can simply indicate oversight. But consecutive silences should settle it for you, so move on.

Remember that these people are granting you their time and knowledge; if no answer comes straightaway this need not mean a refusal; ask again as above. The main thing to note is to keep the initial request short and to the point; make quite clear what your topic is (in accessible language – no Big Thinker name-dropping!) and your aims for the interview.

Once a person agrees in principle you need to then gain informed consent; a signed form (adapted to your needs) or as a clear acceptance in an email if this suffices (see Appendix 1). People need to be fully informed of the intent and purpose of an interview; unlike some experimental situations, deception is not an option.

Once again, draft and redraft (if you have to) the questions. It is also customary to offer to send the questions to the interviewee beforehand. Keep the list short (6–10 questions maximum, of which some are basic information and where the key questions are clear and distinct from one another). Too many questions overwhelm your respondent and often indicate a lack of concerted thinking on your part, i.e. avoid sending your first brainstorm list to anyone agreeing to speak with you and, under advisement, before they have accepted or not.

If you only get one or two positive responses, take these on and readjust the interview's role in the overall design if you need to. For BA and MA level projects, be content – and work with what you get. The main rule of thumb at all levels is to note that interviews require time and preparation. They can flow easily and they can be difficult. People can be all too ready to tell you anything they want you to know but others can be evasive and hostile. Sometimes this is for reasons beyond your control.

During

Berg has an overview of ways to troubleshoot if things start to go off-course during an interview (Berg 2009: 117–21). As noted above, interviews can start well and end less happily, and vice versa. Points to note, however obvious, include:

How you start an interview, and how you bring it to an end also requires care, a sense of timing and an awareness of fatigue (on your interviewee's part) and the other person's time restrictions. What was the arrangement? Check with the other person what their timeframe is and do not take too long to get things off the ground.

As noted above, all interviews (and focus-group situations – see below) need to warm up. This is where the information-type questions play a role. It helps both of you settle down. Do a sound check if the interview is being recorded (and check that the interviewee is happy with this – not all people are).

The biggest pitfall is letting an interview go on too long, past the point the other party wants, or can sustain. Set your watch, or ascertain which questions you really want to cover before the end, prior to starting (see Berg 2009: 141–3). You can always approach them for a follow-up or ask supplementary questions by email or phone if need be.

Do your homework well; if this interview is with a government official or someone with management responsibility, be clear as to their area of expertise and portfolio. If you find yourself interviewing someone about an area in which they are not qualified, or permitted to comment upon, both of you will be frustrated.

Cultural sensibilities

Here attitudes, including underlying assumptions or perceptions from both parties, can lead to tensions as well as open doors. For instance, some activists and communities where research does not have a good 'street credibility' can be guarded in their responses. Probing questions are important (as journalists know), however, your job is to encourage responses, not to grill the interviewee as would an investigative news journalist.

When interviewing people from other cultures, backgrounds, or language groups, your ability to negotiate the linguistic and cultural mores underpinning good exchanges is paramount. In some cases you may need to do interviews by proxy. Male researchers interviewing women in some parts of the world may not be welcome, unmarried female researchers may have restricted access, homeless people may not feel comfortable with a stranger, and so on (see inter alia Berg 2009: 136–43.

Afterwards

At the end of the interview do not forget to thank your interviewee for their time, no matter what you may think of the usefulness of the material at that point. More importantly, be sure to send a follow-up thank you, again no matter how well things went or not. If you have arranged for the interview subject to consult the transcripts or eventual use of their material (whether they are named or not, depending on the terms of the consent they grant) be sure to fulfil this obligation.

Final point: sometimes we can exit an interview convinced that it has been no use at all. Given that working with human subjects and the sorts of inquiries conducive to this sort of data-gathering, often our first impressions can be incorrect. An interview can feel like a great success – flowing, affable, lots of material. But on looking more closely we may notice that there is less substance than we imagined. And the converse is true, so note how emotions and interpersonal dynamics, contingencies like hold-ups, the time of the day, or interruptions, can affect our initial judgment. All the more reason for taking time to absorb and analyse the interviews at a later date, and more than once if this material is important to your investigation.[6]

Methodological considerations

When considering whether interviews will allow you to investigate your topic and elucidate your research question, note that not all inquiries lend themselves to interviews: for instance, policy analysis or various forms of textual analysis (for example, in film studies, audio-visual media) in which first-hand information about human subjects' views and experiences are not the main focus.

If interviews do suggest an avenue then you also need to consider what sorts of interviews are best suited. Perhaps a survey/questionnaire can precede this element, or perhaps fewer, more in-depth interviews are better. Perhaps focus groups (see the following section) are a more productive way forward. Neither do all sorts of research with human subjects need to be completed by setting up a face-to-face, or email-based interview. Ask yourself, particularly if you have previous interview experience from another research project or in journalistic work, whether this sort of data-gathering is best-suited, indeed relevant to your current research question (see Berg 2009: 110).

That said, if interviews are going to be the main data-gathering mode for your project there needs to be a clear reason for embarking upon this course; a time-consuming one which requires preparation and due care with the material even in the most unstructured settings. Interviews for research purposes are, by definition, directed and directive; they are intended to flow from the researcher to the research subject, more informal and narrative formats notwithstanding. Interviews are social acts, intersubjective and thereby often unpredictable. They are comprised of a particular sort of listening (from the researcher), speaking and narrating (from the interviewee), and post facto analysis and representation (as cited/verbatim material in the role of substantiating evidence in the findings). For these reasons they provide rich and diverse material, challenge the researcher to reconsider their own operating assumptions (for example, about what people really think or experience as opposed to what we as researchers would like them to tell us!), and create productive tensions between research aims, and research findings; if, and only if interviews are relevant to the research on hand. The ways, and challenges of analysing these data (transcripts, email texts, video footage if pertinent) is the next task, for Chapter 7.

Summing up

The working premise of semi-formal to informal interviews is that the researcher *expects* a wide variance in response – in form, delivery, and substance. For more narrative modes of research, the open-endedness and individuality of the responses are integral to the research question; the ensuing analysis will then emphasize and tease out these nuances and inconsistencies rather than seek to eliminate them as bias or overstate their importance.

Successful interviewing at the more informal end of the spectrum does require an in-depth knowledge if not empathy on behalf of the interviewer; being responsive to the situation and language/idiom of those interviewed.

Across the board it is worth noting before setting out, during, and afterwards that a 'research interview is not a natural communication exchange' (Berg 2009: 127); the utterances of people have been granted for the purposes of a project that will then shape their words into findings and draw conclusions on the part of the researcher.

Interviews – further reading

See Berg (2009: chs 4 and 9) for a discussion of narrative research techniques; Bertrand and Hughes (2004: ch. 4: 74 *passim*, ch. 7: 141–51); Burnham et al. (2004: ch. 4: 80 *passim*, ch. 9: 205 *passim*; C. Davies (2007: ch. 7: 101–11, ch. 10; Gray (2009: ch. 14: 369–95; Silverman (2011: part IV). James and Busher (2009) look at the specifics of online interviewing.

FOCUS GROUPS

Focus groups – a sort of group-based interview – are multilateral conversations as opposed to the bilateral format of the classic interview (see previous section); as such they are often seen as one-stop shops for researchers wanting to gather qualitative, semi-formal interview material.

General principles

Focus groups, small-group discussions led by a facilitator – or *moderator* – have been a mainstay of market research in recent years, making a comeback after a period of disuse (Gunter 2000). In the last few decades many techniques and analytical approaches have been refined for this sort of data-gathering. The establishment of *audience research* and *reception studies* in research on popular culture, the media, and communications saw the establishment of focus groups as a popular form of data-gathering in academic research as well. Researchers in politics looking at gathering qualitative information about how groups perceive political processes, policy-making, or key issues of the hour also make use of focus groups.

Why focus groups?

This sort of data-gathering works for research projects that regard the material generated in a group, by way of people talking together, how interpersonal inter-actions generate more material, as the primary data. By implication this means that a variety of open-ended responses, including the psycho-emotional dimensions that govern any sort of group discussion, are relevant to the research question (Berg 2009: 158–9, Gunter 2000: 42).

This format for getting a range of nuanced information from more than one person at a time can work well on its own or together with other techniques such as surveys or one-to-one interviews; the respective importance of the focus group data will require a comparable degree of justification and working through in the research plan. The key point here is that it is a group-based response, interactively produced ideas and opinions about the topics on hand that matter. In this respect focus groups can provide an extra dimension to face-to-face interviews and more depth than anonymous surveys.[7]

- In market research focus groups are effective ways for ascertaining impressions of a product or service, isolating problems in communicating the latter to general publics or target audiences, or teasing out inchoate opinions and attitudes. In market research they are also a convenient way to target future markets as well as introduce or refine products and services (Berg 2009: 158–9).
- For academic research purposes focus groups come into their own when the researcher is interested in attaining breadth and diversity of responses as part of a 'live' interaction between discussants.
- However, focus groups are not anything-goes, a free-for-all, or a scenario in which the researcher becomes a co-participant.
- The size of each group as well as their composition and how many in total are enlisted all, once again, depend on the research topic and specific question. Just as one or two interviews are not enough on their own to support a whole research project at postgraduate level, neither is one focus group on its own.

Practicalities – formats and organizational concerns

A key element of focus groups is that, in principle, they can gather a lot of data in a relatively short time; organizing this sort of group interview is also both cost-effective and time-effective under certain conditions. However, this assumption can be misleading. Bruce Berg provides a useful list of things to avoid when deciding about whether a focus-group approach is suitable for your research project, echoed by others (Berg 2009: 160–2, 165–6).

1   The first thing to remember is that deciding to run focus groups is not a substitute for other, possibly more suitable methods like surveys (when you want straight-forward, comparable answers to clear questions) or interviews (when individuals' views and experiences are more important on their own terms).

2   Accompanying this faulty, even sloppy reasoning is to set up focus groups as a way to generate your research question. Whilst this approach is not ruled out in the early phases of a research design, it is not adequate as core data-gathering during the research; your reasons for undertaking this way of gathering data need to be coherent and consistent with your inquiry.

3   Vague intentions usually lead to vague questions, a situation in which groups can be 'hijacked' or diverted by group members (Berg 2009: 159, Gray 2009: 389); as focus groups have gained in popularity the emergence of 'professional' focus-group participants has as well.

4   There are other factors in focus-group modes of data-gathering and analysis that are in themselves more rather than less time-consuming: setting up, preparing the questions, execution, and data-handling all take more time than you might think. In other words, focus groups are not in themselves shortcuts.

5   You still need to prepare a focused set of questions, find a venue and organize a day and time in which enough people can take part, have a moderator up to the job (are you?), have a suitable recording device and means to transcribe these recordings (if not yourself then someone else), provide adequate rewards for people taking part in this sort of exercise, and have obtained informed consent according to standard codes of ethics.

Not enough care taken in these areas before and during the session can result in material that has little application for the project; the chance that participants may not show up or that discussions will either not take off, become dominated by one or two dominant members, or stray too far from the topic to generate anything worth analysing. Nonetheless, the effect of getting a group of people together to discuss a topic, consider a set of focused questions, is often a positive one; energy and ideas can emerge in ways that a formal/semi-formal interview between two parties cannot.

The researcher/moderator's role

Like a tutor – even a media anchor person or talk show host, albeit with a clear scholarly outcome in mind – the moderator can make or break a focus group. No matter how fascinating the discussion may be or how strongly you (if you are wearing the researcher/moderator hats at once) feel engaged with the topics and opinions raised, you are not a fully participating member. As Berg notes, professional 'moderators tend to get professional results' (Berg 2009: 163).

The moderator's role is a distinctive element in well-run focus groups; it is not the same as the interviewer's role in that a moderator consciously guides and redirects the conversation. Their rapport with the group is at once more simple – more distant, and more complex – group dynamics work between moderators and participants as well as between the latter. Your participants also need to have a clear idea about the purpose of the group, of how their input will be treated and what the research project is about.

Sorts of questions

One thing that focus groups and interviews have in common, however, is the way in which the moderator/interviewer needs to use their intuition, if not experience, in deciding when to leave one topic and move onto another.

For focus groups in which participants are asked for their ideas about an item – product or TV programme for instance – a checklist of specific questions may be substituted by a single general topic. If the group is assembled to consider a range of issues arising from a more general topic – the effects of gaming or social networking sites in people's everyday life for instance – then a list of questions does need to be devised; more is less in this respect, hence the formulating of clear questions that also inspire discussion takes time, and trying out.

Rules of thumb

Below we encapsulate these practicalities in terms of some do's and don'ts; these points can also be adapted for interviews, face-to-face or computer-mediated. As a rule:

- Don't set up focus groups as a substitute for one-to-one interviewing, as a quick way to conduct surveys, or as a shortcut form of observation. In all three cases, time spent designing the techniques each of these approaches need on their own terms will offer better data respectively.
- Before committing to this sort of data-gathering do ask yourself whether this approach is best suited to your project; is it sufficient on its own or accompanying other avenues?
- Don't make groups too big; 6–8 participants is more than enough; what the composition of the group/s will be again depends on the research question: age-dependent, socio-economic categories, preferences, gender-specific, or mixed.
- How many groups again depends on the level and ambitions of the project. If you conduct only one focus group then your conclusions, and any generalizations, need to reflect this.
- Don't have sessions go on too long; the usual limit is 30–60 minutes. If you are showing an item (programme, film) then consider the effect this has on the timing.
- Don't assume that everyone taking part has the same motivations or level of interest in your project.
- Do make people as comfortable as possible: do consider your financial resources and venue requirements.
- Do be prepared to have to spend a lot of time transcribing the sessions; for each hour of talk calculate at least 4 hours of transcribing verbatim, as well as including other cues such as hesitations, silences, irritation. If video is used you need permission.

- Do think about whether you are qualified and/or experienced enough to moderate the group/s. If you carry out this role do be prepared to intervene when things go off-topic but also be prepared to let the discussion run.
- Don't intervene substantively, unless you have devised a project/question and corollary focus group that justifies this.
- Do provide clear structure and directions before, during, and after the session.
- Do obtain signed, informed consent from your participants. Confidentiality and respect for the time and input of your participants are high priorities in academic research with/on human subjects.
- Do have a Plan B if a group, or groups do not work though no-shows or lack of viable material; one is beyond your control and the other is up to your level of preparation.
- Do try out your questions, rationale, and ideas on others first; your supervisor as well as classmates are good starts.

Methodological considerations

The latter point is relevant for any sort of interactive research. With these practicalities in mind, here are some observations about the knock-on effect of more unseen, unknowable factors when conducting this sort of research:

1 Even when carrying out interview-based research with your peer group, within your own community, these conversations differ from those you would have with these people normally.

2 While in some areas of inquiry controversial topics are quite popular for focus-group work, they can create friction or personal distress in some participants in ways that are not always foreseeable. People respond in various ways and at varying levels of intensity to certain sorts of questions and issues; for this you need to be prepared. Experience will also make you more aware of various levels of distress signals, but it is worthwhile considering these factors early on; ethics forms often point these aspects out too.

3 Not only are there palpable gender- and power-based hierarchies often at work as group-based discussions unfold, but emotions and potential conflicts are integral to these sorts of face-to-face/one-to-one or one-to-many research encounters. Unlike the anonymity provided in a survey, or distance gained by email-based question and answers, stand-offs in focus group conflicts can affect the outcome if not the range of responses you are looking for. Perhaps, though, such conflicts could constitute the findings; this you need to consider.

4 In most small-scale research projects, people take part in these research set-ups voluntarily; there may be some remuneration or 'reward' (for example, a book token) but on the whole, following standard codes of ethics, they are free to withdraw their cooperation at any point. Most informed consent forms include this provision. Even during a session, participants may leave mid-discussion or not turn up; engage in, or defer to implicit power hierarchies (for example, focus groups held within company departments with line managers present). Others can withdraw into silence, others, as already noted, can dominate.

A well-prepared researcher should be able to cope with these contingencies and interrogate them in light of the research question. In short, you need to think about how this sort of group (collectively)-generated qualitative data relates to your inquiry; what it can, or cannot offer with respect to other approaches.

Summing up

Particularly popular in media and communications, market research, political polling, and current affairs TV programmes,[8] focus groups are an extension of interviewing; they are less time-consuming as they cluster groups by various ways and for various research ends.

A focus group is just that however: a highly selective – focused – *group* and a *focused* set of group-based interactions. They do not produce any sort of representative sample nor are members necessarily coming to the task disinterested (payment, forms of manipulation). They also need to be managed carefully in that generally speaking focus groups are not free-for-all discussions. That said, an astute researcher who takes the requisite amount of time to read and analyse the records closely will notice that sometimes the conversations that are 'off-message' can prove informative, rich material.

Finally, a point for the next chapter, written transcripts and recordings of focus-group sessions, as is also the case with interviews, do not speak for themselves. They generate audio-visual and written matter that is usually characterized by contra-dictions and a lack of standardized responses (*contra* survey work). Theses records constitute the 'raw' data which you, as a researcher, need to collate, filter, and make sense of in some way.

Focus groups – further reading

Berg 2009: 158 *passim*, C. Davies 2007: ch. 11: 178, 202; Gray 2009: 389–95, Gunter 2000: 42.

ETHNOGRAPHIC FIELDWORK AND PARTICIPANT-OBSERVATION

The term *ethnographic* refers to a research context rather than a singular approach to data-gathering or analysis. It describes research that is carried out whilst the researcher is immersed *within* a field of action, usually a geographical location or a community, over a length of time. Here researchers are in direct and continual contact with others, some of whom may become individual research subjects – interviewees or people the researcher pays particular attention to during the course of their stay. Others may play a gate-keeping role in that they grant access to the location (a village, or password-protected discussion group for instance). Others may act as local advisers, hosts, or interpreters. They, or others again may mediate the working relationship between the larger community and the researcher. In short, ethnographic research is an intersubjective activity where observation implies participation by virtue of the researcher being part of the everyday activities and events around them.

General principles

Ethnographic approaches define anthropological research. As George Marcus puts it, the 'ethnographic research project [is a] single site probing of local situations and peoples. . . . Ethnography is predicated upon attention to the everyday, an intimate knowledge of face-to-face communities and groups . . . that habitually focuses upon subaltern subjects, those positioned by systemic domination' (1995: 98, 99, 101; see Fabian 1983, Hakken 1999).

Historically, particularly during the colonial era, this meant knowledge gained by the anthropologist – ethnographer – spending time with a community in a specific location that was foreign to their own. Traditionally:

- Ethnographic research requires a personal commitment in physical and emotional terms that are eschewed in other quarters.
- Part of the skill-set required for carrying out anthropological fieldwork success-fully entails a grasp of the local language, cultural customs, and a commitment to developing close relationships and mutual obligations with the community as a whole; most particularly with your 'local contacts', 'host family', or 'informants'.
- The net result of this close-up and longer-term (i.e. longitudinal) approach to undertaking research is highly nuanced, wide-ranging and produces rich sorts of material that ranges from direct observations of other ways of life, cultural practices, and production as drawings, film or photographs; insights gained from conversations or more formalized interviews with community members; incorporation of various forms of linguistic, textual or visual analysis of images, rituals, speech patterns, or commerce.

What distinguishes this level of close-up, relative 'insider' research and the sorts of *rich description* produced when the fieldwork is formally written up is that the researcher gains – and then claims – particular levels of understanding based on the quality of this 'fly-on-the-wall' access; sometimes to what are often conversations, rituals, or community events that would not be possible by other, more formal or hands-off approaches to data-gathering.

For anthropological projects, the outcome of this approach is an *ethnography,* or *ethnographic study*. This is a report which presents a comprehensive narrative, a picture of life in the respective community, or group. This approach also applies to projects where the researcher may pay close attention to a particular aspect of a broader community's daily life (e.g. coming of age rituals), the role played by particular members (e.g. women, or teenagers), or core activities (e.g. fishing, producing 'zines, basket-weaving, participating in an online discussion group); for example, how gossip works as an integral part of everyday communicative cultures in a Pacific Island country (Besnier 2009), or the daily grind of life as a group of street sellers in Greenwich Village, New York (Duneier 1999).

Whilst the above characterization is central to traditional anthropological projects, the premise has been increasingly adopted by other disciplines – sociologists and media researchers in particular. Any – episodic or extended – time spent with a group of human subjects, sometimes even if this involves carrying out interviews on the spot or attending a gathering (conference, or meeting on a street corner), has nowadays taken on the 'ethnographic' label. Add to this the way anthropologists and other researchers have been engaging in web-based forms of internet/virtual ethnography or ethnographic-inflected sorts of data-gathering since the early days of the internet, and we see how this approach is no longer confined to anthropology departments. Nor is it confined to face-to-face, exotic locations as anthropologists – 'virtual ethnographers' – study web-based cultures and communities.

The double-edged effects of research *in* and *on* the field, changes in the location and nature of the 'field' itself, and emerging ethical practicalities around online modes of participant-observation permeate ongoing debates within anthropology; about the nature and limits of the field, cultural practices as global rather than local phenomena, the privileging of a single-sited approach to ethnographic studies. As other disciplines develop their own versions of ethnographic research and respective notions of what can or cannot be achieved by this sort of inclusive and composite mode of data-gathering, the section below looks at the key characteristics for non-anthropologists.

The brief excursion above into what is a vast literature and established academic discipline indicates how the term *ethnographic* has a number of applications, and is more elastic that the stricter notion of ethnography, understood largely as a particular sort of writing based on a specific sort of engagement and locus for the researcher (see Fabian 1983, Ulin 1984).

The governing premise of any sort of project aiming or claiming to be ethnographic is that the data-gathering is based on *participant-observation*. What this means, in contrast to the varying degrees of distanced observational modes adopted for (quasi) experimental research, surveys, or even focus groups, is that the researcher is deliberately in the thick of it; getting the 'seats of their pants dirty' (Paccagnella 1997). Visible and with permission to be there in on-the-ground situations; not necessarily visible, yet also with access granted in online ones.

Three other working principles distinguish ethnographic participant-observation and corollary data-gathering from other approaches:

1   The *where*: 'I am doing fieldwork'; this statement covers a range of data-gathering about and with human subjects that takes researchers outside their institutional and geographical working environment; for example, travelling to where people live or work to conduct interviews or focus groups. What we are talking about here though is a more marked notion of fieldwork/the field, one that can entail the observation of people in a public place like a railway station or city square for a specified length of time – 'non-participant' observation (see C. Davies 2007: 174–6), being granted access to a particular event (for example, a ritual) or location reserved for insiders (a board meeting, private club), or spending long periods within – living in – a community. In the last three instances, fieldwork, whether or not its parameters are geographical, physical or, nowadays, digital, presupposes a time commitment over an extended period, or episodes.

2   The *how*: With the exception of where physical invisibility or physical distance governs the vantage point from which researchers are observing (for example, experiments, observation points in public places, web-based communities), extended periods of observation are premised on the researcher being inside the field, known if not visible to those s/he is interacting with. The researcher is a tacit, if not active participant in their surroundings. As a rule, carrying out any period of participant-observation satisfactorily cannot happen without consent; permission from those whose activities, ways of life, or customs are the object of study – the 'locals' – in general, and in particular respective leaderships, gate-keepers, or guardians (as is the case with minors). This sort of research is longitudinal in the sense that time spent in the field matters; anthropologists speak of entering, exiting, and revisiting the field.

3   *Ethical obligations*: Chapters 3 and 5 address the issue of research ethics; many of the principles are also foundational to anthropological rules and procedures. In short, research subjects in ethnographic work can, and do talk back; fields can and do become closed to the researcher later on. For this reason, ethical considerations play a major role in the design and execution of the research, as do local and historical contexts.

In light of those specifics, note that:

- This fly-on-the-wall work is where the material gathered, analysis made, and knowledge produced are all defined by up-closeness.
- Stronger still, the researcher is presenting their findings premised on their understanding of a *relative* – or *reflexive* – objectivity that emerges from their interrelationship within and with the field and its inhabitants; ethnographic knowledge is thereby regarded as distinct from 'subjective experience' even though personal experiences do colour the final analysis (see di Leonardo 1991, Fabian 1983, Marcus 1995).
- For these reasons, some of the detail and nuance can threaten to overwhelm the researcher if not the eventual report under the 'weight of its own detail'.[9] Just as statistics don't speak for themselves, the wealth of observations and experiences forming any extended and in-depth ethnographic encounter in the field need shaping into a narrative related to the core research inquiry.
- Precisely because the sort of information gathered, and insights gained by the researcher are effectively a sort of 'first-hand' knowledge, this approach is in sharp contrast to experimental research, large survey work, and focus group-based research.
- The legitimacy, replicability, and thereby transparency of the scholarly product rests on the ability of the researcher to present and ground their findings in the integrity of relationships forged whilst in the field and those maintained afterwards with their hosts.

As there is a large literature within anthropology and also related disciplines covering theoretical (for example, conceptualizing the 'field') as well as practical issues (debates about 'going native' or neo-colonialist relations between western researchers and non-western cultures) for this sort of research the sections below select several aspects that non-anthropologists can overlook or underestimate. As participant-observation techniques, from 'non-participatory' to 'full immersion', have become par for the course, the fine line between this sort of data-gathering and ethnographic research proper is the subject of ongoing debates amongst anthropologists and those working from other disciplinary frameworks 'borrowing' from the ethnographic tradition.

For our purposes, the three following practical distinctions need addressing if your research inquiry is served by spending time with a community, or group of people beyond the time it takes to interview or survey them, or set up focus-group work:

(i)   getting into, and working 'in the field';
(ii)   exiting and returning to the field;
(iii) changing fields; 'multi-sited' ethnographic research on the ground and online; global and local contexts.[10]

Practicalities

In terms of gaining, and sustaining access, the principles of informed consent and related ethical points govern how you need to approach any potential site, or community for both on-the-ground and online scenarios (see Chapters 3 and 5). The main points to note once you have access, and particularly if you intend to observe/participate for any extended length of time, involve you in (1) varying shades of (digitized or embodied) visibility; (2) developing relationships as you consciously engage, or find yourself drawn into interactions; (3) keeping your bearings and records of what you see, hear, and feel;[11] and (4) exiting and returning to a field.

Whilst traditional settings, face-to-face and in a clearly demarcated site of action, dominate this literature, the points below also pertain to online, computer-mediated participant-observation in varying degrees of immersion, and visibility.

Visibility/invisibility

Here most fly-on-the-wall approaches are characterized by the visibility of any initial 'entrance' (a group meets you for the first time; your avatar and/or IP address becomes registered on an online discussion group; a moderator, or you introduce yourself as a new member/researcher) becoming less prominent as time goes on.

- In traditional, on-the-ground settings, we are always ' there', visible to those others who are at the end of the day part of our inquiry. Even then, the fear that many novice researchers have about their presence disturbing proceedings is less significant than imagined. First, people get used to having you there. Second our presence is less important to people engaged in everyday cultural or social relationships then we imagine. Only if our presence, or participation, and perhaps eventual misuse of what we may learn there creates tensions might we need to reconsider, adjust, and respond.

- Online, it is still moot about how far a researcher needs to worry about this aspect. The basic rule of thumb is that each community has its own limits and 'netiquette' concerns about accepting observers, or having members become researchers. You need to work this out as your project proceeds, having gained access and informed consent initially. Sometimes you simply need to '"show up" and reveal [your identity as a researcher]' and that will suffice.[12]
- Given ongoing debates, it is best not to assume that the permission from an administrator online is enough. Indeed many moderators defer on this matter when first approached.
- On the ground, and online in particular, there could be moments when a researcher becomes almost too invisible. This is as relationships, allegiances, and perhaps conflicts take on a role of their own.

Developing relationships

Being in the thick of it means of course that no researcher is immune, or untouched by what goes on around them. Here, you may find that your initial impressions, allegiances, and perception of what is 'really' going on change over time. You may yourself become the object of 'flaming', either by participating in a discussion (online) or having your presence objected to by others. You may also develop friendships, debts of gratitude, and dislikes for others.

- Here, the best advice is to actually remember that you are still a researcher; being allowed inside, or coming into a situation as an insider brings its own degree of accountability and unexpected shifts in view. In short, just as an interview is not a naturalistic conversation per se, neither is any degree of participant-observation the same as everyday community membership.
- These two dimensions may well overlap during the fieldwork. However, on getting back to 'homebase' (your institution, home/office) your analysis and writing up of your findings constitute a shift in power (you become an author) and vantage-point (your observations at the time become 'data' to be analysed and applied later on).
- For these reasons alone, ethnographic research reports are not only full of 'rich description' but they are also to some extent autobiographical accounts; the researcher needs to 'flag' this reflexive dimension in various ways.[13] Clearly, a very different notion of observation, and avoiding bias, to those practised in other disciplines (see Chapter 1).
- Be aware, and prepared for access to be denied (at the outset), challenged, or perhaps needing to be renegotiated.
- Informed consent is thereby the first step in evolving, and devolving relationships. The bottom line is that in most situations, if people know what you are doing there and are assured their words and deeds will be treated with respect, there is little to worry about.

Keeping your bearings

As noted above, the main difference between participant-observation and other data-gathering methods covered in this chapter is the way in which the researcher is involved in various sorts and levels of observation, gathering, and recording.

- This is what people are referring to with the term *field notes*; the means by which an observer/participant records what they see, experience, hear whilst there. After all these are not controlled experiments or standardized surveys, or even moderated focus groups. We are in a field, with others, engaging and being exposed to a range of interactions. This applies to online settings as well, albeit in different forms and with different sorts of incarnations (i.e. an avatar, a digital footprint, a hyperlinked set of relationships, texts and photos) and effects.
- The main point is *keep a record*. Decide beforehand in what form: handwritten notes? On your laptop? Taped/video diaries? Which means are the most unobtrusive? Consider this.[14]
- What sorts of records? There are many places for advice on this matter (see Berg 2009 for instance, Paccagnella 1997, Miller and Slater 2000). However, the key thing is to note down anything you think is worth recalling. Why? Because you *will* forget; our memories for times, dates, places, who said what, get hazy over time.[15] As you write up the fieldwork the scholarly side of things starts to matter: transparency, precision, and an eye for detail are no good if you have forgotten key dates, places, or locations. These include
  - maps (where people sit, how a place looks, for websites what the key features are, and what changes);
  - dates, start times, moments of change or tension;
  - impressions – these are distinct from recording (in note form or otherwise – with permission); for example, I usually square-bracket impressions I have of proceedings to differentiate later between these (personal responses) and what went on;
  - names, positions, kinship structures, or other hierarchies can also be recorded in graphic or textual form;
  - interviews, and other sorts of formalized data-gathering require a clear demarcation;
  - counting: for qualitatively minded participant-observers, knowing how many (for example, registered on a listserv, in a community) is invaluable.

There are any number of ways to keep field notes but the main thing is to be consistent and set up an approach that works for you, and is suited to the context. Also, be aware that these ways of keeping notes and what you note will also develop over time.

Finally: how to keep your bearings when conducting work that involves multi-sited fields? For example, between online and offline meetings of a community, or for groups who move around the world. As George Marcus, and others note, the notion of the local has been largely offset (arguably) by global geographies; for example, migratory patterns, communities who travel between locations (e.g. athletes, activists, business people). What if your field is both digital, as in web-mediated, and traditional (face-to-face)?

- The first thing to be clear about is the research question and its relationship with you chosen object of analysis. In other words, as today much ethnographically inspired research is less about a full ethnographic study (for example, of a village, a tribe, a subculture) you need to ascertain an anchor point. Sometimes this is singular, clear from the outset. Sometimes though this anchor (for example, a particular file-sharing community) can prove to be more complex, more multidimensional than envisaged. Here, note where you start, and note where you end up and where you change focus.
- More consciously though, having established your initial parameters – another reason why pilot research, and even fully developed pilot studies are worth their while, there is an approach put forward by George Marcus for just these occasions. His is a six-point schematic for research inquiries that defines 'their objects of study through several modes or techniques' (Marcus 1995: 106). He sees these as baselines that can be 'preplanned or opportunistic' (ibid.):
  - Follow the people
  - Follow the thing
  - Follow the metaphor
  - Follow the plot, story, allegory
  - Follow the life or biography
  - Follow the conflict.   (Marcus 1995: 106–12)[16]

Exits and returns – afterwards

The key point here is that ethnographic research entails a commitment of time from both the researcher and research subjects. The researcher in a sense becomes part of that community for the duration of the fieldwork, and in many cases this relationship is continued or maintained throughout a career, if not a lifetime. For non-anthropologists though this mutuality can be overlooked.

- For student researchers embarking in fieldwork participant-observation for lengths of time, sending regular reports back to their supervisors is a useful way to sift and shift all these notes up a level of abstraction. Once back, these observations need to be reactivated, and then incorporated into an analytical (rather than a stream of consciousness) account in various ways.[17]
- Once exiting for the purposes of writing up the findings for the project on hand, as with interviews, gratitude and interaction with those you have worked with afterwards go a long way.
- If access was granted on the basis of people being able to view your results, check your use of their words, then follow though.
- Even for shorter projects, it is a good idea to revisit, if feasible, or get in touch with key people as you finalize the work. The depth of analysis, and nuances of the report can greatly benefit, at the very least, from being up to date. In online settings where things change quickly, this is even more important.
- The main factor afterwards is what to do with all those notes: impressions, accounts, photos, details. This is where we enter the analysis and writing-up

phase; the lion's share of the work for all the approaches covered here (see Chapters 7 and 8).

- One preliminary here is on returning to 'base' to readdress the research question, your aims and objectives in light of the fieldwork; this may be in the form of a report (for yourself, or supervisor) or a revised methodological chapter.

Whilst many of the practicalities above are things a researcher learns as they go, there are some that require preplanning, or commitment before you enter. Others can be adjusted as you go, for example, interviews or observational points developed as their significance arises. Preparation, awareness, and spontaneity go hand-in-hand in ethnographic research. For these reasons, there are some particular methodological issues to bear in mind.

Methodological considerations

Some may ask, why go this far? Research projects that explore phenomena from the point of view of those closest to the action, those that wish to get a sense of how people, in groups or communities, make sense of their world in their own terms, those that examine how cultural practices are created and expressed by their indigenous actors, or projects with a socio-political engagement, engage in participation-observation from *within*. Because of its efficacy in exploring research questions that require close-up, longer-term forms of observation (for example, those following people's attitudes over time, minority groups or subcultures) this approach has become popular across the disciplinary spectrum. Indeed at times the term 'ethnographic', not unlike references to 'qualitative' research, is more suggestive than elucidating.

Intradisciplinary debates aside, researchers differ on the respective amount of participation that may be entailed, by default, or requisite to the inquiry. In this respect, we return to the notion of varying degrees of participation as active or passive, depending on the research question.

A corollary to this preconception is that no matter how passive your initial participation may be, spending time in the company of others as a researcher involves a more interpersonal level of interaction, requires more attention to ethical implications: your responsibility to others – your research subjects on the one hand and, on the other, where your presence may expose you to legal or physical precariousness. This level of close-up observation may not serve your inquiry; at the very least it can result in some fundamental reconsiderations of the research question you entered the field with. One of the strengths here of this approach is that it is acceptable to change, and so chart this journey. Indeed, in many respects this is what the ethnographic encounter is; one between researcher and researched where both sides are affected (for better or worse).

Finally, given the depth and range of what counts as ethnographic, and also the intensity of ongoing debates within anthropology and elsewhere about the influence of computer-mediated research encounters, the following points can serve as both caveats and orientation points.

1   Because this term derives from anthropology's early days, at the height of colonial rule (the mid-nineteenth century to the mid-twentieth century), its central aim – the 'primitive other' (Besnier 2011) – has been thoroughly critiqued and revised in the wake of decolonization and twentieth-century social movements (feminism, civil rights). This is why we need to be clear about the distinction between ethnography and research in which participant-observation may play a role. Nonetheless both entail a research design that 'places researchers in the midst of whatever it is they study' (Berg 2009: 191).

2   Whilst the empirical material gathered under these conditions can cover various combinations of quantitative and qualitative data, a key characteristic of the eventual study is its emphasis on generating a written narrative. Diagrams and other graphical representations play a role, but the primary characteristic of fieldwork-based projects in this mode is their textuality; narrative is a stylistic feature wherein both researcher and researched are protagonists. I have noted these issues already above. The implications for the eventual product is that the time it takes to write up the research can be as long as time spent in the field; there is another dimension to this sort of research that only really takes place afterwards that is particularly acute for ethnographic inquiries.

3   What the above point means in practice is that a researcher engaged in an ethnographic project even outside anthropological codes of conduct, enters the field in a different state of mind, and intention, to one they would have in the administration of a survey, focus group, or experiment. In particular, informed consent, gaining and maintaining access, and exiting in sustainable ways are paramount, which is why anthropological codes of ethics are so detailed. Bottom line is that you are there as a guest, and the local conventions of hospitality, including 'netiquette', govern what you can achieve.

4   This very proximity at the time and the distance taken to produce the 'rich description' mode of analysis, and the shades of participation the researcher engages in, can create disconnects. It is natural for student researchers, even the more experienced, to iron out these in the course of the narrative, as if the account is of a smooth journey. If undertaking this sort of work in settings where objectivity in its strictest sense, observational forms of data-gathering where 'observer bias' is to be avoided, and statistical forms of analysis are all privileged, then this close-up account may be received with scepticism, indeed hostility. This embracing of a micro-level, interpersonal take on data-gathering is still a contested one in some parts of social research.

5   In short, the uptake of fieldwork-based immersed observations by other disciplines, and ongoing debates within anthropology about the pros and cons of 'multi-sited ethnography' (see Marcus 1995), or studies of virtual worlds, gaming, or the everyday practices of internet communities, has meant that the term ethnographic works these days as a shorthand for research designs that emphasize reflexivity – whereby researchers 'embrace the challenge of revealing and correcting their own mediation' (Abdelal et al. 2009: 7). The upshot is that: 'researchers can believe themselves to be doing ethnographic research when they are not. Students often have a stereotype of ethnography that is any form of participant observation, or any form of qualitative research that involves being a bit "touchy feely" . . .' (Jones and Watt 2010: 4).

Whilst participant-observation is integral to ethnographic modes of research, the latter is more than 'a form of participant observation (which it is) that entails a bit of reflexivity' (Jones and Watt 2010: 4). In other words, the effectiveness of the analysis brought to bear on data gathered cannot be reduced simply to having gained access mindful of codes of ethics and reassurances that the researcher spent time 'being there' (Marcus 1995: 114).

Summing up

Traditionally, ethnographic research was by western anthropologists, intent upon 'capturing', studying non-western societies and their cultural practices. Nowadays anthropologists also study their own societies, neighbourhoods, and even family groups (see Berg 2009: 192–4). Moreover, in a digital age there is a burgeoning field of 'virtual' or 'digital' forms of ethnographic research: participation-observation in either fully-immersed or combined online/offline worlds and communities (Franklin 2004, Hine 2000).

Designing an ethnographic research project is distinct from incorporating empirical material collected through participant-observation alone; the research question and underlying assumptions about the nature of knowledge and observation bring with them particular obligations. Ethnography 'involves the scholar being situated within a social context [the field] to become part of its discourse – its language and practices – the research that results has the advantage of conveying social meanings as they are experienced' (Abdelal et al. 2009: 7).

The basic premise, in distinction to content analysis conducted within shorter time-windows, is that the sort of in-depth data – and trust – built up with respondents and local contacts, provides an unrivalled degree of insight, giving rise to studies rich in detail, nuance, and insights for projects focusing on the particular and infinite variations of human experience and practices.

Ethnographic approaches – further reading

Berg 2009: ch. 6: 190 *passim*; on analysis of fieldwork material see also 2009: 228 *passim*; M. Davies 2007: 168 *passim*; Gray 2009: 396 *passim*, where he focuses on observational techniques; Jones and Watt (2010) and C. Davies (2007) provide also invaluable suggestions.

For critical interventions about the ethos of ethnographic work during and since the colonial era, see Fabian (1983), Giri (2004), Tuhiwai-Smith (1999), Ulin (1984).

References related to how ethnographic approaches have evolved with the web are listed in the online research section of Chapter 5. See also Hakken (1999) and Jones (1999) for constructive and still current observations related to the practicalities of online forms of participant-observation and researching live in cyberspatial fields.

SUMMING UP: REPOSITIONING THE DIVIDE?

As a segue to Chapter 7, it should be apparent by now that in practice sweeping allusions to 'quantitative' or 'qualitative' methodologies as polar opposites do not suffice. Whilst mindful of how just such allusions work as an undertow in everyday research settings in mixed departments, the goal for all researchers is articulating and then executing the research in ways that make sense for, and of the project. The points below recap the discussion so far as we move on to the last two chapters: analysing and writingup the material:

1   How to go about gathering and analysing data is related to the object of inquiry, researcher's intentions, and the research question; data-gathering methods serve our inquiry, not the other way around.

2   That said, in practice positing this interrelationship as entirely one-way is too simplistic as well. For example, even the most elegant hypothesis or pristine research proposal will not proceed snag-free; conditions of access may change, the data gathered/material read may be less interesting than you expected should 'subsidiary' ideas or findings emerge as more significant, or your conceptual framework or working hypothesis may need revisiting.

3   In short, a negative outcome, or reconsideration of your initial premises, depending on the context, may in fact be as valuable.

4   No data-gathering method or mode of analysis is perfect, bullet-proof or above criticism. There are always advantages and disadvantages, trade-offs to make, limitations to recognize.

5   Any particular method or methodological 'family' of data-gathering brings its own do's and don'ts to the task on hand: criteria for ascertaining legitimacy, replicability, objectivity, and conventions around writingup the results.

6   However the primary data comes to us, or we generate it, and whether or not it is qualitative (not in numerical form) or quantitative (in numerical form), measurable or immeasurable, differences in outcome and conclusions drawn lie in *why* a researcher sets out to work with these sorts of data, to what ends, and how they present and defend these outcomes. All researchers need to navigate overlapping and competing conversations about the form and substance of the enterprise within any chosen mode of data-gathering and analysis.

7   Certain methods require specialized skills. If you need to get additional training (for example, how to use statistical programs such as SPSS, basic spreadsheet programs, or online tutorials for tools such as Web Crawler), *do so*. Finding out more about these 'mechanics' even if you don't proceed can stand you in good stead for the future.

8   When considering collecting data from human subjects directly, most of the techniques laid out above require the researcher do some initial research, if not design a pilot study to iron out any inconsistent thinking and refine basic administration skills during and after the data has been gathered; this can range from a mini-survey to a preliminary discussion of a key thinker's work.

9   Ruling out a data-gathering method because it looks too daunting or does not fit your (fledgling or ingrained) scholarly identity is not sound thinking in any way.

As we move into modes of *analysis*, and in particular those approaches where analysis features prominently as researchers work with texts (however defined) – the focus of the next chapter – I would urge readers to let go of absolutist markers of disciplinary identity, for the time being at least. At this point in the proceedings these obscure rather than clarify exactly what you are doing; your task is to pursue the research question in ways that make sense for this inquiry, carried out in as rigorous and transparent a fashion as possible. In short, to show you can 'walk the walk' as opposed to 'talk the talk'.

NOTES

1   The (quasi)experimental cluster falls outside the purview of this book.
2   Thanks to Susan Banducci for providing supporting material and ongoing feedback to quantitative research data-gathering sections.
3   To extrapolate: for probability samples, the larger the population means that the confidence intervals narrow; this is where margins of error in statistical terms play a role. Conversely, the more homogeneous the sample is, the more precise the results will be. The formula for a standard margin of error looks like this:

$$\text{Standard error} = \frac{\sqrt{p\,(1-p)}}{n}$$

4   Thanks to Marieke Riethof for this input. *Action research* is a methodology that takes a leaf out of several books, with its own set of ethical and operational rules and procedures; see C. Davies (2007: 172 *passim*), McLeod and Thomson (2009), Smith (1999).
5   For instance: the UK Data Archive: www.data-archive.ac.uk/; Leibniz Institute for the Social Sciences (GESIS): www.gesis.org/en/services/data/retrieval-data-access/; World Values Survey: www.worldvaluessurvey.org/; British Election Study: www.bes2009-10.org (26 August 2011).
6   See also Bruce Berg's 'ten commandments' (Berg 2009: 143–4).
7   In some sorts of inquiry they can also generate ideas about future research directions, provide feedback about research findings, and ground more abstract sorts of questions in day-to-day, ordinary people's lives. This more *action research* oriented incorporation of focus-group based data-gathering needs to make sense for the research question, aims and objectives of research in which researcher and research subjects are collaborators. The finitudes of this approach are beyond the scope of this discussion; see McNiff and Whitehead (2009).
8   For example the BBC current affairs programme *Newsnight* has made regular use of focus groups, as corroborating evidence in an item or 'live' in the studio, for items on high-profile government policy issues. In so doing, these programmes become 'media texts' for researchers to analyse in turn.
9   Thanks to David Morley for this observation.
10 Berg (2009) has an extensive discussion of the practicalities around entering and exiting the field. Appadurai (2002), Clifford (1997) and Marcus (1995) differently address changes to the single-sitedness of traditional ethnographic work in the wake of globalization. See also Inda and Rosaldo (2002) for an overview, Besnier (2011) for a specific example of how these issues work on the ground, Franklin (2004) for online fields, and Hine (2000) for an approach to virtual ethnography.
11 Berg (2009) has an extensive discussion on these matters; these points build on his useful overview based on previous and ongoing research of my own, and that of a number of research students.
12 Thanks to Yu-Kei Tse for this expression.

13 See Fabian (1983) for an extensive discussion; Marcus (1995: 113) on the notion of 'circumstantial activism'; Mitchell Duneier (1999) for a particular way of dealing with this element in an ethnographic note in the appendix. Moreover, feminist and postcolonial anthropologists, as well as those from other disciplines exploring ethnographic approaches, have also contributed to these issues; see Charlotte Davies (2007), di Leonardo (1991), Harding (1998a, 1998b), Henwood et al. (2001).

14 As I had to in one scenario where, unlike a previous setting, my jotting down the main points of the discussion where people were sitting was noticed by the group moderator; as gate-keeper they were concerned about what I was up to. They eventually denied me further access to the meetings. Incidentally, those participating in the group were more curious than concerned about my notes (which I showed them as well). They, however, were not in charge of access.

15 Thanks to Jeannette Hoffman for this reminder.

16 The critiques and limits of this approach to doing and conceptualizing traditional anthropology are beyond the scope of this discussion. Suffice it to say that there is a tension, productive and problematic, between, as Niko Besnier (2011: 6–19) argues, inquires into 'plurals', 'bifocality' between local and/or global, or 'sites' (figurative and literal) for an enterprise premised on encounters with a '"primitive other"' (Besnier 2011: 6; see Certeau 1991, Fabian 1983). Add to these epistemological issues a host of computer-mediated pluralities, and practicalities become even more complex – exciting new terrain I would say.

17 Thanks to Marieke Riethof for this input and her noting how a lot of students returning from their fieldwork 'have friends who ask them what exactly they have to say about their topic. This is where they start to understand that [their project] is more than a report . . . they need an analysis and an argument' (personal correspondence, 18 August 2011).

CHAPTER 7

Doing research – analysing findings

Topics covered in this chapter:

- What is analysis?
- Working with texts
- Content analysis
- Textual/visual analysis
- Discourse analysis
- Deductive and inductive paths to knowledge
- Behaviouralism and its critics
- Data-gathering and analysis: process *and* product

INTRODUCTION

We now turn to the role and specifics of analysis; an integral yet often under-discussed aspect of successfully completing a research project, let alone how this process operates within particular methodological traditions. Ways of going about gathering material and then analysing it are intimately connected. Yet the quality of final reports rated as above average often lies in the strength of the analysis sections; tables of survey results, chunks of interviews cited verbatim, focus-group transcripts, large quotes from the thinker under investigation, or chapters of descriptive prose based on field-work observation are not sufficient in themselves. They all require an analytical dimension. Yet this is where many student projects can suffer from a lack of attention to this aspect; running out of time and 'oomph' playing a major role here.

The chapter has a dual aim: (1) to deal with a broader question that often goes begging for many students: what *is* 'analysis'? and (2) to unpack a cluster of method-ological approaches in which analysis plays a key role. These relate to the data-gathering techniques covered in Chapter 6 as well as departing from them. As analysis is a stage most of us encounter later on in a project, or we are confronted with the limits of our understanding and ability to make sense of more literature-based material as we write, the rest of this chapter looks at corollary issues that arise at this point. With generating or gathering 'raw data', the focus of the last chapter, we see in the discussion here that ways to approach and then 'process' material can produce different sorts of outcomes and accompanying claims of how these critique, or contribute to existing knowledge.

Issues raised here may catapult some readers back to the start; though by now you will be looking back from further down the research road, for better or worse. Others will notice here that they have reached another set of crossroads, where distinctions between analysing and presenting quantifiable and qualitative material require you to make another set of decisions. The power lies in knowing why you are making these choices and being able to deal with the consequences for what you can claim at the end of the day as well as the selections that come with writingup (Chapter 8).

Chapter organization

After taking a look at the whole notion of analysis in terms of the larger research project, the second section gets back to practicalities: working with *texts* in various forms and related analytical 'rules and procedures'. Here I take in turn three large areas of research approaches that are often presented in the literature and classroom as diametrically opposed to one another: content analysis, textual/visual analysis and discourse analysis. In the second instance, as these very categorizations are in themselves the object of some controversy, past and present, they tend to operate as markers of intra- and interdisciplinary pedigree. This in turn affects how the outcome of the research project gets presented in the final dissertation. In these cases, firmly on either side of the trenches so to speak, divisions are as deep within as they are between competing rules and procedures (tacit or codified) and their respective worldviews.

This practical section, a follow-on from those covered in Chapter 6, makes way for a discussion that is often dealt with early on in a project's life-cycle. This is the way presumed and imagined differences between *deductive* and *inductive* modes of reasoning affect how we draw conclusions – or inferences. This returns us to inter-related differences about how research traditions regard the relationship between the observer (that's me and you) and the 'evidence' (facts or fiction, depending on how you see these things). These two lines of reasoning are usually regarded as charac-terizing the difference in how quantitative and qualitative research ticks, one usually positioned as inherently superior to the other. As philosophers and practitioners have been showing for some time, research working realities suggest otherwise. Because flexing our analytical muscles, so to speak, usually follows the collection – or selection – of the material under investigation, this discussion has been held back until now.

To ground these issues in practical research realities, this chapter draws to a close by breaking out in two directions: first the legacy of *behaviouralism* and its critics. Second, we consider some working distinctions between quantitative and qualitative sorts of data as these emerge during a research process and its outcome.

A lot of territory to cover, some of which will be passed over and all of which bears closer scrutiny. A further reading guide will provide some ways to get on with this. At this stage in the project, you will need to bear in mind the limits to what you have done, and what you hope to achieve with the time and resources (still) available to you, so some of the points may need to wait for another time. For others it may be the moment to pause and reconsider some fundamentals of this particular project; progress in this respect is not considered here as forward movement only along a straight road.

WHAT IS ANALYSIS?

Now that you have a clear research question, have isolated what your object of inquiry (the 'what') is, done the lion's share of data-gathering – whatever that entails – the next level is sifting and sorting all this material in order to make sense of it, to yourself but more importantly to shape it in some coherent way for public consumption. What you are entering is the *analysis* phase, a portal through which you pass in order to construct an argument and make it stick as you present your *findings* and draw conclusions about the inquiry. It is at this moment that many a research student often finds themselves leaving a supervision session or seminar presentation with the words 'go analyse this' ringing in their ears.

It is a truism as well that there is more than one way to analyse something; interpretation and analysis are synonyms in many respects (see Harding 1987, Ulin 1984, van Zoonen 1994). Moreover, different modes and *levels of analysis* can lead to distinct if not conflicting outcomes or conclusions based on the same evidence, along with the consequences when these interpretations are then translated into action.

Whatever term we may give it, this phase is when a researcher puts their stamp on the project, makes sense of their material in an original way, however understood. For some modes of research, analysis is synonymous with codified 'rules and procedures'. For others it is tantamount to writing and reflection; the upshot being how effectively and convincingly you can convey the outcome of these reflections to the reader. At the end of the day, for the purposes of completing an academic dissertation, you are looking to make and sustain an argument in a written account of what you did, how, why, and with what sort of outcome.

Even when talking about modes of inquiry identified with *philosophical research*, the primary material referred to here comes in the form of ideas and meanings, usually in written, sometimes multimedia, and increasingly visual *texts*; from philosophical treatises, to images, to sounds. In these scenarios a researcher engages with primary rather than secondary sources; getting to grips with the ideas of Simone de Beauvoir or Hannah Arendt in their own words, or investigating silent movies, is a different prospect from relying entirely on what others have to say.[1]

Whilst all analyses make recourse to the 'facts', the strength of any analysis lies in its ability to combine (counter-)arguments, (counter-)evidence, and a persuasive narrative. For instance:

- In political decisionmaking, how a crisis situation is analysed and recommendations to proceed with any given action (or not proceed as the case may be) has consequences; for example, when countries decide to go to war or not.
- Legislative reforms or international agreements can ensue from experts' analysis of a particular policy issue-area such as that of the International Committee on Climate Change. Academic and other sorts of practitioner expertise have their part to play in the debates that follow.
- Conflicting analyses can play a major role in policy-making outcomes, or the consequences of public inquiries on controversial issues. Take for instance debates about how best to analyse and then reform social services for at-risk children or victims of domestic violence in the aftermath of high-profile deaths, diverging analyses of what went wrong and who is to blame in the wake of financial crises (for example, the global financial crisis of 2008), or acrimony over a religious leader's interpretation of a contentious publication or issue.[2]

The question of what the purpose of analysis is in any particular research undertaking, let alone which – or whose – analysis counts in light of conflicting evidence or contentiousness over procedure, are questions that tend to go begging when students are working in mixed/hybrid or composite disciplinary settings. As Carol Smart notes, these days the work being done in many parts of academe is

> well beyond the old empiricist idea that we simply capture 'reality', condense it, and represent it. We know that knowledge is always knowledge from somewhere, and that different research questions create different realities.
>
> (Smart 2010: 6)

For those projects working with worldviews that would dispute this view (see Chapter 3) the point still remains that analysis, even as the sum total of variable sorts of capturing, condensing, and representing said 'reality', is when the researcher *actively* provides some sense of coherence, *makes informed* and perhaps even inspired *decisions* about the value of any findings (including the means by which they were arrived at), and *sets up parameters* for presenting the material to be included, or excluded, either beforehand or in the course of writing. This is why analysis is more than listing, more than description, more than assertion, more than a compilation of everything a researcher has done, everything we have found out. Analysis entails:

- *Making a commitment*, either taking a conscious stance before the analysis (deduction), developing one as you go along (induction), a mixture of the two ('grounded' analysis/ theorizing), within or despite respective 'disciplinary con-straints' (Smart 2010: 7).

- The act of *thinking*, as a cognitive and intellectual process.
- It is also a lot about *doing*, organizational and literary processes such as writing, tabulating, calculating, coding, sorting, rewriting, deleting, reordering, and representing in graphic forms. All these are elements in any said analysis. Only the most diehard advocate of the power of numbers or direct observations as knowledge in their own right would suggest that there are data requiring no analysis.

What are the trade-offs, then? Researchers, students in particular, at this stage are often confronted with the realization, sometimes too late, that not matter how much material we have, or have not managed to gather, as 'evidence' it needs help in 'speaking for itself'. This boils down to three sorts of trade-offs:

1　However we enter the research domain of our choice, gather or engage with the 'raw' material relevant to our inquiry, we need to render that material in some processed way: to represent it.
2　And that means, effectively, changing the form, if not the substance of that data on the way; statistical analysis of large 'n' surveys are but the first base of this phase for quantitative models; the researcher still needs to engage with these results by making an interpretative intervention.
3　Likewise for those performing any sort of textual analysis: a picture may 'tell a thousand words', but whose words, and what is there to tell?

Before getting into particulars, the next section deals with approaches in which the 'rules and procedures' reside in modes of analysis rather than modes of gathering data.[3]

WORKING WITH TEXTS

In western academe, the large majority of material that is gathered, analysed and presented as scholarly knowledge in the humanities and social sciences takes the form of written texts, as already noted in Chapter 4. Even as industrialized societies have acquired significant dimensions of visual material with the advent of television, film, and increasingly image-laden computer interfaces in the age of the internet, written documents still provide researchers with primary data. Historians deal with archival documents, those looking to investigate policy study written communiqués, White Papers, and legislation as legal scholars dissect legal statutes. Meanwhile, cultural and social anthropologists, media and communications scholars, sociologists, and political scientists have been taking an interest in the 'visual cultures' that constitute how individuals and communities live and make sense of their world.

For these reasons alone, the term 'text' now denotes more than the written word; a photographic image, film, television programme, advertisement, or piece of music can also be regarded as a text. Their multiples also, such as an advertising campaign, musical genre, set of images, novel. That no text emerges from nowhere, out of context, is a basic premise of those forms of analysis focusing on the way texts are produced, who produces them and under what conditions. These demarcations are further complicated when text (literal and otherwise) is accompanied by an interest in attitudes, behaviours, and even outcomes whereby the text/s are treated as causal agents. By the same token, much useful and indeed groundbreaking research has been carried out on texts treated as self-contained data, in which meaning/s are contained, intention and interpretation deducible from this content.

Paths diverge within this larger rubric. On the one hand researchers can treat texts (narrowly and broadly defined) as opaque or transparent. In both instances we see research designs where a body of material (written texts for instance, or advertising images) is treated forensically, being broken down into composite parts, examined, and then reconstituted with an increase in insight or new knowledge emerging. These two forks in the road proceed more or less as follows:

- On the one hand, researchers treat written textual matter as an empirical, contained object comprised of words, phrases, grammar, and syntax. Much can be learnt, according to this approach, by analysing this manifest content in a methodical, consistent, and so comparable way. The cumulative effect of this sort of approach is to
    - ascertain measurable indices of meaning-as-content as a baseline as well as an indicator of significance; for example, frequencies of derogatory terms, news coverage, trends, fashionable ideas;
    - interpret the implications following from there; for example, the appearance of negative terms frequently paired with a particular social grouping (male youths and anti-social behaviour, homeless people and addiction, the Global South and misery) are used to prove hypotheses about *media framing*, social prejudices, the power of newsroom editors, and such like.
- On the other hand, the opacity of the material requires or is taken both as a given and as a riddle. This paradoxical approach means that there are various sorts of interpretative intervention possible, if not preferable. Three broad lines are:
    - by following the line of thought of the analyst who has acquired an intimate understanding of the text in its own right and context (perhaps even translating or transcribing parts of the text) as a *hermeneutic*, namely as one element in a larger set of texts and historical trajectory;
    - by applying strict, or more open-ended forms of interpretative methods, for example, *semiotics*, *conversational analysis*, and other sorts of linguistic approaches to the way languages function by which these architectures – grammar, syntax, and other technicalities – frame how the analyst approaches the selected material including the rules by which they dissect it, from political speeches, to press releases, to literature;
    - by doing a bit of both in order to underscore the way that written, visual, or mixed material are *social texts*; there is more than one interpretation, reception, and meaning or significance contained or striven for; for example, advertising exploits these 'gaps' and 'double meanings' in visual and literary ways, as do painters, poets and novelists.

So where exactly does the divide, if indeed there is but a single one, lie? The main line in the sand for our purposes is, I would argue, between approaches that see

- the whole as a sum of its parts; and
- those that regard the whole as greater than the sum of its parts.

It sounds like a riddle but this distinction has been a fundamental source of friction, both productive and corrosive, in a number of classic and ongoing debates across the arts and humanities, and their counterparts in the social sciences.

In the spirit of pragmatism, the modus operandi here, I will deal with these two pathways and their respective twists and turns in turn, bearing in mind that, as always, these overviews focus on operating principles, practicalities, and wider methodological implications that can be executed as both multi-directional and one-way streets. Moreover, this is a terrain in which terms of reference are often particularly fudged or have different applications; where intellectual fashions come and go. It is also where the polemics of philosophical and interdisciplinary *methodological* grandstanding can hinder creative research, research into not just what people (and now their virtual personae) do or think but also what these activities and ideas produce – as cultural practices, art, media rituals, social institutions, power hierarchies, political regimes, economic exchange, bodies and even the human psyche.

CONTENT ANALYSIS

This term has come to be identified with research that renders written, and in some cases visual material as countable – measurable – *content*. This is understood to mean the words, phrases and images that comprise manifest content as what is visible to the seeing/reading eye; there is a message and that message is decipherable in a number of ways.

- Nowadays this notion of content comes to use in both traditional – written and audio-visual – and digital, web-based formats.
- News and entertainment media, policy documents, literature, and colour spectra lend themselves to this treatment of content as manifest and measurable in quantifiable terms.
- As documents and media messages widely construed become increasingly web-embedded this 'content' can also be broken down into byte-sized data; if not words, then phrases or search results based on keywords.
- As the use and pursuit of web-content as 'keywords' have become the staple of everyday and academic uses of the web, aided and abetted by increasingly able automated search engine software, related products and services (see Chapter 5), pre-digital era notions of content have taken on a new dimension.
  - Indeed they lend themselves very well to automated sorts of analysis, for example, commercial search engines for the open web or more specialized tools for research or surveillance purposes.

- There are some who argue that content – as a product of social and cultural life – has become digitized and with this so has (hyper)textual production and (hypermedia) circulation and their role in how societies reproduce themselves meaningfully and in memory.

For the time being, I am going to refer to the variety or approaches under discussion here as content in a generic sense of the term precisely because of the way that the web has created a swathe of 'content' and interactions for emergent research. This also means resorting to the quantitative–qualitative division to acknowledge their respective research traditions as these set off along the paths sketched above.

Quantitative traditions of content analysis lay the emphasis on forensic analysis of aggregated, countable evidence: keyword frequency, terms, collocations. The unit of analysis is thereby the 'message component' (Abdelal et al., citing Neuendorf, 2009: 5) that is visible to any reader/s. Here, whilst there is a level of opaqueness (otherwise there would no point embarking on a research inquiry), this approach proceeds on the assumption that transparency can be made evident by unpacking and then analysing the content on its own terms. This is basically the 'idea that the individual text is meaningful on its own and that a summary of the message within it is the desirable outcome' (Abdelal et al. 2009: 6).

Qualitative traditions beg to differ. The demarcation line here is that qualitative understandings treat content as opaque by definition; sub-text – the different meanings (and thereby receptions) that lie 'between the lines' of any manifest content – is as important, if not more significant in psychological or political terms than the manifest, explicit message. We will look at how this approach operates for research in due course.

How then do researchers adhering to these broad traditions go about deciphering their material – text/message?

- For quantitative modes this is managed by devising a *coding scheme* as a device for breaking the message down into suitably manageable components: phrases, transitions, single words. These schemes are devised around familiar notions of probability and non-probability sampling (see Chapter 6, surveys and questionnaires section) for particular sorts of research questions.
- For qualitative modes, we see that this literal notion of 'coding' is replaced by a more figurative one: that of 'encoding' and 'decoding', to borrow here from Stuart Hall (1996). This means that the researcher's task is to unearth the inner – perhaps even hidden – significance of the message in context. The assumption here is that there is a hidden meaning, if not several. Texts are treated here as phenomena, representations of thought and experience, and as sociocultural artefacts.
- Nestled somewhere in between are what we could call 'architectural' modes that examine the mechanics and so structure of texts. How they function linguistically is the primary focus. These deep forensic analyses have developed respective procedures for exploring these structures and functionalities based on whether meaning is determined in the final analysis (no pun intended) by these underlying structures or the way language is enacted, or practised; for example, the difference

between looking at grammatical structures (nouns, verbs, prepositional phrases) or inflections of speech such as pauses, accentuation, rhythm.[4]

Back to content analysis within the quantitative tradition. Coding schemes, human or computer-aided, can be divided into two broad forms: (1) frequency counts (key-words, phrases, word pairs) and (2) keyword-in-context analysis. In essence, this is what a search engine on the web does for us every day; based on our search items (in themselves a form of elementary coding), its algorithm sets about sifting and collating millions of texts stored in the service provider's data banks and then presenting the results according to a particular, and highly effective code: the 'top ten hits'. Whilst ordinary web-surfers (including researchers) seldom ask why or how their search engine came up with that particular list, scholars pose just these sorts of questions because of the influence of the top ten on status and significance, to wit *citation indexes*. More on this below.

Practicalities

Let's for the moment treat the term *content analysis* as a rubric under which both qualitative and quantitative approaches make diverse, and sometimes overlapping claims about how societies and cultures make sense of their world.

As noted already, real-life research scenarios and 'texts' now encompass more than words on a page of hard copy. Moreover, in computer-mediated and multimedia settings there are many ways to conduct 'content analysis' by combining quantitative and qualitative indicators of significance in symbolic and pragmatic forms:

Quantitative notions of content analysis

Quantitative notions of content analysis are generally based on research questions that entail hypothesis-testing (see Chapter 2, 000 section) and which regard texts as transparent carriers of meaning. These approaches treat written texts as made up of units of analysis: single words, phrases, or sentences. They also look at positioning as well as context.

- Significance is ascertained in terms of frequency (the number of times a word appears) and/or placement (where in a text keywords appear).
- Whilst words are the traditional unit of analysis, visual texts can also be broken down in this way, albeit not exclusively. For visual texts, for example, a television programme or film fragment, frequency and placement can be coded by looking at timing, frame-lengths, editing, as well as the script.

Coding schemes

Analysing the content in this way requires the researcher to set up some sort of *coding scheme*,[5] which they will then apply to the selection.

- The results are then translated into numerical values, organized and then presented as tables or graphs according to the research question in hand.
- Developing and then applying coding schemes in order to make sense of the material in its manifest form (words on a page or screen, colour frequencies, or images) is based on *deductive reasoning*: an analytical framework is applied to the data in a preconceived form. From there inferences are drawn and the strength of the findings based on the integrity and validity of the coding scheme used.
- To be effective, a coding scheme has to be applied to a clear sample; this could be based on various sorts of selectivity. For research looking to ascertain the frequency of keywords or their placement in a comprehensive way, then the stress here is on ensuring the sampling techniques, the coding scheme, and the findings are in a logical relationship.

A similar approach can be applied to the content analysis of television programmes, newspapers, or policy document-sets whereby the 'content' here is an amalgam of texts, scripts, images, audio (for example, in YouTube clips), and user-produced material. The various sorts of content can also be broken down into quantifiable coding schemes.

- However, different sorts of 'content' require their respective criteria for selection and collation; for example, a news item on television is comprised not only of the script but also of footage; a talk show likewise but this time there is an element of editing and 'live' interaction.
- Audio material is treated as units of sound: rhythm (for example, the 'amen break'), samples (a melodic line), elements of the mix (separating out the drums from lead guitar), riffs, and so on. When a score is a core element this too is treated as a particular sort of text.

In sum, any coding scheme needs to make sense of, and elucidate the underlying research question and objectives on the inquiry. Once the content has had the coding applied

- the results need to be studied and analysed according to the theoretical framework governing the inquiry;
- this may see the researcher moving between an deductive approach to the material (where the hypothesis/research question sets the tone) or a more inductive one (where the outcome of the coding is studied for patterns and insights emerging from there);
- the findings are usually presented in the form of tables or graphs whereby the designated coded content is rendered as numerical values of frequency, volume, duration, or spacing.

Administration

A coding scheme has to be devised, according to the research question. In that respect there is a certain level of trial and error, an aspect often belied by the clarity and graphic elegance of many coding schemes presented as research findings. What exactly comprises a coding scheme is effectively both theory and method (see Chapter 2, theory and method section); frequency, positioning, framing of single terms, pairs or phrases is selected based on an inquiry's respective 'how', 'what', 'where', and 'why'. In any case, this design phase is crucial and requires time and thought.

- Automated programs do not do this for you.
- Moreover, why rush to software when in fact much coding can be done manually – coloured pens and other sorts of drawn graphics work if the rationale behind these selections makes sense.
- That said, for larger chunks of digitized material, software tools, such as Invivo can facilitate these schematics by performing an analysis based on the criteria preset by the researcher.
- All these tools have their own inbuilt defaults and thereby methodological preferences (see Chapter 5) which may affect the degree to which a manually devised scheme 'works'.

Once the results emerge, you need to shift up to another level of analysis; what do these findings (ensuring there are no errors in design or execution) tell you? What inferences can be drawn? What do they not tell us?

Advantages and disadvantages

The advantages of content analysis in this form are:

- The material can be confined: limited to a particular genus, timeframe, or provenance. This works well for written archives, official policy document sets or intergovernmental resolutions, as much is now available on the web.
- Note though that interactive forms of content generation (for example, in discussion forums) need to be pinned down in terms of entry and exit dates.
- Once selected, the material can be reshuffled and examined in many ways, manually or digitally.
- For societies based on written literacy this is a major source of evidential material; for example, policy statements provide insight into political processes, speeches into a political leader's worldview, and news scripts supply an angle on public debates and current events coverage.
- For questions looking into reconstructing important decision-making process as they emerge as policy, content analysis is very useful for navigating and unpacking public and political statements.
- Similarly for media content: current events and controversies, local and global, can be studied through the media content produced by news outlets.
- The coding and eventual analysis, if the selection is manageable and accessible, can be carried out manually and by a single researcher.
- Written texts, unlike human subjects, don't talk back nor do they require informed consent. However – and this is an emerging issue for web-based content and other sorts of analysis – increasingly online texts are falling under conflicting

intellectual property rights regimes, for example, on social networking sites, photos and texts are by default the property of the 'owner' not the user (currently hotly contested by the way).

The last point flags some of the disadvantages, indeed issues around which qualitative approaches part company from these more quantitatively inflections:

- Focusing only on written texts, including visual data, assumes that social phenomena and relationships are contained, and so observable in the written word.
- In increasingly multimedia-saturated societies, conventional forms of investigating content as the written word produced from one source may not be adequate on its own.
- Strictly speaking content analysis focuses on the output of social actions, and interlocutors, as a sort of 'scriptural economy' (Certeau 1991). It is less suited for questions about behaviour, interpersonal interactions, or events, unless these are being reconstructed on the basis of official or eye-witness, informal archival material.
- Effective content analysis is more time-consuming than many realize.
- Issues arising out of selectivity, in terms of what and when, require thought, and access may be assumed rather than possible.
- Whether you develop your own or adopt an existing coding scheme, their application on your selection and then your eventual interpretation of the results is not self-explanatory; graphics produced require more time to consider and come to grips with than many think, often as much as setting up the coding and executing it.
- The focus on the content itself, however it may be approached, may distort other equally important conditions relevant to the inquiry, for example, the conditions of production (e.g. media messages during wartime) or how people (e.g. audiences) receive and respond to the message (e.g. gender-based or class-based differences in responding to news items).
- Meaning, as we will see in the section on textual/visual analysis, does not reside in the manifest, countable content as separated units; meaning resides in the whole rather than in the parts.
- In some political and cultural contexts content may well be misleading, mystifying, or deliberately coded, for example, propaganda, politically sensitive policy documents, or political speeches. Sometimes what is *not* said, or left out of the official record, is as important as the words on the page.
- Turning complex messages and their meanings into numerical values sacrifices understanding to the method, reduces content to numbers when in fact meaning is an *intersubjective* process.

This latter observation is where alternative and competing approaches to researching what humans (and their avatars) produce in written and other sorts of texts come in. What we see on the page, or the screen is not necessarily what we (think we) get.

Methodological implications

Content analysis is generally regarded as a specific term for quantitatively inflected research into written, and now audio-visual texts. But it can also be regarded as a wider term for inquiries into any sort of meaning-making that treats messages, content, and meaning as an interaction between the manifest and latent message/s on the one hand, and reception (how others make sense of these meanings) on the other.

For the time being bear in mind that when opting for a conventional content analysis approach, the following methodological distinctions are in play:

1   In the one instance, researchers treat content primarily as self-contained and unidirectional, i.e. meaning resides in the message itself and largely at the point of its production (the sender and message are in a one-to-one relationship).
2   In the other, researchers regard the meaning as an interplay between what is produced (manifested) and its reception (how others receive and respond to the message); how messages are transmitted and circulated is also studied in other cases.

The difficult part here for anyone interested in this sort of inquiry, from archivists to media researchers and policy analysts, is the way these two paths (and the ever-increasing degrees of specialized techniques and vocabularies that go with them) appear to head off in opposite directions immediately. In many respects this is true; content analysis has developed in Anglo-American media and communications, and political research institutions as a largely quantitative enterprise.

Its counterpart, textual/discourse analysis, has followed a particularly continental path, spliced in turn by changes in the way scholars and theorists have staked various levels of commitment to *structuralist* frameworks. In other words, whether all meaning/s reside in the way language is structured – all is coded and so can be deciphered methodically, or rather in the way language is received – the code is over-determined by a variety of factors, such as the vagaries of human psyche and culture.

Practically however, and contingent upon the inquiry in hand, it is more productive when starting to consider how you might carry out a research project to gather this sort of data that these poles are not necessarily diametrically opposed. For research looking to work primary with texts (broadly defined), consider the following:

(i)   If your project gives you reason to analyse the content of a set of written texts, television programmes, or website content then the outcome may be useful for setting up a workable set of parameters, trying out which criteria comprise your eventual 'coding scheme' or get you more acquainted with the content itself. In all cases as an object of research it needs more than a first reading.
(ii) It could be that your project sees you working entirely from the presumption that this content is the object of inquiry, its examination the lion's share of your original research component, its frequency and placement of key terms, references or framing crucial to your investigation. As such the design and setting-up of your analytical scheme requires time and attention. The methods by which you intend to carry out this sort of content analysis thereby need elucidation, to make sense of your research question.

(iii) It could be that a dual approach is an option. If so, why? What are the limits you need to set to achieving both sorts of analysis?

TEXTUAL/VISUAL ANALYSIS

This section turns to ways of researching 'content' by another name – *texts*;[6] those that regard the latter as not only a product of society and culture but also the means by which culture and society are produced. In short, 'texts' are socially embedded and so emerge out of contexts. By the same token, they become autonomous as symbols, signs, and reflections.

Characterized as quintessentially *qualitative*, the term *textual analysis* includes visual as well as written material. These approaches avoid references to 'content'; meaning is produced by more than what we see or read on the page/screen. Stronger still, breaking meanings down into quantified values for recurring words or phrases mistakes the wood for the trees; meaning is not reducible to frequency indicators alone. It has to be not only interpreted but it is also received, and then circulated in different ways by different actors.

This point of departure is based on an everyday insight: people often do not mean what they say, or write; there are many ways to respond to a film, piece of music, or novel; many more ways in which the interaction between production, content, and reception generate layers of acceptable, and so unacceptable meaning.

Operating principles

These approaches to content use another notion of 'text' whereby the production and reception of a message involves more than one sort of response: this could be emotional, intellectual, or even physical. In addition, these responses generate another set of meanings: texts. In short, this analytical approach is based on the premise that 'no text is an island', stands outside society; hence the frequent use of the term intertextuality.

Based on intersecting but by no means synonymous worldviews, and comparably different emphases on the theory–method relationship in academic research (see Chapter 3), research programmes falling under the rubric of textual analysis treat visual, written, or aural content as latent – hidden levels of meaning-making – the significance of which requires active interpretation that is more than the sum total of frequency of appearance:

- How the researcher goes about interpreting (usually posited as the opposite of counting) the content can follow a number of trajectories, based in linguistics, philosophy, and literary criticism.
- Non-quantified sorts of 'content analysis' – usually called *textual analysis* – are executed on the basis that manifest content – words – are in themselves codes. This means that their frequency or 'preferred placement' has a significance that may be more than face value.

- The emphasis therefore is on inductive reasoning – to conceptualize, 'theorize your way out of' the material[7] rather than impose a coding scheme onto it. In this sense qualitative content analysis, whether this is called discourse or textual analysis, is based on inductive modes of reasoning.
- For this reason the effectiveness of the eventual outcome of these sorts of analyses is dependent on the agility with which the researcher can make an argument by way of handling the material in a more pliable, and plastic way.

Practicalities

Research based on a treatment of the written, visual, and aural production of societies – from hieroglyphics to totem poles, Hollywood or Bollywood musicals, YouTube videos, to government White Papers – still require a researcher to select a 'unit of analysis', have a research question and object of analysis in mind and a theoretical framework by which to make sense of the material they are investigating. It is a caricature of well-conceived and well-executed research in these traditions, to assume that the influence of philosophical heavyweights, particularly those from continental Europe, means that there is no methodological rigour involved. On the contrary, the research question takes on a particularly central role, as does the ability of the researcher to make use of their 'text' in such a way that their argument and evidence hang together. These are not approaches where 'anything goes'.[8]

But the main issue for research students brought up and skilful with the audio-visual media and advertising images that surround them all the time –indeed permeate all our working and everyday lives in hi-tech and visually saturated societies – is that being used to something is not the same as being able to analyse it, or treat it in academic research terms.

The following practicalities may appear straightforward, but as educators and supervisors know, 'seeing' an image or 'hearing' a piece of music is distinct from analysing it. Observation in these sorts of research are based on how the object observed is conceived as something in particular, be it a fossil, an advertising image, or a film scene. How we hear or see something as aural or visual and how we might analyse it requires different levels of engagement. So:

1 What exactly is your *text*?
- Is it a single item? A cluster of similar items? A selection of contrasting items?
- If it is an image, is it a still or moving one? (Photograph or movie still, video or film-clip).
- If it is a piece of audio, how would you characterize it? A musical composition? An environmental sound? A soundtrack? A sample? Pop song, live or recorded?
2 Once selected, or perhaps on the basis of why you think it is relevant to your inquiry, consider the following:
- What do you see initially? In other words, how would you describe it if the image (or clip, audio sample) were not available? For example, how is it organized as colour, form, depth? How long is it? Is there a clear subject (for example, a face, or 'story') or is it more abstract?

- What is your initial, or recurring response to the text (image, sound, clip)?
- Do you think this is the only response possible, i.e. would other people respond in the same way?
- Is this response a negative or positive one? How do you think this affects your eventual understanding of what its significance is? For instance, is the image a controversial one (for example, using nudity, or violent references, or reproducing documentary footage of violence or disaster such as starving children).
- Does the context (of your reception or its production) affect your or others' reactions? For example, if this is an advertisement, is it part of a larger campaign? Does it include references to social issues or current events? If so, in what way?

3   The next step is to consider the exact approach you are going to take in analytical terms, assuming here that you have not already opted for a particular school, for example, *critical discourse analysis* (see Fairclough 2003). This includes addressing questions such as:
- Are you interested primarily in analysing the text on its own terms, as an aesthetic or cultural artefact?
- Have you a clear idea about whether you are interested in the text's socio-cultural, political, or economic significance?
- Or are you more concerned with the way it was produced or the context in which it has been circulated and how others makes sense of it?
  - For example, television newscasts are studied from the point of view of how they are produced (edited, written, timed) as well as how they convey meanings (the item itself), along with how audiences respond (differently) to these programmes.
  - For example, an advertising campaign is one thing, an analysis of the particular images and how they convey various meanings (for example about femininity, aspiration, love and desire) another. Global brands and the advertising industry have been particularly influential in creating particular sorts of images that not only sell something but sell this commodity a certain way (for example, cars with beautiful women, clothes with androgynous models, cigarettes as socially desirable, alcohol as cool).
- Have you an idea about what sort of worldview is at stake in the approach you will be employing? In other words, as a baseline are you taking a
  - *hermeneutic* approach to its meaning?
  - *psychoanalytical* one?
  - *semiotic* one?
  - *structuralist* or *post-structuralist* one?
  - *post-colonial* or *feminist* approach to any of the above?

4   Moving ahead: How are you going to present your 'findings' and substantiating evidence; on what – and whose – authority?
- First, is pasting in an image or frame-by-frame stills of a film scene enough on its own? Will you need to dissect these in some way? If so, what kind of commentary is required for this evidence to ground your analysis in some sort of argument?
- If reproducing an image, have you considered copyright issues?

- How do you envisage lining up your analysis to that of others? What kind of larger discussion (viz. literature) is pertinent to your interpretation?
- Had you considered that there could be a danger of reading too much into an image, a text? In other words, on what authority are you drawing your inferences?
- Do you impute all possible interpretations to this text, or its relationship to the world, the historical context in which it circulates or is consumed?

As you can see from the list above, these terms of reference refer to a large body of literature, and their composite debates, in turn. They also point to a range of world-views, some of which consist of trenchant alternatives to conventional approaches to studying cultural and social production.

By the same token, these approaches have become in other quarters an orthodoxy as well, begging a number of questions about the privileged interpretative position maintained by these authoritative analyses; 'ways of seeing' (see Berger 1990) may indeed be multiple, any one boiling down to many other factors. Emerging in the crucible of the postmodern or, as some call it, 'literary turn' of the last quarter of the twentieth century, these larger debates are beyond our scope. Their echoes and ramifications for how generations of research students approach any given text, however defined, are palpable in books, classrooms, and dissertation work.

Methodological implications

As research students live and study in an image-saturated world, much of which now comes in the form of web-based multimedia, here too we can see longstanding traditions of research under pressure to take account of the different qualities web-mediated, produced and circulated content bring to research endeavours. Add to this the instantaneity and global circulation of images – advertising, news, entertainment – and we see how research incorporating texts (however defined) as an object of analysis is having to deal with new challenges. As Judith Williamson notes in her then groundbreaking structuralist analysis, *Decoding Advertising*:

> It is the images we see in ads which give them significance, which transfer their significance to the product. This is why advertising is so uncontrollable, because whatever restrictions are made in terms of their verbal content or 'false claims', there is no way of getting at their use of images and symbols. . . . [It] is images and not words which ultimately provide the currency in ads.
>
> (Williamson 1978: 175)

As noted above, western academic research is heavily dependent on the written word even though nowadays this is arguably being superseded by visual and audio cultures.

A final note on this generically qualitative approach to researching content as coded, social texts. The distinctions between all the aforementioned philosophical approaches to how people create and represent their world, in figurative and literal terms (documentary evidence) that include commerce, beliefs, and everyday experiences and those that treat content in more quantifiable ways, runs along another dividing line.

To put the distinction rather starkly, this is an *ontological* difference between whether

- the physical world and its representation (in visual or linguistic form) operate in a one-to-one relationship, or
- as the Surrealist and Dadaist movements in early twentieth-century art, and others in psychology, evoked and provoked their viewers to consider, there is a gap not only in our ability to accurately convey what we see (for example, a landscape painting in the realist style) but also in the way the physical, and by association social world is made up of contradictory 'ways of seeing' that include emotions, drives, or cultural sensibilities.

We can see then that the first option above could also apply to quantitative, researcher and coding-scheme driven forms of inquiry even though these treat texts as manifest (not coded) content, strictly speaking. In the second option we can see how in some research scenarios a written or visual 'text' could well be interpreted on its own terms as well as examined in light of what others have to say, for example, by way of surveys, interviews, or focus groups.

If you come down on the second of these options then the next, *epistemological* challenge (particularly if you are ever debating these points with practitioners of the first option) comprises questions about the status and nature of the knowledge produced:

- Which ways are best to interpret gaps, contradictions, double meanings?
- Is only one interpretation possible? Then whose counts?
- And even if this were so, are meanings conveyed and received at the individual level; or
- Are they rather the product of cultural – social – agreement; tacit or institutionalized?
- When did these start, or develop over time? In short where to draw the line if everything is socially embedded, all texts multiple, all interpretations valid?

If your research inquiry, and the question you are addressing, leads you to consider more than one of these options then there is no reason for you not to design the data-gathering and analysis accordingly. Here, as always, it is less a question of piling one approach on top of another but rather showing how exactly a considered application of elements of both would be informative. That, again (and it bears repeating) is where the methodological rationale has an abstract and a practical side.

DISCOURSE ANALYSIS

Before moving into the last set of issues for this chapter, we need to take a look at another large rubric under which a lot of research falls: *discourse analysis*. Whilst this term overlaps with content/textual analysis at first sight, it actually emerges out of the interaction between the 'literary turn' of the late 1960s in which written texts – archives, policy, speeches – predominate as an object of inquiry and that era's social movements, decolonization, and political protest. The point for now is to note that here we see the term discourse as a larger, more malleable rubric covering the above distinctions.

Here content/texts are treated as ways in which powerful elites over time, or in a particular institutional setting, convey and reproduce power; by setting terms of debate, agendas, or simply in the way the historical record, as archives particularly, is selective and not representative of all views. 'History is written by the victors' as the saying goes. For this reason, discourse analysis is an approach that consciously moves the selectivity net outwards to include 'a collection of related texts, constituted as speech, written documents, and social practices, that produce meaning and organize social knowledge' (Abdelal et al. 2009: 7; see Burn and Parker 2003: 77 *passim*).

Whilst references to content/textual analysis imply a relatively contained set of terms and techniques, references to *discourse analysis* are more expansive. And this is where the problems begin. The contentiousness of the very term *discourse* remains an open debate, between successive generations of proponents of this mode of research and between more content-based and more textual-based schools of thought (sometimes, but not always demarcated by the Atlantic Ocean or the English Channel) and their critics.

The main objection, not to put too fine a point on it, is a lack of precision about what parameters of the raw data (speech, documents, practices) are selected as well as how said data is deemed to be significant, beyond the aims of the research questions – given the open-endedness of this approach. A key figure in this body of work, particularly as it found its way into Anglo-American academe, is the French philosopher, provocateur, and godfather of the notion of discourse analysis as a critical alternative to textual analysis, Michel Foucault.

First, the intention of this move away from content, or text strictly conceived in his own words is:

> to raise questions in an effective, genuine way, and to raise them with the greatest possible rigor, with the maximum complexity and difficulty so that a solution doesn't spring from the head of some reformist intellectual or suddenly appear in the head of a party's political bureau.
>
> (Foucault, cited in Faubion 2000: 288)

Next, the notion of *discourse* itself is treated here as not only an object of research, even if a broadly inclusive one, but also the means by which to conduct the analysis. What this boils down to, in Foucault's words, is that in

> every society the production of discourse is at once controlled, selected, organized and redistributed according to a certain number of procedures, whose role is to

avert its powers and its dangers, to cope with chance events, to evade its ponderous, awesome materiality. In a society such as our own we all know the rules of exclusion. The most obvious and familiar of these concerns what is prohibited.

(Foucault 1972: 215–16)

This approach clearly departs company from architectural and content-based procedures for deciphering texts, however defined, in several ways:

- by consciously combining literary techniques with historical research methods (living and archival documents as a focus being a favourite of Foucault's own research);
- by employing sociological and anthropological approaches to connect the above to their sociocultural and institutional contexts: people and practices (elicited through interviews as well as participant-observation).

The sum total is a range of research that investigates these sorts of 'procedures' or 'exclusions' at any given period of time or locale; not only text in literal terms can be focused upon but so can the role of key figures, media coverage, parliamentary debates, and popular culture.

Whilst there is range of conceptualizations and applications of the term 'discourse' currently operating, the bottom line is that these inquiries are premised on designing research that investigates how the way 'we describe reality has an effect on the way we perceive and act upon our environment [and if so, how] new perspectives might lead us to consider alternative courses of action' (Tickner 1995: 61); it is not unthinkable that some of these research designs incorporate equally diverging and converging notions of the status of quantitative and qualitative data as evidence, or units of analysis.

Summing up

So how to make sense of these moving targets, claims, and counterclaims about rigour, selectivity, and replicability as the *sine qua non* of truth claims? How to keep our bearings in the strong ebb and flow of intellectual fashion where these approaches have strong traction for our inquiry?

1   For coping purposes, a key distinction for projects undertaking some kind of discourse analysis is that these can focus purely on literary texts as well as 'place texts and practices in their intersubjective contexts', this being 'the qualitative and interpretive recovery of meaning from the language that actors use to describe and understand social phenomena' (Abdelal et al. 2009: 6).
2   In other words, meaning-making is not locked in the 'text' as a static object; necessary for traditional content analyses. Rather what actors, as individuals but also as institutions, do with these 'texts' also counts.
3   So, discourse also refers to practices as well as the written word, visual signs, or audio cues: to intentions behind a message as well as the way audiences, or in some

cases consumers pick up on these intentions or indeed reinvent them in the way they then talk about, refer to, and reiterate these composite objects.

4   Data gathered in discourse/textual analyses can be quantitative in the sense that a high or low frequency of an item (word, phrase) in a written data set may be significant if taken in context; conversely the absence of keywords can also be significant depending on the underlying relations governing how a text is conceived (for example, diplomatic or politically sensitive policy-making).

5   However, the main emphasis is on the scholar interpreting these texts, placing this interpretation in a larger context and then convincing 'his or her readers that a particular reconstruction of the intersubjective context of some social phenomenon . . . is useful for understanding an empirical outcome' (Abdelal et al. 2009: 7).

To sum up and move on, we can regard the different modes of analysing 'content' along

- Quantitative lines: where manifest content (frequency and/or placement of keywords, phrases, framing, keyword mapping), coding schemes and hypothesis-based research questions predominate, and varying levels of statistical operations are applied once a coding scheme has been devised.
- Qualitative lines: whereby 'content' is treated as irreducible to frequency or placements and there is interpretation of latent content whereby the sub-text or sub-texts are isolated and analysed by the researchers; this can be achieved via open-ended research questions or more structured analytical frameworks based on grammatical and syntactic structures – in linguistic terms, hermeneutics (i.e. interpretation, semiotics), signified/signifier, etc.

Figure 7.1 Surrealist painter meets surrealist plumber

Source: Dan Piraro, http://www.bizarro.com

What is at stake? Wider methodological considerations for this line of research reside in the various theories of communication and language underpinning the above distinctions. For instance:

- It is not unreasonable to proceed by getting to grips with how a text, or set of texts is made up before embarking on an interpretation of its larger meaning.
- This can also provide a manageable approach to generating some original data in cost-effective ways.
- However, just as focus groups don't necessarily provide us with a substitute for the time and effort needed to undertake semi-structured interviews, content analysis in its conventional, more quantitatively understood sense has advantages and disadvantages. These, needless to say, have implications for the role this approach may play in your inquiry, or its relevance for your research question.

Further reading

McQuail (1994) for an overview of content analysis in media and communications; Gunter (2000) for more quantitative extensions; Bertrand and Hughes (2004) for a discussion of texts as an axial aspect of media and communications research; see also Skovmand and Schrøder (1992) for their take on mixed methods in this discipline.

For more detailed discussions within distinct approaches see Atkinson and Coffey (in Silverman 2011: 77–92; Prior (in Silverman 2011: 93–110); Emmison (in Silverman 2011: 233–49); Heath (in Silverman 2011: 250–69). See also Markham (in Silverman 2011: 111–28) for researching web-based content issues.

Overviews include Berg (2009), Burn and Parker (2003), and Sturken and Cartwright (2005), who look at the theory and methodological practicalities of textual/visual analysis as explicitly qualitative methodologies in the round.

Working example: As the theoretical and evidential terrain available for first-timers is huge, intimately connected to the emergence of the moving image, consumer society, and advertising, the following cluster of authors concentrate on photography, a medium that has fascinated philosophers and researchers since it was invented in the late nineteenth century, evolved into the moving image, and was then digitized in the late twentieth century. Images are now a staple of contemporary news and entertainment, PR and advertising, and the way people communicate online: see Benjamin (1973 [1931]), Barthes (1981), Sontag (1977, 2003), Williamson (1978), Freedberg (1989).

DEDUCTIVE AND INDUCTIVE PATHS TO KNOWLEDGE

We now need to spend a moment with the underwater part of the analysis iceberg, distinctions within and between disciplines about which ways of reasoning are the 'key' to knowledge that claim superiority to the knowledge and understanding based on what some call common sense (life experience), others see as residing in formal belief systems and scriptures, and others follow based on knowledge, 'folk wisdom', handed down through the generations from father to son, mother to daughter, elders to younger generations.[9]

There is an implicit yet crucial distinction made between *deductive* and *inductive* modes of reasoning. Induction refers to the process of reasoning from specific observation to general principle or theory. Deduction indicates proceeding from general principle or theory to specific observations. Both are involved in the history and practices of scientific discovery, knowledge production, and the business of academic research. Both are embedded in major philosophical debates in western academe, and popular imaginaries, about what distinguishes scientific knowledge from other truth claims. Because working assumptions about which is the right path to follow, in principle, govern formal and informal expectations about what sorts of inquiry pass muster in respective settings, we need to make a pit stop.

First, think for a moment. Which approach do you tend towards when learning about things?

- Do you begin with a theory – presupposition – about something and assess the evidence, the facts, as supporting or refuting this presupposition?
- Do you prefer to wait until you have all the facts before you draw any conclusions?

In short; deductive modes of reasoning work from the top down. Inductive reasoning works the other way around: conclusions or general laws are drawn only after enough evidence – facts – has been assembled and analysed, from the ground up. Here a 'general law' can only be inferred from 'particular instances'. For deductive reasoning, theoretical formulations effectively precede the data-gathering with the latter functioning as proof or 'falsification' of the original supposition, hypothesis, or general theory. For inductive modes, theories or generalizations emerge out of the raw material much later in the day; certain methods, and methodological issues follow.

Sherlock Holmes – the fictional detective created by Conan Doyle whose method for solving crimes was by 'deduction' (the first scenario above), when he cracked a case would exclaim to his bemused sidekick Dr Watson that it was 'elementary, my dear Watson!'. Holmes was an ardent advocate, fictional as he may be, of what he called *deduction* as a failsafe mode of logical reasoning. His approach and manner to investigation is best summed up in the following way: 'I'm Sherlock Holmes, the world's only consulting detective . . . .This is what I do: * 1. I observe everything. * 2. From what I observe, I deduce everything. * 3. When I've eliminated the impossible, whatever remains, no matter how mad it might seem, must be the truth.'[10]

Taken in the context of early forensic science and at the height of industrialization and the 'Big Science' narrative during the late nineteenth and twentieth centuries, the notion of applying a logical approach to solving problems has come to epitomize and distinguish the 'scientific' from the non-scientific, the methodical from the chaotic, the logical from the irrational.[11] What Holmes was effectively doing, however, was drawing inferences from observational evidence, coming to a 'logical conclusion' about 'particular instances' of a 'general law'.

Some of the 'laws' at work in this sort of detective work, driving many a twist and turn in any whodunit plot, are models of human behaviour (for example, a murderer often returns to the scene of a crime, facial movements or physiological reactions are seen to correlate with lying or telling the truth), the properties of physical matter, and such like. More recent popular television shows like *Silent Witness* (UK) or *CSI Investigation* (USA) write this way of reasoning into the script, making the accompanying computer-facilitated techniques of forensic proof the star of the show. Even when inspiration, intuition, or coincidence contribute – a detective's 'hunch' or sense that they 'have got a feeling about this one', the approach that wins out in the end is this 'Holmesian' emphasis on the close relationship between logical reasoning and observation.

Much ink has been spilled in arguments about what comes first, the facts, their observation, or the frameworks by which such facts can be observed and thereby identified at all. Starting with a law – or an hypothesis – and then substantiating it by recourse to the facts is a basic tenet of the natural sciences, and their strictly quantitative cousins in the social sciences. Starting with the 'facts' and drawing what are often tentative conclusions at a later date is the hallmark of both qualitative and quantitative work. In both cases the strengths and weaknesses of either get used as sticks to beat the other over the head with. Philosophers have provided researchers here with a rich literature and armoury of arguments and counter-arguments. Some are the stuff of legend.

But are these two ways of thinking really that mutually exclusive (see Gray 2009: 14–16)? Most research practice involves a hybrid of inductive and deductive reasoning. So, think again, was Sherlock Holmes really employing a *deductive* mode of reasoning? Perhaps he was doing a bit of both; inferring from the general to the particular as well as the particular to the general. Some pundits would go further by noting how 'Holemsian' deduction is in fact *induction* by another name.[12]

So why does this distinction matter so much in theory and practice, and lie at the heart of major schisms, strategic alliances, and occasional détentes between schools of thought as it does?

The heart of the matter is actually a paradox, or as it is often called, the 'problem of induction' (Popper in Jarvie 2005: 821). In the history of western academe and particularly the rise of 'scientific method' as the arbiter of knowledge, truth, and validity, it is not a minor matter to argue about what comes first, 'theoretical knowledge or experience', 'perceptions' or 'conceptions' of the world (see Chalmers 2004, Radder 2006).

The paradox for everyday research is the realization that hypotheses cannot 'come from observation alone because there is no observation without hypotheses' (Jarvie op cit, see Chalmers 2004: 41 *passim*, Gray 2009: 14–16). If that is the case, then the optimal way to proceed in a *scientific* way, according to Karl Popper's formative reworking of this everyday 'problem of induction' and his answer to it, a way of getting around this conundrum by privileging a particular form of hypothesis-formation, is one that is phrased and executed in such a way that it can be, indeed must be open to being *'falsified'*. To put it another way, scientific research, and by association scholarship aiming to produce a particular sort of knowledge must be able, and willing to be found wrong (Chalmers 2004: 59 *passim*). In other words, researchers are not in the business of being 'right' despite protestations to the contrary (see Schulz 2010).[13]

As Popper put it, what scientists really do is engage in a set of decisions about how to go about doing science according to strict rules about scientific procedure;

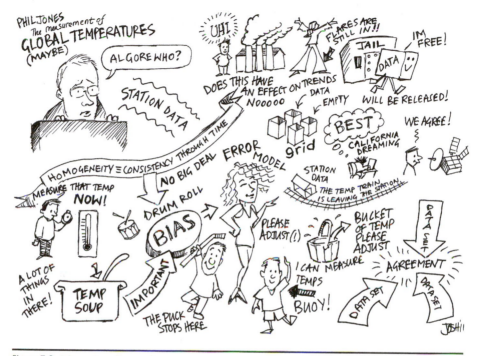

Figure 7.2 Measuring climate change

Source: Josh: http://www.cartoonsbyjosh.com

'designed in such a way that they do not protect any statement in science against falsification' (Popper in Jarvie 2005: 821). This distinguishes scientific knowledge from 'metaphysics', not whether either camp can ever lay claim to the truth at the end of the day. The upshot is, to over-simplify some longstanding and complex debates, that deductive modes of reasoning as an ideal-type now predominate in popular and scholarly imaginaries, research cultures, career-structures, and research questions. More than a rerun of the classic chicken-and-egg conundrum, these preferences amount to a 'policy decision governing action and embodied in norms or "methodological rules"' (ibid.).

The governing consensus, now institutionalized, is that researchers are 'theorising all the time in order to navigate the world, and our encounters with negative evidence are the bumps that deliver information about the shape of reality' (Popper in Jarvie 2005: 821). The constitution, conclusions drawn, and consequences these 'bumps' may or may not have in sociocultural, political, or economic terms are where researchers and commentators stake all manner of claims; the ongoing scholarly and public debates that line up climate change supporters against 'sceptical environmentalists' is a case in point (see Box 2.2).

Back to the 'problem of induction', for those who see this as a problem. Critics of Popper's take on the matters, also covering the spectrum of worldviews and research cultures (see Chapter 3) can include those who favour consciously inductive approaches to empirical research nonetheless. So, here most would have trouble

BOX 7.1 PHILOSOPHICAL RESEARCH

One approach alluded to in these discussions, philosophical research, bears mentioning given its place in philosophy, the oldest scholarly discipline by all accounts, and the way the term refers to research projects that are not primarily involved in gathering and analysing empirical data. For our purposes, let's condense two millennia or more of discussions around the best way to do philosophy per se, to two main principles: 'slow reading' and 'slow writing'.

- These are 'slow' because the aim is not to collect but to consider, and then to present the outcomes as an argument.
- 'Slow reading' is another way of saying 'close reading', i.e. taking time to consider a written text one step at a time, sometimes word by word, paragraph by paragraph. Here the quality of thought is not judged by how much literature is consumed.
- 'Slow writing' follows because the aim of the exercise is to get 'under the skin' of ideas, concepts, and assumptions in themselves rather than treat them as a means to empirical data-gathering ends.
- Writing, rewriting, and building up a 'plausible' argument means that philosophical research is an intrinsically literary activity; genres here are characterized by the various branches of philosophy and their respective views of 'being' (ontology) and 'knowing' (epistemology). The latter term is also a school of philosophy.

So, to sum up, philosophical research distinguishes itself from those forms of research discussed here, yet also informs many other disciplines through its 'general strategy' as Hans Radder (2006: 179) puts it. Following his schematic, there are three criteria for 'plausible' philosophical accounts: (1) presenting the 'basic philosophical claims' you are considering in a coherent way; (2) showing how these claims stand up to and rebut 'existing and potential criticisms'; (3) arguing how any alternatives to your claims are 'inadequate, either for intrinsic reasons or by comparison' with the claims you are advocating (ibid.).

These sorts of inquiries and their governing research questions may well occur within a particular literature; for example, see how Radder articulates his inquiry (2006: 1–3) and so proceeds without any references to 'reality out there'. This is not exclusively the case. Whilst, as another commentator puts it; the 'primary task of philosophical research consists, to my mind, in the clarification of concepts or meanings. . . . [There] are cases where it is not possible to clarify the meaning of a word without empirical research. . .' (Ernst Tugendhat, cited in Wren 1990: 3). In other words, philosophical research can be entirely engaged in by philosophers within the philosophical canon or it can be applied to research projects looking to both 'clarify concepts and meanings' as well as conduct 'empirical research' (ibid.).

disagreeing with the first part of the above statement; that researchers are 'theorising all the time in order to navigate the world'.

Others would take issue at the one-way street implied in the second part; that is, they do not agree that the 'shape of reality', and the bumps encountered are inseparable from theorizing. There is more than one way to produce viable knowledge about what the bumps along the way mean; scientific knowledge can include modes of reasoning that are qualitatively different from the construction of falsifiable hypotheses and experimental research design.

The strict demarcation drawn by Popper and others between science and non-science is also disputed on philosophical but also cultural and political grounds. Worldviews are at stake in what is seen to constitute objective 'reality' at any one time; the formative role reflection and thought plays in all these views of the correct path, or paths to knowledge remains paramount across the board, however.

Meanwhile, in practical terms these intricacies are less about which comes first in retrospect. More to the point, is the way you understand and then manage this fraught relationship at crucial points in the larger process and as you come to grips with your material, the appropriate method for the *phenomena* your research question is looking to study?[14] This is where 'coping with ambiguity' is part of the territory and part of the struggle; albeit more explicitly put forward in certain approaches than others.[15]

Bruce Berg puts it well when he notes that a more productive way of proceeding is working with a 'model that encompasses both the research-before-theory and theory-before-research models' (Berg 2009: 26). This is, not unlike Holmes in fiction and many scientists and scholars in everyday life, a mixture of inductive and deductive modes of reasoning with preferences and their consequences emerging along the way.

BEHAVIOURALISM AND ITS DISCONTENTS: A WORLDVIEW IN ACTION

In the above section we looked at the differences between inductive and deductive modes of reasoning; how these approaches diverge in theory yet also overlap in practice along the course of research projects in which the gathering of primary data is a core activity more or less, but not exclusively, prior to its analysis.

Alongside these two paths runs another set of debates about the nature, the 'special status' claimed by scholarly research. Chapter 3 addressed some of these issues in terms of distinctive worldviews (Chapter 3, 000 section). Chapter 6 and the first part of this chapter also looked at the practical implications of not only divisions but also overlaps between how quantitative and qualitative sorts of evidence relate to particular rules and procedures for gathering and then analysing this evidence, including the sorts of conclusions, generalizations or specific details, that a researcher can expect to make from their findings.

There is a larger issue, one that could be seen as the quintessential marker of the quantitative–qualitative divide if we were to step back and take a bird's eye view: the difference between research based on *behaviouralist* understandings of human nature and behaviour, and research based on *constructivist* ones. How these differences become evident within and across disciplines, even departments, differs from place to place and generation to generation, their more starkly drawn *incommensurability* often emerging during public debates, peer-assessment procedures, or in research seminars.

What are the key differences and why do they matter?

1   Constructivist approaches to understanding research place the explanatory emphasis on a combination of forces, with the claim that ideas (thought), actions (behaviour) and societal-level phenomena are interconnected.
2   Behaviouralist approaches understand research as primarily the pinpointing of a cause-and-effect relationship. They aim to isolate a clear 'variable' that can be observed, measured, and then analysed accordingly based on hypothesis testing.

Working example: if we take *sex-gender roles*, indeed the whole way in which the term gender is conceptualized within these two schools as an example, the implications of these differences are that:

1   Constructivist research examines and then interprets – draws conclusions – about a phenomenon as multidimensional; for example, that social attitudes about sex-gender roles and which tasks around the home are done by women or men, are mutually reinforcing rather than biologically predetermined. At the one end, gender is performed and lived (Butler 1990) and thereby not reducible to chromosomes, genitalia, or brain-size. At the other end, biological bodies, minds – neurological and consciousness – develop in a symbiotic relationship (see Haraway 1990, Swaab 2010).
2   Behaviouralist research concerns itself less with these issues. Rather it looks to isolate specific behaviours and attitudes in controlled ways (see Chapter 6 on surveys). In the case of sex-gender roles, or gender-based behaviour differences that are manifested in actions, or attitudes between men and/or women around the home we can see research to ascertain if, in fact, attitudes about sex-gender roles and who actually does which household chores correlate in observable practice or popular opinion.

Both approaches could rely on the accumulation and use of quantitative or qualitative sorts of evidence, although constructivist research tends to favour the latter. The key difference boils down to diverging ways of drawing conclusions about first how people, individuals or groups, and societies operate and, second, explanations for why they do so.[16]

Let's zoom in on the behavioural approach. For the purposes of this discussion the focus is on the historical link between behaviouralist psychological models and behaviouralist approaches to social research. Both are based on a core question: 'Why do people behave the way they do?' (Sanders, cited in Marsh and Stoker 2002: 58). This is different from asking another core question: Why do people think the way they do? Or: Why do people think, or say one thing and behave in quite another way? Moreover, answers to the first question will differ according to the underlying, if not explicit psychological approaches to why human beings behave the way they do.[17]

Two operating principles distinguish behaviouralist from non-behaviouralist takes:

1 Any analysis has to be based on observable behaviour, individual or group-based. For instance, in political science behaviouralists examine why people participate in politics, what influences voters' political preferences. They also look at political leaders and interest groups, and how they behave at election time or during a crisis. These observations are usually gathered through survey instruments, experiments, or a combination of the two.

2 As this approach is based on a view that empirical data is defined by it being observed, within the larger debates touched on in earlier chapters, this means that behaviouralists position themselves as researchers who take a 'scientific approach' to the way they study social and political phenomena – a source of past and ongoing friction between advocates of this view of what constitutes science and their critics.

Any theory purporting to explain the political (or social) behaviour under study must be empirically, in this case meaning *quantitatively*, verifiable. In behaviouralist psychology, political science, media and communications studies we see then how this interest in why people behave they way they do (based on what they say and observations of what they do) have become equated with quantitative methods and large scale data-gathering techniques.

However, the behavioural movement's embrace of quantitative techniques and with that its claiming of the latter as the only way to understand the notion of empirical (and so 'objective') knowledge has not gone unchallenged from within those disciplines where it has pride of place. For example in political research, theorists and political philosophers were quick to suggest that those working in this tradition had lost touch with the real world of politics and the best way to study it, because of their increased reliance on refining data-gathering techniques (see Barber 2006, Berns 1962, Lippmann 1998 [1922]). As far back as the 1960s the tendency to create sophisticated survey instruments was to some commentators tantamount to 'the sacrifice of political relevance on the altar of methodology. The questions asked and pursued are determined by the limits of the scientific method rather than by the subject matter'(Berns 1962: 55).

This view has been echoed in other parts of academe; critiques have been developed and rich literature and research traditions have evolved out of this fundamental difference about the aim of scholarly research and its claims to produce a particular sort of superior knowledge; from feminists and postcolonial scholars coming of age in the 1960s to generations today who stake their scientific reputation, and thereby claim to engage in scholarship as a socially and politically worthwhile enterprise, on treating the 'subject matter' as the primary objective; method follows these matters.

Whether quantitative or qualitative approaches to investigating these matters do, or should be confined to the behaviouralist side of the divide is a moot point. As I note in the opening chapters of this book and all the way through, endeavouring to quantify something is not in itself a pointless exercise for a non-behaviouralist research project. Nor should the incorporation of survey data or quantitative content analysis necessarily relegate your project to the 'enemy camp'; conversely, neither should undertaking an ethnographic study that includes questionnaires or other uses of statistics turn you into a 'woolly postmodern' thinker. In many respects, research in the humanities and social sciences has moved past these polarizations as the emergence of mixed method, multi-sited analysis, or hybrid research designs and guides show.

BOX 7.2 COMPOSITE APPROACHES TO COMPLEX REALITIES – WORKING EXAMPLE

One response to 'reality out there' is to be pragmatic. Realize that much research today actually incorporates quantitative and qualitative elements. Termed mixed method or hybrid research, this approach has been gaining ground in social science departments. For some, this straddling of the divide points to a third methodology that goes some way in reconciling many imagined differences (see Burn and Parker 2003: 3–4.

For example: in the *Guardian* newspaper (Hattenstone 2009), research on teenage boys actually combines three specific methods: a content analysis (quantitative and qualitative) of terminology and relationships in media reporting on teenage boys; a survey – questionnaire to 1,000 boys (quantitative); and semi-structured interviews (qualitative).

That said, renaming your research design as 'mixed method' versus either quantitative or qualitative does still require a rationale in the context of your inquiry; less may indeed be more in some projects, so methodologies comprised of data-gathering 'clip-ons' for the sake of it serve little purpose unless they have some point. For this reason, now is the time to consider why you are undertaking this sort of data-gathering/analysis as opposed to another one; are you able to articulate the trade-offs, show an understanding of what it is you are *not* going to research?

The polemics surrounding the rights and wrongs of particular methods reduces these procedures to their (mis)application in certain instances, thus caricaturing the subtleties and corresponding debates occurring within any mode of research. Such standoffs actually obfuscate the practical realities of research design decisions, given that no data-gathering as process or product is above reproach. Stronger still, popular imaginaries and media discussions of 'good' or 'bad' science perpetuate caricatures of academic research rather than facilitate productive debate, reproducing some longstanding stereotypes along the way.

In the meantime, academic research continues as debates proliferate. Let's return to some working examples of where practice belies political differences.

DATA-GATHERING AS PROCESS AND PRODUCT

For research projects pursued as part of university degrees, the narrow notion of empirical as synonymous with quantitative modes of data-gathering, quantitative data as facts pure and simple, and then their statistical analysis as ipso facto 'scientific' can result in either an overly reverent or dismissive views of their usefulness before a research project has even got off the ground. Many research students hobble themselves all too early in the day by rushing to characterize their project as either quantitative or qualitative per se, and then launch into the corresponding ways of data-gathering without considering whether these are actually best suited to their research question or even match the purpose of the inquiry. This is effectively research design by prejudice rather than consideration.

Putting it another way: whether you are interested in quantifying in order to make predictions and generalizations about the social world, or interested in symbolic, representational and experiential dimensions to the world, the way you go about gathering and making sense of material pertinent to the research question at hand may require more pragmatism than dogmatism, more use of available knowledge and research findings than overly ambitious claims of originality.

How do these conundrums, and the dead-ends they can create during a project, unpack in the real world of academic research?

1   One of the first questions you may ask is whether there are data already out there somewhere, collected and present, that may already answer your research question or allow you to further refine it.

   (a) There are large data archives that keep, document and distribute both qualitative and quantitative data for secondary use. But if you are going to collect your own – primary – data, compile your own 'data sets' or raw material based on your own labour and collection method, there are some general rules of thumb to bear in mind.

   (b) Recall that 'data' can be understood as either qualitative or quantitative in terms of the nature of the material gathered (see Chapter 1); for example, in-depth personal interviews and focus groups provide data in large chunks of text (recorded or written) whilst large-scale surveys, using questionnaires for instance, provide answers that are designed to be counted up, collated and then analysed statistically.

2   Within the quantitative tradition and to some extent within qualitative research discussions, there is a common misconception that qualitative data only ever refers to that which is immeasurable. First, this overstates the case for research based on statistical – or numerical forms of measurement. As noted in Chapter 2 a certain degree of imprecision is accepted in quantitative data sets. There is plenty of qualitative data that also measures attributes and qualities. It simply does not use numerical categories to do so; recall the discussions about the Body Mass Index (BMI) as an indicator of weight/degrees of thinness or fatness that is both qualitative and quantitative.

3   Not only between but also within both traditions, quantitative are distinct from qualitative data. Whereas the first designates numerical quantities such as measurements or counts, for example, height, weight, price, the second can be used to describe other sorts of attributes, for example, sex, nationality or commodity. In the idiom of quantitative research, these sorts of attributes are referred to as 'soft' data, approximating rather than precisely measuring the characteristics of a thing or phenomenon.

4   What may be referred to as quantitative data can be simply an assignment of numbers to qualitative categories, for example, *gender* – as represented by designations of masculine or feminine/male or female – is often represented as two quantitative categories (1 assigned to women and 0 assigned to men, for example) for the purposes of statistical analysis.

Second, what do such conventions mean for the design and successful execution of the research part of your project?

- More important than privileging one sort of data (and its gathering) over the other is that the theoretical premises – including the research question, or hypothesis if you prefer – underpinning any sort of investigation (measurement, fieldwork) make sense. There needs to be some sort of inner logic to the relationship between the conceptual framework, or *substantive theory*, being put forward, the techniques used to gather data, and the analysis carried out.
- This cuts both ways; if the theoretical side of things, research question and research plan are well thought-out and articulated then so should the data-gathering tools and forms of analysis (measurement or otherwise) be also. This interplay, inner coherence, is what gives researcher, and audiences, confidence in the eventual findings and integrity of the means by which the knowledge has been produced. Others may disagree with your findings or challenge you on these mechanics but that is a different matter (see Chapter 8).
- Once again, with all other choices in the research process, these decisions rest on the question you are asking; do not assume too quickly there is only one best way of doing things. Moreover, not all data and data-gathering are transferable.

Third, what do these principles mean at the analysis stage and how is the handling and eventual presentation of any data gathered, however defined, to make sense in the final report, whether or not your conclusions are negative, positive, categorical or qualified? By way of illustration, the three cases below, drawing on studies of voters and political elites from quantitative research literature, show the ways in which notions of qualitative data are applied within quantitative research traditions. They also highlight how not all sorts of qualitative data lend themselves to quantification.

(a) *Assigning qualities*: A commonly used question in large-scale surveys of citizens and attempts to measure how 'warmly' a voter feels about a political leader is a 'feeling thermometer'. Respondents to the survey are shown a picture of a thermometer marked from 0 to 100 degrees and given the name of a party leader. The respondent then indicates the warmth of feeling he or she has toward the party leader with 100 being the warmest. The thermometer here is a heuristic device to elicit how favourable a voter is toward a party leader, to capture emotion or affection for the party leader rather than how respondents evaluate a party leader based on the policy positions of the party.

This approach recognizes a truism for qualitative research: in practice it is difficult to separate affective judgments from policy-based judgments. The feeling thermometer attempts to measure the former along a quantitative scale so as to make comparisons across a larger sample in order to conduct a statistical analysis (by calculating the mean thermometer ranking for a party leader or candidates across all respondents).

(b) *Gender as an empirical category*: Gender is considered a qualitative category for quantitative researchers as well. It is impossible to talk about an 'average gender'. However, it is possible to talk about the 'quantity' or percentage of women in the population. Researching gender as an empirical category (part of a demographic) is also where research drawing on a range of feminist approaches parts company (see Hughes and Cohen 2010); gender is construed as a relational and analytical category in which quantifying is not the main objective (see Butler 1990, Peterson and Runyan 1999, True 2001).

(c) *Qualitative databases*: The *Economic and Social Data Service* (ESDS) has been running a project to capture qualitative data and make it available to secondary users.[18] While the ESDS has been known for providing access to quantitative data, this newer initiative provides access to a range of social science qualitative data sets. Electoral Reform and British Members of the European Parliament, 1999–2004 (designated in the archive as SN 5372) comprises qualitative interviews with sixty British MEPs of the 1999–2004 European Parliament. The interviews focus on the representative role of the MEP and the impact upon this of the change in the electoral system (from single-member district representation to multi-member regions) in Britain for the 1999 European elections. The available data if downloaded from the data archive consist of the transcribed interviews with the sixty MEPs.[19]

The latter example underscores how transcribed interview material is not amenable to the same mathematical transformations as the quantitative indicators used in the thermometer example. Moreover, analysis that understands *gender* in other ways than a countable empirical category would not be content with numerical assignations such as '0' or '1' particularly for research projects looking at sexuality, social relations based on people living with or being assigned multiple (rather than two) genders, and feminist research approaches that regard gender as a lens, or as a facet of power relations (Peterson and Runyan 1999, Shepherd 2009).

BOX 7.3 SEX, GENDER, AND CHROMOSOMES[20]

There are many topical examples of how the above differences in academic terms work in everyday life; in our daily lives and work we are often confronted with questions about how we 'know' something for sure. In this case, how we know for sure who is female and who is male. As feminist theorists and women's rights activists point out, behaviour and appearance that count as masculine or feminine have differed over time and across cultures. Where quantitative indicators have a powerful influence is in the sporting arena, for centuries divided along male/female lines of physical prowess – a debate in itself. It is a longstanding issue in the Olympic Games, where both gender and race have played major roles (for example, the

Continued

1936 games held in Berlin during the Nazi era; the affect of drugs on female but also male athletes during the Cold War era; whether African/African American men and women jump higher, run faster for genetic reasons, and so on). Sex tests have been a feature of the modern Olympics for female athletes.

One well-known case of gender ambiguity in athletics was only discovered upon the athlete's death. Polish born athlete Stella Walsh (Stanislawa Walasiewicz was her Polish name) was an American national champion and won Olympic gold in the 1932 and 1936 Olympics competing for Poland. She was shot dead during an armed robbery in 1980. The autopsy revealed she possessed both male genitalia along with female characteristics; further investigation revealed that she had both an XX and an XY set of chromosomes. The 2009 athletics World Championships presented a more recent illustration of these complex issues of evidence, method, and interpretation addressed in this and other chapters. During the competition it was reported that South African runner Caster Semenya had been asked to undergo 'gender tests' in South Africa and further tests in Berlin during the competition, to establish whether she was eligible to compete in the *women's* 800-metre track-race.

The goal of gender verification is to prevent an unfair advantage in gender-restricted sports (male athletes have an advantage to date in most events but not all, for example, equestrian). The earliest gender verification tests for athletes amounted to simply verification of the existence of the appropriate genitalia.[21] The sex chromatin test, which identifies only the sex chromosome component of gender, was used but later discredited as it was misleading particularly in cases of individuals who could be considered intersexual. Genetic anomalies can present as having a male genetic makeup while having female physiological characteristics. The International Association of Athletics Federation (IAAF) stopped gender verification testing in 1991, while gender determination tests were abandoned for Olympic competition in 2000. However, the IAAF has reserved the right to invoke the test and Semenya has been the first to be tested by the IAAF since 1991. What we see here is that even when resorting to the evidence provided by the chromosomal model of biological sex there are crucial ambiguities. For example, transgender adults or technical 'hermaphrodites' can be brought up as girl or boy children without knowing otherwise; others undergo 'sexual reassignment at birth' which means that if a gender test reveals their ambiguous chromosomal structure their gender identity, and in the case of sporting events, integrity, becomes a public matter.

Back to academic debates. In this context, gender theorists and feminist biologists such as Judith Butler (1990) and Donna Haraway (1990) respectively argue that neither human – gender-based – behaviour nor the human genome are outside cultural or political influences. These things 'matter' when even scientists cannot categorically support one interpretation (male) or another (female) in terms of social costs for individuals and families. For the huge national and financial stakes in global sporting spectacles such as the Olympics we see how the tension between fact, observation, and interpretation when applied through a dominant interpretation in everyday life and politics is anything but an arcane question of semantics. They are also cultural and political questions about the correct and proper way for boy and girl children to be brought up, and how they (should) behave as adults.

CONCLUDING COMMENTS

To sum up: for practical purposes, and to avoid getting too bogged down, this chapter has treated *analysis* as a moment when the researcher needs to take time to think – pause, contemplate, (re)consider – and then make decisions as they get down to their respective analytical 'business'. The chapter has treated analysis as follows:

- As the moment in a research project when we need to consciously and methodically look at, study, and (re)consider accumulated data on their own terms.
- Some talk about this phase being about letting the data 'speak' to you. As mystical as that may sound, what this really boils down to is moving into a new level of decision making, even confusion. This is because the material does not entirely speak for itself, no matter how badly you wish it did. Some translation and transposing needs to take place as you set about sorting, re-selecting, and sifting what you have gathered, observed, listened to, or read.
- Cross-checking that the results before you are valid, no errors have been made or underlying parameters incorrect; for example, mistaking a dependent variable for an independent one, and vice versa, making sure your arithmetic is correct, ensuring no key item in the policy selection has been overlooked.
- Achieving a reasonable to excellent degree of analysis comes with getting to grips with the material close-up, as it 'presents' itself to you. For example:
  - taking time to read, or re-read interview transcripts, looking at – studying – the figures (if not checking them again);
  - looking more closely again at an image or film sequence or applying a particular way of looking at this material, for example, frame-by-frame, time-sequence breakdowns, sorts of shots used, soundtrack/musical scoring and other mechanics in the montage;
  - 'close reading' of selected passages in key texts alone, or alongside others, for example, applying Derrida's notion of *deconstruction* to parts of the canon;
  - applying a pre-given or tailor-made coding scheme (concept/keyword-based or more interpretative) to the selected material (for example, policy archives or media messages);
  - drawing inferences from the maps or diagrams you have produced, either manually or with software (for example, Invivo results as tables, Issue Crawler maps of web-hubs requiring interpretation as well as legends).

Granted, the particular methodologies covered here treat the gathering and analysis of material as inseparable. De-linking analytical interventions from the process of formulating a research question or written forms of contemplation and argumentation may, for some readers, smack of empirically reductionist (read *positivist*) notions of social inquiry; diametrically opposed to more philosophically or culturally inflected (viz. *critical*) ones (see Chapter 3). However, this implies that research carried out in arts and humanities departments disregards such distinctions on principle. Whilst some claim to do so, others, although eschewing terms such as *data*, *evidence*, or *findings*, do articulate a definable object of inquiry and interrogate the matter in a methodical way, albeit from within particular worldviews and idioms about how best to apprehend the phenomena under investigation: physical, symbolic, or ideational.

There is, I would argue, still a distinction to be made between these moments along a research path; each of which are distinct from what we are doing when embarking on the writing-up phase. This chapter has looked at key analytical interventions along the divide in terms of the way texts are understood and then studied: as quantifiable units of content, or as complex carriers of meaning. In effect, whilst these discussions underscore the divide as introduced at the start of the book, in practice we can see how their various rules and procedures and underlying worldviews, particularly when transposed into online, web-mediated research settings, also reposition this divide.

The main argument underpinning these discussions is that the mechanics and philosophies making up various sorts of methodologies where analysis features by definition are often overlooked and hurried through, wrongly subsumed under either data-gathering rubrics (Chapter 6) or as a self-explanatory element of the writing-up phase (Chapter 8). Granted, all three moments overlap one another; as we generate or gather, and then sort out and consult our data we are already making inferences – drawing some sorts of conclusions if not being challenged by the unexpected as we assess what counts and what does not count as significant to the inquiry. Gathering, engaging with, and writing up the research are all activities that entail 'analysis'; the concrete and the abstract are both implicit in this term, which is why it is so over-used and so under-elucidated. It is a name for physical and abstract research practices, larger methodological labels. But it also invokes a verb in that researchers also 'do' analysis.

NOTES

1   Many undergraduate and postgraduate dissertations do make use of secondary sources; how well and to what end depends on the research question. I would simply note that if a particular thinker is so important to your project then it would be remiss not to have some sort of first-hand experience of reading the relevant parts of their work.

2   For instance, the fatwa issued by Iran's Ayatollah Khomeini on Salman Rushdie after the publication of his book *The Satanic Verses*, the Catholic Church's outlawing of the book published by the astronomer Copernicus in which he proposed a heliocentric model of the cosmos and subsequent indictment of one of its prominent advocates, Leonardo da Vinci. Or, more recently, the growing rift within the Anglican Church over the rights and wrongs of openly homosexual clergy, in the UK and abroad. In all cases, conflicting interpretations – analyses – of holy scriptures and extant knowledge of how the physical or social world does or should work are at stake.

3 These sections take us into philosophical and theoretical literatures that are not only fascinating but also very dense; inseparable from contentious worldviews and positions on the 'what is science?' questions (see Part 1). I have consciously steered away from 'tagging' the points below with Big Names and Big Ideas. Not because I find them irrelevant or uninteresting. Far from it. However, the primary task is to activate independent thinking and enable decision making along a road travelled. Moreover, most readers are pretty well-versed in these issues, theoretical and technical, and the literature well established and evolved enough for a full rehearsal of these issues to warrant separate attention beyond the scope of this one chapter.

4 A current example from political communication and the study of rhetoric: the rise and election of Barak Obama as president of the United States in 2008 brought with it public and academic interest in his oratorical prowess; like his role-model, the civil rights activist Martin Luther King, this includes looking at not just how his speeches are written as literary and persuasive devices but also at their, now famous, delivery: pauses, reiterations, climaxes in volume and pitch. Margaret Thatcher, the former British prime minister, and one of her admirers, Tony Blair, are also examples; for example, note the conscious use of triplets such as Blair's 'education, education, education'.

5 Two examples: (1) coding according to the 'nearest neighbour' principle, e.g. young boys and anti-social behaviour; (2) *Cognitive Mapping* (Abdelal et al. 2009: 7–8).

6 Thanks to Pasi Väliaho for access to teaching material in this section.

7 Thanks to Julian Henriques for this expression.

8 In particular semiotics is a particular form of linguistic analysis defined by both its rigorous, systematic approach to the text; see Scolari (2009), Williamson (1978)

9 These are the terms used in many of the history of science's major polemics. It is beyond the scope of this book to critically discuss the sociocultural dimensions of how western pundits place these terms on the 'wrong' side of the divide between 'science' and 'non-science', 'objective' and 'subjective' knowledge.

10 This citation is taken from one of websites linked to the BBC TV series *Sherlock*, based on the Conan Doyle character, updated for young twenty-first century viewers and entitled *The Science of Deduction* (www.thescienceofdeduction.co.uk/; accessed 20 June 2011).

11 See Canales (2009), Chalmers (2004), Haraway (1990), Harding (1998a,b).

12 See the Wikipedia entry on just this point: 'Methods of Detection: Holmesain Deduction' at http://en.wikipedia.org/wiki/Sherlock_Holmes-Methods_of_Detection (accessed 20 June 2011).

13 For a classic rendition of what is regarded as the 'mainstream/malestream' notion of scientific method, watch the YouTube clip entitled *The Key to Science* showing the physicist Feynman Chaser teaching a class at Cornell University in 1964; www.youtube.com/watch?v=b240PGCMwV0 (accessed 20 June 2011).

14 Thanks to Zlatan Krajina for this nuance; space does not permit more commentary on the implications of this distinction.

15 Thanks for Zeena Feldman for this insight. For those more convinced that their way is the best way, see note 13 above. In the clip, Chaser maintains that if the evidence produced by an experiment countermands the hypothesis then it is the hypothesis that is wrong; the evidence has 'falsified' it. What other commentators note is that such clarity assumes that the experiment, in terms of design and execution, is beyond reproach.

16 For example, see Burchill et al. (2001) for a range of approaches forged in the 'Third Debate' in international relations.

17 The differences between psychological models of human behaviour at stake here are vast. Suffice it to say that they rest on just how far what is observed, or observable to the investigator is related in turn to the sorts of interpretations or inferences drawn from these observations; recall the Sherlock Holmes example above. Another example: Freudian psychoanalytical models of human behaviour based on unconscious drives and how these emerge as a 'psychopathology of everyday life' diverge sharply from those based on innate

neurological features of the human brain. The nature versus nurture debate permeates these differences.

18 The Economic and Social Data Service (ESDS) is a national data service providing access and support for an extensive range of key economic and social data, both quantitative and qualitative, spanning many disciplines and themes. ESDS provides an integrated service offering enhanced support for the secondary use of data across the research, learning and teaching communities; www.esds.ac.uk/

19 For instance, David Farrell and Roger Scully's (2007) study of British MEPs makes use of qualitative data archived at the ESDS.

20 Thanks to Susan Banducci for providing this example and her input into this discussion.

21 Sex/gender verification tests currently involve gynaecologists, endocrinologists, psychologists and internal medicine specialists.

CHAPTER 8

Writing it all up and going public

Topics covered in this chapter:

- What is *academic* writing?
- Writing formalities: citation and style guides
- Feedback: examinations and going public
- Procrastinations and prevarications
- Coping and moving on – creatively
- The final cut – what to remember

INTRODUCTION

It will not have escaped the reader's notice how integral the act – techniques, craft and for many the art of writing is to successfully completing a research project. Academic writing, in a research environment and for scholarly consumption, has particular formalities, stylistic and professional idioms and skill-sets that also merge and diverge from more individualistic notions of personal 'style' or authorship. By the same token, the notion and reverence for authorship in academe is still alive and well despite influential critiques of any notion of 'the author'.[1] Such distinctions and how they are rendered as evaluative criteria, for examining and peer-review purposes, underscore disciplinary boundaries, fuel debates according to changing trends in research cultures and their respective writing conventions (for example, pronoun use – 'we' versus ' I'; role of notes, degrees of citation). Students too often have a number or preconceived ideas about what it means to write *academically* as distinct from writing 'journalistically' or 'creatively'.

Students embarking on a major research project with working experience, journalists in particular, bring with them well-developed writing skills, an ability to work to deadline (in principle) and within a set word-limit. Others come with blog-writing, PR, and/or creative writing experience. Others with experience in the private sector or NGO work may well be able to put together an executive summary or policy-brief statement at the drop of a hat. All these skills are important in that they entail an ability to write in certain ways, for certain audiences, with respective aims and formats. It is when being asked to write more 'critically', or 'analytically' and not 'just descriptively' that uncertainty can set in. Not just because academic writing is seen to be, and in many ways is distinct from these other genres and working practices. But because academic writing includes a number of specific skill-sets that are peculiar to this enterprise: formatting and compiling literature lists, footnotes/endnotes, citation styles, presentation formats, argumentation conventions, and vocabulary. Research students coming through from undergraduate programmes may also find themselves challenged to improve techniques acquired as they went along, or adapt academic writing skills to accommodate other formats.

Currently the influence, generally seen as a negative one, of computer-mediated idioms such as email, blogs, micro-blogging, and the increased reliance on powerful web search engines on writing and thinking standards have been the focus of research attention and popular debate about the implications these have on younger generations (see Chapter 5). Given the predominance of the written word – longhand – in academic research and teaching for legitimizing the production and dissemination of knowledge, *writing* a dissertation is no small matter (see second section, Chapter 2, Box 2.1). Criticisms of our writing at any point can be tough; not only a personal matter but also embedded in disciplinary if not localized institutional norms about what constitutes the most appropriate organization and style for an academic piece of written work. Given the range of views on what counts as coherence, clarity, accessibility in any literary genre, the first point to note at this stage is that, as is the case with non-academic discussions in these matters, what counts as 'well written' is a contentious category within and across the divide.

Second, students often ask 'when is the right time to start writing my dissertation?' Although discussions about this aspect of the process usually come towards the end, writing has been taking place from Day One of your project. Depending on the disciplinary and geographical context in which you are working, you may find that mentors and supervisors regard the act of writing as synonymous with doing research itself. In philosophical and literary-based approaches, this is indeed true; for example, the literature review/theory chapter is considered in many UK institutions as a crucial, formative piece of writing quite early on; producing chapters as part of progressive coursework is also seen as indispensable to assessment regimes and feedback sessions. Producing an outline or formal research proposal is one piece of completed work, writing up fieldwork notes or survey results (along with the requisite graphs, tables, or interview material citations) another; handing in a 'methodology chapter' as coursework for methods seminars a distinct piece of work again.

Third, why still this overwhelming emphasis on the written word, particularly in a multimedia and visual age? As you may recall, the 'literature review' elements (process and product) covered in Chapter 4 is all about getting to grips with written texts. Completing a dissertation satisfactorily therefore also includes writing up the work in order to present it to an academic audience; first stop usually being the examiners. From research reports, through to dissertations through to journal articles and books, the written word is still the primary form in which academic research and the knowledge produced 'goes public'. However, a research project can also go public orally; as part of an official defence (Ph.D. level but in some parts of the world, at M.A. level as well), or in a conference/research seminar paper presentation. Nonetheless oral presentations are usually based on a written document, a paper, or PowerPoint presentation, now *de rigueur* in academic research and classroom settings.

For dissertation work, the writing-up stage has its own peculiarities and challenges. Even the most experienced researchers can find their best-laid research planning coming apart, certainties fading, and research question wobbling in the face of large amounts of material, or countermanding evidence that defies attempts to make written – narrative – sense of it. What to leave in, take out, which initial ideas need reviewing – or rejecting, which initial questions require revisiting, can be a daunting prospect. However, it is this transition – if not transformation – of inchoate data (however defined, for ideas need refining too) is the *sine qua non* of academic research; findings and their analysis – or if you prefer, interpretation presented in formal written formats; the inclusion of multimedia, visual, and performance presentations dependent on the sort of degree.

BOX 8.1 WHAT KIND OF WRITER ARE YOU?

What kind of writer are you?

- A planner-drafter?
- A write-as-you-think writer?
- A think-as-you-write writer?
- A rewrite-and-rewrite-again writer?
- A procrastinator?

Which stage in any formal writing assignment produces the most anxiety?

- Getting started?
- Finishing up?
- The whole thing?
- Waiting for the feedback?

Aims and objectives

This chapter looks at the later stages of the research process in which writing dominates. Here too there are decisions, organizational and editorial, you need to make as you present the results to others, bring the project to a formal close and, hopefully, make a satisfying and graceful exit. Whilst writing is the main issue at stake here, there are several corollary matters:

- dealing with, and giving feedback to your own and others' presentation of their research work;
- being up to speed on general and institutional formalities about written dissertations;
- coping with countermanding pressures, from within and externally, about originality, creativity, and issues of 'voice';
- navigating competing audiences, and evaluations come into play here as well, given geographical and institutional differences between research traditions.

WHAT IS ACADEMIC WRITING?

As was the case in the previous chapter, this section takes a moment to pin down this elusive yet palpable category, academic writing.

A basic truism of academic work in arts and social science faculties is that this sort of writing is distinct from others; journalism, creative writing, reports in the natural sciences or industry, policy-writing (see discussion in Chapter 1; 'What is academic research?'). As Carol Smart notes, echoing many programme handbooks and study guides to academic writing, the key skills in this area

> appear to be the ability in writing to convey knowledge of a field (i.e. competence), to structure an argument tightly (i.e. literary and intellectual skill), and to arrive at a position based on an evaluation of the material available (i.e. an ability to adopt a defensible and well argued stance).
>
> (Smart 2010: 3)

She then goes on to note a paradox underscoring the everyday realities of academic research in the round for experienced and novice researchers: this model assumes that the researcher already has at their fingertips '*a literary competence* which can not only cover adequate amounts of material but which will form a *convincing argument in an engaging way*' (ibid., emphasis added). This 'literary competence' is also implicitly an analytical one, pulling disparate, copious, and diverse sorts of data into some shape in order to lend some coherence to the final report is the lion's share of the work (see Chapter 7). As I have noted earlier, however much time has been needed to design, read-up, and then carry out the actual research, writing it all up takes just as much time. Let's make three distinctions right now:

1 Whilst creative writing and academic writing are considered distinct, it would be wrong to suggest that the latter is devoid of any level of creativity. Indeed, as

Smart and others note, effective academic writing is also about developing a narrative. When the narrative lines are not provided by set conventions (for example, reports that follow a strict format, those around presentation of large survey results), this aspect is where a particularly tough struggle occurs, and late in the day. No matter how much writing has been done in earlier parts of the final report, these chapters – if this is how they were conceived – or term-essays, proposals, articles or conference papers, all need revising in light of how the research has progressed; in terms of the information gathered and insights gained, and in terms of your more theoretical thinking in general.

2   Giving shape to the analysed material entails not only narrative skills – telling a 'story' of some sort albeit one with certain attributes and claims to accuracy (or even truth-values) and contribution to 'knowledge'. It also requires editorial and meta-level organizational skills. These decisions take place even within the stricter parameters of some dissertation formats (see Chapter 2); in which order to arrange certain sections or chapters for instance, what goes in the main text and what is relegated to notes, indeed whether to include notes at all. You need to be able to hold down one, perhaps more than one, narrative thread throughout the detail, but also be able to move in and out of these details (from literature references, to figures, to quotes, to images and tables of results) to the wider perspective.

3   Moreover, the 'story' you are telling has to do more than describe, more than persuade, and more than generalize. It needs to be original – your own words – yet embedded in, and so cognizant of the work of others; in short the 'field, or 'literature'. You need to show that you have processed and 'analysed' all those data gathered in such a way that others can not only interact with these data on their own terms but also respond to your argument – the findings and conclusions you present. This is why two dissertations, or reports on the same data can be very different; not just in style but also in the conclusions presented.

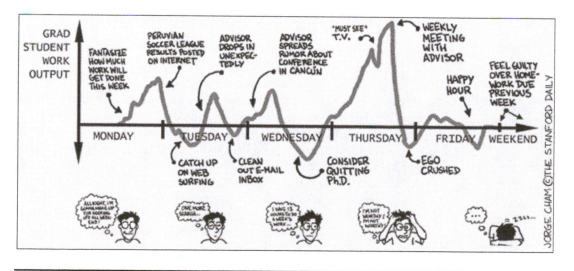

Figure 8.1   Student workout

Source: Jorge Cham: http://www.phdcomics.com/comics.php

WRITING FORMALITIES: CITATION AND STYLE GUIDES

This next section echoes points raised in earlier chapters about the form and objectives of academic research at dissertation levels in particular. All the planning aside, and data gathered notwithstanding, there is no easy way around this; to produce a written report you need to write in a certain way. Here academic writing for degree qualifications adheres across the board to some general principles. More radical innovations and formats aside (for example, practice-based degrees where a film, script, novel or performance are part of the final work, creative writing degrees), your final report will have to show that you have managed the required elements outlined in Chapter 2. In other words, the head, middle, and tail ends of the final piece moves, on the whole, from the general and more abstract through to the concrete and specific (your empirical findings/philosophical exegesis, or fieldwork depiction) and then back to the more general and abstract.

Because this area of academic work is quite complex in technical and legal terms this section looks at citation conventions as different levels of difficulty. Not unlike computer games, getting to grips with the mechanics of citation, how these relate to issues around how best to acknowledge sources, written and unwritten, sees most of us moving up a level as we become more adept. In addition, gaining fluency in different citation conventions helps avoid accidental forms of plagiarism (see Chapter 4). The way in which these formalities are also carriers of various expectations, even prescriptions about style for academic writing will become clearer as well; from formal sorts of 'house-style' required by journals and book publishers to informal understandings about the role played by footnotes, graphics, and written text.

Level 1

First, some basic rules of thumb, whatever the citation conventions you opt to choose, formalized and codified by a number of academic associations and institutions:

1 All verbatim quotes need to be clearly indicated and fully referenced; according to the citation convention adopted.
2 When citing a source cited by someone else you are reading, you need to indicate this clearly, unless you have read the original source yourself. The rule here is the initial source of this 'second-hand' citation as (x, cited in y, [date]).
   - There are more than a few students who 'crib' in this respect for some high-profile thinkers (Foucault, Bourdieu, Butler, Habermas, Beauvoir are names that immediately come to mind) by passing over this point and so implying that they are directly informed about the work cited.
   - This is sloppy because it 'lifts' the work of one from the work of another without due context or acknowledgement. It can also catch you out if you are ever quizzed on the author in question; it happens and it really should not.
3 Direct quotes need to be unedited, deletions notwithstanding (indicated by an ellipsis). Now, in the case of gender-exclusive language (where 'he' no longer suffices as representing all humankind) or socio-politically sensitive terminology, use of 'sic' (Latin, 'thus') can indicate this without excessive intervention.

4   When not directly *citing* the text as such, if your text is directly referring to, or influenced by someone else, then you need to provide an exact reference even when only alluding. This means that page numbers are primary; specific page/s where the reader can find the passage quoted, or alluded to.

5   Any neologisms, or 'cool ideas' or expressions picked up during the course of conversations or in lectures you want to use in your own work, and when you know where it came from or who said it, deserve due recognition; it is a courtesy and best practice which requires sometimes some deft use of notes.

6   Bottom line: anyone reading your work should be able to follow your reference trail. For online sources, given their fluidity, if you cannot keep track then no-one else will. There is a fine line between legal and nominal forms of mutual recognition.

Level 2

Now, on the specific technicalities. With the above principles in mind, the following brief summaries of the main citation/style guides available to researchers hopefully will make more sense. The details, however, are important for you to get under your belt. Here practice makes perfect and consistency is your best ally; after all if consistent even errors are easy to correct. Very briefly the main guides are as follows:

The American Psychological Association (APA) style guide: This is based on the author acknowledging 'a source within your text by providing a reference to exactly where in that source you found the information. The reader can then follow up on the complete reference in the Reference List page at the end of your paper'.[2]

The Chicago Manual of Style: This breaks down into two sorts of citation formats; one similar to the APA above and the other which places all citations into the notes. To cite Concordia University once again, *The Chicago Manual of Style* has

two basic documentation systems: (1) notes and bibliography and (2) author-date. . . . The notes and bibliography style. . . . presents bibliographic information in notes and, often, a bibliography. It accommodates a variety of sources, including esoteric ones less appropriate to the author-date system.

The author-date system . . . sources are briefly cited in the text, usually in parentheses, by author's last name and date of publication.[3]

Figure 8.2 You need some boundaries
Source: Nina Paley: http://www.ninapaley.com

The Modern Languages Association (MLA) style guide: This guide, popular in languages and humanities, also favours citations in the text ('parenthetical references') with the full reference being provided in the literature list; the MLA stipulates that

> The alphabetical list of works cited that appears at the end of your paper contains more information about all of the sources you've cited allowing readers to refer to them, as needed. The main characteristics are: The list of Works Cited must be on a new page at the end of your text; Entries are arranged alphabetically by the author's last name or by the title if there is no author; Titles are italicized (not underlined) and all important words should be capitalized; Each entry must include the publication medium. Examples include: Print, Web, DVD, and Television.[4]

Finally the Harvard Referencing System: As you can see references in this book follow this system, the preferred house-style of the publisher. Namely, 'if you use this system you cite the author's surname, the year of publication and the page reference immediately after the quoted material'.[5] Extrapolations aside for online and other sorts of sources, this system is a distillation of those above.

Some departments, if not institutions, and this depends again on geography and disciplines, have mandatory citation requirements following one of the above codes or another combination. Learn these first. You can acquire the next citation 'language' another time. For those working in places where more then one citation convention is permitted, settle on the one that suits you and stick to that for the duration of that project. If you change halfway you need to go back and adjust backwards.

You will see that for citations of over forty words, the usual practice is to indent the paragraph. For less than forty words, 'quotation marks' and then the reference (in brackets or in the note) will suffice. As for online citation conventions, most style guides now incorporate these into their guidelines. However, there are resources that focus on these sorts of material because, as most readers will know, the web is comprised of more than straightforward literary material: multimedia, images, people's words, links, and hypertext.[6]

Before moving up to Level 3, and because most research dissertations for university degrees are completed without the benefit of a professional copy-editor from a publisher, coming to grips with citation technicalities also takes us into question of academic style in general and preferred disciplinary conventions in particular. Not only students but teaching and research staff have difficulty maintaining consistency. It's not only a skill but also an aptitude; some are better at this than others. Nonetheless paying attention to these formalities is part of the territory.

Level 3

Now, the Top Ten Tips on what to remember when checking and tidying up how you cite any sources for academic purposes, in the main text, in notes, and in the literature list:

1   Consistency is the rule; even if the format you apply turns out to be not quite right, if you apply it consistently throughout then corrections are easier.

2   Practice makes perfect; writing academically involves the ability to recall, and then call up what others have said. This is why getting a grip of key literature in the field/s within which you are working is a cornerstone (see Chapter 4).

3   Page numbers matter. Dates matter. Correct spelling of authors' names matter (a lot).

4   Publishers are part of the citation, as is (strictly speaking) where publishers are based. All this information is provided inside the book cover (the 'copyright' or 'imprint' page), the top or bottom of a journal article.

5   Authors can be one person or several, so all names have to be cited at least once and in the literature list. Authors can also be associations (for example, The Internet Society), organizations (for example, the World Bank) and, if there is no other indication, web-page/newspaper/media organizations (for example, the *Guardian*, Fox News). Look closer, though, when citing online sources, particularly from news and entertainment media: somewhere you may well see the author's name.

6   Online sources are cited the same way as traditional ones. The main difference is that you need to include the full URL (see Chapter 5) and (usually) the access date. Why? Because the latter provides an indication of currency and because web-pages change, move or go offline.

7   Decide whether you want to have a 'clean' main text or want to integrate any citations to references as you go; this book does the latter. This is where footnotes and endnotes come in.

8   Notes can be allocated for citations (depending on the format used) as well as additional comments.

9   All citation formats, save those that include a full reference in the notes, require a fully referenced literature list.

10 Finally, particularly for research students: your 'Bibliography' should actually consist only of works you cite, or refer to in the dissertation. Hence the term 'Literature Cited', 'Literature List', or 'Reference List'. Technically speaking, a 'Bibliography' is a comprehensive reference of all possible literature in the field (see also Chapter 4 on 'undertaking a systematic literature review').

FEEDBACK: EXAMINATIONS AND GOING PUBLIC

'Feedback' is integral to academic life, from the point of view of *learning* (students are assessed in order to progress), *teaching* (marking and commenting on students' work), and *peer assessment* (students/researchers evaluating each others' work). There is a range of types of feedback that vary in terms of who is giving feedback (peers or teachers); how the feedback is given (written or orally) and whether or not we know who is giving the feedback (blind or double-blind). Even those far along in our research careers rely on feedback to improve our work. Students are not the only ones concerned about receiving feedback that in theory provides productive guidance on how we can improve our work; fully fledged academic researchers also receive feedback in the form of reviews of work submitted for publication, discussant's comments on conference presentations and sometimes from research monitoring by our institutions.[7]

As universities require their teaching staff to undergo teacher-training as a co-requisite to tenure, or are providing training for incumbent teaching staff, the notion that feedback is *necessarily* more than a ranking exercise or numbers game, more than scribbling a few curt comments in the margin or cover page of student essays – such as 'excellent work', 'well done', or 'poorly executed', 'inadequate' – or the awarding of a final 'pass' or 'fail' is slowly gaining a foothold. Critics and supporters of quantitative assessment and their corollaries, such as league tables, abound, as do those of purely qualitative forms of feedback; all that comes under 'non-graded assessment' in short. This is why we need to distinguish between feedback in the round and scores assigned to any piece of work; only one part of the feedback. There is a whole other realm of feedback that operates as the underwater part of the visible iceberg that represents quantitative indicators of quality and achievement. This underwater part is in practice the larger part of the research learning curve. It comes to us as both informal and formal written or spoken commentary on our research, either when presenting it as work-in-progress, output, or public defence.

Informal feedback comes to us on a daily basis: in class during question- and -answer sessions, and individual and group tutorials as we encounter on-the-spot reactions not only to our own questioning but also as our responses to others when in debate. Individual and group-based supervisory encounters during the course of a dissertation project also influence how students perceive their own progress; email encounters are becoming increasingly predominant as students and mentors communicate by remote means. The main point here is that as students, and then as educators or budding researchers, we learn from experience and example more than by our grades.

In public – some do's and don'ts

Below are some do's and don'ts for receiving and by implication giving feedback in the form of spoken or written comments on someone else's completed work or ongoing research project. These apply mainly to public settings and examinations but also the work for one-on-one supervisory sessions. Feedback from supervisors most likely will occur when no others are present so you need not feel so constrained by these do's and don'ts aimed at formal public settings. However, for the feedback to be effective many supervisors would argue that the same principles apply.

The do's and don'ts below are a compilation of my own experience, as educator and research supervisor but also as a student. These points also combine valuable input from colleagues and former students (who shared their concerns and perceptions with me after graduating, and some even beforehand). It is also no surprise to note that some of the don'ts have been generated by how supervisors perceive students during a dissertation project; marked by the upward curve of student numbers and use of computer-mediated communication by students (and staff) to interact with their supervisors and teachers; smart phones with mobile web access have been generating additional email traffic; short, text-like communications between students and staff increasingly ending with phrases such as '. . . sent from my beloved [brand] . . .'

Figure 8.3 How not to act like an artist

Source: Nina Paley: http://www.ninapaley.com

Do's and don'ts

Do be prepared for criticism. Expect it. In fact you should be concerned if you don't get any at all.

Why? Criticism is part of doing research. Debate and argumentation are part of the territory; learning to defend your project is an art and a skill. Remember, getting away with no overt criticism at all does not mean your work is without fault. Research designs all improve with feedback from opponents and 'critical friends' so go get it!

Don't, however, take the criticism as an attack.

Why? Good feedback is given as a way to improve your research and to help you meet you goals. Of course, some supervisors, discussants and reviewers are better at giving feedback than others. If you feel that your work is being attacked rather than critiqued then be prepared to still act graciously and take whatever is useful from the feedback.

Do listen, preferably without interrupting.

Why? It is natural to want to defend your choices, correct any apparent misunderstandings of what you're doing straightaway, but you can do this afterwards. Apart from courteousness, waiting also gives you time to consider your response, if not come up with one!

Do be aware that positive comments or compliments can also contain crucial criticism.

Why? Some cultures don't express negative criticism directly. Here you need to understand when different cultural and institutional conventions are at work. For example, 'But I can't help wondering . . .' often precedes a fundamental objection to what you're doing, how, or why you're doing it; likewise with the expression 'with respect'. In some settings praise precedes criticism and in others it comes afterwards; 'this could be better' is another way of saying 'this is poorly executed work' and saying something is 'bad' is in some parts of the world straight-talking. Receiving personal feedback on your work in public is quite commonplace in some settings whereas in others this happens under 'four eyes' so you may need to take account of this shift in register. For instance, the same person's feedback can have a different tenor in a private (supervisory or friendship) and public setting.

Do accept that some people's comments and some sorts of criticism are harder to deal with than others. Some of our toughest critics can come from our support network.

Why? We are all human. Personality clashes, cultural differences, personal or institutional rivalries, grandstanding, and 'unknowables' like fatigue or stress all have a role to play in feedback scenarios, public ones particularly. So do group dynamics and gender/power hierarchies. In some settings official rank and superiority affect who can critique who, where, and in what form. In others, 'friendly fire' is not considered a faux-pas in that some 'edgier' feedback is part of interactions 'offstage'. Besides, those who work in the same or an overlapping area will spot weaknesses and oversights in our work more quickly; it is in their interest – and yours – to do so in fact.

Do try and notice your own responses to negative feedback; do you feel depressed, anxious, misjudged, indignant?

Why? Because negative feedback is not fun; few people relish criticism. Some are happy to hear anything about ongoing work whilst others are more guarded until they have something 'presentable' to hand in. In both cases, the intensity of our emotional response may be in inverse proportion to the critique or intentions behind it. Sometimes we respond most strongly to the fairest criticism. So, if it feels tough, is the criticism fair? Can you do something about it, and so improve your work? If you are the recipient of a personal attack

Figure 8.4 Gate-keepers

Source: xkcd: http://xkcd.com

or an angry response to your work then stay calm if you can (for example don't forget to exhale). Encounters of the more ferocious kind are also part of the territory; a direct attack can be less lethal than one taking a 'softly, softly' approach, so you need to take both in your stride.

Don't sit back and think that you have things sorted on getting positive feedback, compliments and suchlike, especially when this applies to work-in-progress. Take heart for sure but do try not to gloat too much if others around you are having a hard time.

Why? Well you can work this one out for yourself! Recall that the quality of a dissertation is not decided upon by who gets to the finish line first or accumulates the most thumbs-up on the way.

Do try not to fret if a supervisory session or seminar presentation is disappointing.

Why? Maybe it wasn't as bad as you think. In any case, consider all criticism in order to take on board what you need to and under advisement and then MOVE ON. Fretting is a form of procrastination too.

Don't panic if you get a question you are unable to answer (yet); if your over-sight, or attempts to 'bluff' yourself out this corner get called, graciously 'fess up' and move on.

Why? Sometimes you are not at that point; for example, you may not yet have clear findings or it is too soon to provide a definitive set of conclusions. Sometimes, though, the question reveals an aspect of your work that is under-prepared or weak; for example, 'what exactly is your research question?' is not something to which you have no answer at all in an oral examination. If a lack of preparation or a fundamental weakness is exposed, then better it happens sooner rather than later.

Don't try and defend yourself *every* time you get a criticism, reject every suggestion immediately, or try and gain your audience's sympathies by emotional appeals.

Why? In all these cases, things can backfire. In a supervisory setting or research seminar, if you find yourself receiving a lot of criticism – justified or not to your mind, countering every comment or criticism usually means you're not listening. Whatever you do, try and avoid specious responses such as 'but it's difficult', or 'I haven't had time', or 'but my supervisor

www.VADLO.com

"Editor says the manuscript would serve some purpose if it were written on toilet paper."

Figure 8.5
Views and reviews

Source:
http://Vadlo.com

said . . .'. In the last case, emotional appeals or attempts to gain sympathy are not an argument. In exceptional circumstances, deal with these issues with your mentor or personal tutor.

Don't despair if you are ever subjected to a particularly personal attack, or a critique that takes exception to your work on political, social, or cultural grounds.

Why? See above. In the first instance, personal attacks (ad hominem *arguments) are the weakest form of argumentation, as pointed out by the Greek philosopher Aristotle many centuries ago. Good debate and constructive critique interacts with the content, not the person. In football terms, the aim is to play the ball, not the player. In the second case, you are in more complex territory; if the criticisms mounted expose a fundamental weakness in your research, your underlying assumptions, or reveal an ethical or cultural blind-spot on your part, listen first. And if you find yourself without 'a leg to stand on', take note and learn from it.*

Do expect there to be more suggestions and ideas than you can use.

Why? Our colleagues, classmates, and supervisors all have their own ideas. Their comments are also work-in-progress and are generated by what we are doing. Some points may have to be put aside for another time. Others may be more urgent for our current project. The art is to know the difference, for we cannot use all feedback equally at the time. Attempting to respond to everything is not a way to gain focus. Decisions have to be made and priorities set. In some ways, reviewers, discussant or supervisor may confuse giving you constructive feedback on your own work with telling you to do the research they wish you had done. In other words, you may hear that you need to do a different paper or project. If you think you are hearing this it is important to talk with your main supervisor or a second supervisor.

Do give yourself time to think about all comments, ideas, and criticisms before making any major changes.

Why? We all need time to absorb the feedback we are getting, get past any emotional responses to comments, or come to terms with that sinking feeling that our 'original contribution to knowledge' is more modest than we imagined for example, or that our topic is not 'cool' compared to others. So be it. Perspective comes with distance and increases with the benefit of hindsight. Live feedback sessions are nerve-wracking at times. However, written feedback, particularly when it is negative, can sometimes feel more devastating. When required to give a written response, it is even more important to take your time; don't send back your first response, you will regret it!

Do take detailed notes if the feedback is oral rather than written.

We risk losing some important points of the feedback if we do not take careful notes during the sessions. This applies to all live sessions – group presentations, conference presentations and the like.

Don't send endless emails, streams of your digital consciousness and thinking, to supervisors.

Why? They clutter up in-boxes and generate stress because you are not the only one under your supervisor's care. This is endemic to email/SMS-based communications; sometimes these sorts of panic-button mails have their place. But on the whole they do the student more good (by writing/venting) than the supervisory relationship. Continue to write these mails (part of your research diary) but don't send them until the next day. Reread before sending and then ask yourself: do I really need to send this?

Do thank people for their feedback, including your supervisor.

Why? Graciousness and acknowledgement go a long way. For public settings, if a point is well made, then acknowledge this. If a criticism is fair, even fundamental, then take it on the chin. If you are not sure what people mean then ask for clarification. As for your supervisor, well they (we) are also human! Taking notes also allows for time to absorb any broadsides, and prevent an over-hasty retort.

Additional points – between the lines

These do's and don'ts are much easier to list that they are to follow; there are *unwritten and explicit codes and hierarchies in play* including the (necessary) desire of most researchers to put their stamp on a research report they are getting credit for on an individual basis; innovativeness, originality, and 'flair' are highly prized in even the most conventional academic settings. In this aspect of research practice and academic life, the quantitative–qualitative divide operates in particular ways.

The key dividing line is the relative weight government bodies, university managements, and respective constituencies give to *outcome* as opposed to *process*; output is what counts in other words. Most quantitative assessment, also referred to as feedback pure and simple, is of the latter; the final outcome (exam script, essay, or dissertation) is what counts for examined *student* assessment. As many students studying abroad notice, there are geographical and institutional differences between how grades are assigned; higher ceilings can differ by 10–20 per cent in some cases, which is one reason why most academic records provide a guide for translating the home institution's indicators of excellence, whether these are quantitative or qualitative, for other contexts.[8] Many ambitious and high-achieving students can be overly perturbed on receiving a grade that appears lower than what they are used to, taking little comfort in being told that this mark is the highest in the class.

The point here is that grades are conventions, shorthand for ascertaining whether one essay, one thesis is more (or less) original or well executed than another. Of course, these scores need to be backed up by a written justification – feedback – on how to improve the mark; these marking scales and corresponding criteria are usually available in the relevant programme or institutional guidelines. In short, something marked at 75 per cent is considered markedly better than something marked at 55 per cent; whether the latter is close to failing (50 per cent being a common cut-off point but not exclusively) or average (when the pass/fail mark is set at 30 per cent for instance).

Changes in educational fashions and attitudes notwithstanding, the *aim of both praise and criticism* is to lead to improvement in quality in the long run. It is a truism that the best sort of criticism is constructive, namely that there are some reasons provided underpinning any negative comments. In that respect, student feedback and peer reviewing are not well represented by the sorts of personalized or kneejerk reactions that characterize a lot of talkback radio, online readers' comments pages, or vituperative reviewer reports and student course evaluations. That said, *without negative feedback in the case of a research project our work has little chance of improving*; sometimes a piece of work is not up to scratch. Becoming aware of how others see our proposed work-plan or provisional findings helps us to deal with any weaknesses or blind-spots in our argument, underlying assumptions, and practicalities in the research design. It also alerts us to how different audiences, sometimes from other research traditions, regard what we do. It helps us think outside our particular 'box'. So, whilst not all criticism can be taken on board it also means that praise is not sufficient in itself.

Whichever way you look at it, *when the feedback is positive* – a high mark, thumbs-up from our supervisors, colleagues, or classmates, a high ranking in external assessment exercises – it feels good. A good performance is a prime motivator for many people, in competitive societies especially. When the feedback is negative, however, the going can get tough, for student and experienced researchers. As people respond differently to negative feedback, particularly criticism about the aims, organization, or even worth of our project, there is no golden rule. Qualitative feedback in the case of student–teacher or student–supervisor relationships operates within a hierarchy; the teacher/supervisor is in a superior position. Sometimes, though, excessive levels of self-critique (likewise for self-congratulation) can blind our judgment. The reality we have to settle for is usually somewhere in between these two extremes. The same rule of thumb applies to how input from other people influences what, and how we write. Here, over-sensitivity to every criticism or suggestion levelled at us by superiors and our peers can be as counter-productive, as can over-defensiveness.

As for *peer assessment* such as student presentations, research seminars, conference panels, or anonymous reviewing, the relationships between giver and receiver are less clear cut. Personalities, intellectual backgrounds, cultural differences, and social conventions in terms of how criticism is expressed all have a role to play in how the message is sent, received, and then understood or misunderstood. However, peer

Figure 8.6 How to act like an artist II

Source: Nina Paley: http://www.ninapaley.com

assessment is often underestimated as a valuable part of the research process. Not only in terms of receiving input and ideas from our peers but also in terms of giving feedback to others. Both aspects need to be practised, for the ability to give and to receive feedback improves over time. There are also differences according to personal circumstances, and between educational and professional settings.

One *key difference between feedback that takes place in the workplace and in an academic environment*, particularly when it occurs between peers or in a supervisory interaction, is that the latter does not occur within a line-management structure. Your peers in a research setting are not your boss, or team-leader, or desk editor. Their comments are freely given and in the spirit of dialogue. In this respect they do not impact on your final mark. But they do make a difference in other ways. How you give feedback too, harder than it sounds as many novice teaching assistants learn, is also a measure of your ability to be constructive. It also trains you in how to better frame your own work for others.

Academic research in undergraduate and postgraduate degree processes are intrinsically individualistic, sometimes quite self-absorbed and hermetic experiences. Your main contact person is your supervisor/s, who during your project has a double role as your mentor and your examiner at the end of the day. Peer-to-peer assessment, just like P2P sharing on the web in the case of creative cultures and knowledge exchange, can be a synergetic process, not a downward spiral. Ultimately we are all better off, and our projects are stronger, for 'going public' and hearing what others think. That means also that *learning to give constructive feedback* also needs practice; as does learning to receive and then deal with criticism of our work along any research project's lifespan.

PROCRASTINATIONS AND PREVARICATIONS

This penultimate section takes a look at other equally important aspects to the writing-up and completion phases of a larger piece of academic work. I am referring here to all those self-created and unforeseen obstacles along the way to completion, as well as ways of encouraging the creative dimension to your writing and thinking at this stage. For there is scope for flair, perhaps not in all disciplines and dissertation formats or genres in equal amounts; always a degree of 'wriggle room' for letting inspiration and original thought and approaches show. Indeed in the history and philosophy of science literature there have been some renowned studies of the role of creativity and inspiration in the natural sciences, some even arguing that methods in the strictest sense of the term can be counter-productive to the advancement of knowledge (that is deemed scientific).[9]

Recall, the *conventional approach to academic writing* is underscored by the formalities of research dissertation, and funded research report writing (see Chapters 1 and 2) where standard, generic headings provide the outer shell for arranging the various parts in some kind of order; 'introduction', 'lit review', 'theory', 'method', 'empirical chapter/s' – or 'findings', 'discussion' and the 'conclusion'. For many this is enough; following the recipe will do. That said, even for those of you simply wanting to tick the boxes but particularly for anyone striving to successfully complete their research project to high standards of self-satisfaction or external evaluative criteria, keeping up the momentum, particularly as research 'metal fatigue' sets in, can trip you up.

First is, metaphorically speaking, 'altitude sickness'; the feeling that there is still so much to do and still so much you do not yet know, can be overwhelming. This is the first point: how to stay 'on task' for a sustained amount of time (months often) without going off the boil; initial enthusiasms can easily go stale, findings prove less riveting, topics less thrilling after living with them for so long. The second is a form of inertia. For many facing the writing-up phase, as analysis takes shape in the form and act of writing, general procrastination or avoidance of specific sections can be a major hurdle. We all face moments of putting off starting the writing or periods of inaction during the writing. Any long-term degree of 'writer's block' has a way of becoming a self-fulfilling prophecy; inaction perpetuates the cycle of anxiety–no/not enough progress–more anxiety.

What are some ways of responding to these twin perils?

One response is to grit your teeth; realize that once the research design and data-gathering are completed writing up is effectively a whole new stage, mostly uphill. It also occurs in a large part quite late in the process, often too late for many – but more on this in due course. Gathering the data is not the same as being in control of it, cognitively, intellectually or literally. These moments of handling, apprehending, and then (re)presenting the work you have done are distinct processes. As Carol Smart notes, even the most experienced researcher has faced their data (however defined) more as 'recalcitrant mound of wet clay which defies you to shape it into something recognizable' (2010: 5) than something ready-made for writing purposes. This because *working* with data is not the same as 'the ability to *write* with data' (ibid.: 5, emphasis added).

A second response lies in even more contentious territory; the fine line between creative and formal requirements in academic writing practice is a shifting one; talk of striving to write 'well' can appear to be mutually exclusive to the trials of

Figure 8.7 You are here

Source: Chappatte:
http://www.globecartoon.com

writing/working with the material we have gathered, collated, and analysed. Research projects identifying with literary and philosophical traditions often work with a high regard for 'slow writing' – and 'close reading'; others consider simple sentence structures, executive summary-style introductions and conclusions, bullet-points and very short paragraphs as the *sine qua non* of readability. In all cases, without something to report, truckloads of creative writing, journalistic copy, or blogging experience serve little good when this 'mound of clay' or, worse still, pile of feathers (some students have characterized their research findings as flying away from them as they try and pin them down) defies our attempts to tame it.

COPING AND MOVING ON – CREATIVELY

There is such a thing as creativity in academic writing, comparable to how originality and innovativeness are valued highly (see Chapter 2). However, this quality is understood, and then evaluated, a bit differently than in creative writing or composition for instance. At one end of the spectrum, creativity is tantamount to 'anything goes', free associative techniques, or the effect of inspiration, the source of which is the subject of debates in philosophy, theology, and aesthetics as well as other disciplines in the wake of the postmodern – literary – turn in the arts and social sciences. Just how creative you can be in terms of the formalistic requirements of dissertation work and your writing very much depends on the disciplinary context in which you are working; in some settings all the formalities discussed thus far are a mainstream to be resisted, subverted, and transformed. At least in theory if not in practice. Even radically subversive expressions of academic form emerge from some sort of disciplining crucible. The point here is to realize that creativity and originality are not absolutes; they are negotiated and contested at all points.

For some academic contexts, creativity is less about the literary value of the final report, stylistic gymnastics, but more about how *parsimonious* the theorizing is, elegance in research design, or coherence of the argument made. In other cases, creativity is not considered a goal in itself; considered *reports*, there are genres of academic writing that are assessed by standards of what constitutes unambiguous, transparent and so 'accessible' written expression, declamatory as opposed to lyrical. In those parts of academe where literary styles or evidence of creative flair are part of the assessment

Figure 8.8 Help! I'm trapped in a hole!
Source: Nina Paley: http://www.ninapaley.com

here too there may well be limits; the tension between form and substance, prescription and permissiveness varying in degree accordingly. The point is to note that no matter where our work is being done, informal expectations create their own 'holes' that can create obstructions to our thinking and executing the project.

Some tactics for getting yourself out of any hole:

- 'Don't get it right, get it written'; write first and rewrite afterwards is a way to get copy produced, particularly for those who have a hard time putting words onto the page/screen.
- Perfectionism, particularly when wrestling with the data and changes in how we interpret these data, conclusions we make as the data-analysis and writing-up phases merge, can be an obstacle in the early stages of writing the research report. One useful tip is to think about 'four drafts in an hour' rather than 'one draft in four hours'. Whilst this may not work all the time, it is a good way to get past tinkering with that first paragraph, early chapter.
- When working with transcript material, often producing large amounts of text, be aware that there will be a need to tailor the main text (your voice) with the voices of your respondents (the 'evidence'). The latter, if in textual form, can create pressure on the word-limit. So, first get down those citations you have decided matter. Reread and then reconsider. This sort of writing-with-data is always rewriting-with-data or, letting the data write, or speak.
- If you find yourself labouring over the same passage, early chapters over and over again, to the detriment of less well-honed or unwritten sections, take heart; at some point these more refined parts were relatively raw. Apply the above approach for any 'white space' threatening to engulf you in the fog of prevarication by jotting down notes, establishing some section headings, working backwards (we tend to move forwards and then stay stuck when that forward movement stalls).
- Plan! The exclamation mark is deliberate. Writing by planning not only generates copy, but ideas. You may well be surprised at just how much you have written down after a planning session.
- Try different formats to use different body/brain parts if you find your inspiration and attention span waning. Mind-maps using coloured pencils, crayons and other sorts of visuals (draw instead of write) can help shift your thinking and take on the material; for example, tables of figures could be transposed to other graphics if you are unable to see past the number in that pie-chart, and bar-charts convey different angles, if not suggest different interpretations to even immovable quantities.
- Assembling and writing about these data, and in such a way that you are making an argument, could be seen as a puzzle; move the flat screen into three-dimensional space by literally cutting and pasting.
- Take a break, a cat-nap, a walk. These do wonders to our thinking and writing.
- Try monitoring any recurring habits, procrastinating behaviours that get in the way (as opposed to being creatively supportive activities) if you find yourself in danger of not making the deadline; for example, get out of bed earlier, allow yourself these activities as a reward for completing some aspect of the work; alternatively start with the toughest first (sifting through the material one more time) and then reward yourself with the more 'fun' parts (for example, formatting).

- Keep working a bit at a time; writing only happens by writing so by dividing your writing tasks or days up into bite-sized/doable chunks you may well find yourself producing more of what you hope to, even if only in draft form, than sitting down at the start of the session determined to 'not get up until I have written or "x" hours, written "x" amount of words'. That may work for some but for others it may be too daunting. Get a sense of what works, and what does not work for you. Encourage the former and minimize the latter. If you cannot carry out your own diagnostic, ask those around you – they will know.
- Finally, coherence, insight, creativity, and flow even in the most formal document layout or discussions of dry findings, for example, discussing the findings from large 'n' surveys, come in fits and starts. If you expect to be on the ball 100 per cent of the time you will disappoint yourself.
- Be content with being in the flow for any of the time. Even academics over-romanticize the process, practice, and skill of any sort of writing.

REVISING AND EDITING – WHAT TO LOOK FOR

Good writing guides abound so this section highlights recurring points for anyone at these final stages. Even if you are not an Ernest Hemingway (known for his brevity) or Virginia Woolf (known for the effortlessness of her flow-of-consciousness style), there are ways to lift the text up a level. Academic writing is seldom achieved as a steady stream. Whilst there are times when the work and accompanying writing 'flows', and the ideas and grasp of all those data are clear, there are many others when this is not the case. However good you may be as a writer (remember, not everyone is a natural born author) in academic or creative terms, 99 per cent of the time you will need to revise and edit the larger document at least once before handing it in. Not leaving enough time for this final once-over has tripped up many; and will continue to do so because we all overestimate the cogency of that first draft, underestimate the value fresh eyes can provide. This also applies to those submitting this major piece of writing in a foreign language. In fact in the latter case the time you allocate to revising and editing your text should be longer; more on this below.

Below are ten pointers (mini 'commandments') in this respect based on my own and others' experiences. These aim to provide guidance on how to avoid tripping up during the writing-up and revising phases. If you do trip up and it is too late to do much about it, these help you to cope, deal with what you can and still make the deadline:

1 It is a truism but nonetheless, one more time: leave enough time to let the text 'percolate'. Your ability to spot mistakes, redundant repetitions, 'tortured syntax' and other factual oversights and errors (for example, with graphics, notes, and references) will increase with time. Like sending an email too quickly and regretting it the next day, the same applies here.
2 Even if this is but a day or two (preferably a week depending on the size of the project; I'd suggest even longer for Ph.D.s and book-size writing) make sure that you go away and do something completely different. Give your brain a rest;

intense bouts of writing are usually accompanied by equally intense bouts of rerunning and fretting over the text in our heads. Do something physical, embark on a completely different project, go away for a day or two, to the movies, read some pulp fiction – or classics if you prefer. As long as this is something quite different. Then come back to the text with the red pen/highlighter and be your own toughest editor.

3 *Everyone needs to check their spelling and grammar* – everyone! With the software-aided spell-checks (for all their limits) available on all desktop word-processing packages this is easier than ever. Proper nouns (author names, concepts, places) will need a manual check. Assuming you have set up your spell-check to work along the language/dialect you are working with, this basic task is a must.

4 Likewise for *grammar checks*. That said, as grammar and syntax are closely allied to (conflicting) notions of style, good and bad writing, these tools also need to be treated with due care. However, if you are not writing in your first language, applying the basic grammar check can help a lot; you learn something and many of the more jarring issues can be dealt with. If you are able to engage someone to edit your work to render it more idiomatic in the submission language this can work. However, remember that you are the author of this text, legally, so this is not to suggest you engage a ghost-writer; this is something quite different from a good and engaged editor.

5 For all writers, having someone else read all (if you can find someone other than a supervisor) or part of the text can help; copy-editing is a particular skill but an alert reader with no stake in the material (unlike the writer) can locate errors or confused expression. If you do not agree with their verdict, that is your call. But for important sections, enrolling other readers is useful: ready-made fresh eyes and head for a start.

6 Look at balance; within a chapter or section and between them. Extremely long chapters or sections against very short ones might require consideration, reorganizing or cutting.

7 On that note, *cuts and deletions will – and must – happen*. Most of the time anyway. If not of obvious repetition or sentences or sections (sometimes leftovers from incomplete cut-and-paste actions on the text) then perhaps of whole chapters. For Ph.D. projects entering the final drafting stage, sometimes this decision to cut (rather than continue to write) can be a crucial moment, liberating in fact. In short, be prepared and expect to have to let go; leave something out. The final copy is usually better for it.

8 The same goes for reorganization. Changing the order of things alters the flow, clarifies and tightens up an argument, enhances the narrative line or provides a way to reconsider the data you have been writing with. This too can be hard, though, so once again a fresh pair of eyes (yours or another's) and percolating time help here enormously.

9 Expect the revision and editing phase to be emotionally charged. Even researchers with journalistic experience (who have desk editors intervening in the final version) find these decisions tough in an academic project. One clear way to figure this out when contemplating whether to cut a major section is to think 'if in doubt, leave it out'. When this is a large piece of the work, file it away in case.

10 *Word-length restrictions do matter*; make them work for you. If you have too much text, even if you are convinced it is all indispensable, you will have to, and you can cut it back. Again, leave time for this.

A final comment warrants separate treatment, *an 'eleventh' commandment*. That is to consider how the much-heard advice to 'know your audience' applies to you; in terms of recognizing the limits to what you can achieve in literary, or even scholarly terms in the time and comparative level of experience you have. Why?

* For research students completing their first major piece of academic research and then writing (quite distinct from term papers as many a student has lamented to me), uncertainty about who they are addressing is often overlooked.
* This audience need not be a person (though you could consider having supervisor and/or classmates before you in your mind's eye if that facilitates things. It may not though). It could be a group, for example, authors you have read that inspire you or a particular community of ideas within your literature.
* Treat this audience as intelligent and (reasonably) interested in engaging with your findings. That said, you also need to be kind to this audience in that by now you have acquired expertise and knowledge of your own; impart that knowledge without assuming equal knowledge yet without being condescending: a tricky balancing act but bear this in mind.
* One thing is for sure, the final version is not intended for that audience-of-one that is you. Turning your writing outwards, to address those outside your inner-mind's eye is often where the work done with revisions and editing pay off.
* Idioms: Whilst we cannot please all audiences all of the time, we do need to consider who else will be reading the piece. If the context and disciplinary mode you are working in requires certain things, then conforming to these, following convention, may well be advisable for successfully completing the project. If these conventions are counter-intuitive or counter-experiential (for example, some creatively trained writers can find it difficult if not trying to apply section headings or cite the literature consistently), that is tough. If you have time, then why not write up the research as you would like to and then consider creating another version – for academic consumption?

THE FINAL CUT – WHAT TO REMEMBER

Some points about the final cut, particularly as hand-in deadlines for research dissertations in many institutions are very strict. Again, the most important rule is to allocate enough time (after the above revisions and edits are completed) to ensure the following can take place without undue stress:

1 *Printing-out time: never leave this to the last minute*. Something always goes awry – printers break down, toner cartridges empty, printer-shops or services run late or do something wrong. Printing out at home or with a commercial service, always check that all pages are in place; take your time here as haste generates mistakes. Check that:

(a) You are sure about printing formats; for example, single-sided is usually compulsory or expected.

(b) Pages are all there and in sequence; be sure you have pages numbered (many students omit this). If not, do so by hand.

(c) The document is appropriately bound (mandatory usually but students still hand in/try to hand in loose-leaf piles of paper); staples may not be enough for longer documents. How expensive a binding you need is up to you and the degree level.

(d) All other presentation formalities are observed (consult your institutional guidelines): word-spacing, cover page with title, your name/student number and requisite contact information, literature list, appendices, and so on. Don't guess, go check.

(e) You are clear about (how many) hardcopies and/or digital formats are required, and the means and locale for handing in.

2 An additional suggestion, if you have enough time and resources, is to create a first full draft as if it were the final cut; then leave it aside for a while and go back over it for one final check. This is not for everyone but it can help locate any remaining oversights.

3. That said, assuming you have given enough attention to revising and editing the substantive document, do make a point of letting go; there will always be sections you wish were better, could be better written; ideas and conclusions that could be, and will be more clearly expressed. But as the deadline has come, the time has come to really let go.

In short, treat the final version and presentation of your work with consideration. Whilst some students may have the added benefit of graphic design/desktop publishing experience, a clean print-out with decent binding, a cover page and back page creates a good first impression on reader-examiners. It is worth going an extra few metres to achieve this within reason and resources (no coffee stains if you can help it for instance).

Further reading

For some very useful ways of thinking 'outside the box' of your own writing habits, see (quick writing guides) Hall (1993) and Richardson (1990); other writing guides aimed at academic output include Barrass (1982); and Becker (1986), Clanchy and Ballard (1984), Cuba and Cocking (1994) and Turabian and Spine (1984) aim at specifically social science based writing issues; Dummett (1993) is for the more grammatically minded, Hart (1998) muses on the literature review as a way to get writing, whilst Henwood et al. (2001) provide examples of autobiographical modes within science and technology studies. Berg (2009), Creswell (2009) and C. Davies (2007) all have good pointers as well.

NOTES

1 See Michel Foucault's classic essay, 'What is an Author?' (1984 [1977]).

2 Concordia University Library 2011: http://library.concordia.ca/help/howto/apa.php (20 July 2011).

3 Ibid.

4 Concordia University 2011: http://library.concordia.ca/help/howto/mla.php?guid=works (20 July 2011).

5 Taken from Taylor & Francis' (2001: 21) *Instructions for Authors*.

6 The Concordia University Library's online resource, which is linked to the websites of these three systems, is particularly useful. See http://library.concordia.ca/help/howto/citations.html (20 July 2011). It provides more than technical recipes. As for online citing and documentation, see 'Citing Online Research and Documentation' in Hacker and Fisker (2010), available online at http://bcs.bedfordstmartins.com/resdoc5e/ (20 July 2011).

7 This process works along a spectrum of full disclosure and forms of (quasi) anonymity. For journal articles, and research funding applications, peer assessment – external reviewing – is intentionally an anonymous process; double blind reviewing is when neither party is named, the norm for submission to academic journals. Book proposals and funding bids are not necessarily double-blind; reviewers see who the prospective author or funding recipient is, as curriculum vitae form part of the submission process, whilst they as reviewer remain anonymous. There are codes of ethics in place for this role; some specified by funders and others implicit. For example, funding organizations will not accept a review of a proposal from someone within the same institution, reviewers need to declare any conflicts of interest (being married to, or knowing the applicant in a professional capacity for instance). The rule of thumb is that anonymity does not grant a licence to say anything you like about the project, or person; you should be willing and able to say these things in such a way to them face-to-face. Anonymous – external – reviewing has distinct advantages but it also has its own set of occupational hazards.

8 University entrance qualifications and success rates are tied to quantitative measurements, which follow on from various sorts of testing and entrance exams for lower and middle schools (USA); the statistical value called the General Point Average (GPA) noted on an academic record (USA), or the qualifying of a final degree award with 'summa cum laude' or 'cum laude' (Latin for 'double honours' and 'honours' common on the European continent), the awarding of a 'First' or '2.1' degree (the UK) are all cases in point. The preference given to numbers, percentages, or alphabetical values (A through to D) varies as do the lower and upper limits of what constitutes a pass or a fail. These variations create headaches for students and teachers in an international classroom as well as for admissions offices in universities recruiting students who need to make comparisons between degrees and educational systems. Marks, reviewer rankings, and national league tables are something that students, educators and researchers all have to learn to live with. Like it or not these values count. Qualitative commentary is not designed to be processed in this way, unless assessment criteria such as 'feasibility', 'coherence', or 'originality' are assigned a numerical value.

9 Recall Kuhn (1962) and Feyerabend (1978). See also Canales (2009) and Schulz (2010).

CHAPTER 9

Conclusion

> [Researchers] are people of very dissimilar temperaments doing different things in very different ways. Among scientists are collectors, classifiers and compulsive tidiers-up; many are detectives by temperament and many are explorers; some are artists and others artisans. There are poet-scientists and philosopher-scientists and even a few mystics.
>
> (Medawar 1982: 116)

A couple of years ago, one of my master-level research students flew into my office in a panic; the dissertation project was stalled, she had no idea what to read, what her research question really was, or how to start. Whilst this was not the first – nor the last – crisis, this time she paused mid-stream and said, 'I just don't understand; tell me, what *is* research?!'

My heart sank, blood pressure went up, brow furrowed; 'this late in the year and she still doesn't get it?!' I thought. Then I realized this is actually a legitimate question and if I were honest with myself it was probably one (of the many) I too was once too afraid to ask. So, as all supervisors must, I took a deep breath and asked her to take a seat. We then talked through the specific concerns she was struggling with at that particular moment. I am pleased to say that the final result was an excellent one; as accomplished a project as any other submitted that year; including dissertations completed by any number who had made it clear that they knew exactly what the answer is to this question.

In many respects this book has addressed this disconnect: the gap between our real needs for guidance and what we think we already understand, still need to learn about research, taken from – positive or negative – experience, books, mentors, public events, and classmates. There is actually not that much separating a student going through similar anxieties and blocks who thinks they don't understand what the research dissertation element of their degree is about and those who are very clear about what they are doing, in what way, and for what reasons. Either way, my hope is that a student could walk into my, or someone else's office a little less panicked with this book tucked under their arm.

As we have come to the end of this book, though most likely not the end of a particular project or ongoing path of inquiry, this chapter recaps the main themes and rationale of the approach taken here. The final section wraps things up in order for you, and me, to be able to get on with whatever line of inquiry (always open, always cumulative) or particular research project we are currently pursuing.

REAPPRAISING DIVIDES IMAGINED AND REAL

One reader of the manuscript asked me to give a 'friendly hint', a clearer idea of what my 'take' is on where *exactly* the quantitative–qualitative divide at stake in this book lies. However, in practice things are not so clear-cut. First, because pinpointing let alone solving the 'problem of divides' (to borrow from Karl Popper, in Jarvie 2005: 821) is that these are susceptible to the vagaries of time, trends, and economic (dis)incentives. Even in its most trenchant formulations, the notion of which works best, quantitative or qualitative modes of research, has been substantially rethought and fought over in academe over the last half-century. In recent years though, the computational and interconnecting characteristics of computer-mediated communications, web-based research, digital data-gathering and analysis tools, teaching and learning have created a particular edge to these debates. Computers and, moreover, the internet increasingly mediate conventional research, now presenting virtual research fields, digital methods, online communities, and digital subjects as new research terrain.

As real and imagined dichotomies between qualitative and quantitative work are played out in the literature, methods curricula come and go in the classroom. The way implicit positions on research in its more narrow rendition as method is one of the more sensitive aspects to success in gaining research funding, accreditation, and legitimacy – within academe and beyond. This disconnect between what gets taught – or not, and what gets funded – or not, crystallizes in university recruitment strategies and postgraduate employment opportunities the world over. Students are expected to align themselves accordingly, and often without question. These relationships mesh with important debates about 'good' or 'bad' scholarship, good or bad science; about what sort of research is the most relevant at the time for society at large. Meanwhile, money and kudos outside research institutions flow accordingly in that think tanks, policy-making circles, educational curricula, access to decision making, and faculty recruitment strategies reproduce these power relations in latent and explicit ways.

The literatures underwriting these distinctions are made up of an amalgam of mutually exclusive and intersecting worldviews, theoretical brand names, and a myriad interrelated as well as sharply diverging techniques for gathering, analysing and then assembling evidence. Stronger still differences about what counts as evidence per se inform these practicalities. All of these unfold along various disciplinary codes of conduct and research ethics. Gate-keepers and defenders of any approach claiming to have found the 'philosopher's stone' for conducting research purport that this way brings us closer to some sort of truth about the object of study in question.[1] Funding flows, personal and professional standing, careers, and respective orbits of power, influence, and privilege crystallize accordingly.

In the meantime as students or supervisors we all have to deal with the research project at hand, get it off the ground, executed, wrapped up, and out the door. There is little time or motivation to navigate the rich and diverse research methods/research skills literature. So, I shall defer for the time being on stating categorically where I think these divides really matter, and who calls the shots precisely because they move and differ according to project, researcher, institutional context, geographical place, and timing. Students and researchers too, as individuals and community members, experience and reproduce any number of divides, take part in their resolution or codification as we move through, or out of academe.

TO THE EXIT AND AFTERLIFE OF A RESEARCH PROJECT

[It] will sometimes strike a scientific [person] that the philosophers have been less intent on finding out what the facts are, than on inquiring what belief is most in harmony with their system. . . . On the other hand, all the followers of science are animated by a cheerful hope that the processes of investigation, if only pushed far enough, will give one certain solution to each question to which they apply it. . . . It is certainly important to make our ideas clear, but they may be ever so clear without being true.

(Charles S. Peirce, in Cahoone 1996: 152, 154)

Doing research today takes place in an atmosphere of initiatives that ostensibly aim to foster disciplinary cross-pollination and collaboration even as disciplinary specialization and exclusive, single-method approaches are becoming arguably even more entrenched. Beyond inter-departmental initiatives and international research platforms, important geographic alignments of research funding streams, such as the European Research Area and related educational European Union member-state agreements to standardize higher education *outputs* along with an increased emphasis on a particular understanding of *impacts* have implications for the interaction between research institutions, government organs, business, and society at large. Regional histories, job markets, and funding economies make themselves felt at the methods baseline; the USA differs markedly from the UK, and the latter two differ from (western) continental Europe for instance. Students need to understand where and why they are doing their research in the ways they opt to do so, and how to navigate and negotiate where needed as they embark upon and then, hopefully, exit a research process.

Moreover, shifts within university funding streams have seen department restructurings that throw scholars from very different 'worldviews' together. 'Hardcore Quants' find themselves rubbing shoulders with 'Fuzzy Theorists' in the staff common-room, or conferring on student assessment, or co-supervising a research student. Finally, there is the explosion in digital research tools and online fields along with computer-mediated research techniques and multimedia-based applications being put to use in many ways. These also have varying implications for both the entrenchment and redrawing of this divide, for the ethics of doing research in virtual and classical fields, and for shifting patterns of scholarly accountability that cannot be reduced to simplistic duels between *mainstream* vs. *critical* or *virtual* vs. *material* social relations, *normative* vs. *positivist* theory. Providing sustenance – practical and intellectual – for researchers who need to be able to travel to and fro across these real-existing divisions, let alone in cross-cultural, international research settings, a different approach is called for; we all need to be able to converse with those from the 'other side'.

In this sense the book has aimed to speak to the daily realities of the research in what are fluid, demographically diverse albeit unequal terrains. It recognizes that disciplines and sub-disciplines speak with various methodological-theoretical voices and these draw students accordingly, academic fashions and wider societal trends included. By the same token, the often combative if not outright hostile tenor of many debates around about 'good' and 'bad' research that students witness, or experience first-hand, tends to obscure the fact that, at some point decisions need to be made. Knowing why and at what cost is more the point.

In the spirit of dialogue and open-ended puzzling, the book has offered practical guidance rather than prescription based on experience-based and philosophical insights into what makes everyday life as a researcher tick. However, it has also recognized that students often first enter the process by way of a particular methodological preference or set of debates, if not through being trained in a particular school of thought about 'best practices', 'scientific reasoning' or 'critical theory'. It looked at a range of tactics and tools for not only solving puzzles along this path but also dealing with more intransigent conundrums as it links these on-the-job research skills to competencies students should have in order to talk with, and work across any number of divides.

Along with others who take a more holistic approach to research as a practical and intellectual endeavour, one that unfolds in historically and socioculturally drenched settings (ivory towers included) this book sees these activities as not just dry, arcane exercises but also as endeavours that offer researchers a lot on a personal and professional level. As well as dispassionate observers of social phenomena, technicians, disciplinary specialists or generalists, researchers can be passionate. We bring to our projects attributes we already have (Medawar 1982) but also, hopefully, we gain new ones. Moreover, the things we discover about the world, our society, and ourselves can often prove to be as fascinating and provocative as they are confirmations or extensions of existing knowledge. The skills acquired during a research project are specific to that endeavour – its academic ecosystem – to be sure. But they are also 'transferable' to other parts of everyday life and work. It is often only much later that students realize this for themselves.

Whatever your baseline position may be about the point or social relevance of academic modes of generating knowledge, or the role played by your own choices for your future career path, understanding is not a pre-given. Nor is the divide informing this book, and the way we need to reposition ourselves along its shifting sands immutable, no matter how much it appears to define what sort of scholar we (think) we want to become. When entering and then exiting the now interconnected physical and computer-mediated domains in which all sorts of researchers engage with their objects of inquiry we are all also engaging in any number of sociocultural relationship and power hierarchies. These go hand-in-hand with longstanding and newer debates about the pursuit of knowledge (scholarly, scientific, common sense) or, if you prefer, truth.

NOTE

1   The 'philosopher's stone', along with being the title of the first *Harry Potter* book by J. K. Rowling, refers to a term in alchemy for a substance that can turn base metals, lead for example, into precious ones like gold; a metaphor for levels of excellence in effect.

Appendix 1

Informed consent form template

Below is a template for composing your own consent form relevant to the sort of interview and context.

CONSENT FORM FOR INTERVIEW

Thank you for agreeing to this interview. As previously discussed, these questions relate to a . . . in . . . at [institution]. The dissertation investigates . . .

Your responses will be treated with the appropriate levels of confidentiality, i.e. anonymous unless prior permission granted to be named; interviewees have access to the dissertation if they so choose . . .

The material gained from the [interviews] will be used specifically in relation to the aforementioned dissertation topic only.

Signed: . . .

Print name: . . .

Date: . . .

Appendix 2

Guidelines for internet research/ researching cyberspace[1]

Prescriptive and proscriptive ethical duties and obligations for the academic researching of cyberspace or the 'internet' are not significantly different to those applying to traditional qualitative and/or quantitative research in human and animal communities. There are areas of consensus about right and wrong and good and bad in relation to researching and researchers. In the UK there are also legal considerations particularly in any research concerning the process of establishing and developing human relationships online. There are also well-established research centres and journals exploring internet and cyberspace ethics and many academic institutions have publicly published their own guidelines.

NOTE

1 'Draft Ethical Guidelines for Internet Research/Researching Cyberspace' (June 15th 2010); reproduced here with kind permission from Tim Crook.

Table A2.1 Guidelines for internet research/researching cyberspace

Internet/cyberspace	*Textual analysis*. Access by 'going online' using search engines and retrieving internet page impressions without the need for registration, username and password.	*Ethical obligations*: Attribution, URLs, date and time 'retrieved/visited'. Disclosure not needed in visits to web-pages, but permission for inclusion of quotations and multi-media recommended. *Legal risks*: Indecency, anti-terrorism crimes. Breach of copyright/intellectual property laws.
Internet communities and macro-membership networks Large-scale, e.g. Facebook, MySpace, Friendsreunited, YouTube, Second Life. Computer games such as Fairyland and Farmville.	*Textual analysis*. Access by joining the large-scale network via registration, username and password. Opinion is divided on whether permission should be obtained by the companies owning these cyberspace 'networks' prior to conducting textual analysis research or 'ethnographic observation'. *Ethnographic observation without participation.* *Ethnographic participation*. It is advisable to disclose and seek permission not only from the network 'gate-keepers' but also from individuals and group forums that are being observed and are responding to your participation.	*Ethical obligations*: Attribution, URLs, date and time 'retrieved/visited'. Disclosure that registration is being made for the purposes of research is advisable. *Legal risks*: Mainly breach of copyright/intellectual property laws as issues of indecency and terrorism crimes tend to be excluded or met through the networks' own pre-moderation and reporting protocols. Participant-observation must avoid the infliction or causation of emotional and/or social harm. Legal risks include communication crimes and torts such as generating racial, religious, or gender orientation hatred, defamation and breach of privacy.
Closed membership Bulletin boards, email exchanges, chat-rooms.	For *textual analysis and non-participating observation or participant-observation*, prior permission and notification is considered essential.	*Ethical obligations*: Full and explicit disclosure of identity. The avoidance of social and emotional harm in all communications. *Legal risks*: These may have been excluded by the adoption of ethical principles cited above. UK law prohibits communication crimes and torts such as generating racial, religious, or gender orientation hatred, harassment, defamation and breach of privacy.
Subterfuge and 'undercover' techniques of investigation	These are generally discouraged in the field of academic research and belong to the daredevil world of journalism or intelligence. It is rare indeed to find any justification for such research behaviour in textual analysis, qualitative interviewing, quantitative surveying or participant and non-participant ethnographic observation. In cyberspace and internet communications this could involve 'infiltrating' communities without prior disclosure and permission, adopting fake identities and social participation in cyber communications and behaviour via an avatar.	*Ethical obligations*: Such methodology has to be considered at college research sub-committee level and will only be discussed after the furnishing of compelling evidence that there is no other means of undertaking the research; the purpose involves the research of unlawful, anti-social and unethical textual communication and human behaviour. Ethical issues arising involve the acute consideration of justifiable behaviour, utilitarian and deontological analysis, and human rights issues.

Continued

Table A2.1 Continued

		There are very serious *legal risks* including fraud, sexual offences, as well as serious civil wrongs in relation to defamation and breaches of privacy and contract. Researching some areas of human sexuality in cyberspace may require registration with the police under the 2003 Sexual Offences Act, and highly specialized academic supervision.
Consent protocols	These consents must be in writing, and where established by email exchanges should be supported by credible and recognizable electronic signatures.	*Ethical obligations*: Researchers must be conscious that their research subjects and participants are capable of providing informed consent. Issues do arise where the research subjects are persuaded to consent to any textual or observational analysis that is likely to cause emotional, social, or physical harm. In these circumstances issues of ethics may also give rise to *legal risks* such as incitement, joint enterprise, and strict liability for sexual and terrorism offences.
Issues of anonymity These are rather complex in the realm of cyberspace and should be simplified by clarity of promise, expression of obligation and explicit explanation of the limitations and extent of 'anonymity' confidentiality. Internet and cyberspace communications leave a digital trail in being retrievable and traceable via search engines, and are 'saved' on hard disk servers. Internet texts, authors and behaviour are much more capable of being electronically triangulated and 'jigsaw' identified than in the analogue world. Internet identities are usually capable of exposure and confirmation via IP addresses unless they have been communicating using proxy servers. In these circumstances the degree of confidentiality available needs to be qualified.	It is advisable that the authors of textual communications, qualitative interviewees, and individuals and social groups subject to ethnographic observation agree to be identified and that this is obtained in writing to cover inclusion and publication of the research subjects should be informed about the nature of academic publication, e.g. adoption by university library, access via inter-library loans, ProQuest and future public academic book publication. Anonymity protocols need to be by written consent with force majeure declarations and qualified assurances based on the nature of the internet medium.	*Ethical obligations*: Promises concerning confidentiality and anonymity need to be either guaranteed or qualified. A time-limit as well as arrangements for the protection and storage of research data needs to be determined prior to the start of any project. *Legal risks*: Breach of privacy, contract and confidentiality.

Source: 'Draft Ethical Guidelines for Internet Research/Researching Cyberspace' (June 15th 2010); reproduced here with kind permission from Tim Crook.

Appendix 3

Sample (master-level) ethics form[1]

- Name of student
- ID number
- Email address
- Date
- Programme of study
- Project (e.g. dissertation)
- Working title of project
- Supervisor

OVERVIEW

Does the proposed research involve working with human subjects, on the ground or online? Yes/No

Examples of research involving human subjects include (but are not limited to): carrying out interviews; conducting a survey; distributing a questionnaire; carrying out focus groups; and observation of individuals or groups. Where this research can take place can be in conventional, on-the-ground settings, on the web, or a combination of the two.

If so please respond to the questions below in Part A, and Part B where necessary. If not please proceed to sign and date the form and attach to your project the following items [for example]:

- Project description (50–100 words)
- Purpose (50–100 words)
- Research methodology (100–150 words).

PART A

1 Human subjects: does the research proposal involve:

(a) Any person under the age of 18? Yes/No
(b) Adult patients? Yes/No
(c) Adults with psychological impairments? Yes/No
(d) Adults with learning difficulties? Yes/No
(e) Adults under the protection/control/influence of others (e.g. in care/in prison)? Yes/No
(f) Relatives of ill people (e.g. parents of sick children)? Yes/No
(g) People who may only have a basic knowledge of English? Yes/No

2 Subject matter: does the research proposal involve:

(a) Sensitive personal issues (e.g. suicide, bereavement, gender identity, sexuality, fertility, abortion, gambling)? Yes/No
(b) Illegal activities, illicit drug taking, substance abuse or the self-reporting of criminal behaviour? Yes/No
(c) Any act that might diminish self-respect or cause shame, embarrassment or regret? Yes/No
(d) Research into politically and/or racially/ethically sensitive areas? Yes/No

3 Procedures: does the proposal involve:

(a) Use of personal or company records without consent? Yes/No
(b) Deception of participants? Yes/No
(c) The offer of disproportionately large inducements to participate? Yes/No
(d) Audio or visual recordings without consent? Yes/No
(e) Invasive physical interventions or treatments? Yes/No
(f) Research which might put researchers or participants at risk? Yes/No

If you have answered YES to any of the questions in PART A, sections 1–3, you will also need to comply with the requirements of PART B of this form.

4 Research subjects (informants):

(a) Who will your informants be?

(b) Do you have a pre-existing relationship with the informants and, if so, what is the nature of that relationship?

(c) How do you plan to gain access to/contact/approach potential informants?

(d) What arrangements have you made for anonymity and confidentiality?

(e) What, if any, is the particular vulnerability of your informants?

(f) What arrangements are in place to ensure that informants know the purpose of the research and what they are going to inform about?

(g) How will you ensure that informants are aware of their right to refuse to participate or withdraw at any time?

(h) What are the safety issues (if any) arising from this research, and how will you deal with them?

(i) How do you propose to store the information?

Checklist

If you have answered 'NO' to all of the questions in sections 1–3 above, please ignore PART B of the form.

You should return a hard and soft-copy to your supervisor for approval or further consultation.

As noted above, the supervisor can contact the Departmental Ethics Sub-committee about any issues arising.

This form should be considered and completed before research begins.

- Student signature:
- Date:
- Supervisor signature:
- Date:

PART B

This part of the application form is only relevant where researchers have answered 'YES' to any of the questions in sections 1–3 of PART A.

As you design and plan your project the question below will help you make some decisions and ensure you are aware of relevant elements.

A: Justification – ethical issues

1 What are the ethical issues involved in your research?

2 Please explain why the use of human participants is essential to your research project.

3 How will you ensure that informed consent is freely given by human participants?

Please attach a preliminary Consent Form, or provide an indication of a culturally appropriate form of consent that applies to this project.

B: Data-storage and privacy matters

Please consider and answer the following questions *where relevant to your research project* as well as you can. These may best be completed after consultation with your supervisor:

4   How will you protect human participants if your research deals with sensitive issues?
5   How will you ensure that vulnerable research participants are protected? (Please state clearly if you abide by the child protection guidelines and/or have police clearance where necessary.)
6   How will you protect human participants if your research uses sensitive research procedures?
7   Outline any points arising from your project in light of the College's code of practice for research ethics.
8   How will you comply any data protection issues according to the College's guidelines?
9   If relevant, how will you deal with your obligations in relation to the processing of sensitive personal data (special restrictions)?

NOTE

1   This form is similar to one used by the Department of Media and Communications, Goldsmiths (UK) designed for master students to consider for their research projects, as an educative and research design tool.

GLOSSARY

Note: Glossaries at the end of books may appear quaint in an age where many students start and end their referencing and research projects online. This glossary dovetails these online sources alongside those provided by other books in this field.

Academic misconduct This term encompasses a number of transgressions within formal and informal codes of conduct in research communities; from accidentally or deliberately citing someone else's work without providing a full reference, claiming the ideas or expressions of someone else as your own, getting someone else to write the work instead of you, to making up data or manipulating results. The increased use of the cut-and-paste functions of word-processing software in tandem with the ease of web-based access to written texts, images, and other media has raised the stakes in this regard.

Action research This approach takes the full immersion model of ethnographic work one step further by the researcher engaging their research subjects, or community (e.g. a government or company department, or a professional group such as health professionals) in the design, execution, and analysis of the project. The project design is in this respect goal-directed and requires the full cooperation of all parties. See also **Participatory action research**.

ARPAnet An abbreviation for the precursor of the internet as we know it today, the US-based Advanced Research Projects Agency Network.

Avatar Sanskrit for manifestation or appearance, this term has been adopted for web-based and computer-mediated communications whereby a user nominates or designs an image to represent them online; e.g. a comic figure on your social networking site home page, your own creation or character through which you take part in a computer game or virtual world.

Behavioural A designation for social science research that studies how human actors behave by gathering data based on either direct or indirect observation, in controlled experimental or semi-experimental settings, or through surveys. Behavioural research findings are predominately rendered in quantitative forms although not exclusively. Behaviouralist project designs focus on the individual as the unit of analysis, as opposed to groups, communities, or institutions.

Bias In statistical terms, bias is a systematic error in the results. More generally the term is used to designate how 'objective' research projects, based on the gathering of empirical evidence to test a hypothesis, strive to avoid distortions of any kind, e.g. observational or cognitive interference, or expressing or revealing their personal views or involvement during and after carrying out the research. In this view bias is something to be eliminated as far as possible if not accounted for in formal terms; e.g. establishing the *margin of error*, or avoiding the first-person pronoun ('I') in academic writing.

Case study   A research topic that concentrates on a specific issue, group, organization, event, or individual within a defined time and place is called a case study. Comparative case studies involve two or more instances. A case study will engage a researcher in more than one approach to data-gathering and analysis. The aim and benefit of case-study work is the focus, depth of detail and richness of evidential material. Just how far any conclusions drawn can be generalized to other instances is a question methodologists debate, and students can find themselves being corrected on.

Coding   A general term for setting up ways to ascertain patterns in written – and visual – texts in order to draw inferences about significance by analysis of recurring instances. Coding schemes can be quantitative (how many times a word or phrase appears) and qualitative (the position of a term in a larger text). The term tends to be employed in quantitative modes of content analysis based on standardized coding schemes. However, qualitative research projects can also code a text based on interpreting the position or recurrence of words, phrases, or themes.

Coefficient   In mathematics this shorthand refers to the number used to multiply a variant; e.g. '2T' means '2 × T' ('T' stands for the thing you are multiplying – the variant). Put it another way, whatever represents the variant in the equation, the coefficient is the multiplying number before it. When applied to a research situation, a coefficient indicates the size of an effect; e.g. age and its effect on the probability of voting. In this case the effect multiplied by the age indicates how much age contributes to the overall probability of that person voting; the coefficient indicates the 'size of that effect'. See also **correlation coefficient**.

Confidence interval   In statistical terms this refers to the estimation of the highest and lowest statistical values for the observed data; a confidence interval should be high (usually around 95 per cent).

Constructivism   A move with various inflections in social research that takes a different stance to the relationship between the researcher (as observer or analyst) and the object of research. In contrast to research that aims to consciously eliminate all forms of *bias* (see above), constructivist approaches maintain that researchers and that which they observe are mutually dependent. Stronger forms of constructivism argue that the social (and for some even the physical and biological) world does not exist outside human society and history.

Content analysis   A form of textual analysis where the manifest content is collected and analysed according to a pre-designed coding scheme (see **coding**).

Control group   In experimental research this is the group not subjected to the actions under investigation (e.g. a medical treatment or media effect) in order to permit comparison with those groups who are subject to the intervention.

Conversational analysis   A form of linguistics in which conversations can be analysed not just in terms of the manifest content (see **content analysis**) but also in terms of speech rhythms, pauses and their meaning, inflections, and idiomatic phrases within a linguistic or cultural group.

Correlation/correlation coefficient   When two variables are interdependent a change in one means a change in the other. A correlation is the extent to which this association can be measured; see **coefficient**). Independent variables do not correlate. The term in general usage refers to some sort of relationship between two or more values, or phenomena. However, in statistics, a correlation is a mathematical calculation (programs like SPSS do this for you) that establishes either a positive or negative value between measurements; minus one (-1) is negative, zero (0) means no outcome, and one (1) is a positive correlation. As M. Davies (2007: 261) notes, in real research scenarios the calculations usually lie somewhere in between these two values, the significance of which needs to be ascertained in turn. See Rummel (1976) for an extended, and helpful discussion in his guide to the uninitiated.

Critical discourse analysis   This approach is usually identified with the work of Norman Fairclough and colleagues which combines linguistics (see **semiotics**) with **discourse analysis** techniques.

Data   For many schools of thought, data are, by definition, quantitative; facts and figures gained by way of observational means (direct and indirect) that are then rendered in numerical values for statistical analysis. Notwithstanding debates about what does, or should, count as data or not, any sort of observation that is recorded (e.g. from field notes, quantities or tasks listed in a spreadsheet) could be regarded as a data point.

Deconstruction   The French philosopher Jacques Derrida pioneered this critical approach to the relationship between writing, meaning-production, and the transmission of knowledge in western philosophy. All meaning-making and its interpretation is problematic by this account in that the very act of writing and reading are complicit in the legacy of western imperialism and its worldview. Derrida then subjected key texts in the canon to a radical exposé (deconstruction) of their underlying assumptions and pretexts. See also **structuralism**, **semiotics**, **postcolonial research**.

Dependent variable   This variable changes according to another – independent – variable. Dependent variables form the focus of research in hypothesis formulation and testing. See **independent variable**.

Discourse analysis   In contrast to **content analysis**, this approach treats the written (and spoken) word as more than the sum of its parts (countable words or phrases). It takes the manifest content and the larger social, cultural, political or economic context together in order to present an interpretation of both its explicit and hidden meanings.

End-user license agreement (EULA)   The long legal contract that users sign when downloading or installing any new software; no installation can take place without clicking the 'yes' box. As is the case with all legally binding contracts, beware of the small print. Computer game and Virtual World players have discovered many things to contest and reconsider in the respective EULAs of their game/virtual world of choice.

Epistemic community   A phrase to designate scholars or experts working closely together or sharing a common set of assumptions about the form and substance of their respective research enterprise. An epistemic community can be geographically or philosophically delineated, large or small, inclusive or highly specialized.

Ethical codes of practice   These codes, maintained and developed by the professional associations of respective disciplines, aim to codify and guide the development of 'good practice', deter researchers from engaging in forms of **academic misconduct**, or inadvertently being socially irresponsible or culturally insensitive. Codes of ethics differ in content from institution to institution, and between countries and disciplines. National research bodies and funding organizations also maintain their respective codes, to which funded research projects are bound.

Falsification   This term, coined and codified by Karl Popper, is the understanding that the benchmark of scientific research is through the testing of hypotheses that must be able to be proven wrong – 'falsified'. According to Popper, if a hypothesis is phrased in such a way that it can never be proven 'wrong' by countermanding (observational) evidence then it cannot purport to be scientific.

Feminist research   Since the women's rights movement of the 1960s, academic research across the board has been influenced, critiqued, and remodelled by various streams of feminist thought and politics. Feminist research varies in terms of the weight it gives to qualitative or quantitative modes of research from discipline to discipline (e.g. feminist economics, media studies), between different persuasions and generations of feminist scholarship (e.g. postmodern feminism and its critics), and political ideologies (e.g. liberal, Marxist, or socialist feminism). What all feminist research has in common is an emphasis on studying women (as a group) or gender (as an analytical or empirical category).

Formal theory   In political science this term refers to theories based on the modelling of relationships, or social systems, that can elicit hypothesis-testing; e.g. game theory.

FTP   'File Transfer Protocol' allows the downloading and uploading of files from a remote computer system without encryption.

FTTP   This is the abbreviation for 'Fibre To The Premises' (or to the home) whereby a carrier installs a fibreoptic cable; these form the internet's transmission infrastructure, directly into the home, or office.

Gopher   This is the name for an internet protocol that was a popular tool for searching for information on the internet in the early days of the world-wide web (the 1990s) before user-friendly browsers and powerful multimedia search engines took off. A gopher search result presents a 'no-frills' text-based index of 'hits'.

Hermeneutics   This term, 'the art of interpretation' and derived from Greek for interpreter (*hermeneus*) originally referred to the interpretation of Biblical scripture. It now refers to theories of interpretation more generally in which researchers aim to understand the complexity of human actions and their cultural production (e.g. literary and other sorts of 'social texts', institutions). It is closely allied to textual analysis traditions. Research falling under either rubric assumes that meaning is difficult to ascertain – hence the need for interpretation; observational evidence also by this account.

HTTP   'HyperText Transfer Protocol' is one of the fundamental protocols governing the inner-workings of the web. It mediates between computers, servers, and users by processing requests and responses in a uniform way across different systems; e.g. by instructing a server or web-browser what to do in response to a user command (e.g. retrieve a web-page based on the web address command).

Hybrid research   As the term suggests, this is research that synthesizes several approaches to data-gathering and analysis within a single project; often used as a synonym for **mixed method** research.

Ideal type   This term, coined by the German sociologist Max Weber, refers to the distillation of the main characteristics of a particular social instance, or entity, in order for the researcher to extrapolate from the particular to the general and so make comparisons, e.g. between 'traditional' or 'charismatic' authority. Using the term in this way, according to Weber, is not putting the entity under discussion as an ideal in terms of a 'better' type. It is an analytical device rather than a normative evaluation.

Incommensurability   This term, coined by Thomas Kuhn (1962), refers to the way in which research traditions, between generations or epochs even, do not communicate with each other because they cannot find common ground; not only are terms of reference foreign to one another but so are worldviews; e.g. the Ptolemaic view of the universe in ancient Greece and medieval Europe in which the sun revolved around the earth is incommensurable with the Copernican view that the earth revolves around the sun.

Independent variable   This variable is the factor that explains or predicts the outcome of actions performed on a **dependent variable**. An independent variable therefore does not change; it induces change. Causal inferences are drawn based on the statistical measurements of the relationship between independent and dependent variables.

Informed consent   This is the means by which, usually based on a signed form, a researcher makes clear to anyone they wish to interview, survey, or perform and experiment on, what the purpose of the research is; a cornerstone of codes of ethics in all areas of social research and the medical sciences.

Margin of error   When ascertaining whether the outcome of a set of measurements is statistically significant (see M. Davies 2007: 246 *passim*), an acceptable margin of error needs to be taken into account in your analysis. Conventionally this is set at 5 per cent. In other words, this indicates that only 1 in 20 instances has arisen by chance. This is the baseline for ascertaining whether the relationship or finding (e.g. survey result) is indeed significant and not a random occurrence.

Minitel   A videotext precursor to the world-wide web designed in France and made available in the late 1980s and early 1990s through the French public telephone network.

Mixed methods   This term, currently popular in social research, refers to methodologies where more than one sort of data-gathering and analysis is used; e.g. surveys and content analysis. They usually include both quantitative and qualitative modes, with one or the other predominating according to the underlying worldview and theoretical influences of the project's rationale. See **hybrid research**.

Narrative research   This approach investigates how people make sense of their world through stories – narratives. It draws on the oral history tradition as well as hermeneutic understandings of meaning-making as a personal and intersubjective activity; e.g. narrative interview work lays the stress on the interviewee being allowed to 'tell their story', with little input from the researcher.

Nearest neighbour An algorithm for calculating and classifying patterns of relationships. The term is also found in content analysis coding looking to examine the occurrence of target collocations (word pairs). For instance, word pairs in which a term, such as 'boys' or 'homeless', is linked to a negative reference, such as 'anti-social behaviour' or 'disgusting', respectively.

Paradigm shift See also **incommensurability.** According to Thomas Kuhn (1962), major changes in the history of science come about when scholars as a community undergo a major change in their way of thinking – when the 'disciplinary matrix' by which they observe phenomena alters in such a way as to transform the enterprise. Such changes are incremental in Kuhn's view: they occur over time and through debate, although they can come about through a major discovery. The term has been adopted in the humanities and social sciences to denote more localized moments when mindsets, ways of doing research or articulating key issues, undergo change or are subject to fundamental criticism.

Parsimoniousness A particular view of theory-building in which 'less is more'. In political science and international relations theory, this school of thought sees theory as hypothesis-testing – a quantitative rather than an interpretative, language-based undertaking.

Participatory action research This approach, part of **action research** modes of research, puts the emphasis on research subjects also participating in the investigation; to what extent depends on prior as well as ongoing agreements made with the principle researcher or team during the project. In these projects ethical considerations and implications are central to the design, execution and discussion of the findings.

Peer-to-peer sharing (P2P) A term that refers to the sharing of information online within a community of like-minded participants, pioneered by tools that enable the easy downloading and sharing of music, and nowadays films, television and other media. P2P practices and their legal implications for intellectual property rights have come to characterize debates about the social and economic impact of 'social media' since the first decade of the century. See also **Web 2.0.**

Postcolonial research The decolonisation period of the mid-twentieth century, together with the civil rights and women's movements, brought to the fore a range of new themes and critiques of western academe as part of the legacy of previous colonial empires. Postcolonial studies in literature departments brought non-western writers and thinkers onto the curriculum and discussed racialized tropes and stereotypes in the literary and academic canon. Postcolonial research across the disciplinary spectrum continues in this spirit by studying communities, individuals and events in former colonies and their postcolonial populations. It also looks at how race, gender, and class differentials affect the demography and substance of scholarly knowledge and scientific inquiry in academic institutions largely based on the Anglo-Euro-American model. See also **feminist research, deconstruction.**

Probability sampling See **random sampling.**

Psychoanalysis Founded by Sigmund Freud a century ago, this school of thought and clinical practice considers human behaviour and actions through the workings of the unconscious. It is diametrically opposed to **behavioural** models in that it considers that human actions require decoding, interpretation. Psychoanalysis as a research tradition, theoretical pursuit, and profession has had a long history and has led to a wide variety of offshoots (e.g. Jungian or Kleinian psychoanalysis) and competing schools (e.g. 'neo-Freudian', 'post-Freudian').

Random sampling Also known as probability sampling. Large-scale survey research is based on the principle that participants are selected randomly, i.e. that each member of that population has an equal chance of being selected (at least at the start in the event of multi-stage sampling), to ensure that a sample is as representative as possible in order to be able to generalize. If a survey is carried out on a sample in which participants are selected by non-random means, then claims based on statistical probability outcomes do not make sense. Only when probability samples have been established can probability theory be applied to estimations of the population's parameters and statistical analysis of the findings (see **margin of error**).

Reliability This term applies to consistency in the administration, calculating, and internal scoring of a research instrument, e.g. a survey questionnaire or coding scheme. Reliable instruments need to be internally consistent (e.g. a coding scheme yields the same results for different coders most of the time), reliable for different time periods (e.g. a survey from one year to the next) and not susceptible to ambiguity or errors of measurement. Reliability in qualitative research refers to the relative transparency and attention to detail the researcher pays to articulating and outlining their methodological design, as well as the way they approach their analysis of the material. See also **replicability**.

Replicability The principle by which a research project should be designed in order that it can be executed in the same way by someone else, thus enabling an experiment to be replicated in order to test the original findings, or a survey to be administered in another place or later date for comparison or evaluation.

Rich description A term, synonymous with 'thick description', that characterizes anthropological research reports, or those based on ethnographic fieldwork. Close attention to detail governs the narrative account of the research and findings: personalities, sensations, sounds, relationships, rituals. This term designates the form of observation and engagement during the research as well as a genre of writing within the anthropological tradition.

Sample A selection, whether produced randomly or by other means (e.g. **snowballing** samples), of a population of individuals, objects, or occurrences (e.g. phrases) for the purposes of the study.

Semiotics A tradition of linguistic research that concentrates on the way language is structured in order to ascertain how meaning is generated and conveyed through these linguistic structures. The various schools of semiotic method see all human-generated language (speech and written) as made up of patterns, e.g. signs and symbol systems, or codes, which can be broken down for analytical purposes. See **structuralism**.

Snowballing A sampling technique, useful for smaller-scale surveys or semi-structured interview designs, by which the researcher generates a sample from a population generated by personal or professional contacts, e.g. friends or classmates, who then provide their contacts, and so on.

Statistical significance   See **random sampling, correlation coefficient**.

Structuralism   This is an analytical approach as well as a disciplinary tradition in sociology and other social sciences in which social, cultural, political and economic phenomena are explained by reference to larger (macro) structures on the one hand and, on the other, underlying (micro) ones. Microbiology, linguistics, cultural anthropology, sociology and psychology have all been heavily influenced by structuralist accounts of human morphologies, meaning-making, culture, society, and human behaviour. Explaining the social and physical as the result of large-scale, linguistic, or microscopic structures alone has been consistently critiqued by post-structuralist approaches across academia which contend the determinism of structuralist accounts.

Terms of use   The **end-user license agreement** includes the terms of use – part of the contractual conditions a manufacturer or software owner sets, and needing a user's agreement before downloading or play can begin.

Triangulation   Borrowed from trigonometry and land surveying, this term in social research refers to a researcher using more than one data source or data-gathering approach in order to check a claim or strengthen the findings, from checking the robustness of a conceptual definition or statistical reference from multiple sources (e.g. not relying entirely on Wikipedia) to consciously combining data-gathering methods in order to gain a more rounded picture of the object of study.

Usenet   One of the earliest forms of social networking – online forums, still in existence today. News lists for interest-based communities of users are based on Usenet's network of computer servers.

Validity   In quantitative research, 'measurement validity' refers to whether the indicator being used actually measures what it is intended to measure. This is distinct from reliability, in that whilst the indicator in question could be reliable (consistent and thus replicable) it is not actually the appropriate form of measurement. 'Internal validity' refers to ascertaining whether a research design can establish causation as it intends to do.

Variable   A measurable characteristic or category. See **dependent variable, independent variable**.

Variance   When repeating a procedure, variance is the calculation of any differences recorded.

VOIP   'Voice Over Internet Protocol' is the means by which people can telephone each other over the internet, as opposed to using traditional telecommunications networks. At present much cheaper than using the telephone for long distance phone calls. At time of writing, Skype is the world leader in offering free, if not very cheap VOIP services.

Web 2.0   This term designates the current generation of largely commercially maintained platforms – goods and services – that combine previously separately delivered and accessed services under one rubric or entry point. The convergence of these online media, offers users a level of interactivity combining services such as email, live chat, professional and personal contacts, and personal archives within a single integrated platform.

LITERATURE LIST

Abdelal, R., Herrera, Y. M., Johnston, A. I. and McDermott, R. (eds), 2009, *Measuring Identity: A Guide for Social Scientists*. Cambridge: Cambridge University Press.

Adorno, T. W. (ed.), 1976, *The Positivist Dispute in German Sociology*. London: Harper and Row.

Anderson, Benedict, 1991, *Imagined Communities: Reflections on the Origin and Spread of Nationalism*. Revised edition. London and New York: Verso.

Appadurai, Arjun, 2002, 'Disjuncture and Difference in the Global Cultural Economy', *Public Culture* 2(2): 1–24.

Arendt, Hannah, 1953, 'Understanding and Politics', *Partisan Review* 20(4): 377–92.

Baehr, Peter R., 1980, 'The Dutch Foreign Policy Elite: A Descriptive Study of Perceptions and Attitudes', *International Studies Quarterly* 24(2): 223–61.

Barber, Benjamin R., 2006, 'The Politics of Political Science: "Value-Free" Theory and the Wolin-Strauss Dust-Up of 1963', *American Political Science Review* 100(4): 539–45.

Barrass, Robert, 1982, *Students Must Write*. London: Methuen.

Barthes, Roland, 1981, *Camera Lucida*. New York: Hill and Wang.

Beauvoir, Simone de, 1949, *Le deuxième sexe* [The Second Sex]. Paris: Gallimard.

Becker, H. S., 1986, *Writing for Social Scientists: How to Start and Finish Your Thesis, Book or Article*. Chicago, IL: University of Chicago Press.

Benjamin, Walter, 1973 [1931], 'The Work of Art in the Age of Mechanical Reproduction', in *Walter Benjamin, Illuminations*, Hannah Arendt (ed.), London: Fontana Press, 211–44.

Berg, Bruce L., 2007, *Qualitative Research Methods for the Social Sciences*. Boston, MA: Allyn & Bacon.

—— 2009, *Qualitative Research Methods for the Social Sciences*. Seventh edition. Boston: Pearson Education.

Berger, John, 1990, *Ways of Seeing*. London: Penguin Books.

Berns, Walter, 1962, ' Voting Studies', in *Essays on the Scientific Study of Politics*, Herbert J. Storing (ed.), New York: Holt, Rinehart and Winston.

Berry, David, (ed.), 2000, *Ethics and Media Culture: Practices and Representations*. Oxford: Focal Press.

Bertrand, Ina and Hughes, Peter, 2004, *Media Research Methods: Audiences, Institutions, Texts*. London and New York: Palgrave Macmillan.

Besnier, Niko, 2009, *Gossip and the Everyday Production of Politics*. Honolulu, Hawaii: University of Hawaii Press.

—— 2011, *On the Edge of the Global: Modern Anxieties in a Pacific Island Nation*. Stanford, CA: Stanford University Press.

Blaxter, Loraine, Hughes, Christina and Tight, Malcolm, 2006, *How to Research*. Third edition. Maidenhead and New York: Open University Press.

Bleiker, Roland, 2009, *Aesthetics and World Politics*. London and New York: Palgrave Macmillan.

Bourdieu, Pierre, 1977, *Outline of a Theory of Practice*. Cambridge: Cambridge University Press.

—— 1984, *Homo Academicus*. Paris: Editions de Minuit.

Brabazon, Tara, 2007, *The University of Google: Education in the (Post) Information Age*. Aldershot: Ashgate.

Bradbury, Malcolm, 1975, *The History Man*. London: Picador.

Buckler, Steve and Dolowitz, David, 2005, *Politics on the Internet: A Student Guide*. London and New York: Routledge.

Burchill, S., Devetak, R., Linklater, A., Paterson, M., Reus-Smit, C. and True, J., 2001, *Theories of International Relations*. Second edition. Basingstoke and New York: Palgrave Macmillan.

Burn, Andrew and Parker, David, 2003, *Analysing Media Texts*. London and New York: Continuum.

Burnham, Peter, Gilland, Karin, Grant, Wyn and Layton-Henry, Zig, 2004, *Research Methods in Politic*s. London and New York: Palgrave Macmillan.

Busfield, Joan and E. Stina Lyon (eds), 1996, *Methodological Imaginations*. London and New York: Palgrave Macmillan.

Butler, J., 1990, 'Gender Trouble, Feminist Theory, and Psychoanalytic Discourse', in *Feminism/Postmodernism*, Linda Nicholson (ed.), London and New York: Routledge, 324–40.

Cahoone, Lawrence (ed.), 1996, *From Modernism to Postmodernism: An Anthology*. Cambridge, MA and Oxford: Blackwell.

Callon, M. and Latour, B., 1981, 'Unscrewing the Big Leviathan: How Actors Macro-Structure Reality and How Sociologists Help Them Do It', in *Advances in Social Theory and Methodology: Toward an Integration of Micro- and Macro-Sociologies*, K. Knorr-Cetina and A. V. Cicourel (eds), Boston and London: Routledge and Kegan Paul, 277–303.

Canales, Jimena, 2009, *A Tenth of a Second: A History*. Chicago, IL: University of Chicago Press.

Carver, Terrell, 2004, 'War of the Worlds/Invasion of the Body Snatchers', *International Affairs* 80(1): 92–4.

Carver, Terrell and Hyvarinen, Matti (eds), 1997, *Interpreting the Political: New Methodologies*. London and New York: Routledge.

Certeau, Michel de, 1991, 'Travel Narratives of the French to Brazil: Sixteenth to Eighteenth Centuries', *Representations, Special Issue: The New World* 33, Winter: 221–6.

Chalmers, A. F., 2004, *What is this thing called Science?* Queensland, Australia: University of Queensland Press.

Chowdhry, Geeta and Nair, Sheila (eds), 2002, *Power, Postcolonialism and International Relations: Reading Race, Gender and Class*. London and New York: Routledge.

Cinquegrani, Riccardo, 2002, 'Futurist Networks: Cases of Epistemic Community?', *Futures* 34(8): 779–83.

Clanchy, John and Ballard, Brigid, 1984, *How to Write Essays: A Practical Guide for Students*. Melbourne, Australia: Longman Cheshire.

Clifford, James, 1997, *Routes: Travel and Translation in the Late Twentieth Century*. Cambridge, MA and London: Harvard University Press.

Couldry, Nick, 2000, *Inside Culture: Re-imagining the Method of Cultural Studies*. Thousand Oaks, CA and London: Sage.

Couper, M., 2000, 'Web Surveys: A Review of Issues and Approaches', *Public Opinion Quarterly* 64: 464–94.

Craig, Edward (ed.), 2005, *The Shorter Routledge Encyclopedia of Philosophy*. London and New York: Routledge.

Creswell, John W., 2009, *Research Design: Qualitative, Quantitative, and Mixed Methods Approaches*. Third edition. Thousand Oaks, CA and London: Sage.

Cuba, L and Cocking, J, 1994, *How to Write about the Social Sciences*. London: Harper and Row.

Davies, Charlotte Aull, 2007, *Reflexive Ethnography: A Guide to Researching Ourselves and Others*. London and New York: Routledge.

Davies, Martin Brett, 2007, *Doing a Successful Research Project: Using Qualitative or Quantitative Methods*. London and New York: Palgrave Macmillan.

Deacon, D., 2008, 'Why Counting Counts', in *Research Methods for Cultural Studies*, M. Pickering (ed.), Edinburgh: Edinburgh University Press.

Deacon, D., Pickering, M., Golding, P. and Murdock, G., 2007, *Researching Communications*. Second edition. London: Arnold.

Denzin, Norman K. and Lincoln, Yvonne S., 2005, *The Sage Handbook of Qualitative Research*. Third edition. Thousand Oaks, CA and London: Sage.

Dicks, Bella, Mason, Bruce, Coffey, Amanda Jane, and Atkinson, Paul A., 2005, *Qualitative Research and Hypermedia: Ethnography for the Digital Age*. Thousand Oaks, CA and London: Sage.

di Leonardo, M. (ed.), 1991, *Gender at the Crossroads of Knowledge: Feminist Anthropology in the Postmodern Era*. Berkeley and Los Angeles, CA: University of California Press.

Dummett, M., 1993, *Grammar and Style*. London: Duckworth.

Duneier, Mitchell, 1999, *Sidewalk*. New York: Farrar, Straus and Giroux.

Eberstadt, Nicholas, 1995, *The Tyranny of Numbers: Mismeasurement and Misrule*. Washington, DC: AEI Press.

Eco, Umberto, 1983, *The Name of the Rose*. New York: Harcourt.

Elman, Colin and Fendius Elman, Miriam (eds), 2001, *Bridges and Boundaries: Historians, Political Scientists and the Study of International Relations*. Cambridge, MA: MIT Press.

Fabian, J., 1983, *Time and the Other: How Anthropology makes its Object*. New York: Columbia University Press.

Fairclough, Norman, 1989, *Language and Power*. Berkeley, LA: University of California Press.

—— 2003, *Analysing Discourse: Textual Analysis for Social Research*. London and New York: Routledge.

Farrell, David M. and Scully, Roger, 2007, *Representing Europe's Citizens? Electoral Institutions and the Failure of Parliamentary Representation*. Oxford: Oxford University Press.

Faubion, James D. (ed.), 2000, *Power: The Essential Works of Michel Foucault, 1954–1984*. Vol. 3. New York: New Press.

Feyerabend, Paul, 1978, *Against Method: Towards an Anarchistic Theory of Knowledge*. London: Verso.

Fierke, Karin M. and Jørgensen, Knud Erik (eds), 2001, *Constructing International Relations: The Next Generation (International Relations in a Constructed World)*. New York: M. E. Sharpe.

Fink, Arlene, 2009, *Conducting Research Literature Reviews: From the Internet to Paper*. Third edition. Thousand Oaks, CA and London: Sage.

Foucault, Michel, 1972, *The Archaeology of Knowledge and the Discourse on Language*, trans. A. M. Sheridan-Smith. New York: Pantheon Books.

—— 1973 [1966], *The Order of Things: An Archaeology of the Human Sciences*. New York: Vintage Books.

—— 1984 [1977], 'The Author Function [What is An Author?]', available at http://foucault.info/documents.foucault.authorFunction.en.html (19 April 2012)

—— 1984 [1983], 'Interview with Paul Rabinow: Polemics, Politics and Problematizations', available at http://foucault.info/foucault/interview.html (accessed 26 August 2011).

—— 1995 [1975], *Discipline and Punish*. New York: Vintage Books.

Fowler, Floyd J., 2002, *Survey Research Methods*. Third edition. Thousand Oaks, CA and London: Sage.

Frankfort-Nachmias, Chava and Nachmias, David, 1996, *Research Methods in the Social Sciences*. Fifth edition. New York: Hodder Arnold.

Franklin, M. I., 2004, *Postcolonial Politics, the Internet, and Everyday Life: Pacific Traversals Online*. London and New York: Routledge.

—— 2007, 'NGO's and the "Information Society": Grassroots Advocacy at the UN – a Cautionary Tale', *Review of Policy Research* 24(4): 309–30. Available at http://onlinelibrary.wiley.com/doi/10.1111/j.1541-1338.2007.00285.x/abstract (accessed 26 August 2011).

—— 2010, 'Media research in the 21st Century', in *Journalism: Cutting Edge Commentaries on the Critical Issues Facing Journalism at the Practical, Theoretical and Media Industry Level*, Paul Lashmar (ed.), The Marketing and Management Collection, London: Henry Stewart Talks Ltd. Available at http://hstalks.com/?t=MM1072565-Franklin (accessed 26 August 2011).

Franklin, M. I. and Wilkinson, Kenton T., 2011, 'Transnational Communications in Action: A Critical Praxis', *Communication, Culture and Critique* 4(4): 361–81.

Freedberg, David, 1989, *The Power of Images. Studies in the History and Theory of Response*. Chicago, IL and London: University of Chicago Press.

Freeland, Cynthia, 2001, *Art Theory: A Very Short Introduction*. Oxford: Oxford University Press.

Gaiser, Ted J. and Schreiner, Anthony E., 2009, *A Guide to Conducting Online Research*. Thousand Oaks, CA and London: Sage.

Geddes, Barbara, 2003, *Paradigms and Sand Castles: Theory Building and Research Design in Comparative Politics*. Ann Arbor, MI: University of Michigan Press.

George, Alexander L. and Bennett, Andrew, 2005, *Case Studies and Theory Development in the Social Sciences* (BCSIA Studies in International Security). Cambridge, MA: MIT Press.

Gibson, William and Brown, Andrew, 2009. *Working with Qualitative Data*. Thousand Oaks, CA and London: Sage.

Ginsberg, Benjamin, 1986, *The Captive Public: How Mass Opinion Promotes State Power*. New York: Basic Books.

Giri, Ananta Kumar, 2004, *Creative Social Research: Rethinking Theories and Methods*. Lanham, MD: Lexington Books.

Glynos, Jason and Howarth, David, 2007, *Logics of Critical Explanation in Social and Political Theory*. London and New York: Routledge.

Golden, Patricia M. (ed.), 1976, *The Research Experience*. Itasca, IL: F. E. Peacock.

Gray, David E., 2009, *Doing Research in the Real World*. Second edition. Thousand Oaks, CA and London: Sage.

Gunter, Barrie, 2000, *Media Research Methods: Measuring Audiences, Reactions, and Impact*. London, Thousand Oaks, CA and New Delhi: Sage.

Habermas, J., 1998, *The Postnational Constellation*. Cambridge, MA: MIT Press.

Hacker, Diana and Fisker, Barbara, 2010, *Research and Documentation in the Electronic Age*. Fifth edition. Boston, MA and New York: Bedford/St. Martins.

Hakken, D., 1999, *Cyborgs@Cyberspace? An Ethnographer Looks to the Future*. New York and London: Routledge.

Hall, C., 1993, *Getting Down to Writing: A Students' Guide to Overcoming Writer's Block*. Cambridge: Centre for Research into Human Communication and Learning.

Hall, Stuart, 1996, 'What is this "Black" in Black Popular Culture?' in *Stuart Hall: Critical Dialogues in Cultural Studies*, D. Morley and K-H. Chen (eds), London and New York: Routledge, 465–75.

Haraway, Donna J., 1990, 'A Manifesto for Cyborgs: Science, Technology, and Socialist Feminism in the 1980s', in *Feminism/Postmodernism*, Linda Nicholson (ed.), New York and London: Routledge, 190–233.

Harding, S., 1998a, 'Gender, Development, and Post-Enlightenment Philosophies of Science', *Hypatia* 13(3): 146–67.

—— 1998b, *Is Science Multicultural? Postcolonialisms, Feminisms, and Epistemologies*. Bloomington and Indianapolis, IN: Indiana University Press.

Harding, Sandra (ed.), 1987, *Feminism and Methodology: Social Science Issues*. Bloomington and Indianapolis: Indiana University Press.

Harkness, A., van de Vijver, F. J. R. and Mohler, P. P. (eds), 2003, *Cross-Cultural Survey Methods*. Hoboken, NJ: Wiley Interscience.

Harrison, Lisa, 2001, *Political Research: An Introduction*. London and New York: Routledge.

Hart, Chris, 1998, *Doing a Literature Review: Releasing the Social Research Imagination*. London: Sage.

Hattenstone, Simon, 2009, 'Teen Spirit: The Secret Life of Britain's Teenage Boys', *Guardian*, 10 October.

Hay, Colin, 2002, *Political Analysis: A Critical Introduction*. London and New York: Palgrave.

Hayles, Kathleen N., 1999, *How We Became Posthuman: Virtual Bodies in Cybernetics, Literature, and Informatics*. Chicago, IL: University of Chicago Press.

Henwood, Fliss, Hughes, G., Kennedy, Helen, Miller, N. and Wyatt, Sally, 2001, 'Cyborg Lives in Context: Writing Women's Technobiographies', in *Cyborg Lives: Women's Technobiographies*, F. Henwood, H. Kennedy and N. Miller (eds), York: Raw Nerve Books, 11–34.

Hewson, Claire, Yule, Peter, Laurent, Dianna and Vogel, Carl, 2002, *Internet Research Methods: A Practical Guide for the Social and Behavioural Sciences*. London, Thousand Oaks, CA and New Delhi: Sage.

Hine, Christine, 2000, *Virtual Ethnography*. London, Thousand Oaks, CA and New Delhi: Sage.

Hinton, Perry R., 2004, *Statistics Explained: A Guide for Social Science Students*. London and New York: Routledge.

Holmes, Brian, 2007, 'Future Map or How the Cyborgs Learned to Stop Worrying and Learned to Love Surveillance', available at http://brianholmes. wordpress.com/2007/09/09/future-map/ (accessed 26 August 2011).

Hughes, C. L. and Cohen, R. L., 2010, 'Feminists Really Do Count: The Complexity of Feminist Methods', *International Journal of Social Research Methodology* 13(3): 189–96.

Hughes, John and Sharrock, Wes, 2007, *Theory and Methods in Sociology: An Introduction to Sociological Thinking and Practice*. London and New York: Palgrave Macmillan.

Huxley, Aldous, 1954, *The Doors of Perception*. London: Harper Brothers.

Inda, J. X. and Rosaldo, R., (eds), 2002, *The Anthropology of Globalisation: A Reader*. Cambridge, MA and Oxford: Blackwell.

James, Nalita and Busher, Hugh, 2009, *Online Interviewing*. Thousand Oaks, CA and London: Sage.

Jarvie, Ian C., 2005, 'Popper, Karl Raimond', in *The Shorter Routledge Encyclopedia of Philosophy*, Edward Craig (ed.), London and New York: Routledge, 820–5.

Jones, Julie Scott and Watt, Sal (eds), 2010, *Ethnography in Social Science Practice*. London and New York: Routledge.

Jones, Steve (ed.), 1999, *Doing Internet Research: Critical Issues and Methods for Examining the Net*. London, Thousand Oaks, CA and New Delhi: Sage.

Jordan, Tim, 1999, *Cyberpower*. London and New York: Routledge.

Kuhn, Thomas, 1962, *The Structure of Scientific Revolutions*. Chicago, IL: University of Chicago Press.

Lanchester, John, 2010, *Whoops!: Why Everyone Owes Everyone and No One Can Pay*. London: Allen Lane/Penguin.

Latour, Bruno, 2007, 'Beware, Your Imagination Leaves Digital Traces', *Times Higher Literary Supplement*, 6 April. Available at http://www.bruno-latour.fr/sites/default/files/P-129-THES-GB.pdf (accessed 19 April 2012)

Lazuly, Pierre, 2003, 'Telling Google What to Think: How an Online Search Engine Influences Access to Information', *Le Monde Diplomatique* (English edition), November. Original French version, 'Le monde selon Google', *Le Monde Diplomatique*, November. Available at http://www.monde-diplomatique.fr/2003/10/LAZULY/10471 (accessed 20 January 2012).

Lewis, Justin, 2001, *Constructing Public Opinion: How Political Elites Do What They Like and Why We Seem to Go Along With It*. New York: Columbia University Press.

Lippmann, Walter, 1998 [1922], *Public Opinion*. New Brunswick, NJ and London: Transaction Publishers.

Lipsey, M. W. and Wilson, D. B., 1996, *Practical Meta-Analysis*. Newbury Park, CA: Sage.

Lodge, David, 1993, *A David Lodge Trilogy: Changing Places, Small World, Nice Work*. London and New York: Penguin Books.

Lovelock, William, 2000, *Gaia: A New Look at Life on Earth*. Oxford: Oxford University Press.

Marcus, George E., 1995, 'Ethnography in/of the World System: The Emergence of Multi-Sited Ethnography', *Annual Review of Anthropology* 24 (1995): 95–117.

Marsh, David and Stoker, Gerry, (eds), 2002, *Theory and Methods in Political Science*. Second Edition. London and New York: Palgrave Macmillan.

Maslin, Mark, 2009, *Global Warming: A Very Short Introduction*. Oxford: Oxford University Press.

McLeod, Julie and Thomson, Rachel, 2009, *Researching Social Change: Qualitative Approaches*. Thousand Oaks, CA and London: Sage.

McNiff, Jean and Whitehead, Jack, 2009, *Doing and Writing Action Research*. Thousand Oaks, CA and London: Sage.

McQuail, Dennis, 1994, *Mass Communication Theory: An Introduction*. London, Thousand Oaks, CA and New Delhi: Sage.

Medawar, Peter, 1982, *Pluto's Republic*. New York: Oxford University Press.

Miller, D. and Slater, D., 2000, *The Internet: An Ethnographic Approach*. Oxford: Berg.

Morley, David, 2006, *Media, Modernity, and Technology: The Geography of the New*. London and New York: Routledge.

Moses, Jonathan W. and Knutsen, Torbjørn, 2007, *Ways of Knowing: Competing Methodologies in Social and Political Research*. London and New York: Palgrave Macmillan.

Neuman, W. Lawrence, 1997, *Social Research Methods: Qualitative and Quantitative Approaches*. Third edition. Needham Heights, MA: Allyn and Bacon.

Norris, Pippa, and Inglehart, Ronald, 2003, 'Islamic Culture and Democracy: Testing the "Clash of Civilizations" Thesis', *Comparative Sociology* 1(3–4): 235–65.

—— 2006, 'God, Guns and Gays: The Supply and Demand for Religion in the U.S. and Western Europe', *Public Policy Research* 12(4): 224–33.

Oakes, J. Michael and Kaufman, Jay S., 2006, 'Introduction: Advancing Methods in Social Epidemiology', in *Methods in Social Epidemiology*. San Francisco, CA: Jossey-Bass, 3–20.

Ó Dochartaigh, Niall, 2009, *How To Do Your Literature Search and Find Research Information Online*. Second edition. Thousand Oaks, CA and London: Sage.

O'Neill, M., 2009, *Cyberchiefs: Autonomy and Authority in Online Tribes*. London: Pluto Press.

O'Reilly, Karen, 2009, *Key Concepts in Ethnography*. Thousand Oaks, CA and London: Sage.

Paccagnella, Luciano, 1997, 'Getting the Seats of Your Pants Dirty: Strategies for Ethnographic Research on Virtual Communities', *Journal of Computer Mediated Communication* 3(1). Available at: http://jcmc.indiana.edu/vol3/issue1/paccagnella.html (accessed 22 August 2011).

Peterson, V. Spike and Runyan, Anne Sisson, 1999, *Global Gender Issues*. Second edition. Dilemmas in World Politics Series, Boulder, CO, San Francisco and Oxford: Westview Press.

Petrocik, John R. and Steeper, Frederick T., 2010, 'The Politics Missed by Political Science', *The Forum* 8(3): Article 1. Available at http://www.bepress.com/forum/vol8/iss3/art1 (accessed 19 April 2012).

Pole, Christopher and Lampard, Richard, 2001, *Practical Social Investigation: Qualitative and Quantitative Methods in Social Research*. Atlantic Highlands, NJ: Prentice Hall.

Putnam, Robert D., 2000, *Bowling Alone: The Collapse and Revival of American Community*. New York: Simon & Schuster.

Radder, Hans, 2006, *The World Observed/The World Conceived*. Pittsburgh, PA: University of Pittsburgh Press.

Ragin, Charles C., 1987, *The Comparative Method: Moving Beyond Qualitative and Quantitative Strategies*. Berkeley, CA, Los Angeles, CA and London: University of California Press.

Ramage, Magnus, 2009, 'Norbert and Gregory: Two Strands of Cybernetics', *Information, Communication and Society* 12(5): 735–49.

Ratcliffe, Peter (ed.), 2001, *The Politics of Social Science Research*. London and New York: Palgrave Macmillan.

Richardson, L., 1990, *Writing Strategies*. Newbury Park, CA: Sage.

Ritchie, Jane and Lewis, Jane, 2003, *Qualitative Research Practice: A Guide for Social Science Students and Researchers*. Thousand Oaks, CA and London: Sage.

Rogers, Richard (ed.), 2000, *Preferred Placement*. Maastricht, the Netherlands: Jan van Eyck Akademie Editions.

Rosenau, James, 1999, 'Thinking Theory Thoroughly', in *International Relations Theory: Realism, Pluralism, Globalism, and Beyond*, Mark V. Kauppi and Paul R. Viotti (eds), Third edition. Atlantic Highlands, NJ: Prentice Hall, 29–37.

Rosenthal, R., 1991, *Meta-Analytic Procedures for Social Research*. Newbury Park, CA: Sage.

Ross, Michael, 2008, 'Oil, Islam and Women', *American Political Science Review* 102(1): 107–23.

Rudestam, K. E and Newton, R. R., 1992, *Surviving Your Dissertation*. London: Sage.

Rummel, R. J., 1976, *Understanding Correlation*. Honolulu, Hawaii: Political Science Department, University of Hawaii.

Said, Edward, 1994, *Orientalism*. New York: Vintage Books.

Sanders, David, 1995, 'The Behavioural Approach', in *Theory and Methods in Political Science*, David Marsh and Gerry Stoker (eds), London and New York: Palgrave Macmillan, 45–64.

Sayer, Andrew, 1999, *Method in Social Science: A Realistic Approach*. Thousand Oaks, CA and London: Sage.

Schulz, Kathryn, 2010, *Being Wrong: Adventures in the Margin of Error*. New York: HarperCollins.

Scolari, Carlos, 2009, 'Digital Eco_Logy: Umberto Eco and a Semiotic Approach to Digital Communication', *Information, Communication and Society* 12(1): 129–48.

Shepherd, Laura (ed.), 2009, *Gender Matters in Global Politics: A Feminist Introduction to International Relations*. London and New York: Routledge.

Silverman, David (ed.), 2011, *Qualitative Research: Issues of Theory, Method and Practice*. Third edition. London, Thousand Oaks, CA, New Delhi and Singapore: Sage.

Skovmand, Michael and Schrøder, Kim Christian (eds), 1992, *Media Cultures: Reappraising Transnational Media*. London and New York: Routledge.

Sloman, Aeron, 1977, 'Methodology', in *The Fontana Dictionary of Modern Thought*, Alan Bullock and Oliver Stallybrass (eds), London: HarperCollins, 387–8.

Smart, Carol, 2010, 'Disciplined Writing: On the Problem of Writing Sociologically', NCRM Working Paper Series 02/10: ESRC National Centre for Research Methods, January. Manchester: University of Manchester Press.

Smith, Linda Tuhiwai, 1999, *Decolonising Methodologies: Research and Indigenous Peoples*. London: Zed Books.

Snow, C. P., 1993 [1959], *The Two Cultures and the Scientific Revolution*, with an introduction by Stephan Collini. Cambridge: Cambridge University Press.

Social Research Association, 2003, *Ethical Guidelines: Social Research Association*. Available at http://www.the-sra.org.uk/documents/pdfs/ethics03.pdf (accessed 19 January 2012).

Sontag, Susan, 1977, *On Photography*. New York: Farrar, Straus and Giroux.

——, 2003, *Regarding the Pain of Others*. New York: Picador.

Spiller, Neill, (ed.), 2002, *Cyber_Reader: Critical Writings for the Digital Era*. London and New York: Phaidon Press.

Sturken, Marita and Cartwright, Lisa, 2005, *Practices of Looking: An Introduction to Visual Culture*. Oxford: Oxford University Press.

Swaab, Dick, 2010, *Wij zijn ons brein: Van baarmoeder tot Alzheimer*. Amsterdam, the Netherlands: Uitgeverij Contact.

Taylor & Francis Books, 2001, *Instructions for Authors*. London: Taylor & Francis.

Tickner, J. Ann, 1995, 'Hans Morgenthau's Principles of Political Realism: A Feminist Reformulation', in *International Theory: Critical Investigations*, James der Derian (ed.), London: Macmillan Press, 53–74.

Tourangeau, Roger and Smith, Tom W., 1996, 'Asking Sensitive Questions: The Impact of Data Collection Mode, Question Format, and Question Context', *Public Opinion Quarterly* 60 (1996): 275–304.

True, Jacqui, 2001, 'Feminism', in *Theories of International Relations*, Steven Burchill, Richard Devetak, Andrew Linklater, Matthew Paterson, Christian Reus-Smit and Jacqui True (eds), Second edition. New York: Palgrave, 231–76.

True, Jacqui and Ackerly, Brooke (eds), 2010, *Doing Feminist Research in Political and Social Science*. New York: Palgrave Macmillan.

Turabian, Kate L. and Spine, John E., 1984, *A Manual for Writers of Research Papers, Thesis and Dissertations*. London: Heinemann.

Ulin, Robert C., 1984, *Understanding Cultures: Perspectives in Anthropology and Social Theory*. Austin, TX: University of Texas Press.

UCL (University College London), 2008, 'Information Behaviour of the Researcher of the Future: A Cyber Briefing Paper' (11 January). A British Library/ JISC Study. London. Available at http://pressandpolicy.bl.uk/Press-Releases/ Pioneering-research-shows-Google-Generation-is-a-myth-32b.aspx (26 August 2011).

Wallerstein, Immanuel, 1974, *The Modern World-System I: Capitalist Agriculture and the European World-Economy of the Sixteenth Century*. New York: Academic Press.

Wallman, Nicholas, 2000, *Your Research Project: A Step By Step Guide for the First Time Researcher*. Thousand Oaks, CA and London: Sage.

Williamson, Judith, 1978, *Decoding Advertisements: Ideology and Meaning in Advertising*. London and New York: Marion Boyars.

Wilson, Edward O., 1998, *Consilience: The Unity of Knowledge*. New York: Knopf.

Wren, Thomas (ed.), 1990, *The Moral Domain: Essays in the Ongoing Discussion Between Philosophy and the Social Sciences*. Cambridge, MA: MIT Press.

Zoonen, Liesbeth van, 1994, *Feminist Media Studies (Media, Culture and Society)*. London, Thousand Oaks, CA and New Delhi: Sage.

INDEX

accountability 81–2, 92, 130, 152, 202, 277
action research 60, 74, 153, 178, 287; definition of 209
American Political Science Association (APSA) 96
American Political Science Review 102
American Psychological Association (APA) 255
analysis, textual and visual 224–8
approaches *see* ethnographic research; interviews; surveys and questionnaires; worldviews
Aristotle 10, 22, 96, 262
ARPAnet (Advanced Research Projects Agency Network) 132, 287
Association of Internet Researchers (AoIR) 153
avatar 77, 78, 124, 151–4, 189, 201–3, 222, 281

bachelor degree 4, 30, 32, 78, 82, 100, 109, 152
Behaviouralism 213, 237–40, 287; and sex-gender roles 243
Berg, Bruce 68, 169–70, 182–5, 187–8, 190–4, 203, 206–7, 209, 237
Berners-Lee, Tim 133, N 163
bias, possibilities of 17, 153, 179, 192, 202, 206, 287–8
blogs 93, 140, 146, 161
Boolean search terms 144
British International Studies Association (BISA) 97
BUBL Information Service 140
Bulletin Board Services (BBS) 146
Butler, Judith 244

case-study, definition of 288
Chalmers, Alan 42, 70–1, 234
Chicago Manual of Style 255
citation, styles of and referencing 136, 138–40, 254–7
climate change, debates around 46, 118, 214, 235
codes of practice *see* ethics

coding, definition of 288
coding schemes 147, 148, 170, 184, 218–25, 227–8, 231, 245, 288, 292
coefficient 288
confidence interval 209, 288
consent form, sample 279
consilience 117
constructivism 288
content analysis 49, 124, 146, 170–1, 212, 217–25, 232, 239–40, 288; methodological implications 223–4; qualitative and quantitative traditions 146–7, 156, 218; *see also* coding schemes; analysis, textual and visual
control group 40, 288
conversational analysis 216, 288
correlation coefficient 288
Creswell, John 8, 19, 41–3, 47, 51–3, 64, 91, 101, 106
critical discourse analysis 246, 289
cybernetics 132, 164
cyberspace 77, 84, 133–4, 154, 156–8, 163

data, definition of 289
databases: electronic 109–11, 137–41, 144–6, 160; public 177; qualitative 243
data-gathering 6–7, 48–50, 56–63, 69–70, 79–80
data-gathering techniques: and ethical obligations 82; ethnographic fieldwork 197–207; and focus groups 192–7; interviews 183–92; methodology of 101–2, qualitative and quantitative issues 59–60, 90, 238–40; *see also* participant-observation; surveys and questionnaires
data set 18, 42, 45–6, 170, 231, 241–3
Davies, Martin 28, 34, 35, 289
deadlines 29, 36, 85–6, 268–9, 271–2
deconstruction 245, 289
deductive reasoning 72, 212–13, 220, 232–7

CPSIA information can be obtained
at www.ICGtesting.com
Printed in the USA
FFHW012330091218
49812354-54334FF